Prospects for the 2020 Iron Ore Ma

Schriften zu MANAGEMENT,
ORGANISATION UND INFORMATION

Herausgegeben von
Hagen Lindstädt

Band 36

Marc P. Bielitza

Prospects for the 2020 Iron Ore Market

Quantitative Analysis of Market Dynamics
and Risk Mitigation Strategies

Rainer Hampp Verlag   München, Mering 2012

Bibliographic information published by the Deutsche Nationalbibliothek

Deutsche Nationalbibliothek lists this publication in the Deutsche Nationalbibliografie; detailed bibliographic data are available in the Internet at http://dnb.d-nb.de.

ISBN 978-3-86618-679-8 (print)
ISBN 978-3-86618-779-5 (e-book)
Schriften zu Management, Organisation und Information: ISSN 1612-1767
DOI 10.1688/9783866187702
First published 2012

Von der Fakultät für Wirtschaftswissenschaften des Karlsruher Instituts für Technologie (KIT) genehmigte Dissertation.
Tag der mündlichen Prüfung: 13. Januar 2012
Referent: Prof. Dr. Hagen Lindstädt
Korreferent: Prof. Dr. Frank Schultmann

© 2012   Rainer Hampp Verlag   München und Mering
         Marktplatz 5   86415 Mering, Germany

         www.Hampp-Verlag.de

Acknowledgments

This dissertation was written during my time as a PhD student at the Karlsruhe Institute of Technology (KIT), during an educational leave from McKinsey & Company. A number of people have contributed significantly to this dissertation and I would like to take this opportunity to extend my sincere thanks to them.

Foremost, I express my profound gratitude to Prof. Dr. Hagen Lindstädt, for giving me the opportunity to work in such a stimulating research context and for allowing me to learn from his impressive theoretical, methodological and empirical knowledge. The inspiring discussions with him as well as his constructive criticism significantly widened my scientific understanding of oligopolies and market modeling. Also, I would like to thank Prof. Dr. Frank Schultmann for taking on the role of co-referee.

My special thanks go to Dr. Ilse Kenis from the McKinsey Basic Materials Institute, for serving as a sounding board for my ideas and letting me benefit from her vast knowledge of the global iron ore and steel industries. I would also like to thank the McKinsey GEM leadership, particularly Dr. Peter Feldhaus, Dr. Heiner Frankemölle, Dr. Lorenz Jüngling, Dr. Sigurd Mareels, Dr. Stefan Rehbach, Dr. Carsten Sürig and Dr. Benedikt Zeumer, for their guidance and support.

Furthermore, I am grateful for the experience of being a part of the vibrant Fellow community in the Munich office. I thank all colleagues for the many helpful discussions as well as their insightful comments. There is no telling how much my dissertation has profited from working in such an environment that is at the same time friendly and professional. I will always remember the good times we had.

Great appreciation goes to my parents for their continuous support in many different ways. They have laid the foundation for this dissertation by providing the upbringing and education that make up much of who I am today. Finally, I would like to thank Christina for her relentless encouragement and affectionate support which is so strongly coupled with the success of this dissertation.

Marc P. Bielitza   Karlsruhe, January 2012

Contents

List of Figures

List of Tables

Abbreviations

APEF	Association of Iron Ore Exporting Countries
BF	Blast furnace
BOF	Basic oxygen furnace
BRIC	Brazil, Russia, India and China
CFR	Cost-and-freight
CISA	China Iron and Steel Association
CVRD	Companhia Vale do Rio Doce
dmtu	Dry metric ton unit
DR	Direct reduction
DRI	Direct reduced iron
DSO	Direct shipping ore
dwt	Deadweight ton(s)
EAF	Electric arc furnace
EBIT	Earnings before interest and taxes
EBITDA	Earnings before interest, taxes, depreciation and amortization
etc.	Et cetera (and so forth)
et al.	Et alii (and others)
ETF	Exchange-traded fund
e.g.	Exempli gratia (for example)
FDI	Foreign direct investment
Fe	Ferrum (iron)
FOB	Free-on-board
GDP	Gross domestic product
HHI	Herfindahl-Hirschman Index
HRC	Hot rolled coil
Inc.	Incorporated
ISSB	Iron and Steel Statistics Bureau
i.e.	It est (that is)
JORC	Australasian Joint Ore Reserves Committee
kg	Kilograms
MERCOSUR	Common Southern Market
Mt	Million metric ton(s)

Mtpa	Million metric ton(s) per year
Mdwt	Million deadweight ton(s)
NAFTA	North American Free Trade Agreement
nmi	Nautical mile(s)
NPV	Net present value
OEM	Original equipment manufacturer
OHF	Open hearth furnace
OLS	Ordinary least squares
OPEC	Organization of Petroleum Exporting Countries
OTC	Over-the-counter
p.a.	Per annum (per year)
p.	Page
pp.	Pages
ppt	Percentage points
PPP	Purchasing power parity
PVC	Polyvinyl chloride
R&D	Research and development
ROM	Run of mine
SAIL	Steel Authority of India
t	metric ton(s)
UNCTAD	United Nations Conference on Trade and Development
USD	U.S. dollar(s)
USDc	U.S. dollar cent(s)
VAT	Value-added tax
VBA	Visual Basic for Applications
VLOC	Very Large Ore Carrier
vs.	Versus
WTO	World Trade Organization

Symbols

c_{mij}^{CFR}	Standardized CFR cost of ore from mine segment m in region i shipped to region j, in USD per dry metric ton with 62.0% Fe
c_m^{ex}	Export taxes on iron ore from mine segment m, in USD/t
c_m^{FOB}	Standardized FOB cost of ore from mine segment m, in USD per dry metric ton with 62.0% Fe
$c_{ij}^{freight}$	Voyage freight rate from port of region i to port of region j, in USD/t
$c_{mij}^{freight}$	Standardized voyage freight rate of ore from mine segment m in region i to port of region j, in USD/t
c_m^{mining}	Standardized mining cost of mine segment m, in USD per dry metric ton with 62.0% Fe
$c_m^{mining,ROM}$	Actual run of mine mining cost of mine segment m for ore with moisture content mc_m and Fe content fc_m, in USD/t
$c_m^{royalty}$	Mining royalty cost for ore from mine segment m, in USD/t
$corr_m^{grade}$	Grade correction for ore from mine segment m, in USD/t
$corr_m^{VIU}$	Value-in-use correction for ore from mine segment m, in USD/t
d_j	Total annual iron ore demand of region j, in Mt
d_j^{steel}	Total annual net steel demand of region j, in Mt
fc_m	Fe content of ore from mine segment m, in %
M	Set of mine segments
mc_m	Moisture content of ore from mine segment m, in %
n_{ij}	Length of shipping route between port of region i and port of region j, in nautical miles
p_m	Offered price for capacity of mine segment m, in USD/t
λ_j	Market price of region j, in USD/t
$\bar{\lambda}_j$	Arbitrage-free market price of region j, in USD/t
π_m	Profit contribution of mine segment m, in USD millions
r	Interest rate, in %
R	Set of regions
s_j^{BOF}	Share of BOF steel of total steel production in region j, in %
s_j^{DR}	Share of DR steel of total steel production in region j, in %
s_j^{OHF}	Share of OHF steel of total steel production in region j, in %

x_m	Standardized production volume of mine segment m, in dry Mt with 62.0% Fe
x_m^{ROM}	Actual run of mine production volume of mine segment m with moisture content mc_m and Fe content fc_m, in Mt
$\bar{x}_m$	Annual production capacity of mine segment m, in Mt
x_{mj}	Quantity of iron ore mined in mine segment m and shipped to region j, in Mt

1 Introduction

1.1 Motivation

If DNA is the building block of life, then iron ore is the building block of the world's industrialized economies.[1] As the key ingredient for steelmaking, iron ore's importance for our everyday lives is tremendous. Steel, due to its strength, durability, versatile properties and recycling possibilities, represents almost 95% of the metal used in the world each year. It enjoys a broad range of applications and underpins almost all aspects of human activity, infrastructure and standard of living. From skyscrapers to home appliances, from automobiles to cutlery, from beverage cans to heavy machinery, steel, and therefore iron ore, is omnipresent.[2] Put simply, iron ore is a bare necessity and a fundamental ingredient in the economy.[3] Iron ore may, in fact, be more integral to the global economy than any other raw material, other than perhaps oil.[4] For this reason iron ore is rightfully referred to as the "king of resources".[5]

Consequently, the market for iron ore is a market of superlatives. In 2009, almost 1,600 Mt of iron ore were mined around the world,[6] enough to make roughly 14,000 times the amount of steel used to build San Francisco's Golden Gate Bridge.[7] However, the iron ore mining industry is not only large by volume, it also represents a huge value pool. The iron ore mined and sold in 2009 had a total market value of roughly USD 140 billion.[8] That is equivalent to almost 5% of the GDP of Germany[9] and only slightly less than the total

---

[1]See Jeffrey (2006), p. 3 on industrial minerals.
[2]See Degner et al. (2007), p. 2; Geoscience Australia (2011); Jeffrey (2006), p. 3.
[3]See Frost (1986), p. 97.
[4]See Blas (2009).
[5]Sergeant (2008).
[6]See United Nations Conference on Trade and Development (2010).
[7]Based on a comparison of magnitude in Ellsworth (2011).
[8]Calculated based on volume data from United Nations Conference on Trade and Development (2010) and annual average spot market price from The Steel Index (2011).
[9]Germany's GDP equaled USD 3,330.0 billion in 2009, see The World Bank (2011).

market value of the entire real estate in Manhattan.[10]   The market for iron ore therefore represents the world's second-largest natural resource market by value, after the market for crude oil.[11]

The extremely capital-intensive iron ore mining business has traditionally been dominated by three mining conglomerates: Vale, Rio Tinto and BHP Billiton. These companies, termed "the world's quietest, greatest franchise"[12] or simply the "Big Three", controlled approximately one third of iron ore production in 2009.[13] For decades, the iron ore market was characterized by overcapacity as well as stability and continuous high returns, thus being known as the market "where boom times slow but never end."[14] Essential for this stability was the iron ore benchmark pricing mechanism, traditionally reflecting the dynamics of a gentlemen's agreement. Prices were determined in annual negotiations between parties of about equal strength, miners on one side and steelmakers in Europe and developed Asia on the other side, an approach that offered stability in sales and supply for both parties.[15]

However, the iron ore market has recently undergone various radical changes, driven primarily by a global demand shock caused by the rapid industrialization of China. Within just a few years, surging construction and infrastructure investments have transformed China into the by far largest steel producing economy in the world and, due to the low quality of its domestic iron ore resources, the major buyer of iron ore on the seaborne market.[16] In combination with sustained economic growth in the other BRIC countries,[17] this immense increase in iron ore demand has led to an iron ore and bulk freight capacity supercycle[18] that was only temporarily suspended by the financial crisis and is now picking up again.[19]

With iron ore prices climbing to ever greater heights, the biggest profiteers have been miners with a claim on iron ore. The prospect of high profits means miners

---

[10]Valued at approximately USD 169 billion in 2004, see Rankin (2006).

[11]See Blas et al. (2009).

[12]Sergeant (2009).

[13]See Sergeant (2008); United Nations Conference on Trade and Development (2010).

[14]The New York Times (2009).

[15]See, e.g., Hellmer (1997a), pp. 7–8; Kästner et al. (1979), p. 206; Sukagawa (2010); Verhoeven et al. (2010).

[16]See Steel Business Briefing (2011c); Taube and in der Heiden (2010), p. 17; Woetzel (2001).

[17]Brazil, Russia, India and China. First defined by Goldman Sachs's former chief economist Jim O'Neill in O'Neill (2001).

[18]A supercycle is a multi-decade growth cycle in a market as described by the Elliott Wave Principle, originally proposed by Ralph Nelson Elliott. See Frost and Prechter (1998), pp. 155–158.

[19]See Verhoeven et al. (2010).

cannot shovel iron ore out of the ground quickly enough. Consequently, iron ore miners big and small are making huge investments to expand global production capacity. Lured by high market prices, numerous small mining companies are entering the market, many with the help of Chinese seed money.[20] As can be expected, steelmakers are not so jubilant. Driven especially by increased iron ore prices, raw material costs now make up a larger portion of the final steel price. Steelmakers thus face a price-cost squeeze that is threatening their margins.[21]

While the iron ore miners are enjoying this once-in-a-century boom, the overall market structure and dynamics have changed fundamentally. The substantial shift in demand geography, combined with increased global capacity utilization and the supply-demand discontinuity around the financial crisis, have triggered a disruptive collapse of the 40-year-old benchmark pricing system. In the 2009 price negotiations, encouraged by iron ore spot prices below long-term contract prices for the first time, steelmakers in Asia called for a contract price reduction of approximately 40%.[22] The price talks went through a procrastinated deadlock associated with the world's economic downturn and the arrest and conviction of Rio Tinto employees in Shanghai charged with industrial espionage and bribery.[23] In consequence, negotiations were halted and, with Chinese steel mills and the Big Three failing to agree to a 2009 benchmark price, all following iron ore deliveries were sold at spot market prices.[24]

When Chinese steel demand recovered surprisingly fast starting in mid-2009, iron ore spot prices soared past even historically high 2008 contract prices, forcing Chinese steel mills to suffer unprecedentedly high iron ore procurement costs.[25] With Chinese steelmakers' backs against the wall, the Big Three used their considerably increased negotiating power to fulfill their long-held desire for a new pricing mechanism that reflects market conditions more immediately than the negotiation-based benchmark system.[26] Thus, in early 2010, the Big Three announced the complete abandonment of benchmark pricing, opting instead for a quarterly index-based pricing model, operating on the basis of the average spot price for iron ore supplied to China, quoted in a regularly published iron ore index. This newly adopted pricing mechanism has brought an abrupt end

---

[20]See Regan (2011).
[21]See Pilling (2011); Regan (2011); Verhoeven et al. (2010).
[22]See Sato (2010), p. 3; The Economist (2010c); The Financial Times (2010c).
[23]See The Financial Times (2010c); Treadgold (2009).
[24]See Sato (2010), p. 4.
[25]See United Nations Conference on Trade and Development (2010), p. 4.
[26]See Verhoeven et al. (2010); Woolrich (2010).

to the traditional stability of the iron ore market, with iron ore price dynamics now experiencing ever shorter cycles and greater volatility.[27]

1.2 Ambition

The above described recent developments in the global iron ore market are not of a temporary nature. They rather mark the beginning of irreversible and deep changes in the structure and dynamics of the market. Given iron ore's fundamental role in the industrialized global economy, these developments, especially the change of the pricing mechanism, are relevant not only for iron ore miners, but also for steelmakers and major end-users, such as the automobile and construction industries. This situation of general uncertainty has market participants seeking indications as to what direction the development of the iron ore industry will take in the coming years.

This paper aims to answer two fundamental questions against the background of the recent developments and trends in the iron ore market:

- What general structure and dynamics will characterize the global iron ore market in the year 2020?

- How can demand-side players mitigate the risks arising from higher and more volatile iron ore prices?

Providing a comprehensive answer to the first question, i.e. giving an extensive overview of the key characteristics and dynamics of the 2020 iron ore market, represents the main focus of this paper. Of course, speculation about the future is always a hazardous exercise. However, it is natural, against the background of the radical changes and the economic importance of iron ore, to inquire in which direction the market is developing, and to ask what the effects will be on various market participants.

However, prior to setting out on this journey into the future, it is important to gain an in-depth understanding of the iron ore market in general, its current structure and fundamental mechanics. This requires a detailed analysis of the iron ore value chain and relevant technical details of iron ore as a product, as well as its role in the steelmaking process. Also, the status quo of the market must be described, taking into account the current supply and demand situation, as well as identifying key market participants. Having done so, the recent radical

---

[27]See, e.g., The Financial Times (2010a); The New York Times (2010); United Nations Conference on Trade and Development (2010), p. 4; Verhoeven et al. (2010).

developments and trends outlined above must be defined in greater detail and set into the perspective of the status quo.

Based on this solid foundation, this paper then aims to develop a prospect for the 2020 iron ore market, taking into account different vantage points. First of all, the general market setup in the year 2020 must be characterized. This includes the availability and geography of iron ore mining capacity, the level and geography of demand for iron ore, the level of dry bulk freight rates, as well as the resulting iron ore production, trade flows and market prices. It is within this general market setting that the specific outcomes for iron ore miners and steelmakers can be described in greater detail. This entails the analysis of miners' production figures and payoffs as well as steelmakers' iron ore procurement costs.[28] In addition to these structural analyses, this paper also aims to highlight the dynamics of the 2020 iron ore market by evaluating the impact of changes in key market parameters affected by the visible market trends.

The enormous difficulties inherent in quantitative forecast over such a time period make it tempting to avoid numbers and simply make statements on major tendencies in the market together with purely qualitative observations about the prospects for the iron ore market. However, there can be little doubt that, despite their limitations, numerical, model-based forecasts, set alongside qualitative discussions, permit a more focused examination of future developments in the market by suggesting a magnitude to various key market figures and effects of market parameters changes. Therefore, this paper will base the characterization of the 2020 iron ore market on an iron ore market model reflecting the market's fundamental structure and mechanics, including the changes caused by the recent developments. In doing so, it is necessary to make clear that the goal of this paper is not to precisely forecast the 2020 iron ore market, but rather to simulate possible market settings under various input factors.

The second research question, though only a secondary objective of this paper, is equally important from a market perspective. As outlined in Section 1.1, the recent developments in the iron ore market, in particular the surge in demand and the change in the pricing mechanism, have had an especially negative effect on the demand-side players in the market, principally steelmakers. They are now facing not only considerably higher iron ore prices, but also an increased price volatility due to the change from annual to quarterly price revisions. Though

---

[28]Note that the policymaker's perspective on the iron ore market is explicitly not in the focus of this paper. Unless necessary to achieve the goals set forth, this paper will therefore not touch on the question of national resource strategy, optimal public policy, macroeconomic welfare effects of market participants' actions, nor the optimal production path of exhaustible resources.

steelmakers are used to coping with the cyclicality of the markets in general, such short-term price fluctuations fundamentally contradict the nature of the steel industry and the business relations further downstream. Consequently, steelmakers, as well as governments of countries with considerably sized steel industries, are seeking to develop and implement strategies to mitigate the risks arising from this new market situation.

Addressing these considerations, this paper aims to propose and evaluate selected risk mitigation strategies for demand-side players. In doing so, this paper will engage into a detailed analysis of the recent developments and trends in the iron ore market from a steelmaker's perspective, aiming to define and quantify the exact risks to which demand-side players are exposed. With these risks laid out, potential strategies targeted at mitigating these risks will be proposed. Using the above described iron ore market model, this paper finally aims to analyze the effectiveness of selected strategies as well as their effects on the general iron ore market setting and the remaining market participants.

Therefore, based on the two central research questions defined above, the practical goals of this paper can be summarized as follows:

1. Describe in detail the iron ore value chain, the relevant technical characteristics of iron ore as a product and its role in the steelmaking process

2. Gain an in-depth understanding of the current structure and fundamental mechanics of the iron ore market, taking into account the status quo supply and demand situation, as well as identifying key market participants

3. Describe in detail the recent developments and trends in the market and determine the effects especially on demand-side players. Derive potential risk mitigation strategies for these players and select those to be analyzed in greater detail

4. Propose a 2020 iron ore market model reflecting the market's fundamental structure and mechanics, including the changes caused by the recent developments

5. Employ the proposed model to derive and discuss quantitative results with respect to the structure and dynamics of the 2020 iron ore market as well as the effectiveness and influences of the selected risk mitigation strategies for demand-side players

1.3 Structure of the present paper

This paper is split into a total of seven chapters, including the present chapter. Chapters 2 through 6 correspond to the five above defined practical goals.

Chapter 2 provides a technical introduction to iron ore, touching on its key characteristics and its role in the steelmaking process. Section 2.1 provides a precise definition of iron ore and examines the nature and occurrence of the material in the form of resources and reserves. Also, various differentiating factors of natural iron ores are outlined. Subsequently, Section 2.2 describes in detail the mine-to-market supply route of iron ore. Finally, Section 2.3 highlights iron ore's economic importance by describing its significance for iron- and steelmaking. The section includes an overview of the most common steelmaking process routes and discusses the quality of iron ores with respect to their use in these process routes.

Chapter 3 aims to give an overview of the current structure and mechanics of the global iron ore market by describing the 2009 market situation. First, Section 3.1 provides some introductory comments regarding the accepted routines and practices for presenting iron ore data and statistics. Then, Section 3.2 describes the global demand situation for iron ore in 2009 by discussing the geographic distribution of demand and portraying key demand-side players. Section 3.3 describes the global supply situation in a similar manner. Section 3.4 briefly touches on the market for dry bulk freight and highlights its influence on the iron ore market. Section 3.5 deals with the actual iron ore market mechanism, including a description of the modes of iron ore transactions as well as the pricing of iron ore. Also, the 2009 iron ore trade flows are described. Finally, Section 3.6 outlines the effects of public policy on the iron ore market, with a strong focus on the taxation of the industry.

Chapter 4 provides a comprehensive overview of the recent developments and trends in the global iron ore market. First, the respective market developments and trends are described in detail in Section 4.1. Subsequently, Section 4.2 highlights the impact of those market changes on the steel industry. Based on this impact, Section 4.3 gives an overview of potential risk mitigating strategies for demand-side players and selects two to be analyzed in greater detail going forward.

Based on the fundamental characteristics and mechanics of the market described in Chapters 2 and 3, Chapter 5 proposes a model for the 2020 iron ore market. Section 5.1 gives an overview of the general structure of the model and describes in detail the key input components, the market mechanism and outputs. Section 5.2 outlines the technical implementation of the model with a special focus on the implementation of the supply allocation mechanism. Finally, Section 5.3 presents a validation of the proposed model by comparing selected results to respective 2009 actuals.

The results of the quantitative analyses performed using the market model are described and discussed in Chapter 6. First, Section 6.1 sets the scope of the market evaluation, by defining the key market parameters as well as the exact settings leading to a realistic market constellation for the 2020 base case. Additional market parameter settings are defined for a sensitivity analysis, allowing the evaluation of the impact of changes of key parameters on the market. Also, the scenarios are defined with which the selected risk mitigation strategies are to be evaluated. In Section 6.2, the methodology and depth of the analyses are defined in terms of which output factors are analyzed. Finally, Section 6.3 describes the quantitative model results for the 2020 base case and each of the prior defined scenarios along the criteria presented in Section 6.2. In the discussion in Section 6.4, an effort is made to summarize the characteristics and dynamics of the global iron ore market in 2020 as well as to give an evaluation of the selected risk mitigation strategies for demand-side players.

Chapter 7, the final chapter of this paper, aims to provide a concluding summary of the results as well as to give an outlook regarding possibilities for future related research. Section 7.1 reviews the attainment of the goals originally set out in the present chapter and briefly summarizes the key findings of this paper. Subsequently, Section 7.2 gives a critical appraisal of the methodology used and finally suggests areas for future research with respect to the iron ore market.

1.4 Relevant previous research on the iron ore market

While previous studies of the iron ore market are rare, some do exist. Without aiming to create a taxonomy of existing iron ore market studies, this section gives a brief overview of relevant previous research in chronological order. These studies are summarized in Table 1.1.

Historically, studies of the global iron ore market were of a purely descriptive nature. For example, Manners (1971) describes the key changes in the iron ore market setting from 1950 to 1965 and gives an outlook of trends until 1980. Without suggesting a model of the market, Manners concentrates on a descriptive analysis of the economic geography of iron ore supply and demand as well as changes in iron ore prices and seaborne trade. In his market outlook, Manners summarizes global and regional supply and demand forecasts and provides a perspective on future patterns of iron ore trade.

Paper	Description/objective	Characteristics of modeling of iron ore market
Manners (1971)	Ex-post description of economic geography of iron ore supply and demand, changes in prices and trade from 1950 to 1965. Market outlook through 1980, including supply and demand forecasts and future trade patterns	No iron ore market model proposed, purely descriptive market analysis and outlook
Hashimoto and Sihsobhon (1981)	Projection of market situations in global steel market for 1980, 1985 and 1990, including demand and supply quantities, prices, and required investment in production facilities	No iron ore market model proposed, iron ore price is exogenous variable of steel industry model
Yamawaki (1984)	Ex-post empirical analysis of Japanese steel industry between 1957 and 1983 with focus on pricing, capacity decisions and market structure, including buyer and seller concentration	No iron ore market model proposed, iron ore price is exogenous variable of steel industry model
Priovolos (1987)	Econometric modeling of the global iron ore market, including supply and demand on regional level, imports/exports and prices. Historical simulation from 1974 to 1984 and projection through 1994 quantifying the impact of exogenous shocks	Global iron ore market model with 15 regions, price determined by means of bilateral oligopolistic theory, no trade flows calculated between regions
Toweh and Newcomb (1991)	Ex-post evaluation of efficiency of interregional iron ore trade flows in 1984, projection of iron ore trade flows and market clearing prices for the year 2000 under expansionist and stagnant iron ore demand scenarios	Spatial equilibrium model of global iron ore market taking into account 14 regions, prediction of trade flows between regions using linear programming approach
Labson (1997)	Joint econometric modeling of global iron ore and steel industries, including projection of iron ore supply and demand on regional level, imports/exports and prices from 1994 to 2000	Global iron ore market model with ten regions, no trade flows calculated between regions
Hellmer (1997a)	Historical examination of behavior of participants in the European iron ore market from 1984 to 1992	Oligopoly model of European iron ore market assuming supply from Brazil
Hellmer (1997b)	Extension of behavioral analysis to global scale and analysis of competitive strength of iron ore miners with focus on Swedish miner LKAB	Oligopoly model of European and Asian iron ore markets, introduction of product differentiation and mining cost structures

Table 1.1: Chronological overview of relevant previous research on the iron ore market [Own illustration]

Initial efforts to model the iron ore market were not independent of efforts to model the steel industry. A review of these earlier iron ore and steel studies, such as Hashimoto and Sihsobhon (1981) and Yamawaki (1984), shows that many focus on estimating the demand for iron ore. In most cases, iron ore prices are determined exogenously. In addition, effective capacity, production, exports, imports and apparent consumption of iron ore by country or region are not explicitly specified, nor are their interrelationships modeled. Furthermore, extremely simplifying generalizations are usually made regarding the competitiveness of the industry.

The first noteworthy attempt to build a model reflecting the dynamics of the global iron ore market comes from Priovolos (1987). Priovolos models market supply and demand for 15 regions and uses game theory principles to determine iron ore prices with the boundaries of the range of price negotiations specified through bilateral oligopolistic theory. The iron ore players in the model are assumed to select their strategies regarding quantity and price on a probabilistic basis, which are then linked into a general model of the industry. While imports and exports of iron ore are derived per region, interregional trade flows are not calculated. Priovolos validates the model by comparing the results of a historical simulation of the market between 1974 and 1984 to the respective actuals. Also, Priovolos uses a multiplier analysis to calculate the impact of sustained changes in selected exogenous variables of the model through 1994. For example, he shows that an increase in Brazilian iron ore capacity would reduce iron ore prices and would lead to a redistribution of market shares among producers.

Using a different approach, Toweh and Newcomb (1991) presents a multi-market spatial equilibrium model depicting world iron ore trade and market prices. Building on research from Samuelson (1952) and Henderson (1958), the model employs a linear program to evaluate the interregional trade flow efficiency between 14 regions of the iron ore industry in 1984 and predicts trade flows and market clearing prices for the year 2000 assuming perfect competition under expansionist and stagnant demand scenarios.

Labson (1997) proposes a joint econometric model of the global iron ore and steel industries. However, in contrast to the other joint iron ore and steel models described above, which include the supply and price of iron ore as exogenous variables, Labson's model actually reflects the specific dynamics of the iron ore market. The global market is split into ten regions and iron ore imports, exports and prices are projected per region through the year 2000. Somewhat similar to the model of Priovolos (1987), it does not take into account trade flows between the defined regions.

The iron ore market model developed by Hellmer (1997a) uses an oligopolistic approach to examine the behavior of players in the European iron ore market between 1984 and 1992. The results support the hypothesis that Brazil acts as a Stackelberg leader and consequently considers the reaction from other countries when making its output decision. The other countries seem to participate in a Cournot game, thus not considering changes in their competitors' outputs when defining their own quantities. Building on these results, Hellmer (1997b) extends the analysis to the world market with a particular focus on the role of Swedish miner LKAB. The utilized model, analyzing the market between 1986 and 1994, differs in that it considers iron ore product differentiation and takes into account supply and demand elasticities as well as the competitive strength of miners in terms of their mining cost structure.

Summarizing, the iron ore industry has only been subject to very limited academic research in the past 40 years. Especially forward-looking models of the iron ore market, reflecting its key characteristics and underlying dynamics, are extremely rare. While Priovolos (1987), Toweh and Newcomb (1991) and Labson (1997) come closest to suggesting a model adequate to achieve the goals of the present paper, all three models do not reflect the recent radical changes in the market structure as described in Section 1.1. Due to the severity of these changes, especially the altered pricing mechanism, none of the existing iron ore market models are unsuitable for an analysis of the 2020 iron ore market as targeted by this paper. Thus, based on helpful suggestions from existing models,[29] the development of a new iron ore market model reflecting these fundamental market changes is mandated.

---

[29]Mentionable is the general structure of the market models in Priovolos (1987) and Labson (1997), the spatial equilibrium approach using linear programming in Toweh and Newcomb (1991) and the introduction of detailed and differentiated mining costs in Hellmer (1997b).

2 Technical introduction to iron ore

This chapter aims to give a technical introduction to iron ore. Section 2.1 provides a precise definition of iron ore and examines the nature and occurrence of the material in the form of resources and reserves. Also, various differentiating factors of natural iron ores are outlined. Subsequently, Section 2.2 describes in detail the mine-to-market supply route of iron ore. Finally, Section 2.3 highlights iron ore's economic importance by describing its significance for iron- and steelmaking. The section includes an overview of the most common steelmaking process routes and discusses the quality of iron ores with respect to their use in these process routes.

2.1 Nature and occurrence of iron and iron ores

2.1.1 Natural iron resources and iron ore reserves

Iron is a chemical element, a metal of transition group VIII of the periodic table, with the symbol Fe from the Latin word "ferrum". Iron has an atomic number of 26, an atomic weight of 55.847 and a melting point of about 1,535°C or lower depending on the purity of the metal.[30]

Iron makes up roughly 5% of the earth's crust, fourth in abundance behind oxygen, silicon and aluminum.[31] Most of the iron, because of its position or concentration in the earth's crust, is not available for industrial use. Geologic processes have concentrated only a small fraction of the crustal iron into deposits that contain as much as 70% of the element.[32] These crustal concentrations of iron are commonly referred to as "iron resources". Identified resources are those whose location, grade, quality and quantity are known or estimated from specific geological evidence. Following the widely accepted JORC code,

---

[30]See Wakelin and Ricketts (1999), p. 2.
[31]See Wakelin and Ricketts (1999), p. 2.
[32]See Kuck (2010).

identified resources can be divided into measured, indicated and inferred, depending on the level of knowledge and confidence with respect to their existence and geological attributes.[33]

However, not all of the iron found in these resources may be correctly termed "iron ore". Poveromo (1999) defines iron ore for commercial purposes as "iron bearing material that can be economically used at a particular place and time under the current cost and market price conditions". Resources containing iron bearing materials that can be economically mined are called "iron ore reserves".[34] Resources therefore include both such minable ore reserves as well as other iron bearing materials that may become profitable to mine under future economic conditions and/or using improved methods of mining, beneficiation, concentration and agglomeration.[35]

Many thousands of iron occurrences are known throughout the world. They range in size from a few tons to many hundreds of millions of tons.[36] Based on the above definitions, Table 2.1 shows the estimate of the identified world reserves in terms of crude ore and contained iron. Since the iron content of different ore resources can vary greatly, it is sensible to compare them on the basis of the iron they contain rather than the total amount of crude ore.[37] As of January 2011 world reserves were estimated at slightly more than 86 billion tons of iron contained within roughly 183 billion tons of crude ore. Estimates of world resources exceeded 800 billion tons of ore containing 230 billion tons of iron.[38]

2.1.2 Depletion of iron ore

In contrast to renewable natural resources such as timber, which can be used in a sustainable manner, iron ore, being an exhaustible resource, is finite.[39] The fear of depletion of the exhaustible natural resources upon which human society builds dates back at least two centuries to Thomas Malthus, David Ricardo and other classical economists.[40] Since then, the scarcity of exhaustible natural resources and its effects has been the topic of various papers and reports.[41]

---

[33]See Sato (2010), pp. 383–386; The Joint Ore Reserves Committee (2004).
[34]See The Joint Ore Reserves Committee (2004).
[35]See Poveromo (1999), p. 574.
[36]See Poveromo (1999), p. 571.
[37]See Sato (2010), pp. 383–386.
[38]See Jorgenson (2011), p. 85.
[39]See Eckel (1914), pp. 414–416.
[40]See Tilton (2003); World Economic Forum (2011).
[41]See, e.g., Barnett and Morse (1963); Meadows et al. (1972); Simon (1981); Simon (1996).

Country	Reserves		
	Pure iron Mt	**Crude ore** Mt	**Average Fe content**
Brazil	16,000	29,000	55%
Australia	15,000	24,000	63%
Russia	14,000	25,000	56%
Ukraine	9,000	30,000	30%
China	6,400	23,000	28%
India	4,500	7,000	64%
Kazakhstan	3,300	8,300	40%
Venezuela	2,400	4,000	60%
Canada	2,300	6,300	37%
Sweden	2,200	3,500	63%
Other	11,450	23,200	49%
World total	**86,550**	**183,300**	**47%**

Table 2.1: World iron ore reserves by country as of January 2011 [Own illustration based on Jorgenson (2011), p. 85; McKinsey & Company (2011b)]

The most recent wave of concern emerged in the early 1970s, thanks in part to well-publicized forecasts of possible rapid exhaustion of the world's natural resources in such studies as the Club of Rome's "The Limits to Growth" (Meadows et al. (1972)).[42] Using a sophisticated computer simulation model, the study argued that the exhaustion of mineral commodities could cause the collapse of the high living standards enjoyed by the developed world by the middle of the 21st century.[43]

The study listed iron ore as one of the "more important mineral and fuel resources, the vital raw materials for today's major industrial processes."[44] It predicted iron ore resources to last until the year 2210 at the 1972 rate of consumption and until the year 2063 assuming a projected average growth rate of consumption of 1.8% per year.[45] While these figures are meanwhile outdated, more recent calculations forecast global iron ore depletion in the year 2090 given the current rate of consumption.[46]

Though depletion of global iron ore resources therefore may seem a probable scenario, it must be taken into account that iron ore production may not indefinitely continue at current rates. This is due to the fact that iron ore, once it has been transformed into steel, can be easily recycled without loss of quality.

---

[42]See Crowson (1992), p. 86; Tilton (2003). For an overview of the economics of exhaustible resource depletion, see Radetzki (2008), pp. 111–125.
[43]See Meadows et al. (1972), pp. 63–69.
[44]Meadows et al. (1972), p. 69.
[45]See Meadows et al. (1972), p. 64.
[46]See Yellishetty et al. (2011).

Therefore, iron ore can be referred to as a "durable" resource.[47] In contrast to other exhaustible natural resources, such as crude oil for example, it does not vanish after use.[48] Therefore, assuming that recycling of steel will play an increasingly important role with growing environmental awareness and that in the far future steel may anyhow be replaced by a more advanced material, there is a chance that the amount of iron ore remaining in the earth's crust will be sufficient to supply humanity with all the steel it will ever need.

2.1.3 Differentiating factors of natural iron ores

Though we generally refer to "iron ore" as if it were a homogeneous product, in reality no two iron ore deposits in the world are identical.[49] Therefore, iron ore is not a commodity, though it is often colloquially referred to as one.[50] The most important differentiating factors of iron ore are

- *Physical form (particle size)* – Iron ore is found in two natural forms: fines and lump. Fines are defined as iron ore with the majority of individual particles measuring less than 4.75 millimeters in diameter. Conversely, lump is iron ore with the majority of individual particles measuring more than 4.75 millimeters in diameter. Fines and lump are often found in the same deposit and are separated by screening and sorting[51]

- *Iron content (grade)* – Iron ore resources never contain 100% pure iron, but rather iron in the form of various chemical compositions.[52] Therefore, the iron content of natural ores ranges from approximately 20–70%, with ores containing more than 60% Fe termed "high grade".[53] Minerals containing significant amounts of iron may be grouped into oxides, carbonates, sulfides and silicates.[54] The oxide minerals hematite (Fe_2O_3, approximately 60–70% Fe) and magnetite (Fe_3O_4, approximately 20–30% Fe) are the most common sources of industrially used iron[55]

---

[47]Note that, with respect to scarcity, iron ore is therefore not to be compared with rare earths, which are less abundant and harder to recycle (see, e.g., Hook (2011); Köhn (2011)).

[48]See Degner et al. (2007), p. 24; World Steel Association (2008).

[49]See Peel (2009).

[50]Merriam-Webster, Inc. (2011) defines a commodity as "a good [...] whose wide availability typically [...] diminishes the importance of factors [...] other than price." For a broader commodity definition, see Radetzki (2008), pp. 22–26.

[51]See Kirk (1999).

[52]See Degner et al. (2007), p. 16.

[53]See Peel (2009).

[54]See Poveromo (1999), pp. 569–570.

[55]See Peel (2009).

- *Moisture content* – Depending on their region of origin and position in the rock bed, natural iron ores contain different levels of moisture. The moisture content of natural ores roughly ranges from 2–10%[56]

- *Content of trace elements and compounds* – Iron has the natural affinity to unite with other chemical elements. Therefore, iron ores commonly contain small amounts of other elements and chemical compounds, such as alumina, manganese, phosphorus, silica, sulfur and vanadium[57]

2.2 Iron ore value chain from mine to market

In this section, the key steps of the mine-to-market supply route of iron ore are described:

- Discovery of iron ore deposits

- Buildup of mining infrastructure

- Mining of iron ore

- Beneficiation and agglomeration or iron ore (processing and upgrading)

- Transportation of iron ore to the market

2.2.1 Discovery of iron ore deposits

The general occurrence, size and shape of an iron ore deposit is determined during the exploration phase. Geophysical techniques are the primary reconnaissance tools in the search for iron ore bodies. These techniques are based on the presence of measurable contrasts of physical properties, mostly magnetism and density, between the iron ore minerals and the surrounding rocks. Magnetometers are commonly used to determine the strength of the earth's magnetic field or its vertical component at a given location. Variations of this field from magnetic disturbances caused by concentrations of magnetic material near the surface give evidence for the presence of iron ore. Though hand-held magnetometers exist, airborne magnetic surveys are more economical for large areas. The evaluation of the detailed data from magnetometer and other geophysical surveys is usually followed by a carefully worked out drilling program. The so provided samples, through geological and mineralogical studies, establish the

---

[56]See McKinsey & Company (2011b); Poveromo (1999), pp. 642–657.
[57]See Poveromo (1999), pp. 640–642; Wakelin and Ricketts (1999), p. 2.

grade, quality and extent of the ore body and the nature and quantity of the overburden or rock formations associated with the ore.[58]

2.2.2 Buildup of mining infrastructure

Once the presence and nature of an iron ore body has been determined, the required infrastructure must be set up before the ore can be mined. The required infrastructure primarily includes mining facilities, materials handling and processing plants as well as supporting infrastructure such as telecommunication systems, energy and water supply. In addition, administrative offices and accommodations for miners are often needed. Also, to allow for adequate transportation, roads, railway lines and possibly an airstrip must be built. Generally, the amount and type of infrastructure to be set up depends on whether or not existing mine sites are within proximity, allowing for joint use of some facilities and systems. Due to this immense amount of required infrastructure, new mining projects are commonly extremely capital intensive and often take three to seven years to complete.[59]

2.2.3 Mining of iron ore

With the required infrastructure in place, the ore can be mined either by means of open pit or underground mining. Since open pit mining offers the lowest cost of operation, it is employed wherever the stripping ratio (the amount of overburden and waste that has to be handled for each unit of ore mined) does not exceed an economical limit. Nearly all large iron ore mines in the world, with the exception of some in Europe, are worked by open pit methods. The overburden is stripped from the underlying ore and unconsolidated materials are excavated by power shovels, draglines or power scrapers, depending on the local conditions. Consolidated materials are broken into handleable sizes by means of drilling and blasting. The ore is then transported out of the pit by railroad cars, trucks, belt conveyors or a combination of these.[60]

When the stripping ratio becomes too high for open pit mining, underground mining methods are employed. Underground mining requires a larger capital investment per ton of annual capacity than open pit mining due to required costly shafts or tunnels, underground haulage and elaborate pumping facilities. Moreover, the production of iron ore per man per day in an underground mine

---

[58]See Poveromo (1999), pp. 608–609.
[59]See GHD Pty Ltd. (2011); Poveromo (1999), p. 609.
[60]See Poveromo (1999), pp. 610–612.

is only a fraction of that in open pit operations. In most cases, access to underground mines in obtained though inclined or vertical shafts sunk adjacent to the ore deposit. After the ore has been extracted by means of caving, stoping or slicing, it is hoisted to the surface.[61]

2.2.4 Beneficiation and agglomeration of iron ore

As described in Section 2.1.3, iron ore resources differ greatly from one another. While some naturally occurring ores can be sold directly, others require further upgrading in order to be marketed efficiently. From a market perspective, natural iron ores may be grouped broadly as[62]

- *Direct shipping ore (DSO)* – Natural fines or lump ore with more than 60% Fe content and low levels of trace elements are referred to as "direct shipping ore (DSO)". These ores, usually hematite, can be sold on the market without further treatment

- *Beneficiable ore* – Natural fines or lump ore containing less than 60% Fe and/or high levels of trace elements are termed "beneficiable ores". They require upgrading through beneficiation and/or agglomeration prior to marketing

During beneficiation, also referred to as "ore dressing", undesirable elements, such as gangue and chemical impurities, are removed from the crude ore by means of grinding, washing, filtration and concentration by magnetic, gravity or flotation techniques. The resulting end product, fine grained ore with more than 60% Fe, is termed "concentrate".[63] Although the beneficiation methods described above are commonly used to increase the Fe content of low grade fines or lump ore, they are also used to improve the quality of high grade ores by controlling particle size and reducing the content of gangue materials.[64]

Pelletizing is the common method used to agglomerate very fine and powdery ores and concentrates at mining sites. Agglomeration often becomes necessary in order to reduce the loss of ore during further handling and transportation.[65] In the pelletizing process, a binding agent, often clay, is added to the ore, which is agglomerated into balls. These balls then pass through a furnace where they

---

[61]See Poveromo (1999), p. 612.
[62]See Kirk (1999); Peel (2009).
[63]See Kirk (1999); Sato (2010), p. 387.
[64]See Poveromo (1999), p. 574.
[65]See Peel (2009).

are indurated at temperatures of more than 1,000°C and become pellets, usually measuring from 9.55 to 16.0 millimeters.[66]

Therefore, summarizing, four types of iron ore can be found on the market:

- Naturally high grade fines
- Naturally high grade lump ores
- Concentrates
- Pellets

Figure 2.1 gives an overview of these marketable ore types and their origination.

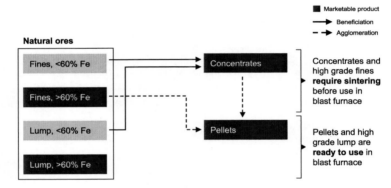

Figure 2.1: Classification of natural and marketable iron ores [Own illustration]

2.2.5 Transportation of iron ore to the market

Historically, steelmaking facilities were located adjacent to iron ore mines. Since 1945, however, the seaborne trade of iron ore has grown dramatically. This is due to higher grade ore deposits being developed in the southern hemisphere and reduced shipping cost thanks to the construction of larger seagoing vessels.[67] Today, iron ore mining is an industry in its own right which is linked to the steelmaking industry by sophisticated bulk transport systems. The transportation of iron ore within these systems is commonly performed with a combined use of railroads and ships.[68]

---

[66]See Burgo (1999), p. 727; Kirk (1999).
[67]See Poveromo (1999), pp. 637–639.
[68]See Frost (1986); Speltz (2006), pp. 79–94.

The distances of most of the world's major iron ore mines from the nearest deepwater ports are considerable. This has resulted in the development of some of the largest dedicated railway lines in the world.[69] Kilometer long megatrains are capable of hauling up to 17,500 tons of iron ore from the mines to the ports.[70] Two of the longest iron ore bearing railway lines are the 853 km long track from Sishen to the port at Saldanha Bay (South Africa) and the 925 km long line between Carajás and Ponta da Madeira (Brazil).[71] After arrival at the port, the ore is loaded onto ships referred to as "dry bulk carriers" or "dry bulk freighters".[72] These are merchant vessels specially designed to transport unpackaged bulk cargo in their cargo holds. Because of the high density of ore, these carriers have a relatively high center of gravity to prevent them from rolling heavily with possible stress to the hull.[73]

Most commonly, Capesize vessels are used in the transportation of iron ore.[74] These ships have a tonnage of 110,000–200,000 dwt (166,500 dwt average) and an average length of 280 meters.[75] Only a limited number of port terminals in the world are large enough to accommodate such vessels.[76] The name "Capesize" comes from the vessels' historic characteristic of being incapable of using the Panama and Suez Canals due to their draft and thus requiring transit via South America's Cape Horn or South Africa's Cape of Good Hope.[77] However, with the upgrading of the Suez Canal (completed in 2010) and the Panama Canal (estimated completion in 2014), both canals will allow the passage of Capesize vessels.[78] By extension, the Capesize category includes VLOC (Very Large Ore Carrier) vessels. These even larger ships (more then 200,000 dwt, 243,000 dwt average) are also used to transport iron ore on certain routes. In 2009, 763 Capesize and 107 VLOC vessels were in service with a total tonnage of 127 and 43 Mdwt respectively.[79]

---

[69]See Frost (1986).
[70]See Isern and Pung (2007); Kästner et al. (1979), p. 199.
[71]See Bottke (1981), p. 15.
[72]See Parker (2006), pp. 99–100.
[73]See Branch (2007), p. 251.
[74]See Branch (2007), pp. 60–61; Gardiner (2011), p. 34.
[75]See Gardiner (2011), p. 24; Parker (2006), p. 100.
[76]See United Nations Conference on Trade and Development (1974), p. 40.
[77]See Parker (2006), p. 107; Taube and in der Heiden (2010), p. 43.
[78]See Panama Canal Authority (2010); Suez Canal Authority (2010).
[79]See Gardiner (2011), p. 24.

2.3 Significance of iron ore for steelmaking

98% of the iron ore that is mined globally is used for iron- and steelmaking.[80] The remaining 2% are used to manufacture cement, heavy-medium materials, pigments, ballast, agricultural products and specialty chemicals.[81] Iron ore is the most important of the many natural raw materials required for the making of iron and steel.[82]

Steel is the most useful metal known, being used 20 times more than all other metals put together. Steel is strong, durable and extremely versatile. The many different kinds of steel consist almost entirely of iron with the addition of small amounts of carbon (usually less than 1%) and of other metals to form different alloys (e.g., stainless steel). Pure iron is quite soft, but adding a small amount of carbon makes it significantly harder and stronger. Most of the additional elements in steel are added deliberately in the steelmaking process (e.g., chromium, manganese, nickel, molybdenum). By changing the proportions of these additional elements, it is possible to make steels suitable for a great variety of uses. Steel's desirable properties make it the main structural metal in engineering and building projects. About 60% of iron and steel products are used in transportation and construction, 20% in machinery manufacture, and most of the remainder in cans and containers, in the oil and gas industries and in various appliances and other equipment.[83]

2.3.1 Overview of iron- and steelmaking process routes

As shown in Figure 2.2, steel can be produced using various different production methods or "process routes":[84]

- *Primary steel production* (approximately 75% of global steel production in 2009), also referred to as "integrated steelmaking",[85] is carried out by reducing iron ores to iron and further converting iron to steel. Although some steel scrap is used in the process, iron ore is the main source of iron in primary steel production. The main routes and their shares of 2009 global steel production are:

    – Blast furnace (BF) – basic oxygen furnace (BOF): 71%

---

[80]See Kästner et al. (1979), p. 213; Kirk (1999).
[81]See Kästner et al. (1979), pp. 213–218; Kuck (2010).
[82]See Poveromo (1999), p. 569.
[83]See Geoscience Australia (2011).
[84]See World Steel Association (2008); World Steel Association (2010), pp. 22–25.
[85]See Barnett and Crandall (1986), pp. 3–6.

> – Blast furnace (BF) – open hearth furnace (OHF): 1%
>
> – Direct reduction (DR) – electric arc furnace (EAF): 3%

- *Secondary steel production* (approximately 25% of global steel production
  in 2009), also called the "minimill route",[86] refers to the melting of recycled
  steel scrap in electric arc furnaces (EAF). In the EAF, graphite electrodes
  conduct an electric current of high voltage to create an electric arc that
  melts the scrap. No iron ore is used in the process

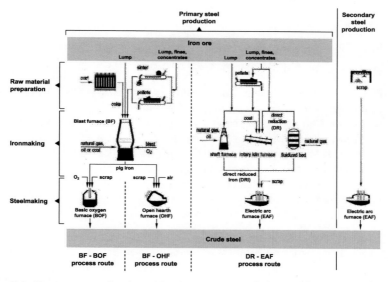

Figure 2.2: Process routes for the production of crude steel [Own illustration, adapted from
Barnett and Crandall (1986), p. 4; Degner et al. (2007), p. 28; World Steel Association (2008)]

For the remaining part of this subsection, the most common steel production
method, the blast furnace – basic oxygen furnace route (also known as "integrated steelmaking")[87], will be described along its value chain in more detail.
This value chain can be roughly split into three steps:[88]

- Preparation of raw materials to be charged into the blast furnace

- Ironmaking: Reduction of iron ore to iron through removal of oxygen in
  the blast furnace

---

[86]See Barnett and Crandall (1986), pp. 3–6.
[87]See Degner et al. (2007), p. 77.
[88]See Frondel et al. (2007).

- Steelmaking: Conversion of iron to steel through removal of carbon in the basic oxygen furnace

2.3.1.1 Preparation of raw materials

The raw materials required for integrated steelmaking can be split into four groups:[89]

- Iron-bearing material (iron ore)
- Reducing agent (coke)
- Flux (limestone and dolomite)
- Fuel (typically oil or gas)

In order to ensure an efficient ironmaking process, these charge materials require some preparation prior to being charged into the blast furnace. The blast furnace is a countercurrent gas-solid reactor in which the solid charge materials move downward while the hot reducing gases flow upward. The best possible contact between the solids and the reducing gas is obtained with a permeable burden, which permits a uniform high rate of gas flow with a minimum of channeling of the gas. Therefore, it is essential that fine grained materials are agglomerated before being charged into the furnace. Otherwise, these materials would clot and obstruct the flow of the reducing gases in the furnace.[90]

While iron ore pellets and lump ores are coarse enough to be charged directly into the blast furnace, iron ore concentrate and fines require prior sintering. This agglomeration is commonly performed at sintering plants often located in proximity of the blast furnaces on the sites of the steel producers. The sintering process is carried out on a continuous traveling grate that conveys a roughly 500 mm thick bed of iron ore concentrate or fines mixed with approximately 5% coke breeze and fluxes. The coke breeze is ignited on the surface by gas burners and, as the mixture moves along on the traveling grate, air is pulled down through the mixture burning the fuel by downward combustion. This creates sufficient temperature, about 1,300–1,480°C, to agglomerate the mix into coarse porouse chunks, referred to as "sinter".[91] This agglomeration of fine

---

[89]See Degner et al. (2007), p. 16.
[90]See Bottke (1981), pp. 155–158; Poveromo (1999), p. 625.
[91]See Degner et al. (2007), pp. 20–23; Poveromo (1999), p. 629.

ores not only improves the flow of gas in the blast furnace, but also improves the transport and storage characteristics of the ore.[92]

2.3.1.2 Fundamentals of ironmaking

The blast furnace is a continuously operating tall shaft-type furnace with a vertical stack on top of a crucible-like hearth. Iron-bearing materials (iron ore sinter, lump or pellets), a reducing agent (coke) and flux (limestone and dolomite) are charged into the top of the shaft. A blast of heated air and, in most cases, a gaseous, liquid or powdered fuel are introduced through openings at the bottom of the shaft just above the hearth.[93] The solid materials move downward and the coke, essentially impure carbon, burns with the injected fuel in the blast of hot air to form carbon dioxide, a strongly exothermic reaction which is the main source of heat in the furnace:[94]

$$C + O_2 \rightarrow CO_2$$

At the high temperature at the bottom of the furnace, the carbon dioxide is not stable and reacts with carbon to produce carbon monoxide:[95]

$$CO_2 + C \rightarrow 2CO$$

The reducing gas carbon monoxide flows upward, binding the oxygen in the iron ore to form carbon dioxide and brings about the reduction of the ore:[96]

$$\text{Hematite: } Fe_2O_3 + 3CO \rightarrow 2Fe + 3CO_2$$
$$\text{Magnetite: } Fe_3O_4 + 4CO \rightarrow 3Fe + 4CO_2$$

The reduced iron melts and runs down to the bottom of the hearth. The flux combines with the impurities in the ore to produce a slag which also melts and accumulates on the top of the liquid iron in the hearth. The liquid iron and slag are drained out of the furnace through tapholes and separated by way of refractory-lined trough and runner system.[97] Large-capacity blast furnaces produce some 12,000 tons of raw iron per day. For each net ton of raw iron

---

[92]See Bottke (1981), pp. 158–159.
[93]See Burgo (1999), p. 725; Degner et al. (2007), pp. 31–35.
[94]See Burgo (1999), p. 729.
[95]See Burgo (1999), p. 729.
[96]See Burgo (1999), pp. 729–730.
[97]See Burgo (1999), p. 725; Degner et al. (2007), pp. 37–38.

produced, approximately 1.6 tons of iron ore, 0.5 tons of coke and other fuel, 0.3 tons of limestone or dolomite and 1,000 m^3 of air are consumed.[98]

The so produced raw iron, referred to also as "pig iron" or "hot metal", contains approximately 4.0–4.7% carbon.[99] Due to this high level of carbon, it is too brittle to be formed by forging or rolling.[100] It can however be used as "cast iron" or "foundry iron" by being poured into a mold, the shape of which it will retain after it cools and solidifies.[101] Approximately 10% of the globally produced pig iron is used as cast iron in foundries, while 90% is further processed to crude steel.[102]

2.3.1.3 Fundamentals of steelmaking

By definition, only ferrous materials that contain less than 2% carbon are referred to as steel.[103] Therefore, the next step in the steelmaking process is the reduction of the carbon content of the liquid iron as well as the removal of various other undesirable trace elements such as silicon, sulfur and phosphorus.[104]

In the Linz-Donawitz process, these impurities are oxidized in the blast oxygen furnace, also known as the "O_2 converter", by top-blowing oxygen onto the hot metal through a water-cooled lance with a pressure of up to 12 bar. The carbon in the raw iron reacts with the oxygen to form carbon monoxide, reducing the carbon content of the liquid to less than 2%. Certain quantities of recycled steel scrap, accounting in average for approximately 10% of the total charge, are added as cooling agents and to influence the final chemical composition of the produced steel.[105] The liquid steel is immediately cast into slabs, ingots, billets or blooms, depending on the intended end product.[106]

2.3.2 Quality of iron ores with respect to their use for steelmaking

As stated in Section 2.3, 98% of the iron ore mined is used for steelmaking. Therefore, it is necessary to review the differentiating characteristics of iron ores described in Section 2.1.3 and define the criteria for the quality of iron

---

[98]See Degner et al. (2007), pp. 38–39.

[99]See Degner et al. (2007), p. 37.

[100]See Kirk (1999).

[101]See Wakelin and Ricketts (1999), p. 2.

[102]See Dillinger Hütte GTS (2011).

[103]See Deutsches Institut für Normung e. V. (2000).

[104]See Degner et al. (2007), p. 53.

[105]See Degner et al. (2007), pp. 24, 53–54.

[106]See Degner et al. (2007), pp. 78–88.

ore based on the desired physical and chemical attributes for the steelmaking process:[107]

- *Physical form (particle size)* – As described in Section 2.3.1.1, steelmakers will ultimately charge their blast furnaces with coarse chunks of ore in order to ensure best possible contact between the ore and the reducing gas. Because of this, natural lump ore and pellets are preferential as they can be charged directly into the blast furnace as purchased. Fines and concentrates, also referred to jointly as "sinter feed", are somewhat less preferential as they require agglomeration by the steelmaker prior to use

- *Iron content (grade)* – From a steelmaker's perspective, the iron content of the ore is to be as high as possible. High iron content of the ore increases the yield of the blast furnace and reduces cost for transportation and storage of the ore. More than 60% Fe content is preferable, 50–60% is adequate and less than 50% is considered low grade

- *Moisture content* – Lowest possible levels of moisture in the ore are preferable as they increase blast furnace yield and reduce transportation and storage cost. High moisture content leads to handling problems in the winter as well as increased sinter fuel requirements

- *Content of trace elements and compounds* – Trace elements and compounds bound in the ore must be viewed from a differentiated metallurgical perspective. While some levels of trace elements and chemical compounds are beneficial for the steelmaking process (e.g., alumina and silica) others are undesirable (e.g., manganese, phosphorus, sulfur and vanadium). High levels of undesired elements and compounds can reduce steel quality, increase flux requirements and cause blast furnace operating problems

---

[107]See Bottke (1981), pp. 155–168; Degner et al. (2007), p. 18; Kirk (1999); Poveromo (1999), pp. 640–642.

3 Structure and characteristics of the 2009 iron ore market

Following the technical introduction to iron ore in the previous chapter, the present chapter aims to give an overview of the current structure and mechanics of the global iron ore market by describing the 2009 market situation.[108] In doing so, this chapter is structured into six sections. First, Section 3.1 provides some introductory comments regarding the accepted routines and practices for presenting iron ore data and statistics. The remaining five sections of this chapter correspond to the five key elements of the framework defining the global iron ore market as shown in Figure 3.1:

- *Iron ore demand* – Section 3.2 describes the global demand situation for iron ore in 2009. The geographic distribution of demand is discussed and key demand-side players are portrayed

- *Iron ore supply* – Section 3.3 describes the global supply situation for iron ore in 2009. The geographic distribution of supply is discussed and key supply-side players are portrayed

- *Dry bulk freight rates* – Section 3.4 briefly describes the market for dry bulk freight and highlights the influence of freight rates on the iron ore market

- *Iron ore trade flows and market mechanism* – Section 3.5 deals with the actual iron ore market mechanism, moderating the economic forces of supply, demand and freight rates. The section includes a description of the modes of iron ore transactions as well as pricing of iron ore. Also, the 2009 iron ore trade flows resulting from the combination of supply and demand geographies are described

- *Public policy* – Section 3.6 outlines the effects of public policy on the iron ore market, with a strong focus on the taxation of the industry. The

---

[108]The 2009 market situation is defined as the status quo of the iron ore market in this paper due to the fact that it is the latest year for which complete market statistics are available.

key objectives of taxes are discussed and the most common tax types are described

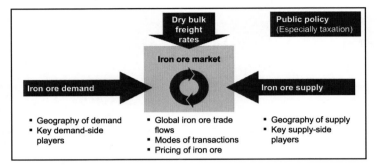

Figure 3.1: Framework defining the iron ore market structure [Own illustration based on O'Driscoll (2006), p. 51; Porter (2008)]

3.1 Introductory comments regarding iron ore market data and statistics

In describing the status quo of the market, this chapter presents a cross-section of various iron ore industry statistics. Supply data is derived from United Nations Conference on Trade and Development (2010), Jorgenson (2011) and Indiastat (2010) as well as corporate sources, while demand data originates from World Steel Association (2010) and McKinsey & Company (2011a). Iron and Steel Statistics Bureau (2010) is used as source for trade flow data. Due to inconsistencies between these different data sources, individual country figures for supply, demand and trade flows are not directly comparable. Also, the difficulties of collecting precise data in this field must be emphasized. There exists general confusion between data concerning extracted crude iron ore and marketable iron ores as are used in the steel industry. Also, most data sources show a lack of precision regarding the definition of moisture and iron contents of tonnages extracted, transported or sold.[109] Routines and practices for presenting iron ore statistics have evolved over a period of several decades. These practices reflect limitations and constraints imposed by the available source data as well as industry conventions.[110] These practices are discussed in the following for iron ore volume and price statistics.

---

[109]See Astier (2001).

[110]See United Nations Conference on Trade and Development (2010), p. 92.

3.1.1 Units of measure for volume data

Contrary to the practice used for statistics on other metals, figures for iron ore production and trade flows are normally presented in gross or natural weight, also referred to as "run of mine" (ROM), and not as the metal content of the ore produced. Though this may seem sensible from a production or shipping point of view, this practice raises several problems regarding the comparability of data from different mines or countries:[111]

- *Fe content* – The natural iron content of ore varies dramatically, with mines in China at one extreme producing ore with an average iron content of less than 30% while other countries produce ore with an iron content of above 60%

- *Moisture content* – Reported figures may refer to either wet or dry ore, i.e. including or excluding moisture. The difference between the two measures ranges roughly from 0–12% with the average being 7.1%[112]

- *Tonnage* – Most statistical sources report iron ore volume figures in metric tons (1,000 kg). However, there are sources that report in gross or long tons (1,016.0 kg), while others use net or short tons (907.2 kg)[113]

In order to guarantee comparability, all weight figures in this paper (unless explicitly stated otherwise) are given in metric tons (1,000.0 kg) of dry ore with 62.0% Fe content.[114] Figures from sources reporting in wet tons and/or with other Fe contents have been recalculated accordingly using the following formula:

$$x = x^{ROM} \cdot (1 - mc) \cdot \frac{fc}{62.0\%}$$

where

$$
\begin{aligned}
x &= \text{Standardized volume, in dry Mt with 62.0\% Fe} \\
x^{ROM} &= \text{Actual run of mine volume with moisture content } mc \\
& \quad \text{and Fe content } fc, \text{ in Mt} \\
mc &= \text{Moisture content of ore, in \%} \\
fc &= \text{Fe content of ore, in \%}
\end{aligned}
$$

---

[111]See United Nations Conference on Trade and Development (2010), p. 92.

[112]See McKinsey & Company (2011b); Poveromo (1999), pp. 642–657.

[113]See Poveromo (1999), p. 569.

[114]The industry has adopted the 62.0% Fe specification as a standard benchmark, e.g. for price indices and derivative transactions (see Section 3.5.2.3).

For example, a reported volume of 10.0 million metric tons containing 7.0% moisture and 60.0% Fe would be standardized to roughly 8.9 million dry metric tons containing 62.0% Fe.

3.1.2 Units of measure for price data

Iron ore on the global market is commonly priced in U.S. dollars (USD), thus facilitating comparison.[115] The "unit pricing system" is typically used to accommodate variations in iron content. This system calls for prices to be quoted in U.S. dollar cents per dry metric ton unit (USDc/dmtu). A unit hereby refers to 1% of iron per ton of ore. Based on the market price, prices for ores with specific levels of iron contents are calculated as follows:[116]

$$\lambda_{fc} = \lambda \cdot fc$$

where

$$
\begin{aligned}
\lambda_{fc} &= \text{Price for one dry ton of specific ore grade with Fe content of } fc, \\
&\quad \text{in USD} \\
\lambda &= \text{Market price, in USDc/dmtu} \\
fc &= \text{Fe content of ore, in \%}
\end{aligned}
$$

Therefore, at a market price of 100.00 USDc/dmtu, one dry metric ton of ore containing 62.0% Fe would be traded at USD 62.00. On the other hand, a steelmaker requiring one ton of pure iron would need to purchase about 1.61 tons of ore at 62.0% Fe with a total market value of USD 100.00.

3.2 Iron ore demand

Any analysis of a raw materials market reveals the essential dynamic that drives international trade: market supply equals market demand. According to O'Driscoll (2006), "[w]ithout a market, a mineral deposit is merely a geological curiosity." So, put simply, no market demand for iron ore means no iron ore mining and no iron ore trade.

---

[115]For reasons of simplicity and comparability, all financial data in this paper is given in 2009 real U.S. dollars. Thus, no monetary inflation is reflected in values representing 2020 data. Also, exchange rate effects are not taken into account.

[116]See Hellmer (1997b), pp. 34–35; Kirk (1999).

The purchasers in the iron ore market are few. In most of the major iron ore consuming countries, the control of buying is in the hands of a small number of organizations. This is partly due to the fact that in several countries, e.g. China, the steel industry is partly or wholly owned by large state-owned companies. Furthermore, in some countries, associations have been formed to act on behalf of the steel companies to coordinate the purchases of iron ore.[117]

3.2.1 Geography of iron ore demand

As described in Section 2.3, iron ore is used almost exclusively for steelmaking. The main iron ore consuming countries are therefore those that have considerable steel production.

Thus, North America and Europe, the industrialized economies along the Atlantic Basin, followed later by Japan and Korea, have traditionally been the major centers of iron ore demand.[118] In the 1980s and 1990s, these established markets were joined by the emerging "Asian Tiger" and Pacific Rim economies of Indonesia, Malaysia, Singapore, Taiwan and Thailand.[119] Since the year 2000, however, the explosion of Chinese steel production volumes, thus triggering immense Chinese iron ore demand, has dwarfed the demand figures of all other economies.[120] Therefore, in terms of iron ore demand and trade, China stands out as a leader not only in the Asia-Pacific region, but also in an international context.[121]

Table 3.1 gives an overview of the iron ore demand by country in 2009. While more than 45 countries consumed iron ore,[122] the top five consuming nations accounted for about 75% of demand. China was by far the largest consumer, with a demand of over 910 Mt. This corresponds to more than half of global production. The degree of Chinese dominance is further stressed by the fact that second-placed Japan consumed only 90.9 Mt, less than 10% of Chinese consumption. Japan is followed in the ranking by Russia (75.7 Mt), India (75.5 Mt) and South Korea (50.5 Mt). The top ten are completed by Brazil, the United States, Ukraine, Germany and Turkey.

---

[117]See Rogers et al. (1987).

[118]See Smith (1988).

[119]See O'Driscoll (2006), pp. 49–50.

[120]See Taube and in der Heiden (2010), p. 39.

[121]Note that, due to this development, it has been argued that the geographic center of gravity of demand has continued to shift away from the Atlantic Basin towards the Pacific (see Crowson (1997)).

[122]See World Steel Association (2010).

Country	Iron ore demand Mtpa	Share of world total	
China	910.7	57.1%	
Japan	90.9	5.7%	
Russia	75.7	4.7%	Σ 75.4%
India	75.5	4.7%	
South Korea	50.5	3.2%	
Brazil	49.5	3.1%	
USA	42.4	2.7%	
Ukraine	37.7	2.4%	
Germany	29.1	1.8%	
Turkey	24.9	1.6%	
Other	207.5	13.0%	
World total	**1,594.4**	**100.0%**	

Table 3.1: Iron ore demand by country, 2009 [Estimated based on McKinsey & Company (2011a); World Steel Association (2010)]

Figure 3.2 shows the geographic distribution of the top ten iron ore consuming countries, together accounting for approximately 87% of global iron ore consumption. As can be seen, this consumption is highly concentrated on the Asian continent. Asia is home to four of the top five iron ore consuming nations. China, Japan, India and South Korea jointly account for roughly 70% of global demand.

3.2.2 Chinese steel industry as key source of iron ore demand

Having multiplied its steel production in an astonishingly short time, China cannot but have had a significant impact on the absolute availability as well as the prices of raw materials relevant to steelmaking, above all iron ore. The so-called "China factor" has been the central parameter of recent dynamics in the iron ore market.[123] Therefore, in order to understand global demand for iron ore, it is important to understand the history, structure and characteristics of the Chinese steel industry at its current stage of economic development.

3.2.2.1 Ramp-up of Chinese steel production

For most of the 20th century, China was considered a sleeping dragon. Despite its attempts to stimulate domestic economic development, it was not an easy task under the strict communist regime.[124] However, with its opening up to

---

[123]See Taube and in der Heiden (2010), p. 38.
[124]See Sukagawa (2010).

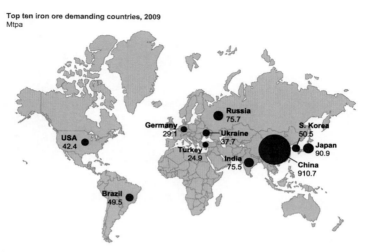

Top ten iron ore demanding countries, 2009
Mtpa

Figure 3.2: Geographic distribution of top ten iron ore consuming countries, 2009 [McKinsey & Company (2011a); World Steel Association (2010)]

the world market in 1978, the Chinese government decided to take a pragmatic approach. By the year 2000, China's economy was starting to take off and with it the demand for steel. In early 2005, China's economy was growing at 9.5% per year.[125] On the back of surging construction and infrastructure investments, demand for steel in China has more than quadrupled since 1980.[126] Since then, the country within just a few years has transformed itself into the by far largest steel producing economy in the world.[127]

Figure 3.3 shows the remarkable growth of China's steel industry since the early 1980s. Steel output rose at an average of 6.4% per year from 37.1 Mt in 1980 to 128.5 Mt in 2000. After the start of the new millennium, the average year-on-year growth rate increased to astonishing 18.0%, catapulting Chinese crude steel production to 567.8 Mt in 2009. In terms of share of global crude steel production, China went from a mere 5.2% in 1980 to 46.4% in 2009.

3.2.2.2 Structure of Chinese steel industry

The structure of China's steel industry differs greatly from that of the steel industries of Japan, Korea or Europe. In China, there is only a limited number

---

[125]See O'Driscoll (2006), p. 54.

[126]See Steel Business Briefing (2011c); Woetzel (2001).

[127]See Taube and in der Heiden (2010), p. 17.

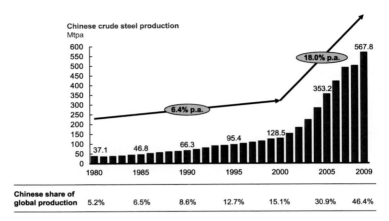

Figure 3.3: Chinese crude steel production and share of world total, 1980–2009 [Own illustration based on data from World Steel Association (1990); World Steel Association (2000); World Steel Association (2010)]

of major players. However, there are countless small and medium-size steel companies.[128]

According to estimates, over 1,000 steel producing enterprises exist in China.[129] Chinese steel producers generate approximately 3% of the nations gross domestic product and employ more than 3 million people.[130] As of 2005, the top 5 players, Shanghai Baosteel Group, Tangshan Steel Group, Wuhan Steel Group, Anshan Steel Group, Jiangsu Shagang Group and Shougang Group, produced roughly 21% of Chinese crude steel. The top 18 steel groups accounted for 50% of national production. The rest was produced by smaller steelmakers, many of them loss-making. The size of the blast furnaces at these steel mills range from 1 m^3 (so-called "backyard mills") up to 1,500 m^3. It is particularly difficult or even impractical for the government to control their activities.[131]

This extreme degree of fragmentation is a result of China's 1960s-era policy of regional self-sufficiency. Since then, Beijing has pushed to close obsolete and underperforming plants, part of its strategy to shift state industry to a more investment-friendly market footing.[132] Recent Chinese government plans called for the shutdown of all blast furnaces below 300 m^3 capacity. The newly

---

[128]See Sukagawa (2010).
[129]See Movshuk (2004); Woetzel (2001).
[130]See Woetzel (2001).
[131]See Sukagawa (2010).
[132]See Movshuk (2004); Woetzel (2001).

announced government target is even to rationalize approximately 100 Mt of capacity.[133]

China's steelmakers have become increasingly dependent on the import of iron ore and are facing dramatic price increases of these raw materials. In order to ease the pressure of escalating cost increases, the Chinese government and the China Iron and Steel Association (CISA) in particular have launched a whole range of initiatives designed to create a Chinese buying cartel and increase the negotiating power of Chinese enterprises vis-à-vis international iron ore miners. In a first move, CISA has been entrusted to participate in the delineation of a catalog of requirements Chinese enterprises must meet in order to qualify as iron ore importers. In the meantime, the number of originally more than 500 importers has been greatly reduced. In 2007, the Chinese iron ore import cartel consisted of no more than 90 members.[134]

3.2.2.3 Government control of Chinese steel industry

China's iron and steel industry is not governed by market principles. The Chinese steel industry is firmly embedded in a powerful state-business cartel. China's steel enterprises are not operating in a competition-based domestic market environment, but rather uphold very close relationships to government agencies on local, provincial as well as central levels. As a result, all major developments regarding overall industry organization, concentration levels, as well as individual firm strategies regarding import/export activities, outward bound FDI initiatives etc. are co-determined and directed by government organizations.[135] As such the Chinese steel industry is not playing according to the same rules as firms in established market economies like the European Union.[136]

The government directs the developments of the Chinese steel industry via the "Eleventh Five Year Program for Economic and Social Development" and especially the "Iron and Steel Industry Development Policy" which constitutes the centerpiece of all steel-related policy initiatives by China's government authorities. At the national (central government) level, the Chinese steel industry is being directed and more or less micro-managed by a politico-business cartel often referred to as "China Steel Inc.". "China Steel Inc." consists of the National Development and Reform Commission (NDRC), the China Iron and

---

[133]See Sukagawa (2010).
[134]See Taube and in der Heiden (2010), pp. 190–191.
[135]See Taube and in der Heiden (2010), p. 15.
[136]See Taube and in der Heiden (2010), p. 217.

Steel Association (CISA), the State-owned Asset Supervision and Administration Commission of the State Council (SASAC) as well as the top management of China's leading steel enterprises.[137]

CISA is nominally the lobbying arm of China's steel industry vis-à-vis the government and other market participants. In reality, however, CISA stands in the middle between being a lobbyist for the industry and a spokesman for the government. The semi-governmental role of CISA becomes obvious in the Association's substantial entanglement in the design and execution of regulatory measures: Since 2005, CISA has taken an active part in the definition of the requirements Chinese enterprises have to meet in order to qualify as iron ore importers. In the campaign to reduce the number of then 523 iron ore importers and curb "blind competition", i.e., install an iron ore import cartel, CISA has also taken up the role of checking the qualifications of the importers and determining those enterprises which would lose their import licenses. The number of qualified iron ore importers was cut to 118 in 2006 and 90 in 2007. Steel enterprises wishing to obtain an iron ore importing license are obliged to formerly report both to CISA and the China Chamber of Commerce of Metals, Minerals & Chemicals Importers & Exporters (CCCMC) in how far they comply with the requirements.[138]

China's leading steel conglomerates are basically government controlled. Among the top 20 corporations, only Jiangsu Shagang and Fosun Hightech Co., Ltd. are not explicitly state-owned on a majority basis. But even these "private" corporations have become co-opted to state interests as state organizations have injected equity capital and now own minority shares in these corporations.[139] Many members of the top-management of China's leading steel conglomerates belong to the Communist Party elite. The top positions (CEO, CFO, Chief Engineer) of China's leading state-owned steel corporations are filled exclusively with members of the Communist Party who may rank very high in party and government hierarchy.[140]

The relationship between state and business in China's steel industry goes beyond joint planning, protection and decision making processes, but involves substantial monetary and non-monetary support and protection by government agencies as well. A broad array of mechanisms can be identified, including access to systematically under-priced raw materials.[141] The necessity for these

---

[137]See Taube and in der Heiden (2010), pp. 15–16.
[138]See Taube and in der Heiden (2010), pp. 58–59.
[139]See Taube and in der Heiden (2010), pp. 58–59.
[140]See Taube and in der Heiden (2010), p. 62.
[141]See Taube and in der Heiden (2010), p. 16.

Country	Iron ore production Mtpa	Share of world total	
China	397.4	24.2%	
Australia	366.0	22.3%	
Brazil	278.6	17.0%	▶ Σ 82.4%
India	226.6	13.8%	
Russia	84.5	5.1%	
Ukraine	61.2	3.7%	
South Africa	51.5	3.1%	
Canada	30.6	1.9%	
USA	24.6	1.5%	
Iran	22.3	1.4%	
Other	99.7	6.1%	
World total	**1,643.0**	**100.0%**	

Table 3.2: Iron ore production by country, 2009 [Based on data from United Nations Conference on Trade and Development (2010), 7.1% moisture content deducted; Chinese data recalculated based on crude ore production data from Jorgenson (2011), assuming 28% Fe average; Indian data from Indiastat (2010)]

mechanisms can be found in the lacking efficiency and deteriorating performance among the largest state-owned enterprises in the Chinese steel industry.[142]

3.3 Iron ore supply

3.3.1 Geography of iron ore supply

Although iron ore is produced in more than 30 countries, five countries accounted for more than 80% of the total world output in 2009 (see Table 3.2). China was the leader in production with 397.4 Mt, equaling 24.2% of the world total. Following closely behind China, Australia mined 366.0 Mt in 2009 (22.3% of total). The top five are completed by Brazil (278.6 Mt), India (226.6 Mt) and Russia (84.5 Mt). The top ten iron ore producing countries further include Ukraine, South Africa, Canada, the United States and Iran.

Figure 3.4 shows the geographic distribution of the top ten iron ore mining countries, together accounting for 94% of global production in 2009.

In the following, the top three producers' iron ore industries are described in brief.

---

[142]See, e.g., Jefferson (1990); Movshuk (2004); Steinfeld (1998); Wu (2000).

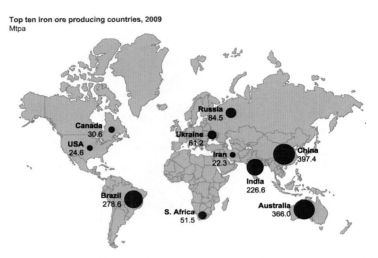

Figure 3.4: Geographic distribution of top ten iron ore producing countries, 2009 [Based on data from United Nations Conference on Trade and Development (2010), 7.1% moisture content deducted. Chinese data recalculated based on crude ore production data from Jorgenson (2011), assuming 28% Fe average]

3.3.1.1 China's iron ore industry

With a production of almost 400 Mt in 2009, China is the largest producer of iron ore in the world. Though this seems normal today, this has not always been the case. Prior to the economic boom of the past century, China was self-sufficient with respect to iron ore, mining just enough domestically to supply its small steel industry.[143] However, with the rapid growth of the Chinese steel industry to accommodate economic growth since 2000, domestic iron ore production has no longer been able to meet domestic demand. As Chinese steelmakers were forced to import iron ore, feeling the heat of rising iron ore prices on the world market, they struggled to offset cost pressures by pushing the domestic iron ore sector. The Chinese government encouraged domestic iron ore producers to increase their output.[144] With large proven reserves of the mineral and a long tradition in mining, Chinese iron ore mines have since expanded at great speed to catch up with excessive demand growth.[145] During

---

[143]See Feng (1994).
[144]See U.S. Geological Survey (2010c).
[145]See Taube and in der Heiden (2010), p. 39.

the past five years, the volume of domestic iron ore output increased sharply, leading China to the number one position in iron ore production rankings.[146]

Though China has managed to boost its domestic iron ore production, its ores remain of relatively low quality compared to those of other large producers. This is due to naturally low iron contents and high levels of impurities in Chinese ore reserves.[147] Furthermore, the average ferrous content of domestically mined Chinese iron ore has been declining rapidly, down from over 30% to between 27–28% in 2008.[148] Reports indicate that the high relevance of iron ore for the domestic steel industry have encouraged Chinese mine operators to even tap reserves with ferrous contents as low as 17%. In comparison, ores from Australia and Brazil boast a iron content of 60–70%.[149] This suggests that China will not attain a comparative advantage in iron ore production, given that the iron content is an important determinant of mining cost as well as efficiency in usage for steelmaking.[150]

The specific geological parameters of China, with mostly small and low grade deposits, lead to the structure of the Chinese iron ore industry being extremely fragmented. Perhaps as many as 8,000 small mining companies have titles to patches of ore-bearing lands, but some large players also exist.[151] The most significant are Anshan Mining Co., Shoudu Mining Co., Benxi Iron and Steel Co., Panzhihua Mining Co. and Ma'anshan Iron and Steel Co.[152] Chinese iron ore mining is concentrated in northeastern and central China. Liaoning province leads the domestic production ranking, followed by Hebei, Sichuan and Anhui provinces.[153]

3.3.1.2 Australia's iron ore industry

In addition to being the world's number two producer of iron ore, Australia also holds the second largest amount of iron ore reserves. As of January 2011, Australia's reserves totaled 24,000 Mt of crude ore with an average iron content of of 63%.[154] This high level of iron gives Australia a comparative advantage in the iron ore market, as it reduces beneficiation and freight costs. 96% of the

---

[146]See U.S. Geological Survey (2010c).
[147]See U.S. Geological Survey (2010c).
[148]See Ericsson (2009).
[149]See Feng (1994); Taube and in der Heiden (2010), p. 39.
[150]See Feng (1994).
[151]See Ericsson (2009).
[152]See U.S. Geological Survey (2010c), p. 20.
[153]See U.S. Geological Survey (2010c), p. 20.
[154]See Jorgenson (2011), p. 85.

iron ore produced in Australia in 2009 was high-grade hematite with over 60% Fe content.[155]

Although iron ore resources occur in all of the Australian States and Territories, the country's most significant iron ore mines are located in the Pilbara region of Western Australia. The Pilbara accounts for 96.7% of the country's total iron ore production followed by South Australia (2.3%), Tasmania (0.7%) and Northern Territory (0.3%).[156] The Pilbara region is situated approximately 1,200 km north of Perth in the northwestern part of Western Australia.[157] Located within the Pilbara, the Hamersley Iron Province is home to roughly 80% of the Australia's iron ore production, making it one of the world's major iron ore centers.[158]

The dawn of iron ore development in the Pilbara started with the lifting of an iron ore export embargo from Australia in the mid-1960s. Before this, the Australian government believed that iron ore was not an abundant resource and should be maintained as a strategic resource for future national security. With mining companies investing heavily in the following years, the Pilbara soon became one of the world's leading source of iron ore.[159]

The majority of mines in the Pilbara are located near the town of Newman. Established in 1968, the massive Mount Whaleback mine is the biggest single-pit iron ore mine in the world. Adjacent to the Mount Whaleback mine are smaller deposits with satellite mines located outside the town of Newman. Other major Pilbara mines, located 200–300 km to the northwest of Newman, include the Brockman, Marandoo, Mount Tom Price, Nammuldi and Yandicoogina mines. The bulk of these mines are owned by mining giants BHP Billiton and Rio Tinto, but many junior companies have begun iron ore operations in the region during the past years.[160] In addition to numerous ore bodies, the Pilbara region boasts iron ore related infrastructure including railways (operated mainly by BHP Billiton and Rio Tinto) as well as 3 deepwater ports at Cape Lambert, Dampier and Port Hedland.[161]

---

[155]See Peel (2009).
[156]See Australian Bureau of Agricultural and Resource Economics (2009b), p. 22.
[157]See Fehling (1977), p. 44.
[158]See Fehling (1977), p. 38; Geoscience Australia (2011).
[159]See Frost (1986); Sukagawa (2010).
[160]See U.S. Geological Survey (2010a), p. 7.
[161]See Fehling (1977), p. 39; U.S. Geological Survey (2010a), p. 7.

3.3.1.3 Brazil's iron ore industry

As already shown in Table 2.1, Brazil has the largest iron ore reserves in the world. Its crude ore reserves total an estimated 29,000 Mt, with an average grade of 55% Fe.[162] The wide-scale tapping of these deposits began as a result of aggressive economic policy in Japan, where crude steel production dramatically increased commencing in the mid-1950s. This economic growth rubbed off on Brazil as it started exporting iron ore to Japan in 1955. [163]

In the decades that followed, a healthy combination of economic stability, structural advantages and a superior position in global cost curves has rapidly made Brazil an upstream supply base for iron ore and positioned it among the top three global producers.[164]

Almost 85% of the Brazilian iron ore production in 2009 stemmed from four iron ore producers: Vale, Minerações Brasileiras Reunidas S/A (MBR), Samarco Mineração S/A. and Companhia Siderúrgica Nacional (CSN).[165] Major mines are located in the Carajás province in northern Brazil and in the Brazilian state of Minas Gerais in the south. Each of the two ore-rich regions has railway systems running from the mines to maritime terminals and ports. In Carajás province, the majority of iron ore is shippped from Ponta da Madeira Maritime Terminal. In the south, Itaguai, Guaiba and Tubarão are the main port facilities.[166]

3.3.2 Corporate control in iron ore mining

In general terms, owners of iron ore mines can be split into the following four categories:

- *Mining conglomerates* – Large, multinational companies with a vast capital base, active in the mining of a variety of minerals at several different mine sites across the globe (e.g., Vale, Rio Tinto and BHP Billiton)

- *"Junior miners"* – Small to medium-size mining companies, often specializing in the mining of few minerals with only a limited number of mining properties (e.g., Gindalbie Metals)

---

[162]See Jorgenson (2011), p. 85.
[163]See Sukagawa (2010).
[164]See Andrade et al. (2007).
[165]See U.S. Geological Survey (2010b), p. 4.
[166]See Vale (2010), pp. 24–27.

- *Steelmakers* – Steel mills that own an equity share in iron ore mines in order to secure the ore mined to satisfy their iron ore demand (e.g., ArcelorMittal)

- *Governments* – National governments owning mines (usually domestic, but also abroad) either for investment purposes or for reasons of national resource strategy (e.g., the Steel Authority of India (SAIL))

As described in detail in Section 2.2.2, the setup of the required infrastructure for new iron ore mining projects is commonly extremely capital intensive. These necessary investments often represent an effective barrier to entry. Even junior miners financially capable of setting up functioning mining operations are often not able to efficiently sell their ore on the world market, as the additional capital required to build own railway lines to port is immense.[167] For example, in Western Australia, only Rio Tinto, BHP Billiton and Fortescue Metals Group have own rail infrastructure. All other miners either transport their ore by road or are dependent on selling capacity chunks to one of the larger miners in return for rail haulage. However, the majors so far have often been reluctant to engage in such deals, leaving numerous junior miners without real access to the world market.[168]

The capital-intensive nature of the iron ore mining business is the main reason why iron ore mining is dominated by three mining conglomerates: Vale, Rio Tinto and BHP Billiton. These companies, known in the industry as the "Big Three", controlled approximately one third of iron ore production in 2009 (see Table 3.3). Brazilian Vale holds the position as the world's largest iron ore producer with 234.7 Mt in 2009, leaving second and third place to Anglo-Australian miners Rio Tinto and BHP Billiton with 162.2 and 106.4 Mt respectively.[169] However, Vale's position as the undisputed industry leader is seriously challenged. Not only have the volumes controlled by Vale decreased from a peak of 308.0 Mt in 2007, but its closest rivals Rio Tinto and BHP Billiton have managed to increase their controlled production, therefore recapturing market shares.[170]

The seemingly high level of corporate concentration on the supply side has been repeatedly criticized in the past by steelmakers and anti-monopoly authorities.

---

[167]Analysts estimate that, for example, building a new railway line from a mine in Australia's Pilbara region to Port Hedland would cost around USD 5.0 to 6.0 billion (see Steel Business Briefing (2010c); Treadgold (2009)).

[168]See Regan (2009); Steel Business Briefing (2010c). For more details on the importance of infrastructure access for the emergence and success of junior miners, see Ernst & Young (2011a), pp. 14–15.

[169]See BHP Billiton (2010), p. 53; Rio Tinto (2010), pp. 66–67; Vale (2010), p. 26.

[170]See United Nations Conference on Trade and Development (2010), p. 50.

Controlling entity	Controlled iron ore production Mtpa	Share of world total	
Vale	234.7	14.3%	
Rio Tinto	162.2	9.9%	Σ 30.7%
BHP Billiton	106.4	6.5%	
State of India (incl. SAIL, NMDC)	55.3	3.4%	
Anglo American	43.8	2.7%	
ArcelorMittal	38.7	2.4%	
Metalloinvest	35.5	2.1%	
Fortescue Metals Group	34.9	2.1%	
System Capital Management	27.0	1.6%	
Cliffs Natural Resources	23.9	1.4%	
Other	880.4	53.6%	
World total	**1,643.0**	**100.0%**	

Table 3.3: Iron ore production by controlling entity, 2009 [United Nations Conference on Trade and Development (2010); BHP Billiton (2010), p. 53; Rio Tinto (2010), pp. 66–67; Vale (2010), p. 26]

Especially steelmakers blame the dominance of the Big Three for surging iron ore prices. Some even draw parallels to the market power of the Organization of the Petroleum Exporting Countries (OPEC).[171] Steelmakers are calling for new players to enter the market to improve the competitive environment and create "reasonable competition".[172] As the largest dependent, China is considering anti-monopoly investigations to remedy "growing signs of monopolistic behavior by the iron ore miners" including some "monopolistic-colored moves".[173]

Though the level of concentration in the iron ore mining has actually increased in the past 35 years,[174] referring to the Herfindahl-Hirschman Index (HHI) as developed by Herfindahl (1950), the supply-side concentration in the iron ore market is far from critical. The HHI is a standard tool used by the worlds' antitrust watchdogs to measure the level of concentration in a market. It is a function that summarizes the structure of an entire industry, calculated as the sum of the squared market shares of each company.[175] For the ten largest controlling iron ore companies the index for 2009 was 375, far below the 1,000 mark that the United States Federal Trade Commission uses as the lower limit for a "moderately concentrated" market.[176]

---

[171]See Kaiser (2010).

[172]See The Financial Times (2010b)

[173]China Daily (2010).

[174]See respective analysis of iron ore miners' market shares from 1975 to 2009 in United Nations Conference on Trade and Development (2010), p. 51.

[175]See also Cabral (2000), p. 155.

[176]See United Nations Conference on Trade and Development (2010), p. 51.

Nevertheless, the iron ore industry remains under the scrutiny of the world's competition watchdogs, who recently stepped in to prevent an attempted merger in the industry. In 2008 BHP Billiton approached Rio Tinto with an offer to buy its Anglo-Australian rival at a price that valued the company at nearly USD 150 billion. Rio Tinto's board rejected the deal, but BHP Billiton kept up its pursuit. The combination would have created the world's largest minerals company and one of the largest companies of any sort in terms of market capitalization. Months later though, at the end of a year dominated by the global economic meltdown, BHP Billiton announced that the deal no longer provided value to its shareholders and, so, called it off. Instead, both companies went for a 50/50 joint venture that would have combined the two companies' iron ore projects in Western Australia. However, that deal fell through after the German Federal Cartel Office ruled in 2010 that it was anti-competitive.[177]

When touching on the topic of supply-side concentration, it must also be mentioned that, in 1975, an attempt was made to establish an iron ore cartel, the Association of Iron Ore Exporting Countries (APEF). Modeled after the OPEC, the APEF aimed to set export prices for iron ore. The effort was unsuccessful because two important members, Australia and Sweden, were unwilling to implement price-influencing measures and because Brazil and Canada, both significant exporters at the time, refused even to join. Failing to institute effective price-raising measures, the APEF consequently reduced its role to collecting statistics on market trends and was terminated in 1989.[178]

In the following, the Big Three are described with respect to their corporate structure, financial performance, production footprint and strategic outlook.

3.3.2.1 Vale

Vale S.A, named "Companhia Vale do Rio Doce" (CVRD) until 2007, is by far the world's leading iron ore miner. In 2009, Vale produced 234.7 Mt of iron ore and iron ore pellets, giving it a share of 14.3% of global production.[179] Apart from iron ore, Vale is active in the production of many different ferrous and non-ferrous minerals including nickel, manganese ore, ferroalloys, bauxite, alumina, aluminum, copper, coal, potash, cobalt and platinum group metals. With this diverse portfolio and over 60,000 employees, Vale is the second-largest metals and mining company in the world based on market capitalization.[180] The

---

[177]See Hoovers (2011a), p. 3; The Economist (2010c).
[178]See Crowson (2006), p. 158; Jones (1986); Radetzki (2008).
[179]See Vale (2010), p. 26, adjusted for moisture and Fe content.
[180]See Datamonitor (2010d), p. 4.

diversified product portfolio and geographically diversified revenue base are seen as Vale's key strengths.[181] Although a publicly traded company, the Brazilian government holds veto power on any changes to the company's purpose as regards to mining activities.[182]

In the financial year ending December 31, 2009, Vale achieved total operating revenues of approximately USD 23.9 billion (down from USD 38.5 billion in 2008) and a net income of USD 5.5 billion (USD 13.5 billion in 2008). The iron ore and iron ore pellets lines of business accounted for a total of USD 14.2 billion in revenues (59.2% of Vale total), down from USD 22.1 billion in 2008.[183]

Based in Rio de Janeiro, Brazil,[184] Vale is actively engaged in mineral exploration and mining efforts in 21 countries around the globe.[185] Vale's iron ore operations, however, are focused entirely in South America, with all active mines and pellet plants situated in Brazil. Vale operates three systems for the mining and distribution of iron ore. The Northern System, situated in Carajás province, contains some of the largest iron ore deposits in the world and comprises three open pit mines. The Southeastern System, located in the Iron Quadrangle region of the state of Minas Gerais, consists of twelve open pit mines grouped into three mining complexes (Itabira, Minas Centrais and Mariana). The Southern System, also in the Iron Quadrangle region, is made up of three major complexes (Minas Itabirito, Vargem Grande and Paraopeda) with a total of eleven mines and seven beneficiation plants. The Northern and Southeastern Systems are fully integrated, consisting of mines, railroads, a maritime terminal and a port (Tubarão). The Southern System relies on freight contracts with an external railway company to transport ore to maritime terminals. In addition to its iron ore mines, Vale runs ten iron ore pellet-producing plants in Brazil and owns a 50% share of Samarco, which operates three integrated pellet plants near the Southeastern System.[186]

3.3.2.2 Rio Tinto

Melbourne-based Rio Tinto Limited is the Australian half of dual-listed sister companies, with Rio Tinto plc taking up residence in London. Although each company trades separately, they operate as one business and are in the

---

[181]See Datamonitor (2010d), pp. 6–7.
[182]See Datamonitor (2010d), p. 7; Hoovers (2011c), p. 3.
[183]See Vale (2010), pp. 13–15.
[184]See Hoovers (2011c), p. 1.
[185]See Vale (2010), p. 15.
[186]See Vale (2010), pp. 24–27.

following referred to jointly as "Rio Tinto".[187] Rio Tinto is one of the world's leading mining operations and the number two iron ore miner with 162.2 Mt of controlled production in 2009 (9.9% of global iron ore production).[188] With slightly over 100,000 employees globally (thereof approximately 11,000 in iron ore operations), Rio Tinto mines not only iron ore, but also copper, uranium, industrial minerals, gold and diamonds.[189]

In 2009, Rio Tinto's revenue totaled approximately USD 44.0 billion (down from USD 58.1 billion in 2008) with net earnings of USD 4.9 billion (USD 3.7 billion in 2008). The iron ore product group accounted for a total of USD 12.6 billion in revenues and USD 4.1 billion in net earnings (28.6% and 83.7% of Rio Tinto total respectively). 2008 revenue had been USD 16.5 billion with earnings totaling USD 6.0 billion.[190]

The company sells globally, but the majority of its operations are located in Australia and the Americas.[191] Since the sale of the Brazilian Corumbá mine to Vale in 2009, approximately 95% of Rio Tinto's iron ore production capacity is to be found in Australia, the remainder being in Newfoundland (Canada). With a network of 14 mines, three shipping terminals and the largest privately owned heavy freight rail network in Australia, Rio Tinto's Pilbara operations make up a major part of its global iron ore activities. The dominant iron ore mining complex with a total capacity of approximately 100 Mt is Hamersley Iron in the Hamersley Ranges of Western Australia. The complex includes six wholly owned open pit mines (Brockman, Marandoo, Mount Tom Price, Nammuldi, Paraburdoo and Yandicoogina) and two partially owned mines (Channar and Eastern Range). The Hamersley complex is fully integrated with a Rio Tinto-owned railway leading to Cape Lambert and Dampier port. Other complexes in which Rio Tinto holds shares include the Hope Downs joint venture and Robe River Iron, both located in the Pilbara region of Western Australia. Rio Tinto's Canadian iron ore subsidiary, the Iron Ore Company of Canada, in which Rio Tinto holds roughly 59%, is the only facility in Rio Tinto's portfolio partially producing iron ore pellets.[192]

In 2008 Alcoa and Aluminum Corporation of China (Chinalco) acquired 14% of Rio Tinto for USD 14 billion. Early the next year Chinalco stepped in with an offer to assist Rio Tinto out of a portion of its debt, which was considerable. The complicated arrangement would have given Rio Tinto USD 19.5 billion

---

[187]See Hoovers (2011b), p. 1.
[188]See Rio Tinto (2010), pp. 66–67, adjusted for moisture and Fe content.
[189]See Datamonitor (2010c), pp. 4–6.
[190]See Rio Tinto (2010), p. 219.
[191]See Hoovers (2011b), p. 1.
[192]See Rio Tinto (2010), pp. 66–67, 80–81.

through investments in aluminum, copper and iron ore joint ventures as well as through convertible bonds. Chinalco's stake in Rio Tinto would have been raised to 19% and the Chinese company would have had the right to name two members to Rio Tinto's board. However, the transaction, never popular with domestic investors, fell through by mid-2009.[193]

3.3.2.3 BHP Billiton

Completing the Big Three is Melbourne-headquartered BHP Billiton. The Australian minerals and oil company Broken Hill Proprietary (BHP) Limited acquired UK miner Billiton plc in 2001. The result is a two-headquartered, dual-listed enterprise consisting of BHP Billiton Limited and BHP Billiton plc. They are run as a single entity with the same board of directors and management and are collectively known as "BHP Billiton".[194]

With a market capitalization of USD 144 billion as of 2009, BHP Billiton is the world's largest diversified natural resources company.[195] The company is the world's number three producer of iron ore, having mined 106.4 Mt in 2009 (6.5% of global production).[196] BHP Billiton's portfolio of export-oriented natural resources is completed by coal (thermal and metallurgical), petroleum products such as crude oil and natural gas, aluminum, base metals, copper, diamonds, manganese, nickel, uranium and stainless steel materials.[197]

In the 2009 financial year, BHP Billiton achieved total operating revenues of approximately USD 50.2 billion (down from USD 59.5 billion in 2008) and an EBIT of USD 12.2 billion (USD 24.1 billion in 2008). The iron ore customer segment group accounted for a total of USD 10.0 billion in revenues (19.9% of BHP Billiton total), up from USD 9.5 billion in 2008. EBIT from iron ore operations in 2009 totaled USD 6.2 billion (50.8% of BHP Billiton total), improving 2008 iron ore EBIT of USD 4.6 billion.[198]

BHP Billiton has some 41,000 employees and more than 100 operations in 25 countries.[199] Its iron ore assets, however, are concentrated in Australia and Brazil. BHP Billiton's Australian iron ore operations account for more than 90% of the company's iron ore capacity. These operations involve a complex

---

[193]See Hoovers (2011b), p. 3.
[194]See Hoovers (2011a), p. 1.
[195]See BHP Billiton (2010), p. 5.
[196]See BHP Billiton (2010), p. 53, adjusted for moisture and Fe content.
[197]See BHP Billiton (2010), p. 5.
[198]See BHP Billiton (2010), p. 110.
[199]See Datamonitor (2010b), p. 4.

integrated system of seven open pit mines and more than 1,000 km of rail as well as port facilities (Port Hedland), all located in the Pilbara region of Western Australia. The mines can be grouped into three joint ventures (Mount Newman, Yandi and Mount Goldsworthy), with BHP Billiton's interest being 85% in each, as well as one wholly owned mine in Jimblebar. Notably, BHP Billiton's Mount Whaleback mine, organized within the Mount Newman JV, is the biggest single-pit open-cut iron ore mine in the world being more than five km long and nearly 1.5 km wide. The company's remaining iron ore capacity emanates from the company's 50% share of Samarco, operating three integrated pellet plants in Brazil.[200]

3.4 Dry bulk freight rates

As described in Section 2.2.5, the iron ore mines are linked to the steelmaking industry by sophisticated bulk transport systems. The main part of the transportation from the mine to the blast furnace is commonly via seaborne routes, using dry bulk freighters, especially Capesize vessels. The influence of freight rates on global iron ore trade therefore cannot be overstressed. The competitive advantage of mines depends to a large degree on the proximity to key markets.[201] Thus, changes in the global freight market have a profound effect on the landed cost of a mine's ore and therefore on the overall trade flows of iron ore.[202]

The bulk freight markets represent a pure economic marketplace with rates determined by the interaction of vessel supply and demand. Bulk freight supply is affected mainly by changes in the world bulk fleet, i.e. demolition of old and building of new ships. The demand for bulk freight represents derived demand, reflecting patterns in the dry bulk materials markets that underpin the demand for bulk freight. As ship owners and cargo interests are located all over the globe, vessel charters are negotiated through shipping brokers who are compensated by commissions paid by the shipowners.[203] Settlement prices for various vessel types and shipping routes are published regularly via the Baltic Exchange, the world's main international shipping exchange.[204]

Interaction of vessel supply and demand on the world market leads to the time charter hire rates (in USD per day) and voyage freight rates (in USD per ton).

---

[200]See BHP Billiton (2010), pp. 37–38.
[201]See Manners (1971), p. 151.
[202]See O'Driscoll (2006), p. 58.
[203]See Lundgren (1996); Parker (2006), pp. 102–106.
[204]See Branch (2007), pp. 172–173.

The rates that are paid by shippers of iron ore are commonly quoted in voyage terms. The rates on a given route depend on many voyage-specific criteria but also on the general levels of the freight market as determined by the supply and demand interaction. The general market levels are indicated by time charter rates which reflect what the charterer will pay, on a USD-per-day basis, for the use of the vessel. These time charter rates are converted by the shipowner into the more familiar USD per ton rates quoted to iron ore shippers. The calculation starts with a USD per day time charter value for the vessel which is multiplied by the estimated number of days of the voyage. Other costs of the voyage (e.g., fuel and port-related cost) are added and the resulting total is divided by the number of tons carried to arrive at the cost per ton.[205]

For example, 2009 average freight rates on major iron ore routes were USD 11.58 per ton for iron ore shipments from Australia to China, USD 16.06 per ton from Brazil to Europe.[206]

3.5 Iron ore trade flows and market mechanism

3.5.1 Global iron ore trade flows

Natural geological endowment dictates that some countries have more iron ore than they require for domestic steelmaking, while others lack iron ore.[207] Before looking at iron ore trade flows, it is therefore necessary to define each country's domestic net balance with respect to iron ore. This can be done by deducting a country's domestic demand for iron ore from its available domestic iron ore production. Economically, a positive net total, or surplus in iron ore production, will generally lead to exports. In turn, a country with a negative balance, i.e., requiring more iron ore for steelmaking than is available from domestic production, will have to import iron ore.

Table 3.4 gives an overview of iron ore exports and imports by country in 2009. As is shown, most of the largest producers of iron ore are net exporters. Australia, owing to its limited domestic steel mill capacity, exported about 90% of its 2009 iron ore output.[208] The country therefore lead global exports with 380.5 Mt in 2009, accounting for more than 40% of total iron ore exports. Following closely behind is Brazil with 266.0 Mt and roughly 30% of global

---

[205]See Branch (2007), p. 194; Galdón-Sánchez and Schmitz (2002); Parker (2006), pp. 103–104.
[206]See Clarkson Research Services Ltd. (2010).
[207]See Jeffrey (2006), p. 4.
[208]See U.S. Geological Survey (2010a).

exports. Therefore, these two countries jointly accounted for almost 70% of world iron ore exports in 2009. The top five exporters are completed by India (90.7 Mt), South Africa (44.6 Mt) and Canada (30.0 Mt).

Iron ore imports are dominated by China. In 2009, China imported 595.7 Mt of iron ore. This translates to 64.0% of global iron ore imports in that year. Japan (98.1 Mt), South Korea (41.1 Mt), Germany (38.1 Mt) and Taiwan (11.6 Mt), placed second to fifth in the import ranking, jointly only accounted for roughly 20% of all iron ore imports.

It is noteworthy that China, although the leading global producer, is also the leading importer of iron ore. Historically, Chinese steel producers relied solely on domestic iron ore supplies.[209] With the rapid growth of the economy since the millennium, however, China's iron and steel producers have increasingly required imported iron ore to meet their demand.[210] In an attempt to offset this development, the Chinese government sharply increased the volume of domestic iron ore output. However, owing to the low iron content and high impurities of domestic ore, this surge in production proved insufficient to maintain self-sufficiency. Since then, domestic iron ore production in China has fallen and imports of high-grade ore to fill the supply/demand gap have increased at a correspondingly high rate.[211] The iron ore supplied by domestic producers decreased to less than 50% of the demand in 2009 compared with 75% in the 1990s.[212]

Country	Iron ore exports Mtpa	Share of total	Country	Iron ore imports Mtpa	Share of total
Australia	380.5	40.9%	China	595.7	64.0%
Brazil	266.0	28.6%	Japan	98.1	10.5%
India	90.7	9.7%	South Korea	41.1	4.4%
South Africa	44.6	4.8%	Germany	38.1	4.1%
Canada	30.0	3.2%	Taiwan	11.6	1.2%
Other	119.4	12.8%	Other	146.6	15.7%
World total	**931.3**	**100.0%**	**World total**	**931.3**	**100.0%**

Table 3.4: Iron ore exports and imports by country, 2009 [Own illustration based on Iron and Steel Statistics Bureau (2010)]

The physical movement of iron ore across the globe is naturally determined by the location of the net importing and net exporting markets.[213] Based on the

---

[209]See Feng (1994); Taube and in der Heiden (2010), p. 39.
[210]See Australian Bureau of Agricultural and Resource Economics (2009a), p. 173.
[211]See Ericsson (2009).
[212]See Taube and in der Heiden (2010), p. 39; U.S. Geological Survey (2010c).
[213]See O'Driscoll (2006), p. 52.

export and import data described above, one may say that, strongly simplified, the focus of available iron ore supply is on the southern hemisphere of the globe, while net demand is concentrated on the northern hemisphere. It can therefore be assumed that the main trade flows in iron ore flow from the southern hemisphere, especially Brazil and Australia, to the northern hemisphere, especially to the Asian continent and, to a lesser extent, Europe.

Table 3.5 shows the interregional iron ore trade flows as they occurred in 2009.[214] The total of all interregional trade flows sums up to 881.4 Mt,[215] more than 50% of the iron ore produced.[216] The average haul length of a ton of ore was approximately 6,500 nautical miles.[217] The by far largest trade flow runs from Oceania (i.e., Australia) to China, with 279.5 Mt of ore transported in 2009. China is also on the receiving end of the second-largest flow; 154.6 Mt of ore were shipped to China from South America (mainly Brazil). The only other flow equaling more than 100 Mt is from Oceania to Other Asia.

■ Top ten trade flows

Mtpa	Destination									Sum of supply
Origin	North America	South America	Europe	Africa & Middle East	CIS	China	India	Other Asia	Oceania	
North America		1.1	13.9	1.7	0.0	9.3		3.1	0.3	29.4
South America	1.4		58.3	14.1	0.0	154.6	0.1	44.8	0.6	273.6
Europe	0.1	0.0		5.3	0.0	1.3	0.0	0.0	0.0	6.8
Africa & Middle East	0.1	0.0	4.2		0.0	34.3	0.0	6.0	0.0	44.6
CIS	0.1	0.0	18.9	2.0		27.0	0.3	0.1	0.0	48.4
China	0.0	0.0	0.0	0.0	0.0		0.0	0.0	0.0	0.0
India	0.0	0.0	0.5	0.1	0.0	83.6		6.2	0.4	90.7
Other Asia	0.0	0.0	0.0	0.0	0.0	6.7	0.0		0.0	6.8
Oceania	0.0	0.0	0.7	0.0	0.0	279.5	0.0	101.0		381.2
Sum of supply	1.7	1.1	95.9	23.8	0.0	597.0	0.4	160.3	1.3	881.4

Table 3.5: Interregional iron ore trade flows, 2009 [Own illustration based on Iron and Steel Statistics Bureau (2010)]

The top ten trade flows in 2009, adding up to 815.9 Mt and thus accounting for 92.6% of total iron ore trade, are further depicted in the world iron ore trade map in Figure 3.5. This geographic layout clearly confirms the above assumption that the world market is split in two along the equator: the iron ore rich southern hemisphere supplies iron ore to the industrially more vibrant northern hemisphere. Since freight rates play a significant role in the cost of the final product, proximity of an iron ore supplier is key. Therefore, China and other Asian countries are supplied mainly from Australian mines, while Brazil satisfies the nearby European market and sends additional volumes to satisfy demand on the Asian continent.

---

[214]To achieve better readability, imports and exports have been aggregated to a regional level. For an overview of the allocation of countries to the geographic regions, see Appendix I.

[215]Note that this is lower than the sum of imports/exports stated in Table 3.4 due to the aggregation to geographic regions.

[216]Note that actual shipping tonnage was higher than stated here, as Fe content has been standardized to 62.0% and moisture content has been deducted to allow comparison with supply and demand data.

[217]See Gardiner (2011), p. 23.

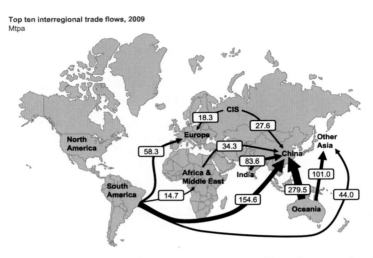

Figure 3.5: Top ten interregional iron ore trade flows, 2009 [Own illustration based on Iron and Steel Statistics Bureau (2010)]

More than half of the iron ore mined in 2009 crossed a country border before being consumed. However, global trade in iron ore has not always been so lively. Historically, iron ore was sourced primarily from local or regional mines. In the last decades, however, seaborne trade of iron ore has increased dramatically.[218] Between 2000 and 2007, e.g., shipments of iron ore increased by over 65% from approximately 500 Mt to around 850 Mt. The reason for this increase is first and foremost to be found in exploding demand of Chinese steel producers combined with low grades of domestic iron ore supplies.[219] However, the development of iron ore trade has also been aided by the construction of large ore-bearing vessels, thus reducing shipping costs. This has set the prerequisite for iron ore from higher-grade ore deposits, e.g. in Australia and South America, to be delivered economically to steel mills worldwide.[220]

---

[218]See Poveromo (2006), p. 1392.
[219]See Taube and in der Heiden (2010), p. 39.
[220]See Poveromo (2006), p. 1392.

3.5.2 Iron ore market mechanism

3.5.2.1 Modes of iron ore transactions

Iron ore suppliers and buyers have two principal options in which to enter into transactions. They can either base trades on the conditions of individual long-term bilateral OTC contracts or enter into an agreement on the physical spot market. Spot trades, with market prices determined on a daily basis, openly expose both parties to price fluctuations occurring between an agreed contract date and physical delivery.[221] Therefore, especially large-scale steel mills choose to negotiate long-term framework contracts with iron ore suppliers in order to secure their ore requirements.[222] Most of the trade in iron ore in the past years has taken place under such contracts, with spot transactions accounting for only approximately 20% of the traded volume.[223] Iron ore supply contracts, with durations ranging from one to twelve or more years, define the annual tonnage, delivery dates and quality of ore that is to be supplied by the miner to its steel mill customers. The prices for these deliveries, however, are defined separately by means of a pricing mechanism.[224] This mechanism is described in the following.

3.5.2.2 Iron ore pricing mechanism

Starting in the early 1970s, iron ore contract prices were settled using an unwritten rule of pricing known as "benchmark pricing". This process centered around lengthy annual "champion negotiations", in which free-on-board (FOB) prices for iron ore fines were set separately for the European and Asian market.[225] The reasons why such a rule was established without the need for systematic coordination or arguments is that the number of players was limited.[226] On the European market, Brazilian iron ore producers and European steel mills traditionally set the reference price, while the Asian market price was negotiated between Australian producers and Japanese steelmakers (championed by Nippon Steel). More recently, due to increased Chinese iron ore demand, the Asian negotiations have been championed by the China Iron and Steel Association

---

[221]See ICAP (2010).

[222]See Millbank (2011); Rogers et al. (1987).

[223]See Frankfurter Allgemeine Sonntagszeitung (2010).

[224]See Banks (1979); Kästner et al. (1979), p. 206; Rogers et al. (1987).

[225]In contrast to cost-and-freight prices (CFR), FOB prices include only the cost of the products being loaded on board the ship, but not the ocean freight to the products' destination. For more details on Incoterms, refer to International Chamber of Commerce (2010).

[226]See Sukagawa (2010).

(CISA) representing the Chinese steel industry. The so determined European and Asian market prices for iron ore fines were commonly regarded as a benchmark for other suppliers, who, depending on the quality of their specific ore, adjusted their FOB price to compete on a landed cost basis in each market. These price adjustments in the form of premiums and penalties applied to the benchmark price reflected the specific quality of the ore and therefore the ore's influence on blast furnace productivity.[227] Prices for iron ore lump and pellets were set by adding negotiated lump and pellet premiums onto the reference price for fines. The market prices agreed on for ore to Europe was applicable for the calendar year effective January 1st of that year. For ore sold to Asia, prices were set for the Japanese fiscal year, beginning April 1st.[228]

This pricing mechanism, untouched for almost 40 years, went through disruptive changes in 2009 and 2010. The price talks for fiscal year 2009 commenced in the midst of the unprecedented economic crisis. Encouraged by historically low iron ore spot prices, below long-term contract prices for the first time, steel companies in Asia abandoned their contracts and resorted to purchasing more iron ore on the spot market.[229] In the negotiations that followed, steelmakers aimed to get new contract prices settled at the levels of fiscal year 2007, calling for a price reduction of approximately 40% for Australian hematite fines, the first price cut in seven years.[230] The price talks went through a procrastinated deadlock associated with the world's economic downturn and the arrest and conviction of Rio Tinto employees in Shanghai charged with industrial espionage and bribery.[231] Iron ore pricing negotiations for fiscal year 2009 finally seemed to reach settlement on May 26, when Japan's Nippon Steel and Anglo-Australian miner Rio Tinto jointly proposed to price Pilbara fine ores at 97 USDc/dmtu FOB (equivalent to approximately USD 71.72 per ton CFR China for 62.0% Fe fines).[232] Though this would have corresponded to a 33% reduction vs. 2008 prices, the Chinese steel industry refused to accept this price, arguing for an even deeper price cut. In consequence, negotiations were halted and, with Chinese steel mills and the Big Three failing to agree to a 2009 benchmark price, all following iron ore deliveries were sold at spot market prices.[233]

---

[227]See Kirk (1999).
[228]See Hellmer (1997a), pp. 7–8; Kästner et al. (1979), p. 206; Kirk (1999). For more details on benchmark pricing (e.g., the brick system and provisional prices) as well as variations of contract conditions (e.g., freight-sharing), see Sukagawa (2010).
[229]See The Economist (2010c); The Financial Times (2010c).
[230]See Sato (2010), p. 3.
[231]See The Financial Times (2010c); Treadgold (2009).
[232]See Sato (2010), pp. 3–4.
[233]See Sato (2010), p. 4.

When Chinese steel demand recovered surprisingly fast starting in mid-2009, iron ore spot prices soared past even historically high 2008 benchmark prices, forcing Chinese steel mills to suffer unprecedentedly high iron ore procurement costs.[234] With Chinese steelmakers' backs against the wall, the Big Three used their considerably increased negotiating power to fulfill their long-held desire for a new pricing mechanism that reflects market conditions more immediately than the benchmark system.[235] Thus, in early 2010, the Big Three announced the complete abandonment of the benchmark pricing system,[236] opting instead to link iron ore contract prices to the spot market with quarterly price revisions.[237] Chinese steel giant Baosteel and CISA tried to hold out on spot prices and even called for a boycott of the Big Three, but this proposal was more an indication of the powerlessness of the Chinese steel industry and its inability to change the course of events, than a real threat.[238]

Miner Vale has since published some details regarding the new system of quarterly pricing for long-term supply contracts:[239]

- All global iron ore prices are based on the cost-and-freight (CFR) spot price for 62% fines to China[240]

- Prices are to be adjusted to reflect differences in ore quality

- The price of the next quarter is calculated as the average of the two first months of the present quarter and the last month of the previous quarter

- If the calculated price is less than 5% higher or lower than the price of the previous quarter, the price remains constant

Despite initial opposition mainly from Chinese steel companies, there seems to be general agreement in the market that future iron ore prices will be linked to the spot market. Current market dynamics suggest that this new pricing model has become the dominant form of iron ore pricing, with quarterly pricing as the norm for the majority of iron ore contract sales entering 2011.[241]

---

[234]See United Nations Conference on Trade and Development (2010), p. 4.

[235]See Verhoeven et al. (2010); Woolrich (2010).

[236]See, e.g., The New York Times (2010); Waldmeir and Farchy (2010).

[237]See, e.g., Tasker (2010); The Financial Times (2010a); The New York Times (2010). Note that the quarterly pricing strikes a compromise between miners' desire to have a market price that reflects market conditions and the fact that steel mills run on thin margins and require some assurance regarding their iron ore procurement costs going forward (see Woolrich (2010)).

[238]See United Nations Conference on Trade and Development (2010), p. 4.

[239]See United Nations Conference on Trade and Development (2010), pp. 4–5.

[240]In contrast to free-on-board prices (FOB), CFR prices include the costs of products being loaded on board the ship as well as the ocean freight to the products' destination. For more details on Incoterms, refer to International Chamber of Commerce (2010).

[241]See Gardiner (2011), p. 14; Oakley and Blas (2010); Verhoeven et al. (2010).

Based on prices for deliveries to China from 2008 to 2010, Figure 3.6 gives an overview of the chronology of the recent changes in iron ore pricing.[242]

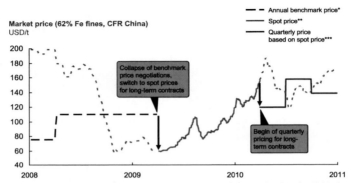

Figure 3.6: Iron ore price levels under changing pricing regimes, 2008–2010 [Own illustration based on data from Intercontinental Exchange (2010); Sato (2010), p. 3; The Steel Index (2011)]

3.5.2.3 Emergence of iron ore indices and derivatives

As the benchmark pricing system based on annual price negotiations is replaced with contract prices linked to the spot market price, there arises the need for independent iron ore spot price indices on which to base the prices of contract deliveries. Consequently, various spot-based iron ore indices have emerged. Though no single index has yet reached a dominant position, the three most common series are[243]

- Metal Bulletin Iron Ore Index (http://www.mbironoreindex.com/)

- Platts IODEX Iron Ore Index (http://www.platts.com/)

- The Steel Index Iron Ore Series (http://www.thesteelindex.com/)

---

[242]To allow comparison, annual average freight costs from Australia to China has been added to the FOB benchmark prices.

[243]See Farthing (2009); ICAP (2010); Steel Business Briefing (2010b); United Nations Conference on Trade and Development (2010), p. 4. For spot prices in this paper, a combination of the Platts IODEX Iron Ore Index and The Steel Index Iron Ore Series is used.

The details of these indices are displayed in Table 3.6. All have in common that they are based on CFR prices for 62% Fe content fines delivered to Chinese ports. However, the indices differ as to the port of destination, minimum volume and publishing frequency.

Index	Basis	Minimum cargo	Published
Metal Bulletin Iron Ore Index	62% Fe content fines, CFR Qingdao, China	30,000 t	Weekly, Friday, 8:00 GMT
Platts IODEX Iron Ore Index	62% Fe content fines, CFR Qingdao, China	35,000 t	Daily, 12:00 GMT
The Steel Index Iron Ore Series	62% Fe content fines, CFR Tianjin, China	25,000 t	Daily, 12:00 GMT

Table 3.6: Overview of three main spot-based iron ore indices [Adapted from ICAP (2010)]

With the growing importance of the spot market price and the resulting emergence of iron ore price indices, financial institutions are gearing up to exploit the new iron ore pricing system by developing a derivatives market similar to the ones that exist for crude oil, aluminum and coal.[244] First iron ore derivatives emerged in May 2008, when Deutsche Bank and Credit Suisse launched the iron ore's first over-the-counter cash-settled swaps in the expectation that the benchmark system would come to an end.[245] Since then, other banks have joined in, including Morgan Stanley.[246] Also, exchanges, clearing houses and renowned raw materials brokers are offering related services.[247] Figure 3.7 gives an overview of the key players currently involved in the development and trading of iron ore derivatives.

It is noteworthy that, until 2008, iron ore was one of the last significant global materials absent of an efficient and flexible hedging mechanism.[248] As with the development of the derivatives markets in oil in the early 1980s and other commodities during the past ten years, the emergence of iron ore derivatives will allow miners and consumers to hedge their positions in the physical market in order to offset price risks. Especially junior iron ore miners are likely to hedge their output as a way to raise finance more easily, while steelmakers can hedge their input costs.[249]

---

[244]See Oakley and Blas (2010).
[245]See The Economist (2010b). For a comprehensive overview of characteristics and financial mechanics of swaps refer to Hull (2006), pp. 149–180.
[246]See Oakley and Blas (2010).
[247]See Verhoeven et al. (2010).
[248]See ICAP (2010).
[249]See Bain & Company (2010); Oakley and Blas (2010).

Banks	Exchanges and clearing houses	Brokers
▪ Barclays Capital	▪ Chicago Mercantile Exchange (CME)	▪ Freight Investor Services (FIS)
▪ Credit Suisse		
▪ Deutsche Bank	▪ Hong Kong Mercantile Exchange (HKMEx)	▪ GFI
▪ Goldman Sachs		▪ ICAP
▪ J.P. Morgan	▪ Intercontinental Exchange (ICE)	▪ London Dry Bulk
▪ Morgan Stanley		
	▪ LCH.Clearnet	
	▪ London Metal Exchange (LME)	
	▪ Singapore Exchange (SGX)	

Figure 3.7: Key players active in the development and trading of iron ore derivatives [See Crust (2010); Czerwensky Intern (2009); Farthing (2009); Kinch (2009); Oakley and Blas (2010); Pamuk (2010); The Economist (2010b)]

3.6 Public policy

A further significant factor affecting the iron ore industry is public policy, especially in the form of taxation. Taxes have historically been one of the largest cost items in the iron ore mining industry, often being charged at local, provincial and federal levels. Taxation therefore has a major influence on production, trade and consumption of iron ore and thus on the iron ore market as a whole.[250] Without going into detail on general aspects regarding public policy in mining, this section gives an overview of the taxes affecting the iron ore industry.[251]

Iron ore mining normally creates wealth or economic surpluses, providing the incentive for private companies to explore for, develop and then exploit iron ore deposits. Although companies generally are driven by the pursuit of profits, the goals and objectives of the governments that control the terms and conditions under which private investors have access to iron ore deposits are quite different.[252] Their actions and policies, including the taxes they impose on the iron ore mining sector, generally meet three primary objectives:

---

[250]See Manners (1971), pp. 150–151; PriceWaterhouseCoopers (2010).

[251]Note that this paper explicitly does not aim to analyze the iron ore market from a policy maker's perspective. Thus, aspects such as optimal taxation of mining activities and effects of different taxation methods are not discussed. For information on these aspects, refer to, e.g., Krugman and Obstfeld (1988); O'Sullivan and Sheffrin (2002); Otto (2000); Otto et al. (2006); Peck et al. (1992).

[252]See Otto et al. (2006), p. 7.

- *Redistribution of economic rent* – Generally, iron ore miners exploit a non-renewable resources in order to obtain an economic rent.[253] A tax on iron ore rents is socially equitable, since economic rent is an unearned surplus (or windfall) in excess of normal rates of return, caused by the finiteness of the resource and market prices far above the cost of extraction. Thus, governments have just as much right to claim it as private mineral producers. Also, in the majority of nations, natural resources are owned by the state or by the people in general. Taxes applied to iron ore mining activities thus are charges incurred by mining companies for exploiting a resource they do not own. The nature of taxation is therefore to ensure that the people have a direct share in the wealth produced by exploiting a country's mineral resources[254]

- *Compensation for negative impacts of mining* – Iron ore mining, like any other form of mining, inevitably generates significant impacts on the natural environment. Open-pit mining destroys large areas of natural habitat, causes complete alterations of soils, ground and surface water hydrology, destroys plants and can, in extreme cases, even change entire ecosystems. Thus, in combination with increased environmental regulation, taxation of iron ore mining activities aims to create compensation for these damages to the landscape and the environment. Tax-generated revenues also act as a reserve fund to finance the environmental reclamation of the land after the mine has closed[255]

- *Influence of taxpayer behavior* – As is the general character of any public policy, taxation of the mining industry aims to influence market behavior by providing an incentive to behave in a manner preferred by the government. For example, to encourage investors to run a more environmentally friendly mine, a tax credit may be granted by the government for the installation of pollution control devices, or a high tax may be imposed on the discharge of harmful effluents. Also, taxes may be levied in order to encourage or discourage the development of iron ore deposits, trade of iron ore as well as financial investments into the industry[256]

In order to reach these objectives, governments in different countries choose to levy different types of taxes on the iron ore industry. Table 3.7 gives an overview of common tax types, including their basis for calculation, a short description and their prevalence with respect to iron ore mining. As is shown, these taxes

---

[253]See Otto et al. (2006), pp. 19–29 for a detailed definition and discussion of economic rent.
[254]See Eggert (1992); González (2004); Otto (2000); Pizarro (2004); The Financial Times (2010e).
[255]See Consiglieri (2004); Crowson (1992), p. 92; Dvořáček (2005); González (2004).
[256]See Manners (1971), pp. 150–151; Otto (2000); Radetzki (2008), pp. 48–51.

can be split into three categories. "In rem" taxes are charges assessed against the iron ore deposit or against the inputs and actions needed to exploit it. These charges can in turn be divided into two groups: in rem taxes that affect the variable costs of the mining project (such as royalty and export taxes) and taxes that affect the fixed costs of the mining project (such as registration fees, property taxes and VAT on mining supplies). In rem taxes therefore do not take into account the concept of profitability. In contrast, "in personam" taxes are charges against some definition of net revenues, that is, revenues less qualifying costs. Examples include corporate income tax and additional/excess profits tax. Generally, in rem taxes that concern the variable costs of mining directly affect a mine's competitiveness. Therefore, these taxes have a greater likelihood of influencing miners' business decisions regarding mine development, production and iron ore trade than other tax types.[257] For an overview of mining tax levels in different countries, refer to Otto (2000).

	Tax type	Basis	Description/objective	Prevalence
In rem taxes, variable (unit or value based)	Royalty tax	Charge per unit or percent of iron ore value (ad-valorem)	Tax on the extraction of iron ore, an ownership transfer payment for iron ore extracted	Commonly used, though some countries forgo royalty taxes on iron ore
	Export tax	Percent of value of exported iron ore (ad-valorem)	Tax on exports, an incentive to satisfy local iron ore demand	Eliminated on iron ore in most countries, particularly relevant for China and India
In rem taxes, fixed (unit or value based)	Registration fees	Set charge per unit area	Administration fees for licenses and permits	Commonly used, usually minor
	Property tax	Percent of value of property or capital	Tax on the ownership and use of real an intangible property	Commonly used
	Land rent or usage fees	Set charge per unit area	Charge for use of land owned by government, often to local authority	Commonly used, usually minor
	Value-added tax (VAT)	Percent of value of the good or service	Tax to capture a portion of value added	Relevant for procurement of mining inputs and supplies
In personam taxes (net revenue based)	Corporate income/profit tax	Percent of income/profit	Tax to provide revenue based on ability to pay	Universally used
	Capital gains tax	Percent of profit on disposal of capital assets	Tax to capture profits on disposal of capital assets	Common in developed nations, not applied in many developing nations
	Additional/excess profits tax	Percent of add'l/ excess profits	Tax to capture a part of profits above high rate of returns	Extremely rare, introduction recently discussed in Australia ("Resource Super Profits Tax")

Table 3.7: Overview of tax types affecting iron ore mining [Own illustration based on Kuyek (2004); Otto (2000); Otto et al. (2006), pp. 32–34; PriceWaterhouseCoopers (2010)]

---

[257]See Otto et al. (2006), pp. 30–31.

4 Analysis of recent market developments and derivation of risk mitigation strategies

Having described the fundamental characteristics as well as the status quo of the iron ore market in the previous chapters, the present chapter aims to give a comprehensive overview of the recent developments and trends in the global iron ore market. First of all, these respective market developments and trends are presented in Section 4.1. Subsequently, Section 4.2 highlights the impact of those market changes on the steel industry. Based on this impact, Section 4.3 gives an overview of potential risk mitigating counter-moves by demand-side players and selects two to be analyzed in greater detail.

4.1 Recent developments and trends in the iron ore market

In recent years, the iron ore market has undergone several substantial changes and developments:

- *Increased iron ore market price* resulting from increase in Chinese demand

- *Increased amount of iron ore capacity expansion projects* as response to higher demand and market price

- *Increased iron ore market price volatility* due to the new pricing mechanism and increasing speculation

- *Increased freight rates and freight rate volatility* due to China-driven surge in seaborne trade

These developments, along with the corresponding market trends, will be described in detail in the following sections.[258]

---

[258]Note that, although there exist dependencies between the observed developments, these will not be discussed here.

4.1.1 Increased iron ore market price

As described in Section 3.2.2.1, with its opening up to the world market in 1978, China's economic growth has shown a remarkable development. On the back of industrialization and urbanization on a scale never seen before, demand for steel in China has more than quadrupled since 1980. Consequently, China has evolved to become the world's leading consumer of iron ore. Due to the low quality of domestic Chinese ore, however, China has been unable to maintain its self-sufficiency in iron ore, thus leading to a surge in imports of high-grade ore.[259] Therefore, China's increase in iron ore demand has caused a profound structural shift in the global iron ore market. For decades, the world iron ore market was characterized by overcapacity.[260] Now, global iron ore mining capacity utilization is peaking and with it, the price for iron ore. As a matter of fact, the "China factor" has been the central force behind price movements in the market.[261]

Figure 4.1 aims to illustrate the effect of China's economic awakening on global steel production as well as on the iron ore price. As is shown, global crude steel production remained more or less stable between 1980 and 2000, cycling roughly between lows of 650 Mtpa and highs of 800 Mtpa. During the same period, the iron ore market price showed a similar stability at levels between 26.35 and 37.86 USDc/dmtu (FOB), while mirroring the minor steel production fluctuations with a small time lag. After the start of the new millennium, however, China's annual crude steel production catapulted from 128.5 Mt in 2000 to 567.8 Mt in 2009 (see also Figure 3.3) and even higher to 626.7 Mt in 2010.[262] Consequently, global crude steel production peaked in 2010 at 1,413.5 Mt, with China's share equaling 44.3%.[263] This global steel production boom, triggered by Chinese construction and infrastructure investments, has sent the iron price skywards. While at a moderate level of 27.06 USDc/dmtu (FOB) in 2000, the price increased more than sevenfold to 222.93 USDc/dmtu (FOB) in 2010.[264]

China is still only in the early stages of economic development and thus industrialization and urbanization trends are still strong. Goldman Sachs expects China's economy to grow by 5–8% per year through 2020.[265] Plenty more

---

[259]See Ericsson (2009).
[260]See Verhoeven et al. (2010).
[261]See Taube and in der Heiden (2010), p. 38.
[262]2010 figure from World Steel Association (2011).
[263]See World Steel Association (2011).
[264]Note that, as of April 2009, iron ore prices are no longer given in FOB, but rather in CFR terms. However, in order to allow comparability, 2009 and 2010 average market prices mentioned here have been recalculated to FOB terms.
[265]See Wilson and Purushothaman (2003).

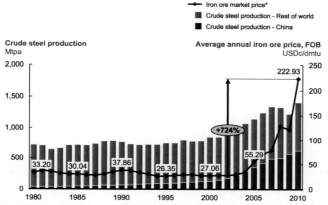

Figure 4.1: Global crude steel production and average annual iron ore market price, 1980–2010 [Own illustration based on production data from Sato (2010), pp. 6–7; The Steel Index (2011); World Steel Association (1990); World Steel Association (2000); World Steel Association (2010); World Steel Association (2011)]

young Chinese, eager for new opportunities, are due to make their way from their rural homes to vast cities yet to be built, on roads and railways that currently only exist on the drawing boards of central planners.[266] Though growth in steel-intensive fixed asset investments has continued since the early 1980s, saturation levels have not yet been reached. Massive infrastructure projects still absorb huge amounts of steel every year.[267] Also, China still consumes relatively little steel on a per capita basis. Measures of steel intensity, the relationship between GDP per capita and consumption of steel, show that China still lags far behind not only North American and European economies, but also neighbors such as South Korea.[268]

On a global scale, annual blast furnace production is expected to rise by about 300 Mt in the coming years. While China alone is expected to account for roughly 60% of this total increase, other economies are also showing increased industrial activity and infrastructure buildup.[269] Where there is evidence of a growing population combined with a developing economy, these countries and regions become earmarked as growing and future markets for steel and therefore

---

[266]See The Economist (2011c).
[267]See Bisson et al. (2010); Taube and in der Heiden (2010), p. 40.
[268]See The Economist (2011c); Woetzel (2001); Wu (2000).
[269]See The Financial Times (2011a).

for iron ore. [270] Following this pattern, especially the other BRIC countries Brazil, Russia and India are showing good prospects for increased demand for iron ore going forward.[271] Over the next decade, these four economies are aiming to jointly move about one billion people from poverty into the world of consumerism.[272] By 2020, it is expected that the BRICs will account for a third of the global economy (in PPP terms) and contribute about 49% of global GDP growth.[273]

Having already described China's economic outlook above, it is necessary to briefly touch on the expected economic developments of the remaining three BRIC countries from a steel/iron ore market perspective:

- *Brazil* – Brazil's steel consumption has a high potential for growth due to its current low per capita consumption and strong macroeconomic factors combined with great needs for investments in infrastructure. Also, Brazil's government is seeking to expand domestic steelmaking activities in order to create jobs in the country. Thus, it is considering levying an iron ore export tax in addition to an import tax on steel products as well as a removal of taxes on finished and value-added goods such as steel and steel plates. As a result, Brazilian annual crude steel capacity is expected to grow by as much as 70 Mt by 2015 through green- and brownfield investments[274]

- *Russia* – Russia's growth projections, though somewhat hampered by a shrinking population, are strong, with annual GDP growth calculated at 3–6% through 2020. The growth of Russia's steel industry is being pushed additionally by the government's support of steel-intensive industries, such as automotive, manufacturing and machine building. Additional steelmaking capacities will be utilized as a result of the expected boost in exports after Russia's admittance into the WTO. Also, the country's booming oil, gas and energy industries are expected to increase steel demand going forward[275]

- *India* – India has the potential to show the fastest economic growth of all BRICs over the coming decade. Annual GDP growth could be be-

---

[270]See Feng (1994); O'Driscoll (2006), pp. 49–54.

[271]See, e.g., Ernst & Young (2011b); Goldman Sachs Global Economics Group (2007); Wilson et al. (2010); Wilson and Purushothaman (2003).

[272]See Jeffrey (2006), p. 4; Woolley (2010).

[273]See Wilson et al. (2010).

[274]See Brazil Steel Institute (2010); Ebeling (2011); Ernst & Young (2011b); Wilson and Purushothaman (2003).

[275]See Ernst & Young (2011b); Wilson and Purushothaman (2003); World Economic Forum (2010c).

tween 6–10% if economic development proceeds at current rates. With a growing population, an imminent urbanization process, greater focus on infrastructure and more vehicles and cities emerging, India's steel demand is expected to cross 100 Mt by 2012 and continue to grow. This strong growth has attracted many global steel players, including POSCO and ArcelorMittal who are establishing large greenfield steel projects in India[276]

Thus, given a still rising world population, dominantly within BRIC countries, advocates of the supercycle theory suggest that the upward trend of global steel production, and thus of the iron ore price, will continue.[277]

4.1.2 Increased amount of iron ore capacity expansion projects

The prospect of rising iron ore prices and resulting higher profits means mining companies cannot shovel iron ore out of the ground quickly enough.[278] Following China's demand explosion, many iron ore producers are making huge investments in extensive green- and brownfield expansion projects. These projects aim to expand future production capacity in order to provide the iron ore necessary to fuel the BRIC's economic development.[279]

As can be expected, the Big Three are especially active in the buildup of new production capacity:

- Vale has a full pipeline of iron ore and iron ore pellet projects for the upcoming years. These projects are mainly brownfield capacity expansions of existing Brazilian operations (Carajás and Itabirito), but also greenfield projects in Carajás as well as in Africa (Guinea and Mozambique)[280]

- Rio Tinto plans to advance iron ore capacity expansions to achieve a total of 333 Mt per annum capacity in Western Australia by 2015. These expansions, at a total cost of approximately USD 8 billion, include brownfield

---

[276]See Bhaskar (2008); Ernst & Young (2011b); Goldman Sachs Global Economics Group (2007); Wilson and Purushothaman (2003); World Economic Forum (2010b).

[277]See Jeffrey (2006), p. 4; The Economist (2011c).

[278]In accordance with market fundamentals, high iron ore market prices stimulate exploration and development of new iron ore mines as well as the expansion of existing mining operations (see O'Driscoll (2006), p. 53). However, as described in Section 2.2.2, it takes three to seven years to set up or expand an iron ore mining operation. Thus, the available level of iron ore production capacity reacts to demand increases with a certain time lag. This typically leads to the alternation of phases with high capacity utilization and high prices and phases with increased supply and lower prices.

[279]See Pilling (2011).

[280]See Vale (2010), pp. 66–67.

projects at Brockman, Marandoo and Nammuldi mines as well as significant railway and port infrastructure expansions. Abroad, Rio Tinto has invested more than USD 700 million to secure a share in a significant greenfield project at Simandou in Guinea[281]

- BHP Billiton has recently launched expansion projects "Rapid Growth Project 4 and 5". These projects, at a total expenditure of approximately USD 6.7 billion, aim to increase the company's Australian capacity to 205 Mtpa. Apart from brownfield mine expansions, especially in Mount Newman, these projects include handling capacity increases for railroad and port facilities. In terms of geographic diversification of the iron ore portfolio, BHP Billiton is in the early stages of development of its Nimba deposit in Guinea[282]

However, not only the major players are investing. Lured by high market prices, numerous small mining companies are developing new iron ore mines, many with the help of Chinese financing.[283] In order to reduce its dependency on the three largest miners, China has been extremely active in funding junior miners' capacity expansion projects and developing own projects abroad.[284]

In terms of geography, the run for iron ore has lead to a worldwide search for undeveloped iron ore resources. From this search, Africa has emerged as the new iron ore mining "hot spot".[285] Though boasting some of the largest and richest single deposits in the world, Africa has so far been pretty much underdeveloped with respect to iron ore mining. Now, numerous miners are engaging in projects in Africa, despite the high levels of political risk associated with the continent.[286] Especially Chinese firms have signed a number of iron ore deals in Africa, which at best could contribute nearly 250 Mt of iron ore when they come on stream.[287] As described above, also the Big Three, aiming to geographically diversify their iron ore mining portfolios, are investing in numerous large-scale greenfield projects in Africa.[288]

---

[281]See Rio Tinto (2011); Steel Business Briefing (2010d).

[282]See BHP Billiton (2010), p. 39; Steel Business Briefing (2010d); U.S. Geological Survey (2010a), p. 7.

[283]See Regan (2011).

[284]See, e.g., Felix (2011a).

[285]See, e.g., The Financial Times (2011c); The Wall Street Journal (2010).

[286]See Felix (2011c); The Financial Times (2011c).

[287]See Felix (2011a); Felix (2011b).

[288]See The Economist (2011b).

4.1.3 Increased iron ore market price volatility

As can be seen in Figure 4.2, showing the iron ore prices valid for long-term supply contracts from 2004 through 2011, price volatility for such contracts has considerably increased since the change in the pricing system described in Section 3.5.2.2.[289] This increased market price volatility can be traced back to two factors, which will be elaborated in the following:

- New contract pricing mechanism linked to spot market price with shorter pricing periods

- Increased volatility of the underlying spot market price due to speculation effects from new iron ore derivatives market

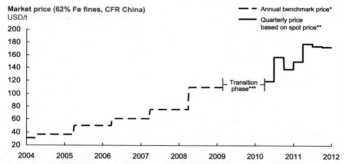

Figure 4.2: Global crude steel production and average annual iron ore market price, 1980–2009 [Own illustration based data from Intercontinental Exchange (2010); Sato (2010), pp. 6–7; The Steel Index (2011)]

4.1.3.1 New contract pricing mechanism linked to spot market price

As described in detail in Section 3.5.2.2, the iron ore pricing mechanism has recently undergone radical changes. For almost 40 years, the prices of long-term supply contracts were set in annual benchmark price negotiations between the major steelmakers and iron ore miners. As of 2010, these negotiations have

---

[289]Prices in the transition phase from April 2009 to April 2010, in which all OTC deliveries were made based on spot market prices, are not shown.

been replaced by a new system, linking contract prices to average trailing spot market index prices with quarterly price revisions.

At present, approximately 80% of the trade in iron ore takes place under such contracts, with spot transactions accounting for only approximately 20% of the traded volume.[290] With contract prices now linked to the much smaller spot market, it only takes a few trades on the spot market to influence the OTC price, thus increasing contract price volatility.[291]

However, it is important to recognize that iron ore pricing therefore has not only gone from negotiation-based to spot-based, but that pricing has moved to shorter time periods. While yearly price revisions were once the norm, now quarterly price updates are common. The move from annual to quarterly pricing has resulted in greater price swings, as the market price is determined by changes in supply and demand on the spot market and the shorter pricing cycle naturally reflects these changes in a more immediate manner. Iron ore producers have quickly realized, however, that in their opinion quarterly pricing is not flexible enough to sufficiently reflect overall market conditions.[292] It therefore seems clear that quarterly pricing is merely a stepping stone on the way to shifting contract terms even closer to the latest spot prices.[293] Thus, contract pricing terms are diverging into many directions, from quarterly to daily price revisions, leading to what the industry calls "the iron ore pricing rainbow".[294] For example, Rio Tinto has recently started to adopt contracts based on monthly price revisions.[295] BHP Billiton, the driving force behind the move to what it calls "market clearing prices", is selling a greater proportion of its iron ore on 30-, 10- and 5-day, or even shorter terms, pegged to average trailing index prices. BHP Billiton has recently stated that it would like its contract prices to move even closer to the daily spot market price.[296] As with the move from annual to quarterly pricing, a monthly or even shorter-term system will result in even greater iron ore contract price volatility.

Though radical, these changes are not a new phenomenon in raw materials markets. Iron ore is simply following other examples, such as the transformation in the crude oil pricing system in the late 1970s, aluminum in the early 1980s and, more recently, thermal coal in the early 2000s.[297] Therefore, though there

---

[290]See Frankfurter Allgemeine Sonntagszeitung (2010).
[291]See Fey (2010). This is also a feature of the crude oil market, where most trading volumes are indexed against spot markets (see Verhoeven et al. (2010)).
[292]See Millbank (2011).
[293]See Gardiner (2011), p. 14; Kinch (2010); Steel Business Briefing (2010a).
[294]See Cavallaro (2010).
[295]See Smith (2011).
[296]See Antonioli (2011a); Millbank (2011); Neely (2011); Serapio (2011).
[297]See ICAP (2010); The Financial Times (2010a).

are still various possible scenarios regarding the future of iron ore pricing,[298] the above described developments are evidence that iron ore "has joined the commodity club".[299] This is meant in the sense that iron ore market dynamics and pricing will more than ever be rooted in microeconomic fundamentals, where the equilibrium price equates market demand and supply.

4.1.3.2 Increased speculation effects from new iron ore derivatives market

As described in Section 3.5.2.3, the new pricing mechanism has triggered the emergence of iron ore indices and derivatives. While until 2008 iron ore was one of the last significant global materials absent of a derivatives market,[300] the presence of iron ore derivatives now allows miners and consumers alike to hedge their positions in the physical market.[301] There is an expectation that the expanding swaps market will evolve into a financial market for iron ore that will rival the liquidity and value of other raw materials, such as crude oil and aluminum.[302] Similarly, over the past several years, global coal markets have experienced a gradual transition from a historical pricing mechanism to that of a vibrant and transparent derivatives system.[303] Figure 4.3 shows an extrapolation of the liquidity of iron ore derivatives trading until 2020, based on the experience from the coal markets.

This increased liquidity going forward will stem not only from steelmakers and suppliers hedging their positions. As with the development of the derivatives markets in oil in the early 1980s and other commodities during the past ten years, the iron ore market is developing into a market that allows speculators to bet on the direction of prices.[304] In many raw materials and commodity markets, such as the markets for cocoa, coffee beans and crude oil, the volume of transactions in the financial markets is significantly higher than the underlying physical trading volume.[305] This high trading multiple is caused by speculative traders, including institutional investors such as banks and pension funds, that seek profit from short-term price volatility as well as longer-term price trends. Although some of these speculative traders may even invest physically in said

---

[298]See, e.g., Sukagawa (2010).

[299]Sukagawa (2010).

[300]See ICAP (2010).

[301]See Oakley and Blas (2010).

[302]See Oakley and Blas (2010).

[303]See ICAP (2010).

[304]For a detailed definition of "speculators" and a general overview of speculation in raw materials and commodity markets, see Radetzki (2008), pp. 100–110.

[305]See Grootjans and Verweij (2009); Miller and Harris (1972).

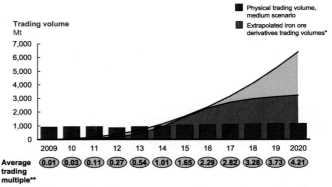

Figure 4.3: Estimation of iron ore derivatives trading volumes vs. physical trading volumes 2009–2020 [Verhoeven et al. (2010)]

goods,[306] the vast majority of investors lack authentic interest in the underlying asset.[307] Thus, speculation can lead to developments in the price of the good that no longer reflect only the supply and demand situation in the actual, physical market.[308]

Despite welcoming iron ore derivatives as a possibility to hedge against price risks, steelmakers fear that increased speculation will make iron ore prices decouple from "real business".[309] The fact that speculation leads to increased price volatility, especially in the case of speculative bubbles, has been subject of numerous studies at both the theoretical and the empirical level.[310]

---

[306]By actually taking physical deliveries of these materials and storing them, known as "cash-and-carry", thus leading to supply shortages in the physical market (see Hajek and Kamp (2010)). Note that, due to its unfavorable ratio of value to volume, such investments are fairly unattractive for iron ore speculators. Also, physically-backed exchange-traded funds, which have gained in popularity in other raw materials markets, do not exist yet for iron ore (see Lam (2011)).

[307]See Grootjans and Verweij (2009); Hajek and Kamp (2010); Hull (2006), pp. 11–14. Note that, although speculators commonly make their bets on derivatives, their actions also affect the physical spot market. For example, the purchase of futures pushes up the futures price, influencing the spot price through the possibility of arbitrage if the market is in contango and through convenience yield in backwardated markets (see Radetzki (2008), p. 106).

[308]See Fischermann (2011); Grootjans and Verweij (2009); Fey (2010).

[309]See Fey (2010); Hajek and Kamp (2010).

[310]See, e.g., de Long et al. (1990); Du et al. (2011); Hart and Kreps (1986); Leach (1991); Stein (1987); Zhou (1998).

4.1.4 Increased freight rates and freight rate volatility

China's economic awakening described above has had significant implications on the global shipping sector, leading to spectacular increases in freight rate levels as well as in freight rate volatility. This is valid especially, but not exclusively, for shipping routes linking China to its most important iron ore suppliers Australia and Brazil.

Based on historical freight rate data from Clarkson Research Services Ltd. (2010), Figure 4.4 shows that shipping companies charged an average of USD 8.84 per ton for transports of dry bulk freight from Brazil's Tubarão port to Qingdao, China between 1999 and 2003. During the same period, transports from Australian Port Hedland to Qingdao cost an average USD 4.80 per ton. Comparing these to the average prices on the same routes for the period between 2003 and 2010 reveals a considerable increase. The average freight rate from Brazil to China increased by 320% to USD 37.19 per ton. While still significantly lower, average rates from Australia to China increased by 226% to USD 15.64 per ton. Starting from a low of USD 4.55 and USD 2.72 per ton respectively in January 1999, prices on both routes rallied, reaching peaks of USD 110.70 and USD 47.50 per ton in May 2008. While freight rates fell considerably during the financial crisis, they were still on a higher level throughout 2009 than before 2003.[311]

However, freight rates not only increased significantly after 2003, they also became much more volatile. While the standard deviation σ for freight rates from Brazil to China averaged 2.64 between 1999 and 2003, the period between 2003 and 2010 showed a standard deviation of 21.68. Similarly on the route from Australia to China, the standard deviation increased from 1.37 for the period between 1999 and 2003 to 8.83 between 2003 and 2010. Despite the overall higher freight levels in the latter period, this is a clear indication that freight rates have become more volatile since 2003.

The increased strength and volatility of dry bulk freight rates can be clearly linked to China's rapidly increasing import demand for iron ore, coal and other raw materials. This has caused the demand for dry bulk transport capacity to increase substantially, on a global scale and in particular for China-bound shipping. Additionally, due to incremental Chinese iron ore demand being sourced from Brazil rather than Australia, the existing fleet can deliver fewer cargoes each year due to the longer haul from Brazil.[312] Combined with a

---

[311]For similar observations of recent freight rate increases, see O'Driscoll (2006), p. 58; Parker (2006), p. 106; Taube and in der Heiden (2010), p. 43.

[312]See O'Driscoll (2006), p. 58; Parker (2006), p. 106; Taube and in der Heiden (2010), p. 43.

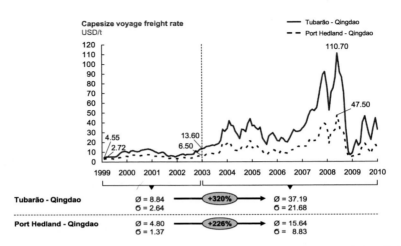

Figure 4.4: Monthly Capesize voyage freight rates for routes from Tubarão and Port Hedland to Qingdao, 1999–2010 [Own illustration based on data from Clarkson Research Services Ltd. (2010)]

general slowdown in fleet regeneration,[313] this leads to a global shortage of dry bulk vessels and thus to higher freight rates.[314]

While this means that the rising Chinese iron ore demand has left a considerable mark on global freight rates, the converse influence of freight rates on global iron ore trade cannot be overstressed. Changes in the global freight market have a profound effect on iron ore trade. Before the above described rally in the markets for dry bulk freight, iron ore miners and consumers had not worried greatly about the movements within the freight market because these changes represented a small percentage of the landed cost.[315] Now, however, freight rates contribute considerably to the price of iron ore.[316]

Although it is impossible to provide a precise forecast for freight rates, a likely pattern for the future is that rates will be considerably lower than in 2009, but

---

[313]See O'Driscoll (2006), p. 58.

[314]Recall that, as described in Section 3.4, settlement prices for various vessel types and shipping routes are based on the interaction of vessel supply and demand on the world market.

[315]See O'Driscoll (2006), p. 58.

[316]Note that freight rates have also moved more into focus of the iron ore industry due to the change of the iron ore pricing mechanism. As described in Section 3.5.2.2, the historic benchmark prices were negotiated on FOB terms, while the new spot-based prices are CFR. It is to be noted that, the new practice of competing on CFR prices means that, in contrast to before the change, miners located closer to a respective destination are in an advantageous position due to lower freight costs (see Creamer (2008); Sukagawa (2010)).

above the market level of before 2003.[317] Also, due to buoyant capacity demand
and volatile raw materials prices, freight rates are also expected to continue to
show increased volatility in the future.[318] Fundamental freight market forecast-
ers, who look at the size of the fleet in relation to capacity demand, point to
an increased supply of new vessels lured by increased freight rates. Over 100
vessels with more than 230,000 dwt are scheduled for delivery between 2011
and 2014, representing more than 10 percent of the total dry bulk orders in
tonnage terms.[319] However, most analysts also expect strong shipping demand
from China, India and other Asian economies, which may continue to fuel the
market and absorb some of the new tonnage.[320]

4.2 Impact of iron ore market developments and trends on the steel industry

As described in the previous sections, the market dynamics in the iron ore
market have changed fundamentally. Driven by fast-growing steel demand,
China has rapidly become the dominant force in steel production globally and,
due to the limited quality of domestic resources, the major buyer of iron ore on
the seaborne market. Additionally, sustained growth in the remaining BRIC
countries has triggered an iron ore and freight capacity supercycle. Also, the
change of the iron ore pricing system from annual benchmark pricing to spot-
linked pricing, leading to the emergence of iron ore indices and derivatives, has
increased price volatility.

Steel producers have had no choice but to accept these changes. The BRIC's
demand boom was simply beyond their power to control and the new pricing
conditions were pushed through by the iron ore miners due to the steelmakers'
weak negotiating position.[321] The present section aims to analyze the effects of
the altered market situation, especially the increased price level as well as the
increased price volatility, on the world's steelmakers.

4.2.1 Impact of increased iron ore prices

The above described change in the iron ore market structure, combined with
the supply-demand discontinuity around the financial crisis, has led to an iron

---

[317]See Gardiner (2011).
[318]See Fischermann (2011). For various shipping scenarios 2030, see Wärtsilä (2010).
[319]See Antonioli (2011b).
[320]See Gardiner (2011); Parker (2006), p. 106.
[321]See Fey (2010); Frankfurter Allgemeine Sonntagszeitung (2010).

ore supercycle that was only temporarily suspended by the financial crisis and is now picking up again. As a result, steelmakers' cost for their raw materials basket, composed mainly of iron ore but also of coking coal and steel scrap,[322] now make up a larger portion of the final steel price.[323] As shown in Figure 4.5, steelmakers' raw material prices have increased fourfold over the past ten years. While a steelmaker's raw materials cost per ton of steel equaled USD 92 in 2000, this cost jumped to USD 464 in 2010. The cost for iron ore within this basket increased even by 480%, rising from USD 46 in 2000 to USD 266 in 2010.[324]

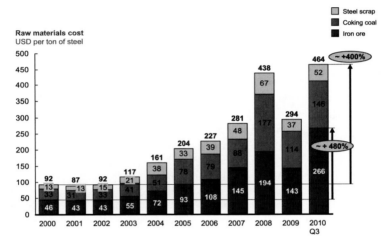

Figure 4.5: Development of hot-rolled coil raw materials basket for Western European steel-maker, 2000–2010 [Adapted from Verhoeven et al. (2010)]

At the same time, these higher raw material price levels have resulted in a significant shift in value creation towards mining. Figure 4.6 shows the roughly five-fold increase of the overall profit pool of the steel value chain from USD 54 billion in 1995 to USD 241 billion in 2008. Due to the global financial crisis, the 2009 profit pool valued only USD 61 billion. A look at the historical evolution of the split in the profit pool between iron ore miners, coking coal miners and steelmakers shows that the relative share of profits of mining companies have risen, while the profits of steelmakers have decreased in relative terms. From 1995 to 2009, the average relative profits attributed to steelmaking fell from 81% to 28%, while the respective profit shares of iron ore miners increased from

---

[322]Note that steel scrap and especially coking coal have recently experienced price increases similar to those for iron ore.

[323]See ArcelorMittal (2011), p. 9; Ernst & Young (2011b); Verhoeven et al. (2010).

[324]See Millbank (2011); Verhoeven et al. (2010).

8% to 41% of the total profit pool. It is expected that increasing raw material price levels will continue to structurally expand profit pools for pure iron ore mining companies and upstream integrated steel players, while decreasing the profit pools of pure steel producers and end-users of steel.[325]

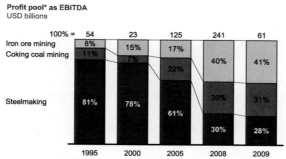

Figure 4.6: Shift in EBITDA profit pools from steelmaking to iron ore mining, 1995–2009 [Adapted from Verhoeven et al. (2010)]

Due to their already tight margins, steelmakers do not consider themselves to be in a position to shoulder the billions in additional expenses and feel they have no choice but to pass on the higher cost of raw materials to their customers. The world's largest steelmaker ArcelorMittal as well as Germany's ThyssenKrupp and Salzgitter have already increased steel prices significantly.[326] As the higher prices in the iron ore market are being passed on to manufacturers of steel products, the entire value chain is being impacted by the changes. Manufacturers and retails are desperate to pass on higher steel prices to their customers. Thus, as a result of higher iron ore prices, consumer goods are also set to become more expensive.[327] For example, in April 2011, white goods producers Whirlpool and Electrolux raised the prices of their washing machines by 8–10%, aiming to pass on the higher cost of steel which had risen by 20% in the past year.[328]

So far, manufacturers of steel products have absorbed most of the increase in raw materials prices. Many doubt however, that they will be able to persuade end customers to pay even higher prices in the future. In consequence, manufac-

---

[325]See Verhoeven et al. (2010).
[326]See Fey (2010); Frankfurter Allgemeine Zeitung (2010); Röttges and Sturbeck (2010).
[327]See Fey (2010).
[328]See The Economist (2011a).

turers have started to push back on anew steel price increases.[329] For example, Japanese steel mills are struggling to persuade their long-term customers to accept higher steel prices. Like their global peers, Japanese steelmakers are citing the need to offset much higher raw materials costs, but larger customers such as Mitsui Shipbuilding & Engineering are not accepting the rise.[330] Many manufacturers are referring to the fact that during the last boom, steel mills were charging increased prices for steel arguing that steel prices were set by supply and demand and not by a cost-plus logic.[331] Thus, steel mills will have to find other ways to cope with higher costs for iron ore.

4.2.2 Impact of increased iron ore price volatility

In addition to higher average prices for iron ore, price volatility is also becoming a real issue for steelmakers. As Heinrich Hiesinger, Chairman of the Executive Board of German steelmaker ThyssenKrupp said regarding iron ore, "It is not so much the price increase, as rather the immense short-term price fluctuations that are worrying us."[332] This iron ore price volatility is, in the view of a number of analysts and steel producers, largely contrary to the character of the steel industry, which by its nature is a long-term business.[333]

Historically, steelmakers were able to protect their margins against iron ore price fluctuations by passing through the cost changes to customers on an annual basis.[334] As iron ore prices are now changing within ever shorter time periods, steelmakers find themselves "squeezed" between increasing cost volatility on the supply side and large customer segments sensitive to price fluctuations on the demand side.[335] Thus, steelmakers seem to be losing their ability to pass on iron ore price changes immediately as they occur, leading to greater planning uncertainty and dramatically volatile EBIT margins.[336] Figure 4.7 shows that steelmakers' profitability reacts extremely sensitive to iron ore price fluctuations. In the example shown, a 20% increase in iron ore price from USD 125 to USD 150 per ton leads to a drop in the steelmaker's unit operating margin of 46%. Assuming an installed steelmaking capacity of 5 Mtpa, this leads to a

---

[329]See Bain & Company (2010); Frankfurter Allgemeine Sonntagszeitung (2010); Röttges and Sturbeck (2010); The Economist (2011a).

[330]See Steel Business Briefing (2011a).

[331]See Röttges and Sturbeck (2010).

[332]Der Spiegel (2011), translated from German: "Es sind nicht so sehr die Preiserhöhungen, die uns Sorge bereiten, sondern die enormen kurzfristigen Preisschwankungen."

[333]See Braid (2011).

[334]This practice was synchronized with the annual iron ore price negotiations.

[335]See Braid (2011); Ernst & Young (2011b); Verhoeven et al. (2010).

[336]See Braid (2011); Fey (2010).

foregone annual profit of USD 141.5 million.[337] Consequently, one of the core
competencies steelmakers will need to emphasize going forward is the management of iron ore price volatility.

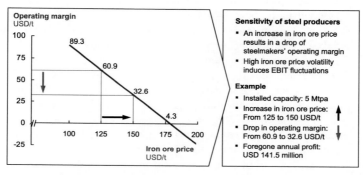

Figure 4.7: Sensitivity of European steel industry's profitability to iron ore price [Adapted
from Verhoeven et al. (2010)]

4.3 Potential risk mitigation strategies for demand-side players

As described in the previous sections, the recent developments in the iron ore
market have had substantial impact on the steel industry. These altered market
conditions are challenging not only steelmakers' margins, but the essence of their
entire business model. Summarizing, steelmakers face two main risks: sustained
high iron ore market prices, with potential for further price increases, and high
iron ore price volatility.[338]

The fact that steel companies can no longer rely on business-as-usual scenarios
when it comes to iron ore should be a call to action. Steelmakers must factor in
higher base-level prices and increased volatility while rethinking their strategies.
To defend current margins, steelmakers can consider a number of mitigation
strategies in the form of commercial, operational and strategic levers:[339]

- Commercial levers

---

[337]See Verhoeven et al. (2010).

[338]Resource security, i.e. physical access to sufficient natural resource supply, is considered a
significant risk in some industries (see, e.g., World Economic Forum (2011), p. 38). However,
as described in Section 2.1.2, this paper argues that availability of iron ore will not be an
issue on a global scale in the foreseeable future.

[339]Structure adapted from Verhoeven et al. (2010).

– *Innovative contract design* – Steelmakers need to focus the design of sales and purchasing contracts on shaping the company's raw materials risk exposure. The resulting strategy can range between two extreme options, depending on whether the steelmaker decides to pass through the raw material price volatility risk to its customers or not. Passing through the risk, e.g. via an index-based raw materials surcharge mechanism, forces steelmakers to explicitly state the cost of the raw material content in order to allow the customers to hedge the resulting exposure. This leads to a considerable increase in customers' negotiating power, as they will be able to calculate steelmakers' markups increasingly accurately. Customers will have the information to challenge cost pass-throughs and demand savings pass-throughs as well. Steelmakers who choose this scenario will thus become commodity producers with profits based solely on their transformation margin. The alternative is for steelmakers to take on the total raw materials price risk by selling steel products at fixed prices. In this case, steelmakers' profits will consist of the operating margin for transforming raw materials into steel, plus a risk premium for taking on the raw materials price risk[340]

– *Hedging* – The transformation activity of a steelmaker generates exposure to risk, as raw materials such as iron ore are procured and end-products are produced and sold. Steelmakers could reduce their volatility risk by actively participating in derivatives markets by means of hedging.[341] Through the hedging process, the steelmaker gains the fundamental freedom to decide when and at which price to buy its raw materials and when and at which price to sell its end-products. As the decisions are typically backed by physical assets, the resulting risk is low, since raw material and end-product volumes can be netted out. Any venture into hedging activities should always be accompanied by the buildup of state-of-the-art risk management and controlling capabilities. Also, the cost of hedging must be taken into account in the pricing of the end-products[342]

• Operational levers

---

[340]See Bain & Company (2010); Ernst & Young (2011b); Fey (2010); Verhoeven et al. (2010); Woolley (2010).

[341]Note that utilities offer a successful example of formerly traditional asset-driven companies that actively pushed the evolution of financial markets for their commodity to enable state-of-the-art portfolio and risk management (see, e.g., Obert (2009)).

[342]See Bain & Company (2010); Ernst & Young (2011a); Radetzki (2008), pp. 98–100; Verhoeven et al. (2010); Woolley (2010). For a detailed overview of the mechanics of hedging and hedging strategies, see Hull (2006), pp. 9–14, 47–69, 116–118.

- *Pooled sourcing* – Subject to regulatory approval, steelmakers could take steps to harmonize their purchasing activities or even join forces to form a shared platform for purchasing raw materials. Currently, one of the main challenges for mid- and downstream steel players is that their relatively scattered companies face the higher corporate concentration in the iron ore mining industry.[343] The consolidation of procurement activities would supposedly increase steelmakers' bargaining power[344]

- *Increased asset base flexibility* – Steelmakers could consider increasing the flexibility in their asset base in order to possibly increase margins by monetizing the flexibilities in the market. This may involve more flexibility in production processes, e.g., by adjusting production to process low-cost material (e.g., sinter feed instead of pellets), not only for the cost savings effect, but also to reduce dependence on the ore suppliers. Similarly, the ability to adjust production assets according to demand and cost structures (with ramp-ups/ramp-downs of assets or modifications to operating procedures) would increase a company's degrees of freedom to absorb unforeseen market movements. This strategy requires the right trade-off between exploiting economies of scale by taking the through-cycle approach and adapting to cyclicality. It also requires a much greater emphasis on flexibility in operating individual assets and a central steering mechanism using key parameters to reduce the resulting risks[345]

• Strategic levers

- *Diversified product strategy* – Steelmakers could escape the commoditization of steel and reduce its exposure to raw material price volatility by pursuing high-value niches, where raw material price volatility plays a less relevant role. Producing high-value specialty products increases the share of products priced on the basis of value and increases the weight of the steelmaker's unique value added in the price of the final product. Moving toward high-value niche markets may allow steelmakers to capture additional margins through value pricing. Such a strategy must be backed by extensive R&D and marketing activities to ensure leading-edge innovation in product development and production processes.[346]

---

[343]See discussion of iron ore market concentration in Section 3.3.2.
[344]See Ernst & Young (2011b); Verhoeven et al. (2010).
[345]See Verhoeven et al. (2010).
[346]See Ernst & Young (2011a); Verhoeven et al. (2010).

- *Upstream integration into iron ore mining* – Buying into the supply chain is certainly one of the most extreme responses to uncertainty. Such a strategy would aim to mitigate the current structural disadvantages of pure midstream steelmakers by tapping into the upstream shift of industry profit pools. Forms of upstream integration can rage from joint ventures or strategic alliances with major mining companies to stakes in smaller mining companies and own greenfield mining projects. In the current high-price environment, it could pay off for midstream steelmakers to integrate upstream and thereby secure iron ore at a competitive price. Additionally captivity of mines reduces steelmakers' dependency on the large suppliers, allowing them to optimize the use of own captive vs. market-sourced ore.[347]

- *Lobbying for protective trade policies* – A more indirect strategy would be for steelmakers to engage in lobbying activities aiming at the introduction of favorable trade policies with respect to raw materials. These could include import subsidies on iron ore (for countries lacking sufficient domestic iron ore mining capacities) or export taxes on iron ore (for countries rich in iron ore). The success of this strategy depends greatly on the joint lobbying power of a country's steelmakers. Also, the respective government will have to consider the steelmaking industry to be of considerable national strategic importance prior to establishing protective measures.[348]

Presumably, none of these levers will be sufficient alone. It will take a combination of actions in all three areas in order for steelmakers to be successful under the altered market conditions. Though all of the above mentioned strategies should be evaluated in detail prior to implementation by a steelmaker, this paper will aim to evaluate the effectiveness of only a selection of these strategies. As the primary goal of this paper remains the analysis of the 2020 iron ore market, those risk mitigation strategies are chosen which are expected to have the greatest impact on the iron market:

- *Upstream integration into iron ore mining* – That is, captivity of iron ore mines

- *Lobbying for protective trade policies* – Specifically, the introduction of iron ore export taxes

---

[347]See Ericsson (2009); Ernst & Young (2011b); Verhoeven et al. (2010); Woolley (2010).
[348]See, e.g., Otto et al. (2006), pp. 32–35; Radetzki (2008), pp. 50–51.

Going forward, these risk mitigation strategies will be analyzed with respect to their effectiveness and their impact on the iron ore market in general as well as on other market participants.

5 A model of the 2020 iron ore market

Based on the fundamental characteristics of the market described in Chapters 2 and 3, the present chapter proposes a model of the 2020 global iron ore market. Due to the immense complexity of the market, the model does not claim to constitute an identical representation of reality. Instead, it aims to capture the key characteristics and dynamics of the market while yielding to certain necessary simplifications. Such generalizations regarding the design of a model of a complex global market must be rather crude, yet it is only through this that the market's essential nature can be grasped.[349] As summarized by Varian (2010), a model is

> [...] a simplified representation of reality. The emphasis here is on the word "simple". Think about how useless a map on a one-to-one scale would be. The same is true of an economic model that attempts to describe every aspect of reality. A model's power stems from the elimination of irrelevant detail, which allows the economist to focus on the essential features of the economic reality he or she is attempting to understand.[350]

The present chapter is structured into three main sections. Section 5.1 gives an overview of the overall structure of the model and describes in detail the key input components, the market mechanism and outputs. Section 5.2 outlines the technical implementation of the model with a special focus on the implementation of the allocation mechanism. Finally, Section 5.3 presents a validation of the proposed model by comparing selected results to respective 2009 actuals.

5.1 Anatomy and mechanisms of the model

Figure 5.1 presents the general structure of the proposed model. As can be seen, the model is split into three main areas:

---

[349]For a detailed discussion of the conflict between generalization and accuracy of models, see Lindstädt (1997), pp. 2–3; Nordhoff (2009), pp. 104–105.
[350]Varian (2010), pp. 1–2.

- *Key input components* – The key necessary inputs to the model are clustered in three groups. Supply must be defined in terms of production capacities and FOB costs per mine as well as information regarding the price elasticity of supply. Building on FOB costs, export taxes and freight rates define the CFR cost for each mine with respect to the consuming regions. From a demand perspective, iron ore demand volumes per region and price elasticity of demand are required[351]

- *Market mechanism* – The market mechanism represents the heart of the model, aiming to simulate the actual marketplace for iron ore by moderating the economic forces of supply, demand and the remaining input components. To this effect, the mechanism is split into two parts. First, the allocation mechanism simulates the global trade of iron ore by allocating iron ore supply to consuming regions using a linear optimization approach. In a second step, the market clearing and pricing mechanism defines the market price per region using a merit order logic

- *Output* – Once all calculations have been completed, the model generates an extensive amount of outputs required to evaluate the respective market situation. Among others, these include production and trade volumes per region, the global iron ore flow matrix, market prices per region, market participants' payoffs as well as industry cost curves per region of destination and origin

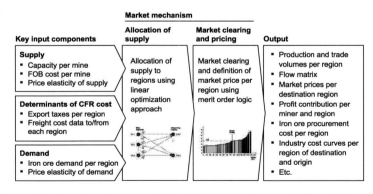

Figure 5.1: Structure of proposed global iron ore market model [Own illustration]

These three areas will also provide the structure for the detailed description of the proposed market model going forward. First, however, the following section

---

[351]For an overview of the key formulae of the input components, see Appendix III.

will define geographic regions in which to split the countries of the world for modeling purposes.

5.1.1 Definition of geographic regions

As shown in Chapter 3, numerous countries play actives roles in the global iron ore market. In 2009, iron ore production took place in more than 30 countries while iron ore demand was generated in more than 45 nations. Modeling the resulting diverse geographic market structure would clearly be extremely complex. Thus, the iron ore model proposed here divides the world into nine geographic regions. Additionally, one major iron ore port is defined in each of these regions:

North America:	Port Duluth, USA
South America:	Tubarão, Brazil
Europe:	Rotterdam, Netherlands
Africa & Middle East:	Saldanha Bay, South Africa
CIS:	Novorossiysk, Russia
China:	Qingdao, China
India:	Mormugao, India
Other Asia:	Fukuyama, Japan
Oceania:	Port Hedland, Australia

As shown in Figure 5.2, all of the world's countries and territories are assigned to one of the regions listed above. The complete list of countries and their allocation can be found in Appendix I. The allocation of countries and territories to a region is dictated not only by the membership in political entities, but also by geographic proximity. Where possible, countries belonging to the same federation (e.g., the European Union) or trade blocs (e.g., MERCOSUR, NAFTA) are assigned to the same region, as these entities might play an important role in terms of joint public policy, especially trade policy. Colonies and overseas territories however, as they mostly play an inferior role in the iron ore market, are mostly allocated to the geographically closest region.

To further simplify the market structure, the named port in each region is defined in this model as the sole iron ore trading hub of the respective region. All supply and demand of a region occurs at this defined port. Therefore, the model simplifies the world iron ore market not into nine regions, but rather into nine punctiform regional markets.

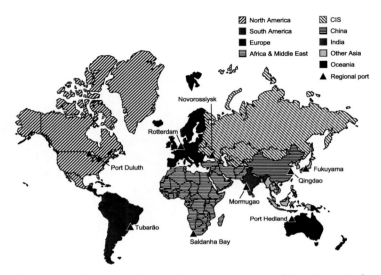

Figure 5.2: Definition of geographic regions and ports [Own illustration]

Since these ports play a central role in the so simplified market structure, special care must be taken in their selection. First of all, only ports capable of accommodating Capesize vessels (see Section 2.2.5) can be considered as hubs.[352] From the so short-listed ports, a region's hub should be selected as to reflect geographically the focal points of the region's iron ore supply, defined in terms of iron ore mining capacity, and demand, defined by the major industrial centers. These points coincide in most regions, e.g. in China, where Qingdao port on the east coast is geographically close to major iron ore mining centers as well as the sites of the major steelmakers. However, a compromise is necessary in some regions. In Oceania, for example, the center of supply lies in the northern part of Western Australia, while the center of demand is located closer to the industrial centers on Australia's eastern and southeastern coasts. In this case, as Oceania is, from a global perspective, clearly more important in terms of iron ore supply than in terms of demand, Port Hedland in Western Australia is selected as Oceania's iron ore hub in this model.

---

[352]Based on port and berth data from Global Ports Ltd. (2010).

5.1.2 Key input components

5.1.2.1 Iron ore supply

The overall quality of the here described iron ore model is considerably driven by the detailed modeling of the supply side and the exceptional quality and uniqueness of the utilized data. In order to grasp the full complexity of global iron ore supply, a bottom-up approach is chosen, modeling the supply side on an individual mine level. The required data for a total of 640 active iron ore mines, brownfield and greenfield expansion projects around the globe is derived from McKinsey & Company (2011b), based on various industry databases, company annual reports and press clippings. This unique data set, accurate as of March 2011,[353] gives an extremely detailed and complete overview of global iron ore mining activities. It consists of the following information per mine and project:[354]

- *Mine ID* – Unique numerical identifier of mine

- *Mine name* – Official name of mine

- *Country* – Country in which mine is located

- *Region* – Region in which mine is located, see Section 5.1.1

- *Owner* – Corporate owner of mine, multiple entries possible

- *Equity share* – Equity share of each of the mine's owners, in percent (totaling 100%)

- *Reserves as of 2009* – Amount of proven iron ore reserves associated with the mine, in Mt, in accordance with the JORC code[355]

- *Depletion year* – Year of expected depletion of the mine's iron ore reserves, assuming production at maximum annual capacity

- *Annual production capacity as of 2009* – Maximum annual production in Mt, reflecting also potential limitations of relevant supply-side value chain steps and supporting infrastructure, detailed below

- *Production volume 2009* – Actual 2009 production volume in Mt

---

[353]Changes in mine and project data, industry structure, legislation and regulations issued after this date are not reflected in this model.

[354]Recall that, for reasons of simplicity and comparability, all financial data in this paper is given in 2009 real U.S. dollars. Thus, no monetary inflation is reflected in values representing 2020 data. Also, exchange rate effects are not taken into account.

[355]See The Joint Ore Reserves Committee (2004).

- *Split of ore types* – Split of output of mine in terms of ore types (fines, lumps, concentrates, pellets), in percent (totaling 100%)

- *Moisture content* – Average moisture content of extracted iron ore, in percent by ore type[356]

- *Fe content* – Average iron content of extracted iron ore, in percent by ore type[357]

- *Status of captivity* – Some mines do not sell their ore to the open market but rather to predefined destinations due to demand-side players holding a production stake in these mines. For example, some mines are owned by steelmakers and are vertically integrated in the respective steelmaker's supply chain[358]

- *Forced destination* – Region to which the ore of the mine is to be shipped depending on the indicated captivity status[359]

- *Mining cost incl. transportation to port* – Cost of mining of ore and transportation to port, in USD/t, detailed below

- *Agglomeration cost* – Cost of agglomeration (pelletizing) of ore, in USD/t, detailed below

- *Beneficiation cost* – Cost of beneficiation of ore, in USD/t, detailed below

For the brownfield and greenfield projects included in the data set, the following additional information is provided:

- *Capacity of project* – Announced annual capacity expansion derived from completed project, in Mtpa

- *Announced start-up* – Announced month and year of expected initial iron ore production

---

[356] In case information is not available for a certain mine, weighted average of respective region is used.

[357] In case information is not available for a certain mine, weighted average of respective region is used.

[358] Note that investors holding equity shares in mines for investment purposes, i.e. without genuine interest in the physical iron ore output, are not considered captive owners. Also mines with joint ventures or strategic alliances with steelmakers that do not provide the steelmaker with access to iron ore at unit production cost are not considered captive in this model.

[359] For mines owned by national governments, the forced destination is set to the region of the respective country. In the case of mines owned by steelmakers, the captive volume is assigned to the regions in which the respective steelmaker has production facilities based on geographic proximity.

- *Project status as of 2009* – Degree of project implementation, reflecting probability of realization and expected delay of project, detailed below

Even though all of the above listed information is required for the precise modeling of global iron ore supply, the bottom line is that supply is finally defined by how much ore is supplied to the market at what cost. Thus, special attention is to be given to the modeling of the production volumes of the mines and the costs involved in extracting the ore from the earth and bringing it to the market. These elements are described in more detail in the following.

5.1.2.1.1 Supply volumes

5.1.2.1.1.1 Reflection of mine ownership structure and split of ore types

As stated above, the supply data set provides information on the ownership structure and split of produced ore types for each of the iron ore mines and projects. In order to reflect this information in the model, each mine is split into "mine segments". Each segment stands for a capacity or production volume block owned by a certain owner and producing a certain type of ore (i.e. either fines, lumps, concentrates or pellets). This is achieved by first splitting the total volume of the mine by owner based on their equity shares. Then each of the owners' capacity/production volume blocks is further broken down according to the overall split of ore types produced by the mine. It is assumed that each owner takes the same share of ore types as stated by the split of the overall mine production.

For example, assume a mine with a 2009 production volume of 10.0 Mt, an overall type split of 70% fines and 30% lumps and two owners, "A" and "B", with 60% and 40% equity share respectively. In the model, this mine would be split into four mine segments: 4.2 Mt of fines and 2.8 Mt of pellets production for owner A as well as 1.8 Mt of fines and 1.2 Mt of pellets for owner B. Note that the total of all four segments again equals the total production volume of the mine.

5.1.2.1.1.2 Price elasticity of iron ore supply

As described above, the 2009 production volumes as well as the maximum annual capacity in Mt is provided for each of the modeled iron ore mining operations. This data reveals that miners produced on average at approximately

86% of their available production capacity in 2009.[360] The reason for this can be found in the impact of the word financial crisis of 2008/2009 and the resulting large decrease in crude steel production and therefore plummeting iron ore demand. Compared to 2008, crude steel production in 2009 dropped by 8% globally and by as much as 30% in Europe and North America.[361]

While this shows that iron ore miners will adapt their production in times of severe demand decline, normal operating practice is to maintain the highest possible capacity utilization rates. This is well founded on two factors:

- *Capital intensity of mine setup* – The high initial capital cost involved in the setup of a mine discourages output reduction in times of decreasing demand. Investments in existing capacities can be regarded as sunk costs, i.e. costs of investments that can never be recouped, but can produce a stream of benefits over a long horizon.[362] Therefore an existing mine has incentives to operate at full capacity regardless of the short-run variations of price and demand[363]

- *Economies of scale in production* – Iron ore mining and processing operations are typically large-scale and involve significant economies of scale, especially in terms of labor cost.[364] Therefore, every reduction in annual production volumes will lead to an increase in variable cost per ton of ore mined[365]

Therefore, as iron ore miners have an incentive not to reduce production, iron ore supply is generally insensitive to fluctuating demand and/or price levels. For the same reasons, it is assumed that miners will not artificially create a shortage of supply for strategic purposes. Such practices, as performed by the OPEC, varying capacity utilization by cutting supply when prices are deemed to be too low and by increasing output when they strengthen to above the desired level, are not seen as practicable in the iron ore industry.[366] Under the hypothesis that the unparalleled demand erosion of 2008/2009 will not repeat in the foreseeable future, this model assumes that all mines will operate at their full available capacity in 2020. For 2009, however, the actual potentially reduced production volume is applied.

---

[360]See McKinsey & Company (2011b).

[361]See World Steel Association (2010).

[362]See Mas-Colell et al. (1995), p. 131; Tirole (1990), pp. 20–23.

[363]See Hellmer (1997a), p. 9; Rogers et al. (1987).

[364]See Crowson (1992); Rogers et al. (1987); Roman and Daneshmend (2000). For a detailed overview of benefits from economies of scale, refer to Lindstädt and Hauser (2004), pp. 12–19.

[365]See Tirole (1990), pp. 23–24.

[366]See Crowson (2006), p. 161.

5.1.2.1.1.3   Modeling of 2020 production capacity

As described above, it is assumed that all miners will aim to produce at maximum capacity in 2020 in order to generate high returns on their initial investment and benefit from economies of scale. Therefore, it is now necessary to derive the expected 2020 capacity for each mine and project from the provided data set.

From a 2009 point of view, the overall expected iron ore output in 2020 can be split into volumes coming from mines that were already active in 2009 and volumes from greenfield and brownfield projects currently being developed. Thus, in order to derive the expected production capacity for 2020, the following factors must be taken into account:

- Potential depletion of mines already active in 2009

- Expected ramp-up of brown- and greenfield projects under development as of 2009

The 2020 capacity of mines already active in 2009 can easily be projected by taking into account their expected depletion. The expected remaining life of a mine is calculated by dividing the amount of proven reserves of a mine by the mine's annual production capacity. Those mines with resulting expected depletion before 2020 are modeled with a capacity of 0.0 Mt in 2020 while all other active mines are modeled with the same production capacity in 2020 as in 2009.[367]

For brown- and greenfield projects, estimating 2020 production capacity is more complicated. As described in detail in Section 2.2.2, new mining projects require immense investments in mining facilities, materials handling and processing plants as well as supporting infrastructure. They often take three to seven years to complete and involve numerous stakeholders such as building contractors, banks, government authorities and the local population. Due to this high degree of complexity, extensive time frame and large number of stakeholders, there is a massive amount of uncertainty associated with mining projects in terms of

---

[367]Special care was taken to validate the actual 2009 production and capacity figures per mine, as these represent the basis for the modeling of the 2020 capacities. All 2009 figures provided in the original data set were calibrated on an individual mine level with figures from respective company annual reports. Additionally, consolidated regional figures were adjusted to match figures from renowned industry reports such as Jorgenson (2011); United Nations Conference on Trade and Development (2010); World Steel Association (2010). The resulting 2009 regional production volumes are listed in detail in Appendix II.

the overall probability and timeliness of their completion.[368] This is reflected in the model by two parameters that have been assigned to each project:

- *Probability of realization* – The probability of realization, in percent, reflects the risk of the project being downsized or completely canceled. Multiplied with the announced project capacity, one arrives at the mathematical expectation of the production capacity of the completed project

- *Expected delay* – The expected delay, in months, reflects the possibility of complications arising along the project time line leading to a delayed completion of the project. The delay is added to the announced start date of the finished mine to arrive at the expected ramp-up date

The value of each of the factors depends considerably on the degree of completion of the project. For example, a project that has just been launched and is due for completion in seven years is subject to more residual risk than a project that is due go online in the coming months. Additionally, at least in early project phases, the proximity of existing mining infrastructure to a project site reduces project risk.

In order to facilitate the assignment of values for the above named parameters, all projects are categorized according to their degree of project completion as of 2009:[369]

- *Category 1* – Projects which have been fully agreed, with infrastructure under construction and proceeding according to plan

- *Category 2* – Projects that are technically defined in terms of ore body to be extracted and planned product flow

- *Category 3* – Uncertain future projects close to existing mining infrastructure

- *Category 4* – Uncertain future projects with no supporting infrastructure nearby

- *Category 5* – Projects announced, but not clearly laid out yet (also optional projects)

As shown in Figure 5.3, three levels of supply stemming from expansion projects have been defined for 2020 by assigning different values for probability of realization and delay of completion to each of these project categories. These levels, combined with the capacity from mines already active in 2009 lead to the total available capacity and therefore maximum iron ore production in 2020. The

---

[368]See, e.g., Cattaneo (2006); Fuentes et al. (2008); Johnston and Reddy (2011).
[369]See McKinsey & Company (2011b).

2020 regional production capacities per supply level are displayed in detail in
Appendix II.

Project category	Low			Medium			High		
	Realization probability Percent	Delay Months		Realization probability Percent	Delay Months		Realization probability Percent	Delay Months	
C1	95%	12		100%	12		100%	6	
C2	75%	30		85%	24		90%	12	
C3	60%	36		70%	30		80%	24	
C4	25%	48		40%	36		50%	30	
C5	10%	54		20%	42		30%	36	

Figure 5.3: Values of parameters defining 2020 iron ore production capacity levels [Own illustration based on McKinsey & Company (2011b)]

5.1.2.1.1.4   Standardization of production and capacity figures

As described in detail in Section 3.1.1, figures for iron ore capacity and production are normally presented in gross or natural weight, also referred to as "run of mine" (ROM), and not as the metal content of the ore produced. This raises several problems regarding the comparability of ore from different mines due to each mine having specific levels of Fe and moisture content.[370]

In order to guarantee comparability between mines, all supply figures in this model are given in metric tons (1,000.0 kg) of dry ore with 62.0% Fe content.[371] The production and capacity figures supplied by McKinsey & Company (2011b) in wet tons and/or with other Fe contents are recalculated accordingly using the following formula:

$$x_m = x_m^{ROM} \cdot (1 - mc_m) \cdot \frac{fc_m}{62.0\%}$$

where

$$
\begin{aligned}
x_m &= \text{Standardized production volume of mine segment } m, \text{ in dry Mt} \\
&\quad \text{ with 62.0\% Fe} \\
x_m^{ROM} &= \text{Actual run of mine production volume of mine segment } m \text{ with} \\
&\quad \text{ moisture content } mc_m \text{ and Fe content } fc_m, \text{ in Mt} \\
mc_m &= \text{Moisture content of ore from mine segment } m, \text{ in \%} \\
fc_m &= \text{Fe content of ore from mine segment } m, \text{ in \%}
\end{aligned}
$$

---

[370]See United Nations Conference on Trade and Development (2010), p. 92.

[371]The industry has adopted the 62.0% Fe specification as a standard benchmark, e.g. for price indices and derivative transactions (see Section 3.5.2.3).

For example, as demonstrated in Figure 5.4 for the fines share of the Minas do Meio mine in Brazil, a capacity of 4.8 million metric tons containing 8.0% moisture and 65.0% Fe is standardized in the model to 4.6 million dry metric tons containing 62.0% Fe.

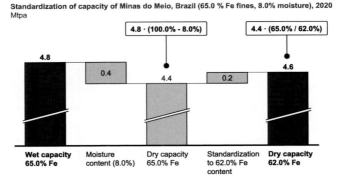

Figure 5.4: Example of standardization of production capacity, Minas do Meio (Brazil) [Own illustration based on supply data from McKinsey & Company (2011b)]

5.1.2.1.2   Determinants of FOB cost of supply

The FOB cost of iron ore delivered to the market is equal to the sum of the costs incurred along the value chain from the extraction of the ore from the earth up to its arrival at the port of shipping.[372] As shown in Figure 5.5, the structure of FOB costs consists of the following three main elements:[373]

- *Mining cost* – Consisting of base mining cost, upgrading cost (i.e., ben-eficiation and pelletizing at the mine site) and cost of transportation to port of shipping

- *Correction factors* – Grade and value-in-use correction factors to reflect chemical and physical attributes the ore

- *Mining royalties* – Charged by governments to miners extracting ore from a country's soil

Each of these cost elements and the influencing factors are described in detail in the following sections. It is to be noted that all costs applied in this model and presented here are variable operating costs, therefore not taking in account

---

[372]See Hakala (1970).
[373]See Hellmer (1997b), pp. 33–54; Manners (1971), p. 149.

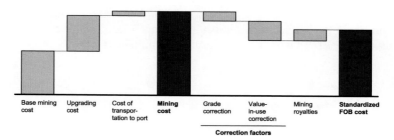

Figure 5.5: Split of FOB cost along the iron ore value chain [Own illustration]

the cost of capital, depreciation or overhead costs. All figures are therefore to be interpreted as the average unit variable cost in USD per ton.[374]

5.1.2.1.2.1 Mining cost

The mining cost consists of the base mining cost, upgrading cost and the cost of transportation to port of shipping. The base mining cost, which is provided for each mine in the data set for 2009, includes all costs involved in extracting iron ore from the earth as well as basic processing of the ore:[375]

- Stripping overburden
- Blasting
- Loading of iron ore and waste, usually on trucks
- Haulage to crusher for primary crushing and screening

While production costs of comparably sized manufacturing plants tend to be similar, the level of mining cost of each iron ore mine is unique. Mining costs are determined largely by geological and geographic circumstances over which the operating company has no control. While manufacturing companies can, within broad limits, choose their plant location, mining companies must go where the ore is found.[376] The level of the base mining cost is affected by the nature of the physical and economic environment, which in turn influences the costs of providing and maintaining essential supplies, such as equipment, water

---

[374]Note that, due to the use of average variable costs, miners' payoffs in this model are given as profit contribution, not profit. In consequence, corporate and profit taxes, as described in Section 3.6, cannot be directly applied to the payoffs in this model. For the interpretation of the model results, however, the presence of such additional taxes must be kept in mind.
[375]See Hellmer (1997b), p. 42.
[376]See Crowson et al. (1978).

and electricity. The nature of the ore body, whether it can be best exploited by open-pit or underground mining, also affects both the level and breakdown of mining expenses.[377] Overall, common factors influencing the base mining cost are:[378]

- Iron ore grade

- Amount of mineralogical constituents

- Size of iron ore deposit and annual mine output (economies of scale)

- Type of mine (underground or open pit)

- Local level of factor cost (especially labor and energy)

Depending on the physical and chemical characteristics of the ore mined (see Section 2.1.3), each mine will decide how much of its ore it can market as fines, lumps, concentrates and pellets. This split of types is given for each mine in the data set and reflected in the modeled "mine segments" as defined in Section 5.1.2.1.1.1. As described in detail in Section 2.2.4, out of the four types of ore found on the market, some are naturally occurring while others have gone through upgrading processes prior to being sold. Fines and lumps are preferable, as they require no further treatment after mining except for basic crushing and screening. Concentrates and pellets, however, are the results of complex upgrading processes. Concentrates are the end product of the beneficiation of low grade ores, whose undesirable elements (gangue and chemical impurities) have been removed from the crude ore by means of grinding, washing, filtration and concentration. Pellets are produced by mixing very fine and powdery ores with a binding agent and agglomerating them into small balls which are indurated in a furnace. Therefore, while only the base mining cost applies to fines and lumps, the cost of beneficiation must be added for concentrates and pelletizing cost for pellets. These upgrading costs are provided for each mine in the data set for 2009.

Once the ore has been mined and possibly upgraded, it is commonly transported by road or rail to a storage stockpile at the port.[379] Transportation costs between the mine and the port are commonly estimated by multiplying the cost per kilometer per ton by the haul length. Rail transportation costs for iron ore are commonly low, ranging from 0.3 to 0.9 USDc per ton per kilometer.[380] The cost level depends on the size of the iron ore deposit as well as on the ownership

---

[377]See Crowson et al. (1978); Manners (1971), p. 150.

[378]See Degner et al. (2007), p. 19; Hellmer (1997b), pp. 35–50.

[379]In the data set used in this model, these transportation costs are already included in the base mining cost of each mine.

[380]See Galdón-Sánchez and Schmitz (2002); Kästner et al. (1979), pp. 199–202.

structure of the railroad. Large deposits usually profit from economies of scale in railroad transportation.[381] Additionally, most large iron ore miners maintain own railroad systems leading from their mines to deepwater ports. The use of these railroads is commonly less expensive than the use of public lines.[382]

As described in Section 5.1.2.1.1.4, supply volumes are standardized to 62.0% Fe and 0.0% moisture in order to guarantee comparability between ores from different mines. In the example used above, the actual fines capacity of the Minas do Meio mine in Brazil, 4.8 million metric tons of ore containing 8.0% moisture and 65.0% Fe, was standardized to 4.6 million dry metric tons containing 62.0% Fe. This means that, although 4.6 million dry tons of 62.0% Fe equivalent ore are sold to the market per year, 4.8 Mt of ore with 65.0% Fe and 8.0% moisture must be mined. If one were to apply Minas do Meio's given mining cost of 15.45 USD/t to the standardized volume, the total mining cost would be lower than in reality. Therefore, the standardization of volumes must be also reflected in the mining cost. The mining cost is therefore recalculated using the following formula:

$$c_m^{mining} = c_m^{mining,ROM} \cdot \frac{62.0\%}{fc_m \cdot (1 - mc_m)}$$

where

$\quad c_m^{mining} \quad = \quad$ Standardized mining cost of mine segment m, in USD per dry metric ton with 62.0% Fe

$\quad c_m^{mining,ROM} \quad = \quad$ Actual run of mine mining cost of mine segment m for ore with moisture content mc_m and Fe content fc_m, in USD/t

$\quad fc_m \quad = \quad$ Fe content of ore from mine segment m, in %

$\quad mc_m \quad = \quad$ Moisture content of ore from mine segment m, in %

In the above example, the original mining cost at Minas do Meio of 15.45 USD/t would be adapted to 16.02 USD/t based on the standardized volume with 62.0% Fe and 0.0% moisture.

The proportions and the breakdown of mining cost vary considerably from mine to mine and from country to country.[383] Figure 5.6 shows a sanitized comparison of the share of major component costs of seven mines in different countries that collectively represent the overall mining cost. On average, energy accounts for approximately 20% of base mining cost while roughly 30% of the cost stems from labor.

---

[381]See Hellmer (1997b), p. 35.
[382]See Hellmer (1997b), pp. 49–50.
[383]See Hellmer (1997b), p. 35; Manners (1971), p. 149.

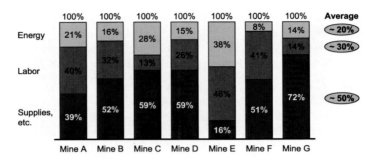

Figure 5.6: Split of mining cost by cost type for seven mines [Own illustration based on data from McKinsey & Company (2011b) (Mines A–C); Anglo American (2010) (Mine D); Hakala (1970) (Mine E); Frost (1986) (Mines F, G)]

Since 2009 mining costs are provided per mine in the data set from McKinsey & Company (2011b), 2020 mining costs can be approximated based on these figures and the expected real factor cost inflation. This model assumes an increase in energy factor costs of about 2% p.a. and an increase in labor factor costs of roughly 3% p.a. based on estimates from McKinsey & Company (2011b).[384] Taking into account the above described average mining cost split, this leads to a real mining cost increase of approximately 16% in 2020 vs. 2009:

$$c_m^{mining,2020} = c_m^{mining,2009} \cdot [0.20 \cdot 1.02^{(2020-2009)} + 0.30 \cdot 1.03^{(2020-2009)} + 0.50]$$

where

$c_m^{mining,2020}$ = Standardized 2020 mining cost of mine segment m, in USD/t
$c_m^{mining,2009}$ = Standardized 2009 mining cost of mine segment m, in USD/t

5.1.2.1.2.2   Correction factors

In discussing mining costs, it has been implicitly assumed that iron ore is a homogeneous product with one market price. As shown in Section 2.1.3, it is not. Iron ore exists in different physical forms and varies in terms of iron and moisture content as well as content of trace elements. As discussed in Section 2.3.2, these differences affect the behavior of iron ore in the ironmaking process, especially in terms of blast furnace productivity, and therefore influence

---

[384]For on overview of the effects of rising costs on miners, see The Wall Street Journal (2011).

the cost of steelmaking.[385] In terms of the commercial evaluation of iron ore, a steelmaker will always take into account the cost of the iron ore plus the cost of its conversion to steel.[386] Hence, if the chemistry and structure of an iron ore are favorable, then iron- and steelmaking costs are reduced, and the steelmaker is willing to pay a higher price for this ore than for one with less favorable properties.[387]

As described in Section 3.5.2.3, a common price basis for iron ore exists in terms of the indices linked to the spot market. The actual price paid by the steelmaker for a specific iron ore, though based on the current price for fines with 62% Fe content, depends on whether the ore in question raises or lowers the costs of producing steel compared to the use of fines with 62% iron content.[388]

To offset these differences in cost of steel production, correction factors are applied to the iron ore base price depending on the physical and chemical attributes of the specific ore. These corrections reflect cost advantages and disadvantages involved in the utilization of certain ore grades and types in iron- and steelmaking. Two common types of price correction factors exist:[389]

- *Grade correction* – Offsets differences in chemical attributes of the ore, mainly with respect to iron content

- *Value-in-use correction* – Offsets differences in physical attributes, i.e. physical form of the ore

This model aims to combine all global iron ore mines into one combined industry cost curve, irrespective of physical form and grade of the mined ore. This requires that the same market price applies for all mines in the cost curve. Therefore, this model takes these correction factors into account on the cost side rather than applying them to the price. For example, an ore that would achieve a 6% higher price on the market than the standard fine ore with 62% iron content due to its quality will be represented in the cost curve with its actual CFR cost minus 6% of the market price.[390] Therefore, since the difference between the CFR cost and the market price, i.e. the individual miner's profit contribution, remains unchanged, this allows the use of one cost curve for all iron

---

[385]See Kirk (1999).

[386]See Degner et al. (2007), p. 19.

[387]See Kirk (1999); Peel (2009).

[388]See Kirk (1999).

[389]See Kästner et al. (1979), p. 206; Kirk (1999).

[390]Note that this approach leads to a circular reference in the market price calculation, as the correction factors applied to the miners' costs are derived from the market price which is in turn derived from the cost curve. This interdependency of cost and price requires recursive modeling of the cost curve.

ore types and grades. Although this may lead to negative FOB costs for some mines, this does not effect the functioning of the model. Thus, by applying inverted correction factors on the cost side and therefore resolving physical and chemical value differences between offerings, iron ore can be modeled as a commodity with one representative market price.

The grade correction factor is applied to ores to reflect their chemical attributes. Though many trace elements may be found in iron ore, the level of iron content is generally considered a good indicator of the general chemical composition of an ore.[391] As described in 2.3.2, from a steelmaker's perspective, the iron content of the ore is to be as high as possible. High iron content of the ore increases the yield of the blast furnace and reduces cost for transportation and storage of the ore. More than 60.0% Fe content is preferable, 50.0–60.0% is adequate and less than 50.0% is considered low grade.[392]

Based on a comparative analysis of prices per dmtu for different ore types in the Asian market between 2001 and 2009 from United Nations Conference on Trade and Development (2010), the following grade classes and respective average correction factors vs. the 62.0% Fe fines price were derived:[393]

$$
\begin{aligned}
67.0\% \ \leq \ & fc_m : & +20.1\% \\
65.0\% \ \leq \ & fc_m & < 67.0\% : & \quad +6.0\% \\
62.0\% \ \leq \ & fc_m & < 65.0\% : & \quad \pm 0.0\% \\
57.0\% \ \leq \ & fc_m & < 62.0\% : & \quad -6.0\% \\
& fc_m & < 57.0\% : & \quad -20.1\%
\end{aligned}
$$

As these price differences are calculated per dmtu, this means that, e.g., fines with 66.0% Fe content will achieve a 6.0% higher price per ton and unit of iron compared to standard 62.0% Fe fines. Thus, even after volume and cost standardization of all ores to 62.0% Fe, the ore with originally 66.0% Fe content will still receive an average price premium of 6.0% (corresponding to a 6.0% lower cost in the model) due to its more favorable chemical attributes.

The value-in-use correction is a price premium applied to certain ores depending on their physical form and their resulting utility with respect to steelmaking. As described in 2.3.1.1, steelmakers will ultimately charge their blast furnaces with coarse chunks of ore in order to ensure best possible contact between the ore and the reducing gas. Based on this, there have been numerous analysis of which ore types are most desirable for steelmaking:

---

[391]See Kirk (1999).
[392]See Bottke (1981), pp. 155–168; Poveromo (1999), pp. 640–642.
[393]See United Nations Conference on Trade and Development (2010).

- *Pellets* – Pellets are considered the most desirable form of iron ore because they can be charged into the blast furnace as purchased and contribute the most to the productivity of the blast furnace.[394] There have been numerous analyses of increased output attributable to pellet furnace charge, ranging from 15% higher productivity to 100%. This is manifested in reduced operating cost, especially in terms of inputs of coke per ton of ore and also over capital costs for furnace and coke ovens[395]

- *Lumps* – While lump ore can also be charged directly into the blast furnace, its productivity increase vs. fines is lower than that of pellets. Also, lump ore is known to decrepitate in the furnace, thereby additionally lowering its value to the steel mill operator[396]

- *Fines and concentrates* – In contrast to the above ore types, fines and concentrates, also referred to as "sinter feed" must be sintered by the steel mill before use in the blast furnace. This leads to an increased cost for the steel mill compared to the use of pellets or lumps[397]

In terms of valuation, it can therefore be assumed that pellets will achieve the highest price premium added to the fines price, followed by lump ore. Concentrates, as they are similar to natural fines from a steelmaking point of view, are expected to have ±0.0% price premium vs. fines.

Based on a comparative analysis of prices per dmtu for different ore types in the Asian market between 2001 and 2009 from United Nations Conference on Trade and Development (2010), the following average value-in-use premiums vs. the fines price were derived:[398]

Pellets:	+66.2%
Lumps (from South America):	+13.0%
Lumps (from other regions):	+29.5%
Fines:	±0.0%
Concentrates:	±0.0%

The results confirm the above stated assumptions. Interestingly, lump premiums differ depending on the geographic origin of the ore. Lump ore from South

---

[394]See Kästner et al. (1979), p. 208; Kirk (1999).

[395]See Hakala (1970).

[396]See Kirk (1999).

[397]See Galdón-Sánchez and Schmitz (2002); Kirk (1999).

[398]Note that, in order to avoid double counting of correction factors, the price series used in this comparison already reflect the chemical correction described above. For example, it was reflected that pellets commonly have a higher Fe content than natural fines and already achieve a slightly higher price due to this.

America achieves a lower price premium vs. fines compared to lump ore from other regions such as Oceania. The reason for this can be found in the difference in average lump size, thus affecting blast furnace performance.[399]

5.1.2.1.2.3   Mining royalties

As described in Section 3.6, mining royalties are charged by governments to miners extracting ores from the country's soil. Royalties are expressed in percent and are commonly applied "ad valorem". This means they are charged as a percentage of the value of the mined ore. However, iron ore does not have an intrinsic value at the mine, nor does it have an inherent value in the ground. Rather, iron ore is worth what a consumer is prepared to pay for it.[400] Thus, mining royalties are based on the current market price for which the ore can be sold.[401] In this model, the highest regional market price is used as basis for royalty calculations. Depending on the region, royalties may differ depending on the physical form of the mined ore.

For 2009, the mining royalties used in this model are derived for each of the iron ore producing countries based on initial data from McKinsey & Company (2011b), supplemented by information from relevant government websites, chambers of commerce as well as industry reports and press clippings.[402] According to this data, 2009 iron ore royalties ranged from 0.00% in Sweden, the USA and Zimbabwe to 10.00% in Germany, India, Iran and Vietnam. Iron ore mining royalties of major producers China (1.85%) and Brazil (2.00%) ranked below the global volume-weighted average of 4.31%. Completing the top three producers, Australia charged its iron ore miners royalties of 5.00% for pellets, 5.63% for fines/concentrates and 7.50% for lump ores.[403]

For the 2020 base case, expected changes vs. 2009 royalties are analyzed based on industry reports and press clippings. However, except for a slight increase in royalties on iron ore fines and concentrates in Australia (from 5.63% to 7.50%),[404] no other probable changes could be identified, thus placing 2020 royalties on the same level as in 2009 for all countries except Australia.

---

[399]See Kirk (1999).

[400]See Manners (1971), pp. 145–146.

[401]Note that this leads to a circular reference in the market price calculation, as the royalties added to the miners' costs are derived from the market price which is in turn derived from the cost curve. This interdependency of cost and price requires recursive modeling of the cost curve.

[402]See, e.g., Bowie (2009); Gravelle et al. (2009); Pizarro (2004).

[403]Royalty levels in Australia differ by state. Due to the geographic concentration of iron ore mining activties, figures for the state of Western Australia are used in this model.

[404]See Steel Business Briefing (2011e).

5.1.2.1.2.4   Calculation of FOB cost

Summarizing, the FOB cost per mine segment is calculated as follows:

$$c_m^{FOB} = c_m^{mining} + corr_m^{grade} + corr_m^{VIU} + c_m^{royalty}$$

where

c_m^{FOB}	=	Standardized FOB cost of ore from mine segment m, in USD per dry metric ton with 62.0% Fe
c_m^{mining}	=	Standardized mining cost of mine segment m, in USD per dry metric ton with 62.0% Fe
$corr_m^{grade}$	=	Grade correction for ore from mine segment m, in USD/t
$corr_m^{VIU}$	=	Value-in-use correction for ore from mine segment m, in USD/t
$c_m^{royalty}$	=	Mining royalty cost for ore from mine segment m, in USD/t

Figure 5.7 shows an example of a FOB cost calculation for the lumps share of Corumbá mine in Brazil with 67.0% Fe and 3.5% moisture content. Starting from the mining cost of USD 51.79 per ton, the iron and moisture content is reflected in recalculating the mining cost to 80.11 USDc/dmtu. On this basis, grade and value-in-use corrections are applied in order to take into account the price premium the ore will achieve due to its advantageous chemical and physical properties compared to 62.0% Fe fines. Finally, 2.0% mining royalties valuing 2.76 USDc/dmtu are added and the cost is transformed back into USD/t on a dry 62.0% Fe basis, resulting in a standardized FOB cost of USD 23.05 per ton.

5.1.2.2   Determinants of CFR cost

In order to arrive at CFR cost for a specific region of destination, export taxes and freight costs must be added to the previously determined FOB cost per mine segment. These cost elements are described in detail in the following.

5.1.2.2.1   Export taxes

As described in Section 3.6, export taxes on iron ore, if levied by a country's government, are applied to all volumes of ore leaving the respective country and must be paid for by the exporter, i.e. commonly the miner. Therefore, these taxes must be acknowledged as part of the cost of bringing the ore to the

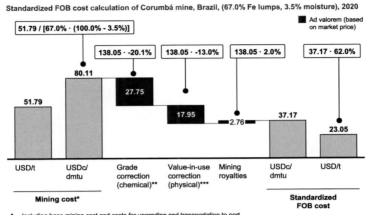

Figure 5.7: Example of standardized FOB cost calculation from mining cost, Corumbá mine (Brazil) [Own illustration]

market.[405] In this model, due to its regional structure, export taxes are defined per region and are applied to ore crossing regional borders.[406] Like mining royalties, these taxes are expressed in percent and are commonly applied ad valorem. Thus, the export tax is based on the current market price.[407] In this model, the highest regional market price is used as basis for export tax calculations. Governments often maintain a tax differential between lump and pellets on the one hand and fines and concentrates on the other hand.[408]

The 2009 export taxes used in this model are derived based on data from McKinsey & Company (2011b), plus additional information from government websites, chambers of commerce as well as press clippings. Ultimately, only two of the nine regions, China and India, were found to levy export taxes on iron ore as of 2009. The tax on iron ore exports from China was 10% ad valorem for all ore types while India charged 5% ad valorem on lump and pellets.[409]

---

[405]See also O'Sullivan and Sheffrin (2002), pp. 450–452.

[406]The potential error, however, is minimized by the fact that the regions were defined along trade blocs, such as MERCOSUR (South America) and NAFTA (North America), which commonly promote free trade between member countries and have a joint public policy with respect to export tariffs. Additionally, the only two countries having levied export taxes on iron ore as of 2009 (China and India) are modeled as discrete regions.

[407]Here, as in the case of royalty calculations, the interdependency of cost and price is also solved by means of recursive modeling of the cost curve.

[408]See, e.g., Mayenkar (2011); Srivats (2009).

[409]See China Customs (2011); Srivats (2009).

For the export taxes in the 2020 base case, implemented or expected changes vs. 2009 taxes are derived from press clippings.[410] Based on the so acquired information, the only change made was to take into account tax hikes to 20% ad valorem for all ore types recently implemented by the Indian government.[411]

5.1.2.2.2   Freight rates

As described in Section 3.4, the influence of freight rates on global iron ore trade cannot be overstressed. The competitive advantage of mines depend to a large degree on the proximity of a mine to its markets. Thus, changes in the global freight market have a profound effect on the landed cost of a mine's ore and therefore on the overall trade flows of iron ore. The freight rates required for the here discussed model are derived in two steps: First, average 2009 freight rates are calculated for all relevant routes based on published settlement prices. Then, 2020 freight rates for these routes are forecasted based on the 2009 values taking into account general projection of freight rate levels.

5.1.2.2.2.1   Derivation of 2009 freight rates

With a total of nine ports defined as hubs in the model, average 2009 freight rates must be calculated for a total of 81 point-to-point connections. In order to reduce the number of connections requiring freight rates, two general assumptions are made:

- Freight cost for trade within the same region is zero. As the FOB cost calculated for each mine already includes the transportation cost from the mine to the region's port (see Section 5.1.2.1.2.1), it can be assumed that iron ore can be transported to any intraregional destination at a similar cost. Therefore, the cost of transportation from the mine to the port is used as an approximation for intraregional transportation cost

- The freight rate between two ports is independent of the direction traveled. For example, the freight rate from Saldanha Bay to Rotterdam is assumed to the same as the rate from Rotterdam to Saldanha Bay. Though certain port-specific costs may apply depending on whether the ship is being loaded or unloaded, the deviation is assumed to be insignificant and is therefore neglected here

---

[410]See, e.g., Reuters News (2010).
[411]See Mayenkar (2011).

Taking these assumptions into account, 36 point-to-point connections remain for which freight rates must be calculated. Research on the Clarkson Shipping Intelligence Network produced average 2009 Capesize ore trip charter rates for six of these routes.[412] For the remaining 30 routes, freight rates are calculated using a linear regression approach. As described above, voyage freight rates are based on trip charter rates and depend in an important way on the duration and therefore the distance of the trip. Thus, a linear correlation between voyage freight rates and length of shipping routes is assumed. Performing a linear OLS regression of the relevant Clarkson data set with voyage freight rates (in USD/t) as dependent variables and length of shipping routes between ports (in nautical miles)[413] as independent variables delivers a slope of 0.002 and an intercept of 4.198 (see Figure 5.8). The coefficient of determination $R^2 = 0.987$ confirms the hypothesis of a linear relationship between the variables. The following formula was therefore used to calculate the 2009 voyage freight rates of the remaining routes:[414]

$$c_{ij}^{freight,2009} = 0.002 \cdot n_{ij} + 4.198$$

where

$$
\begin{aligned}
c_{ij}^{freight,2009} &= \text{2009 voyage freight rate from port of region } i \text{ to port of} \\
&\quad \text{region } j, \text{ in USD/t} \\
n_{ij} &= \text{Length of shipping route between port of region } i \\
&\quad \text{and port of region } j, \text{ in nautical miles}
\end{aligned}
$$

Using this methodology of transportation cost calculation assumed that inter-regional iron ore trade is exclusively carried out using ocean-going vessels. In reality, due to the general geographic setting, this holds true for trade between most of the regions defined in this model. However, some significant iron ore trade is carried out on land-based routes, especially between the regions CIS and China via the inland port city Manzhouli in China's Inner Mongolia Autonomous Region.[415] To reflect this fact, the physical shipping distance in the above calculation, and thus the resulting transportation cost between the two

---

[412]See Clarkson Research Services Ltd. (2010).

[413]It is to be noted that the relevant distance between two ports is not the linear distance, but rather the length of the actual route taken by a ship traveling between these ports. The distances of all shipping routes are derived from Caney and Reynolds (2010); World Shipping Register (2010).

[414]Note that, since based on distance, all derived freight rates fulfill the triangle inequality theorem. This means that for any three given regions i, j and k, the following holds true: $c_{ik}^{freight} < c_{ij}^{freight} + c_{jk}^{freight}$.

[415]See Xinhua News Agency (2010).

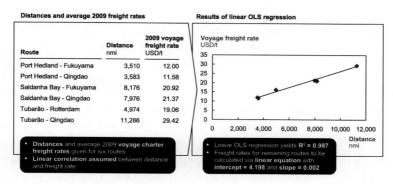

Figure 5.8: Derivation of 2009 average Capesize freight rate per route using linear OLS regression [Own illustration based on data from Caney and Reynolds (2010); Clarkson Research Services Ltd. (2010); World Shipping Register (2010)]

regions in the model has been artificially reduced. The resulting 2009 freight rates for each of the respective routes are shown in Appendix II.

5.1.2.2.2   Forecast of 2020 freight rates

Based on forecasts for the size of the dry bulk fleet in relation to capacity demand, Section 4.1.4 arguments that a likely pattern for the future is that freight rates will be considerably lower than in 2009, but above the market level of before 2003. On a more detailed level, Gardiner (2011) provides a forecast of Capesize time charter rates for routes from Brazil to China and Western Australia to China up to the year 2015. Based on projected fleet growth and future shipping demand, the resulting curves shows a significant initial decrease in freight rates from 2009 to 2012, followed by a gradual increase from 2012 to 2015. This four-year increase was found to be linear with a coefficient of determination $R^2 = 0.947$. Linear extrapolation of the 2012–2015 forecast put 2020 freight rates at approximately 64.9% of respective 2009 rates. This factor was consequently applied to the 2009 freight rates for the six routes from Clarkson Research Services Ltd. (2010) in order to arrive at 2020 base case freight rates for these routes. The corresponding 2020 base case freight rates for the remaining 30 routes are derived via a linear OLS regression using the six calculated rates and the length of the respective shipping routes.[416]

Due to the high volatility of freight rates in the past and the resulting difficulty of forecasting freight rates so far into the future, it is necessary to devise freight

---

[416]The resulting coefficient of determination for the six calculated freight rates is $R^2 = 0.987$.

rate scenarios supplementary to the base case. Based on historical Capesize trip charter rates from Clarkson Research Services Ltd. (2010), the standard deviation σ over a period of ten years (1999–2009) was calculated based on annual average freight rates for six exemplary routes. The 2020 high scenario was constructed by adding $1.0 \cdot \sigma$ to the base case freight rates. The 2020 low scenario rates were calculated by deducting $0.5 \cdot \sigma$ from the base case. The corresponding high and low scenario rates for the remaining routes were again derived via a linear OLS regression using the six calculated rates and the length of the shipping routes.[417]

The exemplary derivation of 2020 freight rates following the above methodology is depicted is depicted in Figure 5.9 for the route from Oceania (Port Hedland, Australia) to China (Qingdao). The 2020 freight rate levels for all routes resulting from this methodology are listed in Appendix II.

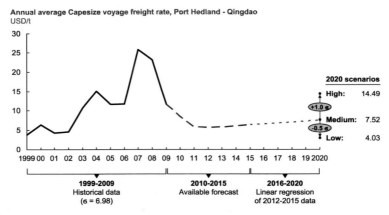

Figure 5.9: Exemplary derivation of 2020 Capesize freight rate scenarios for route Oceania – China [Own illustration based on data from Clarkson Research Services Ltd. (2010); Gardiner (2011)]

5.1.2.2.2.3   Effect of iron ore quality on freight rates

All above defined voyage freight rates are in USD per ton. It is therefore important to recognize the effect of grade and moisture content of an ore on its actual transportation cost. Per unit (i.e. per percentage of natural iron per ton

---

[417]The resulting coefficients of determination for the six calculated freight rates are $R^2 = 0.993$ for the high and $R^2 = 0.969$ for the low scenario.

of ore), the shipping cost of higher grade ores is lower than the rate indicated by the rate per ton.[418]

As described in Section 3.1.1, all iron ore supply and demand figures in this model are standardized to 62.0% Fe and 0.0% moisture content in order to allow for better comparison. For example, a volume of 100.0 metric tons of ore containing 7.0% moisture and 60.0% Fe has been standardized to roughly 88.6 dry metric tons containing 62.0% Fe. While this is sensible practice when seeking to balance supply and demand, the standardization must be reversed when calculating transportation cost. When ore is shipped, it will be shipped with its actual grade and moisture, and therefore its actual tonnage. In the above example, although satisfying only an equivalent of 88.6 tons of standardized demand on the market, the ore will generate the transportation cost of 100.0 tons of ore. One can therefore say that, bringing one ton of this ore from one port to another is approximately 12.9%[419] more expensive than shipping one dry ton of ore with 62.0% Fe. This issue has been reflected in the freight rates used in the model as follows:

$$c_{mij}^{freight} = \frac{c_{ij}^{freight} \cdot x_m^{ROM}}{x_m}$$

where

$c_{mij}^{freight}$ = Standardized voyage freight rate of ore from mine segment m in region i to port of region j, in USD/t

$c_{ij}^{freight}$ = Voyage freight rate from port of region i to port of region j, in USD/t

x_m^{ROM} = Actual run of mine shipping volume with moisture content mc_m and Fe content fc_m, in metric tons

x_m = Standardized shipping volume, in dry metric tons with 62.0% Fe

5.1.2.2.2.4   Calculation of CFR cost

Summarizing, the CFR cost per mine segment is calculated as follows:

$$c_{mij}^{CFR} = c_m^{FOB} + c_m^{ex} + c_{mij}^{freight}$$

---

[418]See Hakala (1970).
[419]Calculated as $\frac{100.0}{88.6} - 1$.

where

c_{mij}^{CFR} = Standardized CFR cost of ore from mine segment m in region i shipped to region j, in USD per dry metric ton with 62.0% Fe

c_m^{FOB} = Standardized FOB cost of ore from mine segment m, in USD per dry metric ton with 62.0% Fe

c_m^{ex} = Export taxes on iron ore from mine segment m, in USD/t

$c_{mij}^{freight}$ = Standardized voyage freight rate of ore from mine segment m in region i to port of region j, in USD/t

5.1.2.3 Iron ore demand

One basic principal must underlie any attempt to forecast the future demand for iron ore. There must be a recognition that the roots of iron ore demands lie in the markets for steel. 98% of the iron ore that is mined globally is used for iron- and steelmaking.[420] As a result, the demand for iron ore is closely and directly related to the performance of the world steel industry. Demand feeds back from the end-use market to the steel market and finally back to the iron ore supplier.[421] Thus it is opportune to work back from forecasts of steel demand in order to reach a satisfactory estimate of iron ore needs.[422]

In general, the demand for iron ore will therefore be influenced on two levels:[423]

- The entire demand for steel products, depending greatly on economic growth and the technological evolution of alternative materials such as aluminum, glass and concrete

- Within the iron and steel industry, in terms of competition between steel-making process routes, each requiring different amounts of iron ore or using collected, obsolete and capital scrap

The influencing factors on both levels as well as the resulting iron ore demand modeling methodology used in this paper are discussed in the following.

---

[420]See Kästner et al. (1979), p. 213; Kirk (1999).
[421]See Kuck (2010); Rogers et al. (1987).
[422]See Manners (1971), p. 288.
[423]See Astier (2001).

5.1.2.3.1   Modeling of steel demand

As laid out in Section 1.1, every industrialized economy requires steel. Steel's
desirable properties make it the main structural metal in engineering and building projects. About 60% of iron and steel products are used in transportation
and construction, 20% in machinery manufacture, and most of the remainder
in cans and containers, in the oil and gas industries and in various appliances
and other equipment.[424]

Although the modeling of steel demand is not to play a central role in this
paper, it is necessary to understand the basics and underlying mechanics in
order to appreciate the dynamics of iron ore demand. While short-term steel
demand can be calculated bottom-up from the performance of the various end-
use segments, long-term demand is best derived using a top-down methodology.
In this paper, steel demand per region in 2020 is derived using the methodology
shown in Figure 5.10.

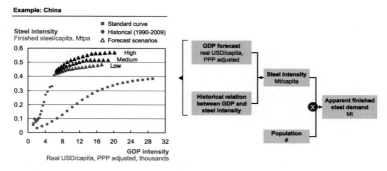

Figure 5.10: Top-down methodology of long-term apparent finished steel demand modeling
[Own illustration based on Feng (1994) and data from McKinsey & Company
(2010b)]

This methodology builds on the fact that there is a well-established relationship
between a country's GDP per capita[425] and its "steel intensity", defined as steel
consumption per capita.[426] It is contended that for countries in the early stages
of economic development with low per capita incomes, the amount of steel

---

[424]See Geoscience Australia (2011).

[425]For GDP, real per capita income is used on the basis of constant purchasing-power-parity
corrected US dollars. Use of purchasing-power-parity corrected dollars instead of exchange
rate based dollars allows for better cross-regional comparison and significantly improves the
capability to represent historical regional metal demand on the basis of trends in regional
population and income.

[426]See Malenbaum (1975).

consumed per capita is quite low. Empirical research in resource economics has found that, as these countries' economies develop, a large number of steel-intensive projects cause the annual per capita use of steel to rise. Therefore, steel intensity can be described as a function of per capita income.[427]

This function has been determined empirically and varies among countries, but its general shape follows an s-shaped curve as depicted as "standard curve" in Figure 5.10. With growing per capita income, the degree of elasticity of an economy's steel consumption has been found to initially increase, but eventually decrease (also called "intensity of use hypothesis").[428] The exact shape of the curve depends on various factors including an economy's degree of urbanization, technological development and speed of infrastructure build-up.[429] China, e.g., consumed significantly more steel along its development path than the "standard" economy due to an increased urbanization rate and massive infrastructure projects.[430]

Therefore, in summary, by combining an economy's historical relation between GDP intensity and steel intensity with GDP forecasts, it is possible to arrive at a reliable forecast for the economy's future steel demand per capita. Multiplied with the population outlook, this leads to the expected apparent annual finished steel demand of the economy.

For the model described in this paper, the above methodology was applied separately to each of the nine regions. Taking into account steel intensity curve scenarios, GDP and population forecasts per region provided by McKinsey & Company (2010a), a low, medium and high demand level for finished steel in 2020 was defined.[431]

One may question whether the above described steel demand modeling methodology, although having proven reliable in the past, will continue to be so in the future. This depends greatly on whether technological evolution will produce significant alternative materials to substitute steel.[432]

In the past, steel has been challenged in some of its many application areas, such as construction and automotive, by a number of competitive substitute materials, including plastics, aluminum, graphite composites, ceramics, glass, wood

---

[427]See, e.g., Crompton (2000); Ghosh (2006); Hatayama et al. (2010).

[428]See Malenbaum (1975).

[429]See Roberts (1996); van Vuuren et al. (1999).

[430]See Feng (1994).

[431]It is also important to recognize that the complex variety of economic forces which are capable of influencing the trend of demand in any single country are to some extent balanced out in a consideration of regions and minimized on a global scale.

[432]See Frost (1986); Rogers (2004), pp. 46–47.

and concrete.[433] Although especially consumer goods manufacturers have in the past successfully substituted steel by state-of-the art plastics, other important industries such as construction and infrastructure have not yet found adequate alternatives.[434] Under aspects of cost effectiveness, many past substitutions of steel by other materials are even being revoked. For example, due to price gains in polymers, many manufacturers are again using steel instead of PVC for pipe applications.[435] In the automotive sector, where lightweight materials such as aluminum have in the past partially squeezed out steel, the "war on cost" has caused some OEMs to reverse substitutions. General Motors, e.g., is now using ultra high strength steel reinforcement beams to replace aluminum extrusions as rear bumpers in several of its models.[436]

Although steel still is prone to the emergence of a material that is capable of serving as an adequate alternative, the current status of material research, combined with the fact that material substitutions normally take several years to implement,[437] suggests that such a wide scale substitution of steel will not take place within the next decade. Therefore, the above described steel demand modeling methodology holds for the foreseeable future.

5.1.2.3.2   Derivation of iron ore demand from steel demand

Having calculated the expected apparent annual finished steel demand per region using the above described methodology, it is possible to define the resulting iron ore demand. First, however, it is necessary to take into account the expected steel trade flows. Expected steel imports must be deducted from and expected exports added onto the apparent steel demand of each region in order to arrive at the region's net crude steel production.[438]

As shown in Section 2.3.1, there is a split in the world steel industry between conventional integrated steel mills, making steel from iron ore with limited additions of scrap, and secondary production in minimills, melting scrap to create steel without the use of iron ore. Global crude steel demand is met through a combined use of primary and secondary production methods.[439] Depending on

---

[433]See Astier (2001); Datamonitor (2006).

[434]See Astier (2001); Fehling (1977), p. 210.

[435]See Coeyman (1994).

[436]See Wilson (2004).

[437]See Tilton (1978).

[438]Note that, although stocktaking has a short-term effect on demand (see Baldursson (1999)), it is not taken into account for long-term demand modeling and therefore not reflected in the here discussed model.

[439]See Astier (2001); World Steel Association (2008).

the chosen steelmaking route and the used reactor, different amounts of iron ore and/or steel scrap are required:

- *Blast furnace (BF) – basic oxygen furnace (BOF)* – BOFs are commonly charged with 90% pig iron and 10% scrap[440]

- *Blast furnace (BF) – open hearth furnace (OHF)* – With an OHF as steelmaking reactor there is a freedom of choice between the share of used pig iron and scrap. However, a mix of 50% pig iron and 50% scrap is widely used[441]

- *Direct reduction (DR) – electric arc furnace (EAF)* – On this route, the EAF is loaded with roughly 90% direct reduced iron made from iron ore and 10% scrap[442]

- *Secondary steelmaking with EAF* – Secondary steel production refers to melting steel scrap in an EAF. It requires 100% steel scrap and 0% iron ore[443]

It can be said that, depending on the used steelmaking reactor, iron ore can be substituted to a certain degree by steel scrap. Therefore, apart from the level of steel demand, a region's iron ore demand is influenced to a great deal by the mix of steelmaking process routes used. In 2009, approximately 71% of global steel was made using the BF-BOF process route, 1% using the BF-OHF route and 3% using the DR-EAF route, while 25% came from secondary production. This mix of routes varies greatly from country to country. For example, in 2009, approximately 92% of China's steel production came from BOFs, with the remaining 8% derived from secondary steelmaking. Some countries, such as Malaysia, Saudi Arabia and Thailand, currently have no primary steelmaking plants and rely completely on the melting of recycled steel scrap.[444]

Based on the above information and taking into account that approximately 1.6 tons of iron ore is required to produce one ton of pig iron or direct reduced iron,[445] annual iron ore demand can be approximated from annual net steel demand using the methodology shown in Figure 5.11.

---

[440]See Degner et al. (2007), p. 24; United Nations Conference on Trade and Development (1994), pp. 3–4.

[441]See United Nations Conference on Trade and Development (1994), p. 3.

[442]See United Nations Conference on Trade and Development (1994), p. 3.

[443]See Degner et al. (2007), p. 24; United Nations Conference on Trade and Development (1994), p. 3.

[444]World Steel Association (2010), pp. 22–25.

[445]$\frac{1}{0.62} \approx 1.6$, due to average 62.0% Fe content of iron ore (see Degner et al. (2007), pp. 38–39).

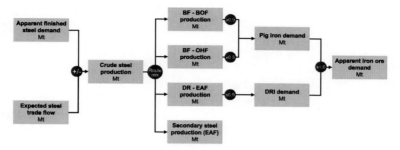

Figure 5.11: Top-down methodology of long-term iron ore demand modeling [Own illustration]

Due to the immense effect of the steel process route mix, it becomes necessary to estimate the future development of the route mix when forecasting long-term iron ore demand from steel demand. The demand for steel scrap and secondary steelmaking is certainly growing as a result of ecological and economic trends.[446] Steel is easily recovered with magnets and is 100% recyclable. It can be infinitely recycled without loss of quality and is among the most recycled materials in the world.[447] Using recycled scrap for steel production reduces the cost of energy and draws down CO_2 emissions.[448] Especially China, as the world's largest steel producer, has encouraged steel mills and society at large to recover more steel scrap to reduce the volume of iron ore imports and lessen the amount of energy consumed in steelmaking.[449] However, scrap volumes will be limited for various reasons, mainly because of the costs of obsolete and capital scrap recovery, including the preparation necessary to obtain the required quality and also the cost of transportation.[450] In particular, China is facing difficulties in terms of its steel scrap cycle. Steel products are commonly used for 20–30 years before they are recycled. China's steel industry, however, only began its present boom around the year 2000. Consequently, the period of scrap high generation has not yet come and this will continue to restrict the development of the Chinese scrap market.[451] Significant amounts of steel scrap are not expected to be available

---

[446]See Söderholm and Ejdemo (2008); United Nations Conference on Trade and Development (1994).

[447]Note that, as described Section 2.1.2, iron ore can therefore be referred to as a "durable" resource, as it, in contrast to other exhaustible natural resources, e.g. crude oil, does not vanish after use.

[448]See Degner et al. (2007), p. 24; World Steel Association (2008).

[449]See U.S. Geological Survey (2010c).

[450]See Astier (2001); Barnes (1974).

[451]See Steel Business Briefing (2009).

in China before 2020.[452] For these reasons, the iron ore model proposed here assumes the same regional steel process route mix in 2020 as in 2009.

Starting from apparent finished steel demand scenarios mentioned in the previous section, low, medium and high iron ore demand parameter values are defined for each region using the following formula:[453]

$$d_j = d_j^{steel} \cdot 1.6 \cdot (s_j^{BOF} \cdot 0.9 + s_j^{OHF} \cdot 0.5 + s_j^{DR} \cdot 0.9)$$

where

$$
\begin{aligned}
d_j &= \text{Total annual iron ore demand of region } j, \text{ in Mt} \\
d_j^{steel} &= \text{Total annual net steel demand of region } j, \text{ in Mt} \\
s_j^{BOF} &= \text{Share of BOF steel of total steel production in region } j, \text{ in \%} \\
s_j^{OHF} &= \text{Share of OHF steel of total steel production in region } j, \text{ in \%} \\
s_j^{DR} &= \text{Share of DR steel of total steel production in region } j, \text{ in \%}
\end{aligned}
$$

It is important to keep in mind that, due to the general complexity of steel-making processes on the one hand (see Section 2.3.1) and the heterogeneity of marketed iron ore on the other hand (see Section 2.3.2), many steel mills will be seeking to buy ore with particular physical and chemical attributes, i.e., particular physical forms, grades and qualities of iron ore for optimum efficiency in their plants. In the most extreme case, a steel mill may only be willing to purchase iron ore from a specific mine due to the chemical attributes of the mine's ore body.[454] In reality, demand for iron ore is therefore split into an almost infinite number of different segments. To simplify matters, demand in the present model, in line with volume and cost standardizations on the supply side as described in Section 5.1.2.1, has been standardized to iron ore fines with 62.0% Fe content and 0% moisture content. What may seem a significant error at first glance is remedied by the fact that demand is modeled on a regional level and not for individual steelmakers. It can therefore be assumed that differences in demand, i.e. demand for iron ore with different chemical and physical properties, will be smoothed out when modeled on a regional level.

---

[452]See Reck et al. (2010).

[453]Note that, as for the modeling of steel demand, stocktaking is not taken into account for long-term iron ore demand modeling. The sum of s_j^{BOF}, s_j^{OHF} and s_j^{DR} equals 100%. The resulting regional iron ore demand per scenario can be found in Appendix II.

[454]See Banks (1979); Frost (1986); Manners (1971), p. 145.

5.1.2.3.3 Price elasticity of iron ore demand

Several market analyses conducted in the past have shown that aggregate demand for iron ore can be expected to be extremely inelastic to changes in its own price in the short run. Three main factors contribute to this price inelasticity of iron ore demand:

- *Price inelasticity of steel demand* – As described in Section 2.3, 98% of iron ore is used for steelmaking. Thus, the price elasticity of iron ore demand depends greatly on the price elasticity of steel demand. Steel is used for construction and infrastructure projects as well as to produce industrial and consumer goods. Thus, steel demand is derived from the demand for these projects and goods. Due to the indispensability of these steel end-uses for our industrialized economy and our everyday lives, demand in the steel industry is relatively inelastic to price changes[455]

- *Lack of substitutes for iron ore in the blast furnace* – There exists no complete substitute for iron ore in blast furnace operations (although the proportion of iron ore can be varied to some extent). Therefore, steel producers with a given process route have limited to no options for adjusting the amount of iron ore in their input mix in response to changes in the price of iron ore[456]

- *High capacity utilization rates of blast furnaces* – Since steelmaking is a highly specific, capital intensive, large-scale operation with significant economies of scale, normal operating practice is to maintain the highest possible capacity utilization rates. Thus, even in the face of rising input costs, steelmakers have an incentive not to cut production[457]

One may argue that aggregate demand for iron ore may become more price sensitive in the long run, as substitutes for iron ore and steel as well as new technologies for producing steel become available.[458] As described above, however, such radical changes are not foreseeable for the near future. Thus, in the model discussed here, iron ore demand is assumed to be perfectly inelastic.

---

[455]Research quantifies the price elasticity of steel demand at approximately -0.2 to -0.3 (see Barnett and Crandall (2002), p. 129; Considine (1991)). See also Lewis (1941); Radetzki (2008), p. 128; Tilton (1978).

[456]See Chang (1994); Radetzki (2008), p. 128; Rogers et al. (1987).

[457]See Chang (1994); Tilton (1978).

[458]See Chang (1994).

5.1.3 Market mechanism

The market mechanism represents the heart of the model. Based on the previously described input components, it aims to simulate the actual marketplace for iron ore by linking supply to demand and determining market prices as well as the payoffs for all market participants. In order to accomplish this task, the market mechanism suggested is split into two discrete steps which will be described in detail in the following:

1. Allocation of available iron ore supply to the regional markets according to their demand

2. Market clearing and determination of the market price in each of the regional markets

5.1.3.1 Allocation of supply

In the above sections, available supply has been laid out on an individual mine basis and each region's demand has been defined. The resulting geographic disparity leads to the necessity of interregional iron ore trade to match supply and demand in each of the model's nine geographic regions. This trade is modeled using the allocation mechanism defined in the following.

International iron ore trade, as described in Section 3.5.1, is based on the fact that some countries have more iron ore than they require for domestic steel-making while others lack iron ore.[459] Though the resulting trade flows can be easily measured, the question of why they are laid out the way they are is not as easily answered. In the end, it can be assumed that the physical flow of iron ore is determined by the preferences of the individual steelmakers when purchasing iron ore on the global market. Frost (1986) names several factors affecting the choice of iron ore purchased, the most relevant being

- *Quality of iron ore* – Quality determined by the desired chemical and physical properties of the ore depending on the steelmaker's type of iron- and steelmaking facilities

- *Cost of iron ore* – Total cost of bringing the ore from the mine to the blast furnace, taking into account not only mining costs, but also cost of transportation and other relevant costs

---

[459]See Jeffrey (2006), p. 4.

As mentioned in Section 5.1.2.3.2, the quality of iron ore has been taken out
of the equation in the here described model due to the standardization of ores
to 62.0% Fe fines with 0.0% moisture content on the supply as well as on the
demand side. This leaves the cost of iron ore as the most relevant basis for
decision. Due to the immense cost-pressures weighing on the steel industry and
the resulting price-cost-squeeze pushing down profits as described in Section 4.2,
cost-efficiency in the purchase of raw materials is key to maintaining profitable
steelmaking operations. It can therefore be assumed, that these pressures will
ensure that the global supply of iron ore will be allocated to the demand in the
most cost-efficient manner.

However, in reality, two factors may offset an allocation based purely on cost-
efficiency:

- *Long-term supply contracts* – As described in Section 3.5.2.1, approximately 80% of iron ore trade in the past years has taken place under
  long-term framework contracts, specifying the quantity of iron ore to be
  purchased over a stated period. The intention of these OTC contracts is
  to increase the stability of the business environment by reducing uncertainty and ensuring the future availability of ore supplies necessary for
  steel production[460]

- *Captivity of mines* – Mines in which market players, including steelmakers[461] and national governments (especially China), hold equity shares in
  order to secure their access to the raw material at low costs. The ore of
  these mines is not sold on the free market, but is shipped to the destination defined by the controlling entity.[462] The price paid for the ore from
  these mines is equal to the marginal cost of production plus transportation
  costs[463]

Information on existing supply contracts between iron ore miners and steelmakers are not publicly available. Even if such information were available,
forecasting the future constellation and validity of such contracts would be extremely complex, if not impossible. Supply contracts are therefore not reflected
in the given iron ore model. In any case, it can be assumed that, in the long-
run, with rising cost pressure, steelmakers will terminate potentially existing

---

[460]See Frankfurter Allgemeine Sonntagszeitung (2010); Rogers et al. (1987).

[461]In the form of vertical upstream integration along the steel value chain, see Fauser (2004),
pp. 9–14; Perry (1989), pp. 185–187.

[462]See Banks (1979); Manners (1971), p. 145.

[463]Note that, while mining units of large steelmakers often sell to their corresponding steel
units at "fair value" or market price (see, e.g., ArcelorMittal (2011), p. 22), from a group
perspective these steelmakers enjoy a cost advantage amounting to the difference between
market prices and unit production plus transportation cost.

adverse contracts in favor of contracts with miners offering more cost-efficient ore. Thus, the existence of supply contracts does not contradict the hypothesis of cost-efficient allocation.

The captivity of mines, however, cannot be neglected, as it may contradict an overall cost-efficient allocation. This is due to the fact that equity shares in iron ore mines do not often become available. Thus, once an opportunity arises, the decision to acquire a production stake in a mine will be based primarily on the characteristics and quality of the mine's ore as well as the cost of the shares. Taking this into account, it may make sense for a Chinese steelmaker to buy a controlling share in a Brazilian mine, even though it would be even more favorable to purchase an Australian mine due to the lower transport costs to China. Therefore, the patterns of iron ore trade are somewhat influenced by the existence of captive mines.[464]

Taking into account the above stated factors, an iron ore allocation mechanism in line with reality must be modeled subject to the following four fundamental requirements:

- The allocation mechanism must define per mine segment[465] exactly how many tons of ore will be produced and transported to what region(s) per year, taking into account the maximum annual capacity of the mine segment

- The annual demand in each region must be satisfied, if possible given available global production capacity

- The allocation should be as cost-efficient as possible based on CFR cost, i.e. the total cost of bringing the ore to the market (i.e., including mining, transportation and other costs incurred between the mine and the blast furnace)

- The captivity of mines and the resulting forced destinations of ore mined at these facilities must be taken into account

Due to the complex allocation requirements outlined above and a total of nine regional markets in the model, a manual allocation of supply cannot be considered. Therefore, this paper suggests a linear optimization approach to allocate

---

[464]See Manners (1971), p. 145.
[465]"Mine segment" is defined in Section 5.1.2.1.1.1 as a capacity segment of a mine that belongs to a certain owner and produces a certain ore type.

iron ore supplies to consuming regions by means of minimization of total cost.[466] Assuming that mine segments $m = 1, \ldots, M$ produce iron ore and supply to consuming regions $j = 1, \ldots, R$, the problem can be defined as a linear problem with a convex objective function:[467]

$$\min \quad \sum_{m=1}^{M} \sum_{j=1}^{R} c_{mij}^{CFR} \cdot x_{mj}$$

$$\text{subject to} \quad \sum_{j=1}^{R} x_{mj} \leq \bar{x}_m \qquad \text{for } m = 1, \ldots, M$$

$$\sum_{m=1}^{M} x_{mj} = d_j \qquad \text{for } j = 1, \ldots, R$$

$$x_{mj} \geq 0 \qquad \text{for } m = 1, \ldots, M; j = 1, \ldots, R$$

where

c_{mij}^{CFR} = Standardized CFR cost of ore from mine segment m in region i shipped to region j, in USD/t[468]

x_{mj} = Quantity of iron ore mined in mine segment m and shipped to region j, in Mt

$\bar{x}_m$ = Annual production capacity of mine segment m, in Mt

d_j = Total annual demand of region j, in Mt

The $M \times R$ matrix of the elements c_{mij}^{CFR} is termed "cost matrix" and the $M \times R$ matrix of elements x_{mj} in referred to as the "flow matrix".

Although this problem, depicted as a network representation in Figure 5.12, resembles a linear programming problem of the transportation problem type, there are two main differences to the classical version:[469]

- The cost c_{mij}^{CFR} is not only the distribution or freight cost, but equals the entire cost of bringing the ore to the market. This includes the min-

---

[466]The use of linear programming to determine trade flows in multi-market spatial equilibrium models was first proposed by Samuelson (1952). The approach was later applied to a model of the coal market by Henderson (1958). For the iron ore industry, Toweh and Newcomb (1991) analyzed the efficiency of 1984 trade flows between 14 regions using a similar linear programming approach (see also Section 1.4).

[467]It must be kept in mind that, due to the fact that demand in this model is defined on a regional level, a mine's ore must be allocated only to a regional destination, not to a specific steelmaker.

[468]Including export taxes if mine segment m is not located in region j.

[469]For details on the classical transportation problem, see Hillier and Lieberman (1995), pp. 304–329; Neumann and Morlock (1993), pp. 325–337.

ing cost, mining royalties, export tax costs, freight costs and other cost elements described in detail in Sections 5.1.2.1.2 and 5.1.2.2

- The total production of a mine segment m, $\sum_{j=1}^{R} x_{mj}$ is not set to a fixed value, but rather constrained to the annual production capacity as an upper bound. This gives each mine the possibility to produce or not to produce[470]

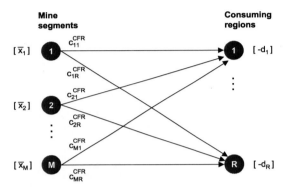

Figure 5.12: Network representation of the allocation mechanism [Own illustration adapted from Hillier and Lieberman (1995), p. 309; Neumann and Morlock (1993), p. 327]

The captivity of mines is reflected in the allocation mechanism by only allowing values greater than zero in the columns corresponding to the respective forced destinations in the flow matrix. For example, for a mine owned by a Chinese steelmaker, only the element in the "China" column of the flow matrix will be a valid decision variable, while all other cells of the row will be confined to zero. This means that the allocation mechanism will decide whether or not this mine is to produce. If the cost of bringing said mine's ore to China is too high, the allocation mechanism will choose to satisfy the Chinese demand using other mines. This decision can be seen as equivalent to the considerations by the respective mine-owning steelmaker. If the market price is below the variable cost of the captive mine, a cost-conscious steelmaker with captive supply will rather purchase inexpensive ore on the open market and save the captive supply for later use. This mechanism does not however, take into account considerations regarding the future development of iron ore prices. In reality, a steelmaker with captive supply may choose to purchase ore on the open market even when the market price is slightly above the variable cost of the captive mine. This

---

[470]It must be kept in mind that, as described in Section 5.1.2.1.1.2, mines have incentives to operate at full capacity.

depends on whether or not it is expected that the market price will rise even further, thus bringing even greater cost savings potential to the captive ore in the future.

5.1.3.2 Market clearing and pricing mechanism

5.1.3.2.1 Discussion of factors affecting the market clearing mechanism

Now that the allocation mechanism has assigned each region sufficient supply to satisfy its respective annual iron ore demand, each regional market must be cleared in order to determine the market price.[471] In determining the suitable clearing mechanism, it is important to take into account the nature of the underlying market regime, as different regimes (such as monopoly, oligopoly and perfect competition) clear the market differently and thus lead to different market prices and payoffs for the market participants.[472] Existing iron ore market models only provide limited guidance in this matter. For example, as described in Section 1.4, the model by Toweh and Newcomb (1991) assumes perfect competition, while Priovolos (1987) and Hellmer (1997a) propose an oligopolistic model.

It is a common fact that the above offered market regimes differ in terms of the number of competing supply-side players.[473] However, it is not only a question of quantity of suppliers, but also a question of market power of these suppliers.[474] Without going into detail on the concept of market power, this paper will make do with the simplified hypothesis that there is a positive relation between market concentration and market power.[475] In other words, the greater the market concentration is, the greater is the degree of market power. Thus, on an extremely simplified basis it can be assumed that the closer the market structure is to a minimum concentration, the closer the performance of the market is to perfect competition.

---

[471] According to Mendelson (1982), a clearing mechanism is a well-defined procedure which uses orders as input and generates as its outputs trades and prices. For a general introduction to clearing mechanisms, refer to Beja and Hakansson (1977); Beja and Hakansson (1979).

[472] See, e.g., Carlton (1989), pp. 912–916.

[473] For example, the performance of the Cournot oligopoly model converges to perfect competition as the number of firms goes to infinity (see Cabral (2000), pp. 151–153; Nordhoff (2009), pp. 24–27).

[474] See Cabral (2000), pp. 156–162.

[475] See Cabral (2000), pp. 154–157.

As measured in Section 3.3.2 using the Herfindahl-Hirschman Index,[476] the level of concentration in the iron ore mining industry in 2009 was 375, far below the 1,000 mark that the United States Federal Trade Commission uses as the lower limit for a "moderately concentrated" market.[477] Therefore, imagining the spectrum of possible market regimes lined up on a continuum with monopoly at one end, oligopoly in the middle and perfect competition on the other end, this paper argues that the market situation in the iron ore market is closer to a situation of perfect competition than to an oligopoly.

In addition to this, it is necessary to take into account the recent changes in the iron pricing system. As described in detail in Section 3.5.2.2, the iron ore pricing mechanism has recently undergone radical changes. As of 2010, the annual benchmark price negotiations have been replaced by a new system, linking contract prices to average trailing spot market index prices with quarterly price revisions. As shown in Section 4.1.3, it is widely assumed that iron ore contract prices, supported by increasing liquidity in the newly emerged market for iron ore derivatives, will move even closer to the daily spot market price in the coming years. Therefore, it can be expected that, if not already, iron ore market dynamics and pricing will in future be rooted in the fundamentals of perfect competition, where the equilibrium price equates market supply and demand.[478]

Prior to describing the proposed market clearing mechanism in the following section, it is necessary to briefly come back to the effect of speculation on iron ore price volatility. As described in Section 4.1.3, the emergence of iron ore derivatives is expected to push speculation on iron ore. This increased speculation, especially in the case of physical or physically-backed investments, may lead to developments in the price of iron ore that no longer reflect only the supply and demand situation in the actual, physical market. This model, however, as it does not aim to simulate potential speculation effects, will be based purely on physical transactions driven by iron ore miners' production capacities and steelmakers' actual demand.

5.1.3.2.2 Definition of the market clearing and pricing mechanism

Based on the above discussion, this paper suggests a market clearing method widely referred to as "market clearing under merit order" or "clearing house procedure". This method has found broad use in the modeling of energy markets

---

[476]Calculated as the sum of the squared market shares of each company (see Cabral (2000), p. 155).

[477]See United Nations Conference on Trade and Development (2010), p. 51.

[478]See, e.g., Mas-Colell et al. (1995) pp. 316–321; Varian (2010) pp. 7–8.

and is an approximate description of the method used in many securities and commodity exchanges around the world.[479]

Somewhat similar to a Walrasian tâtonnement auction,[480] market clearing under merit order is organized as a sealed-bid auction market.[481] It is based on the two simple economic facts that the market price under perfect competition is defined where supply equals demand and that commodities are anchored by their cost of production. This means that producers are generally willing to supply to the market as long as the price they can achieve exceeds their marginal cost of production (including all costs involved in supplying to the market).[482]

Therefore, the main assumptions for the market clearing logic applied to each regional market in this model are as follows:[483]

a) The region j has been assigned M mine segments by the allocation mechanism of the model. These mine segments compete to supply the annual market demand d_j

b) Mine segment m from region i has marginal costs of supplying to the market in region j of c_{mij}^{CFR} which are constant over the segment's annual production capacity range $0 \leq x_m \leq \bar{x}_m$. Mine segments are assumed to be monotonically increasing in their index m, that is, $c_{mij}^{CFR} \leq c_{m+1,ij}^{CFR}$ (Hence, the term "merit order")

c) Miners interact by offering a price for their annual capacity, p_m. Such offers must be at or above the marginal cost c_{mij}^{CFR} of the respective capacity block

d) Fixed and start-up costs of idle mines as well as time-dependent constraints are assumed not to affect the market clearing step

e) Miners simultaneously submit sealed price offers with perfect knowledge of the market demand as well as of each others' marginal costs and capacities

f) Miners do not cooperate

---

[479]See Hasan and Galiana (2010); Mendelson (1982); Sensfuß et al. (2008).

[480]A type of simultaneous auction, developed by Walras (1874), where the auctioneer calls out a provisional price whereupon each agent submits a quantity pledge to buy or sell. The auctioneer adjusts the provisional price in the appropriate direction given aggregate excess demand. The resulting price is such that the total demand across all agents equals the total amount of supply (see Beja and Hakansson (1979)).

[481]See Mendelson (1982).

[482]See Latoff (2009).

[483]Compare the clearing mechanism suggested by Mendelson (1982) as well as the energy market clearing mechanism formulated by Hasan and Galiana (2008a); Supatgiat et al. (2001).

g) Miners are profit-maximizing, but do not have enough market power to "game the system"[484]

h) The annual market demand, d_j, is inelastic[485]

The market clearing problem then minimizes the total production cost over all mine segments at the offered prices subject to the fulfillment of market demand and the respective capacity constraints, that is,[486]

$$
\begin{aligned}
\min \quad & \sum_{m=1}^{M} p_m \cdot x_m \\
\text{subject to} \quad & \sum_{m=1}^{M} x_m = d_j \quad (\lambda) \\
& 0 \leq x_m \leq \bar{x}_m \quad \text{for } m = 1, \ldots, M
\end{aligned}
$$

The market-clearing production levels can be expressed in terms of λ_j, the market price or Lagrange multiplier associated with the fulfillment of demand:

$$
x_m(\lambda) = \left\{ \begin{array}{ll} \bar{x}_m & \text{if } \lambda_j > p_m \\ 0 \leq \Delta d_j \leq \bar{x}_m & \text{if } \lambda_j = p_m \\ 0 & \text{if } \lambda_j < p_m \end{array} \right\} \text{ for } m = 1, \ldots, M
$$

The market price λ_j is found by solving

$$
\sum_{m=1}^{M} x_m(\lambda_j) = d_j
$$

The profit contribution of each mine segment is defined as

$$
\pi_m = \left(\lambda_j - c_{mij}^{CFR} \right) \cdot x_m
$$

The market clearing problem can be solved very efficiently either via an algorithm or graphically by ordering the mining capacity in ascending order of marginal production cost. The so ordered array of capacities form the industry cost curve, which is at its core the supply curve as represented in a classical

---

[484]That is, they do not offer out of merit to force up the market price (see Bor (1999); Hasan and Galiana (2008b); Hasan and Galiana (2010)).

[485]See Section 5.1.2.3.3.

[486]Note that, as the market model is based on annual data, the market is assumed to be cleared on an annual basis.

competitive equilibrium analysis.[487] The industry cost curve shows the relationship between capacity and cost to supply and arrays the capacity from the cheapest to the most expensive to serve a given market.[488]

Figure 5.13 shows an illustrative example of an iron ore mining cost curve. The abscissa of the cost curve represents the available production capacity in the order of increasing cost to service the market.[489] Each individual mine is displayed as its own slab of supply arrayed on the cost curve. As described in Section 5.1.2.1.1.1, most mines, due to the fact that they have multiple owners or produce different ore types with different unit costs, need to be broken into separate entries (mine segments) along the abscissa according to their split of ownership and type of ore produced.

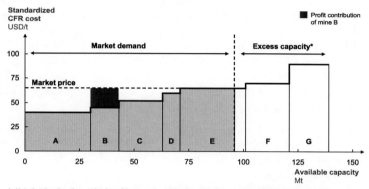

* Note that the allocation mechanism of the present model assigns only the exact amount of production capacity to each region required to meet regional demand. Thus, each region's cost curve ends where demand is fulfilled

Figure 5.13: Illustrative iron ore mining cost curve [Own illustration]

The ordinate stands for the CFR cost, i.e. the cost of bringing one ton of iron ore to the market. As described in detail in Section 5.1.2.1.2, variable costs are used rather than total costs, which would include depreciation, cost of capital and overheads. This is important, as much of the power of the cost curve focuses on the marginal producer and whether this producer receives enough marginal revenue to cover the CFR cost. This cost, in addition to the unit FOB cost of production, includes the export taxes and transportation costs involved in bringing the product to the market in question.

---

[487]See, e.g., Mas-Colell et al. (1995), pp. 316–321.

[488]See Watters (2000).

[489]Note that it is important to precisely define the relevant market. In the case of the present model, the market is geographically defined as one of the nine regions, while the product is defined as the standardized fine ore with 62.0% iron content.

Having arrayed the various slabs of capacity of the mines along the abscissa from lowest to highest marginal cost, the next step is to define the market demand level and place it on the curve against the capacity that is available. Since this model assumes complete price inelasticity of iron ore demand, for reasons described in Section 5.1.2.3.3, the market demand is depicted as a vertical line. In using the merit order market clearing approach, it is important that the demand definition is consistent with the supply definition.

Drawing the vertical demand line on the industry cost curve where the demand is observed, places the capacity to the left of the line to be the most efficient capacity to meet market demand. Capacity to the right of the line is considered excess supply given the demand level and will go idle.[490] Therefore, the marginal cost of production determines which mines can serve the market economically. When a mine cannot operate economically at a given market price, it is priced out of the market. The capacity overhang in the market will exist until the owners of that capacity surrender on the hope that there will be points in time when this capacity will be "in the money", defined as when the marginal revenue of the mine exceeds the marginal cost of supplying to the market. Once a miner comes to the point of view that the excess capacity will never be of value, it will scrap or permanently close the capacity and it will come off of the cost curve.

In line with the above described merit order logic, the equilibrium price is determined based on where demand equals supply.[491] In the cost curve, the market price will be based on where the market demand line intersects with the portions of capacity arrayed on the abscissa. Due to the non-smooth structure of the cost curve, however, the market price cannot be determined as a point on the curve, but rather as a range of prices. This range, also referred to as the "clearing-price range",[492] is bounded on the low side by the marginal cost of the last increment of capacity required to satisfy market demand and on the high side by the marginal cost of the next unit of idle capacity. Within this range, the "invisible hand" will normally set the market equilibrium where the next mine is almost but not quite tempted to operate because it will not quite earn the cash required through marginal revenue to address all of the costs of supplying to the market.[493] However, with respect to the here proposed iron ore market model, it must be taken into account that the allocation mechanism, as described in detail in Section 5.1.3.1, assigns the exact amount of production

---

[490]Note that, in contrast to the cost curve depicted in Figure 5.13, the allocation mechanism of the proposed model, as described in detail in Section 5.1.3.1, assigns only the exact amount of production capacity to each region required to meet regional demand. Thus, each region's cost curve ends where demand is fulfilled.

[491]See Mas-Colell et al. (1995) p. 320.

[492]See Mendelson (1982).

[493]See Mas-Colell et al. (1995), p. 524.

capacity to each region required to meet regional demand. Thus, the last mine segment in the merit order of each region lacks a next best competitor based on which it could calculate its optimal price offering. Therefore, in the model, it is assumed that this player will set its offered price at its own marginal cost of delivery.

With the market price defined, the profit contribution of a mine, equal to its capacity times the difference between the market price and the variable unit cost of production, shows up as the area of a rectangle between its capacity slab on the cost curve and the market price (see Figure 5.13).[494] This rectangle represents the Ricardian rent of the mine.[495] Mines with the lowest marginal production costs in relation to a particular ore market, i.e. mines that are further to the left in the cost curve, have the greatest competitive advantage in satisfying demand there and thus the largest profit contribution.[496]

5.1.3.2.3   Hotelling's rule and user costs

Hotelling (1931) noted that firms exploiting a nonrenewable resource, such as iron ore, incur an opportunity cost in addition to their production costs in the process of mining. This is because increasing output by one more unit today, rather than leaving the required mineral resources in the ground, reduces the mineral resources available to be mined and sold in the future. More specifically, the opportunity cost identified by Hotelling is the net present value (NPV) of the future profits that are lost because mineral resources are reduced by an additional unit of output today. Thus, "Hotelling's rule" states that an equilibrium production path must be such that no firm can increase profit by reassigning a small quantity of production from one time period to another. Therefore, the market price must fulfill the following condition:[497]

$$\lambda(t) = \lambda(0) \cdot (1 + r)^t$$

where

$$
\begin{aligned}
\lambda(t) &= \text{Market price in period } t \\
\lambda(0) &= \text{Present market price} \\
r &= \text{Interest rate}
\end{aligned}
$$

---

[494]Note that, as the present model only takes into account variable production costs, costs of capital and other fixed costs are not included in the cost displayed in the cost curve.

[495]See Otto et al. (2006), pp. 21–23; Ricardo (1821), pp. 53–79.

[496]See Manners (1971), p. 153; Otto et al. (2006), pp. 22–23.

[497]See Erreygers (2009); Hotelling (1931); Otto et al. (2006), pp. 26–27.

Therefore, in theory, mine E, the marginal producer shown in Figure 5.13, will remain in production only if the market price is sufficiently above its variable costs to cover this opportunity cost. Otherwise, the firm's profitability (measured by the NPV of its current plus future profits) is enhanced by decreasing production today and saving its mineral resources for the future.[498] This opportunity cost identified by Hotelling is commonly referred to as Hotelling rent, scarcity rent, or user costs. If the market price does not cover this cost plus the current costs of production, the mine will have an incentive to stop production and keep its mineral resources in the ground for the future.[499]

Empirical studies attempting to measure user costs have shown that they negligible or zero, not only for metals such as iron ore, but also for oil and other energy sources as well.[500] This finding is consistent with the observed behavior of mine managers. Instances are rare if not nonexistent of mine managers deliberately cutting back output when price is greater than production costs in the belief that the increase in future profits, discounted back to the present, more than compensates for the loss in current profits. Indeed, few mine managers are even familiar with the concept of user costs while those that are aware of it deny its relevance.[501] However, mine managers may not consider user costs simply because the exploitation of reserves over time is optimized by the decision regarding mine capacity. As explained above, Hotelling's model assumes that a small quantity of output could be reallocated from time 0 to time t or vice versa. However, if production is at maximum capacity at these times, a reallocation is not possible. Thus, once a mine's maximum capacity is set, it determines the optimal output due to economies of scale (as already discussed in Section 5.1.2.1.1.2).[502] Thus, the model presented here will not take into account user costs.

---

[498] Solow (1974) takes another approach to the problem by considering the capital market. Since mineral deposits are economic assets, in equilibrium they must have the same rate of return as other assets. If their return were lower, investors would sell them in order to buy other assets, thereby lowering their current price and increasing their return. If their return were higher, investors would bid to buy them in asset markets, thereby raising their current price and lowering their return.

[499] Also, under given conditions, user costs can be shown to reflect the current market value of marginal resources in the ground and the expected costs of discovering new marginal resources. As a result, user costs reflect the value of mineral resources arising from the fact that they are nonrenewable. See Otto et al. (2006), pp. 27–28.

[500] See Adelman (1990); Tilton (2003). Kay and Mirrlees (1975) pointed out that, if there was relative abundance of a mineral, i.e. more than 50 years' of supply, then the power of discounting would make user costs negligible.

[501] See Cairns (1998); Otto et al. (2006), p. 29.

[502] See Cairns (1998); Otto et al. (2006), pp. 28–29.

5.1.3.2.4 Adjustment of regional prices to prevent arbitrage opportunities

While each of the nine regional markets has been lead to its individual equilibrium, it is necessary to check whether or not the entire global market, comprised of the total of the nine markets, is also in a state of equilibrium. According to traditional competitive theory, such a state is reached when there are no possibilities for arbitrage between regions.[503] Arbitrage opportunities exist between two regions i and j when the absolute difference between their market prices λ_i and λ_j exceeds the sum of costs incurred in transporting ore from region i to region j, i.e. the sum of freight and export tax costs:

$$\lambda_i + c_{ij}^{freight} + c_i^{ex} \leq \lambda_j$$

In this case, a well-informed market participant would purchase ore in market i at a price of λ_i, transport in to market j, paying $c_{ij}^{freight}$ in freight rates and c_i^{ex} in export taxes, and sell it there at the local market price λ_j for a profit. This practice would lead to additional supply in market j and insufficient supply in market i. Therefore, to ensure that the global market is in a state of equilibrium, all such potential arbitrage opportunities must be eliminated. In this model, the final market price in each of the nine regional markets is thus defined based on the region with the highest market price derived from its industry cost curve. This region is in the following referred to as the "price-setting region", while the others are referred to as "price-following regions". If the market price of the price-setting region p is λ_p, then the market price in the price-following region j is defined in this model as

$$\bar{\lambda}_j = \begin{cases} \lambda_p - c_{pj}^{freight} - c_p^{ex} & \text{if } \lambda_p - c_{pj}^{freight} - c_p^{ex} \geq \lambda_j \\ \lambda_j & \text{if } \lambda_p - c_{pj}^{freight} - c_p^{ex} < \lambda_j \end{cases}$$

5.1.3.3 Overview of market mechanism

The above described market mechanism of the proposed iron ore market model is summarized in Figure 5.14, illustrating the two discrete steps of the mechanism. First, the allocation mechanism assigns available iron ore supply to each of the nine regional markets according to their iron ore demand, taking into account the captivity of mines. This allocation simulates the intraregional iron ore trade flows, which are depicted as arrows. Once each region has been assigned

---

[503]See Stiglitz (1989), pp. 771–772; Varian (2010), pp. 204–205.

a sufficient amount of iron ore to satisfy its demand, each regional market is cleared and the market prices are determined using the respective regional cost curves. As described above, the resulting market prices are further adjusted to prevent arbitrage opportunities between regions. For an overview of the key formulae of the market mechanism, see Appendix III.

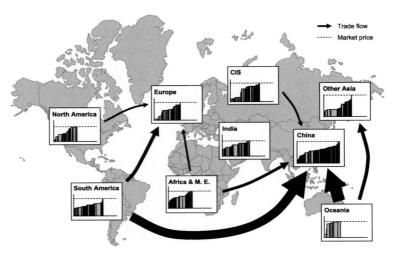

Figure 5.14: Illustrative overview of market mechanism [Own illustration]

5.1.4 Output

The model provides the following key market figures and evaluations necessary to analyze the iron ore market in detail:

- *Split of available capacity by mine owner and region of origin* – Available iron ore mining capacity (in Mtpa), broken down by owner and geographic region of mines, including overall regional split (in percent) and share of Big Three vs. other owners (in percent)

- *Flow matrix* – Mined iron ore volumes broken down by region of origin and region of destination (in Mtpa), including utilization of available production capacity per region (in percent) as well as demand per region (in Mtpa) and satisfaction of demand (in percent)

- *Split of production by mine owner and destination region* – Mined iron ore volumes broken down by owner of mines and region of destination (in

Mtpa), including utilization of available production capacity per owner (in percent) as well as demand per region (in Mtpa) and satisfaction of regional demand (in percent)

- *Production, regional self-sufficiency and trade volumes* – Sum of iron ore production, imports and exports by region (in Mtpa), calculation of net trade balance as well as production/demand ratio per region

- *Market prices per destination region* – Market price of iron ore per region of destination (in USD/t and USDc/dmtu), including definition of price-setting region and calculation of world average market price (weighted by volume)

- *Analysis of profit contribution of iron ore players* – Calculation of individual global profit contribution of Big Three and other iron ore players (in USD millions) as well as per ton of production (in USD/t), including individual values for revenue, FOB cost, freight/export tax cost as well as split of total profit contribution between players

- *Analysis of profit contribution of iron ore players by region of origin* – Calculation of aggregate total profit contribution of all iron ore players by region of origin (in USD millions) as well as per ton of production (in USD/t), including individual values for revenue, FOB cost, freight/export tax cost as well as split of total profit contribution between regions of origin

- *Analysis of profit contribution of iron ore players by region of destination* – Calculation of aggregate total profit contribution of all iron ore players by region of destination (in USD millions) as well as per ton of production (in USD/t), including individual values for revenue, FOB cost, freight/export tax cost as well as split of total profit contribution between regions of destination

- *Iron ore procurement cost of steel players by region of destination* – Total iron ore supply by destination region split into supply from captive sources and supply from the open market (in Mtpa), total cost of procurement per region of destination split into captive and open market supply (in USD millions) as well as average price per ton for captive and open market supply per destination region (in USD/t)

- *Deep dive analysis of procurement cost for ArcelorMittal* – Total iron ore supply for ArcelorMittal by region of origin and destination (in Mtpa), split into supply from captive sources and supply from the open market (in Mtpa), calculation of utilization of captive capacity per region of origin as well as theoretical and actual self-sufficiency (in percent), total cost of procurement per region of destination split into captive and open market supply (in USD millions) as well as average price per ton for captive and open market supply per destination region (in USD/t)

- *Deep dive analysis of procurement cost for Chinese steelmakers* – Total iron ore supply for Chinese steelmakers by region of origin (in Mtpa), split into supply from captive sources and supply from the open market (in Mtpa), calculation of utilization of captive capacity per region of origin as well as theoretical and actual self-sufficiency (in percent), total cost of procurement split into captive and open market supply (in USD millions) as well as average price per ton for captive and open market supply (in USD/t)

- *Deep dive analysis of procurement cost for European steelmakers* – Total iron ore supply for European steelmakers by region of origin (in Mtpa), split into supply from captive sources and supply from the open market (in Mtpa), calculation of utilization of captive capacity per region of origin as well as theoretical and actual self-sufficiency (in percent), total cost of procurement split into captive and open market supply (in USD millions) as well as average price per ton for captive and open market supply (in USD/t)

- *Industry cost curves per region of destination* – Industry cost curves per region of destination, including production volumes on mine segment level (in Mtpa) and CFR cost per mine segment split into FOB cost and freight cost (in USD/t), as well as information on owner and geographic region of each mine segment

- *Industry cost curves per region of origin* – Industry cost curves per region of origin, including production volumes on mine segment level (in Mtpa) and CFR cost per mine segment split into FOB cost and freight cost (in USD/t), as well as information on owner of each mine segment and region of destination of mined ore

5.2 Technical implementation of the model

The here presented iron ore market model is implemented in Microsoft Excel and enhanced using functions and subroutines programmed in "Visual Basic for Applications" (VBA). Various factors were taken into account prior to the selection of this implementation environment. These factors included adaptability of the environment, its ability to process considerable amounts of data as well as the transparency of the resulting model. Though other alternative environments, especially Java-based simulation software, surely outperform Excel/VBA in terms of processing ability, Excel/VBA was finally selected due to its versatility and user-friendliness.[504]

Despite its many advantages, Excel brings with it some difficulties regarding the implementation of the complex allocation mechanism described in Section 5.1.3.1. The largest scenario to be calculated in this paper, scenario C, consists of 431 active mines with a total of 687 mine segments ($M = 687$). Combined with the nine consuming regions ($R = 9$), the flow matrix consists of approximately $M \cdot R = 6,183$ decision variables. Given the scale of the linear program, the standard Microsoft Excel Solver with a maximum handling capability of 200 variables proves to be insufficient.[505] Therefore, the LP/Quadratic Solver engine within the Premium Solver Platform developed by Frontline Systems, Inc. is employed. The Premium Solver Platform is a compatible upgrade that extends the functionality, capacity and speed of the Microsoft Excel Solver to handle large-scale problems up to 8,000 variables.[506] Like the Microsoft Excel Solver, it builds on the Simplex algorithm as described by Dantzig et al. (1954) while additionally relying on a sparse representation of the Jacobian LP coefficient matrix and the LU factorization of the basis with dynamic Markowitz refactorization, yielding better memory usage and improved numerical stability.[507] So equipped, the LP/Quadratic Solver engine requires less than 35 seconds to solve the above described problem with over 6,000 decision variables.[508]

For linear programming problems, the LP/Quadratic Solver engine finds the globally optimal solution. There is no other solution satisfying the constraints that has a better value for the objective. It is possible, however, that there are other solutions with the same objective value. All such solutions are linear combinations of the current decision variable values.[509] Extensive testing of the solver showed that among these linear combinations with the same optimal objective value, the solver will always prefer the solution with the least number of non-zero elements x_{ij} in the flow matrix. This means that it will refrain from allocating the output of a mine segment to more than one consuming region if possible. In multiple runs, the solver will therefore produce the exact same

---

[504]For an extensive comparison of various implementation environments along relevant criteria, see Niedhart (2009), pp. 120–122.

[505]See Microsoft (2006).

[506]See Frontline Systems, Inc. (2010a), p. 14; Nenov and Fylstra (2003).

[507]See Frontline Systems, Inc. (2010b), p. 198; Fylstra et al. (1998).

[508]Using a laptop computer equipped with an Intel Core i5 processor with 2.4 GHz and 3 GB RAM.

[509]See Frontline Systems, Inc. (2010a), p. 17.

solution for a given problem rather than offering different linear combinations with the same optimal objective value.

On the downside, the solver proved to react sensitively to minor changes of the input variables of the model. Being an optimization engine, it will always seek the best possible objective value, even if this means radically realigning the entire allocation to achieve a minuscule improvement of the objective value. Thus, a marginal change of input data from one scenario to another may lead to significant redirection of ore flows in the flow matrix, even though an only slightly adapted allocation would have produced an only insignificantly lower objective value. Though the general output of the allocation mechanism and thus of the entire model appears sound (see results of Section 5.3), it is important to keep this sensitivity in mind. Model results are thus to be treated with caution and interpreted accordingly.

5.3 Validation of the model vs. 2009 actuals

With a market model as complex as the one described above, especially one that has been designed from a bottom-up perspective, good scientific practice requires that the model be validated prior to its use for market analyses. In this sense, "validation" means that a market representation as the one described above may only be correctly referred to as a "model" if its validity regarding the underlying market can be accounted for.[510] Therefore, in the following, the global iron ore market model is validated by means of comparing selected results of the 2009 model run to 2009 actuals as laid out in Chapter 3.[511] Especially the correct functioning of the allocation of supply and the pricing mechanism, both core elements of the model, must be proven. Therefore, the validating comparison will be limited to the global trade flows and market prices, as these best show the accuracy of the allocation and price-setting mechanisms.

5.3.1 Validation of the allocation mechanism

As described in detail in Section 5.1.3.1, the allocation mechanism used in this model is based on complete cost efficiency. It uses linear programming to allocate each mine segment's production volume to a destination region while minimizing the total cost of supply. Thereby it takes into account captivity of

---

[510]See Hanssmann (1987), p. 92; Law and Kelton (2006), pp. 264–272; Liebl (1995), pp. 199–210.
[511]The results of the 2009 model run will not play an important part in this paper, apart from serving as a basis for the validation of the model.

mines, but does not reflect long-term supply contracts that may exist in reality between miners and iron ore consumers. Since the assumption of an almost completely cost-efficient allocation can be considered bold, it is necessary to check the quality of the results of such an allocation. Therefore, Figure 5.15 compares the 2009 trade flows calculated by the model to the actual 2009 iron ore flow matrix as compiled by Iron and Steel Statistics Bureau (2010).[512]

2009 actuals (Mtpa)   ☐ Absolute deviation > 10.0 Mtpa

Origin	North America	South America	Europe	Africa & Middle East	CIS	China	India	Other Asia	Oceania	Sum of supply
North America		1.1	13.9	1.7	0.0	9.3	0.0	3.1	0.3	29.4
South America	1.4	0.0	58.3	14.7	0.0	154.6	0.1	44.0	0.6	273.6
Europe	0.1	0.0		5.3	0.0	1.3	0.0	0.0	0.0	6.8
Africa & Middle East	0.1	0.0	4.2		0.0	34.3	0.0	6.0	0.0	44.6
CIS	0.1	0.0	18.3	2.0	0.0	27.6	0.3	0.1	0.0	48.4
China	0.0	0.0	0.0	0.0	0.0		0.0	0.0	0.0	0.0
India	0.0	0.0	0.5	0.1	0.0	83.6		6.2	0.4	90.7
Other Asia	0.0	0.0	0.0	0.0	0.0	6.7	0.0		0.0	6.8
Oceania	0.0	0.0	0.7	0.0	0.0	279.5	0.0	101.0		381.2
Sum of supply	1.7	1.1	95.9	23.8	0.0	597.0	0.4	160.3	1.3	881.4

2009 model run (Mtpa)

Origin	North America	South America	Europe	Africa & Middle East	CIS	China	India	Other Asia	Oceania	Sum of supply
North America		0.0	13.5	0.0	0.0	1.2	0.0	0.0	0.0	14.6
South America	6.5		58.0	12.1	0.0	156.8	0.7	43.9	0.0	277.9
Europe	0.0	0.0		5.4	0.0	0.0	0.0	0.0	0.0	5.4
Africa & Middle East	0.0	0.0	12.9		0.0	29.5	0.0	16.8	0.0	59.2
CIS	0.0	0.0	21.6	0.0		31.5	0.0	0.0	0.0	53.1
China	0.0	0.0	0.0	0.0	0.0		0.0	0.0	0.0	0.0
India	0.0	0.0	0.0	0.0	0.0	127.0		9.9	0.0	136.9
Other Asia	0.0	0.0	0.0	0.0	0.0	1.9	0.0		0.0	1.9
Oceania	0.0	0.0	0.0	0.0	0.0	256.4	0.0	100.9		357.3
Sum of supply	6.5	0.0	106.0	17.4	0.0	604.2	0.7	171.5	0.0	906.3

Figure 5.15: Comparison of iron ore trade flows from 2009 model run to 2009 actuals [Own illustration based on data from Iron and Steel Statistics Bureau (2010)]

The root mean square deviation (RMSD)[513] is 6.26 Mt, which is low compared to the total trade volume of roughly 900 Mt. Only three of the 72 modeled flows deviate from the actuals by more than 10 Mt. Two of which, iron ore flows from India to China as well as from Oceania to China, are too low by a substantial amount (-43.39 and -23.13 Mt respectively). This may be due to a number of factors, including the non-consideration of long-term supply agreements and the deviation between the regional production and demand volumes assumed by the Iron and Steel Statistics Bureau (ISSB) and the United Nations Conference on Trade and Development (UNCTAD), the latter of which is used to calibrate production and demand figures in the model. Therefore, this validation exercise shows that, despite some deviations between the efficient allocation and actual trade flows, the employed allocation mechanism adequately reflects the trade dynamics in the iron ore market.

---

[512]Note that intraregional trade flows are excluded.

[513]Calculated as $\sqrt{\dfrac{\sum\limits_{i=1}^{R}\sum\limits_{j=1}^{R}(x_{ij}^{model}-x_{ij}^{ISSB})^2}{R\cdot R}}$.

5.3.2 Validation of the pricing mechanism

As the global iron ore market lacks one true market price, the validation of
the pricing mechanism will be conducted based on the CFR market price for
China. The selection of China as the basis for validation seems obvious, as the
Chinese market is the one with the highest level of demand, giving it the role of
the overall price-setting region.[514] In addition, the CFR market price for China
is the price quoted by the three most common iron ore spot price indices as
described in Section 3.5.2.3.

The curve depicted in Figure 5.16 shows the 2009 development of the CFR
spot market price for one ton of 62.0% Fe iron ore fines delivered to China as
determined by The Steel Index Iron Ore Series. As can be seen, the price was
extremely volatile, ranging from a low of USD 59.10 per ton in March to a peak
of USD 119.10 per ton at the end of the calendar year. The average price was
USD 86.28 per ton with a standard deviation of $\sigma = 13.63$.

The global iron ore model suggested in this paper puts the respective 2009 CFR
market price for China at USD 95.44 per ton. When comparing this figure to
the 2009 actuals, it must be taken into account that, as described in detail in
Section 5.1.3.2.2, the model clears markets on an annual basis and therefore
determines one market price per year. It therefore shows an annual snap-shot
of the market, while in reality the spot market price is determined on a daily
basis. With this in mind, the 2009 market price determined by the model is
extremely satisfying. The calculated price lies well between the minimum and
maximum prices quoted during the calendar year and is less than one standard
deviation away from the 2009 average. In addition, the price determined by
the model is situated above the average, thus reflecting the clear upwards price
trend.

---

[514]See Section 5.1.3.2.4 for the definition of "price-setting region".

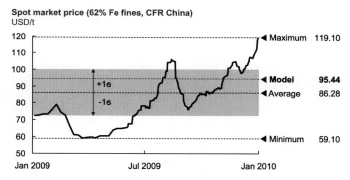

Figure 5.16: Comparison of actual spot market price CFR China in 2009 with calculated price from 2009 model run [Own illustration based on data from The Steel Index (2011)]

6 Quantitative analysis of the 2020 iron ore market and risk mitigation strategies

After having described the recent market developments and trends as well as potential risk mitigation strategies in Chapter 4, Chapter 5 proposed the structure and mechanics for a model of the 2020 iron ore market. Finally, the present chapter delivers the answers to the research questions defined in Chapter 1 on the basis of the proposed market model. It examines the key characteristics and dynamics of the 2020 global iron ore market and, based on this market setting, analyzes the effectiveness of captivity of mines and iron ore exports taxes as risk mitigation strategies of steelmakers as well as their effect on the remaining market participants.

It must be kept in mind that all results in this chapter are based on a market model that, due to the immense complexity of the underlying iron ore market, does not claim to constitute an identical representation of reality. Instead, the model presented in this paper aims to capture the key characteristics and dynamics of the market while yielding to certain necessary simplifications of the real market as described in detail in Chapter 5.[515] Furthermore, the model's bottom-up structure of the supply side, defined on an individual mine level, as well as the general difficulties integral to all quantitative forecasts over considerable time periods give room for certain prediction errors. However, there can be little doubt that, despite these limitations, the numerical results of the model permit a focused examination of the future iron ore market by suggesting a magnitude to key market figures and various trends exposed.

With all the necessary qualifications to the accuracy and reliability of such an approach, the analysis and interpretation of the model results presented in this chapter are structured as follows. First, Section 6.1 sets the scope of the market evaluation, by defining the key market parameters as well as the exact settings leading to a realistic market constellation for the 2020 base case. Additional market parameter settings are defined for a sensitivity analysis, allowing the

---

[515]For example, these simplifications include the regional structuring of the market, the standardization of supply and demand, the allocation mechanism based on total cost minimization and the neglect of exchange rates.

evaluation of the impact of changes of key parameters on the market. Also, the scenarios are defined with which the selected risk mitigation strategies are to be evaluated. In Section 6.2, the methodology and depth of the analyses are defined in terms of which output factors are analyzed. Finally, Section 6.3 describes the quantitative model results for the 2020 base case and each of the prior defined scenarios along the criteria presented in Section 6.2. In the discussion in Section 6.4, an effort is made to summarize the characteristics and dynamics of the global iron ore market in 2020 and to give an evaluation of the effectiveness of the selected risk mitigation strategies for demand-side players as well as their influence on the iron ore market.

6.1 Definition of scenarios based on research questions

Based on the research questions defined in Section 1.2, the analyses in this chapter are conducted in a two-step approach:

- *Quantitative analysis of structure and dynamics of the 2020 iron ore market* – Starting from the market trends described in Chapter 4, key variable market parameters are identified. For each of these parameters, possible values are defined and laid out in detail. Based on this set of parameter values, a 2020 base case is defined by determination of a combination of parameter settings leading to what is considered a realistic 2020 market constellation. By means of variation of these parameter values, additional market scenarios are defined in order to analyze the sensitivities of the model and the implications of the parameter value changes on the key market figures. The quantitative results of the base case and the additional scenarios are described in Section 6.3.1

- *Analysis of effectiveness of selected risk mitigation strategies for demand-side players and their influence on the iron ore market* – In Section 4.3, captivity of mines and iron ore export taxes were selected as the risk mitigation strategies to be evaluated in this chapter. This evaluation is performed by means of slight alterations of the 2020 base case. In doing so, four scenarios are defined. Two of these scenarios are constructed to determine the effectiveness of captivity of mines and two further scenarios evaluate the effectiveness of the introduction of iron ore export taxes. The quantitative evaluation of these scenarios along key market figures is described in Section 6.3.2

In the following Section 6.1.1, the 2020 base case and the remaining scenarios of the sensitivity analysis are defined based on three key market parameters.

Afterwards, the scenarios with which to evaluate the selected risk mitigation strategies in the 2020 base case are presented in detail in Section 6.1.2.

6.1.1 Definition of 2020 base case and determination of scenarios for sensitivity analysis

An intrinsic property of market models is that the results often vary depending on certain parameter settings. In this section, in order to allow the above described analyses, the most critical variable model parameters are defined and a default configuration for these parameters is established. Thereby, a standard scenario is defined, referred to as the base case, which is considered a realistic 2020 market constellation in this paper. By means of variation of the selected parameter values, additional market scenarios are constructed. These scenarios are used to analyze the sensitivities of the model and the implications of the parameter value changes on the key market figures.

The iron ore model proposed in Chapter 5 offers numerous adjustable parameters and therefore a nearly endless amount of combinations of parameter values. However, this paper can touch only on a selection of potentially possible scenarios. Thus, corresponding to the key market trends identified in Chapter 4, the scenarios analyzed in this paper will be based on the three market parameters presumably having the greatest influence on market dynamics in the future:

- *Capacity* – The amount of iron ore production capacity available, in Mtpa

- *Demand* – The amount of iron ore demanded, in Mtpa

- *Freight rates* – The cost incurred in transporting one ton of ore on the 36 routes interconnecting the nine regions, in USD/t[516]

In order to cover as many market constellations as possible, three different possible values, labeled low, medium and high, are defined for each of these parameters. The low and high values represent the minimum and maximum boundary points of the scope of analysis, while the medium value serves as a point of normalization.[517] These values of the variable parameters are shown on the left-hand side of Figure 6.1. They are derived, as described in Chapter 5, based on the potential degree of variation forecasted per parameter for the year

---

[516]Recall that, as described in Section 5.1.2.2.2, freight cost for trade within the same region is zero and the freight cost between two ports is independent of the direction traveled.

[517]Comparable to the origin of a coordinate system.

2020. Therefore, a certain amount of arbitrariness clearly exists.[518] However, this is acceptable at this point as the selected boundary points for each parameter imply a narrowing of the scope of analysis. In terms of the three variable market parameters, this implies the following:

- *Capacity* – The iron ore production capacity in the year 2020, as described in detail in Section 5.1.2.1.1.3, is greatly dependent on the probability of realization (in percent) and expected delay (in months) of the know brown- and greenfield projects. As these factors depend considerably on the degree of completion of the project as of 2009, all projects are categorized accordingly. Each project category is then assigned a low, medium and high value for both factors, resulting in three potential capacity values per mine.[519] On an aggregated level, this leads to a low overall capacity of 2,598.3 Mt, a medium value of 2,798.4 Mt and a high production capacity of 2,937.3 Mt. The corresponding values on a regional level are shown in Appendix II

- *Demand* – As explained in Section 5.1.2.3, each region's demand for iron ore is derived from its underlying demand for steel. This in turn is calculated by exploiting the well-established relationship between an economy's GDP per capita and its steel consumption per capita. Therefore, by taking into account three different GDP growth scenarios per region provided by McKinsey & Company (2010a), a low, medium and high 2020 demand scenario for steel and hence for iron ore is defined.[520] On an aggregated level, this leads to a low global iron ore demand of 2,050.8 Mt, a medium demand of 2,360.5 Mt and a high demand of 2,704.0 Mt. The corresponding values on a regional level are shown in Appendix II

- *Freight* – As described in detail Section 5.1.2.2.2, 2020 medium freight rates per route are derived by performing a linear OLS regression on

---

[518]Due to its subjective component with respect to parameter value selection, a sensitivity analysis may show a lack of meaningfulness with respect to determining the robustness of the respective model (see Fischer (1988), p. 46). Nevertheless, the analysis may provide clues as to critical aspects of the model formulation that may require closer examination.

[519]Note that for mines active as of 2009, apart from depletion which is taken into account, capacity is identical in all three capacity scenarios.

[520]Note that each demand scenario bundles the corresponding GDP growth scenarios per region. Thus, for example, the low demand scenario is comprised of the respective low GDP growth scenarios of all regions. While this makes sense due to general synchronization of the cross-linked global economy, a possible strong divergence in economic development between regions, for example slow economic growth in Europe and North America (corresponding to the low GDP growth scenario in these regions) with simultaneous strong growth in China (corresponding to China's high GDP growth scenario) as suggested in Regan and Smith (2011), is not taken into account.

data provided for six routes with freight rates (in USD/t) as dependent variables and length of shipping routes (in nautical miles) as independent variables.[521] Based on the 1999–2009 annual average freight rates for the six exemplary routes, the 2020 high scenario is constructed by adding one standard deviation to the medium value while the low scenario rates deduct 0.5 standard deviations. Therefore, low 2020 freight rates are calculated using an intercept of 1.5400 and a slope of 0.0007, medium freight rates require an intercept of 2.7249 and a slope of 0.0014 and high freight rates are calculated using an intercept of 5.0946 and a slope of 0.0028. The resulting freight rates per individual route are shown in Appendix II

☐ Base case

Values of variable parameters

Parameter	Low	Med.	High
Capacity (Mt)	2,598.3	2,798.4	2,937.3
Demand (Mt)	2,050.8	2,360.5	2,704.0
Freight rates*			
▪ Intercept (USD)	1.5400	2.7249	5.0946
▪ Slope (USD/nmi)	0.0007	0.0014	0.0028

▪ 27 parameter combinations possible
▪ 7 scenarios selected to analyze parameter sensitivities

Definition of scenarios

Scenario	Capacity	Demand	Freight
Ⓐ Base case	Medium	Medium	Medium
Ⓑ Low capacity	Low	Medium	Medium
Ⓒ High capacity	High	Medium	Medium
Ⓓ Low demand	Medium	Low	Medium
Ⓔ High demand	Medium	High	Medium
Ⓕ Low freight	Medium	Medium	Low
Ⓖ High freight	Medium	Medium	High

* Intercept and slope to be selected in pairs; refers to calculation of freight rates using linear equation: freight rate = slope · distance + intercept

Figure 6.1: Definition of 2020 base case and scenarios [Own illustration]

With these values per parameter defined, it is necessary to determine the 2020 base case as well as the scenarios for the sensitivity analysis. Normally, one would expect to assign the values with the highest probabilities to the base case, resulting in the base case representing the most probable market setting in 2020. However, as this paper does not assign probabilities to the defined parameter values, the base case is pragmatically defined as the combination of the three medium parameter values.[522] Though this does not result in the base case being the most probable market setting, this paper considers the base case to be a "typical" 2020 market constellation on which to base all further analyses.

---

[521] Freight rates are thus given as a combination of intercept and slope with freight rates in USD/t are calculated as slope · distance (in nmi) + intercept.

[522] An ex-post discussion of the probability of the modeled scenarios can be found in Section 6.4.1.

In order to define the scenarios for the sensitivity analysis, starting from the base case, one of the parameter values is changed at a time while the other two parameters remain unchanged (ceteris paribus). Therefore, in order to reduce complexity, the scope is limited to seven of the 27 possible parameter value combinations. Though this does not allow the analysis of cross sensitivities (e.g. the joint effect of high demand and low freight rates),[523] it sufficiently illustrates the impact of changes in the selected market parameters on the output of the model by means of comparison of the scenario results to the results of the base case. This is important as it shows the responsiveness of the model to exogenous changes and because it quantifies the changes' impact on the economics of the iron ore market.[524]

The resulting seven scenarios as shown on the right-hand side of Figure 6.1. It is to be noted that these scenarios are not only labeled with letters A through G, but can also be divided into three groups based on the intended aims of their analysis:

- The 2020 base case (scenario A), representing a "typical" 2020 market constellation, builds the basis for calibration of all further analyses

- Scenarios B through E, showing variations of the capacity and demand parameters, enable the analysis of the 2020 market economics of supply and demand

- The remaining scenarios F and G, defined by variations of the freight rate parameter, are used to analyze the 2020 market economics of freight rates

6.1.2 Definition of 2020 scenarios for evaluation of selected risk mitigation strategies

The following sections introduce the four scenarios with which the selected risk mitigation strategies, captivity of mines and iron ore export taxes, will be analyzed. Each of these strategies will be evaluated based on two explicit examples, constructed by means of slight alterations of the 2020 base case.

---

[523] An analysis of cross sensitivities would go beyond the scope of this paper.

[524] Note that, although the iron ore model used in this paper is static and therefore does not directly reflect market volatility, it suggests a magnitude to the effects of volatility in terms of production capacity, demand and freight rate levels by allowing the comparison of the results of respective sensitivity scenarios.

6.1.2.1 Captivity of iron ore mines

In order to analyze the effectiveness of the captivity of iron ore mines with respect to risk mitigation purposes, two scenarios are defined in the following. These scenarios concern the two largest demand-side entities in the iron ore market: ArcelorMittal, the world's largest steel producer, and China, the largest iron ore consuming economy in the world.[525] In the past, both ArcelorMittal and China have been extremely active in accumulating ownership shares in iron ore mines in order to secure supply at low costs.

Scenario H aims to analyze the effects of the upstream integration of Arcelor-Mittal on the global iron ore market in general as well as on ArcelorMittal's iron ore procurement cost. Similarly, scenario I is defined in order to quantify the effects of China's captivity of foreign iron ore mines on the global iron ore market as well as specifically on the total iron ore procurement cost of the Chinese steel industry.

6.1.2.1.1 ArcelorMittal's captivity of iron ore mines (scenario H)

ArcelorMittal, formed in 2006 through the merger of Arcelor and Mittal Steel Company, is the world's largest steel producer. In 2009, the group produced and shipped 71.1 Mt of steel (101.7 Mt in 2008).[526] ArcelorMittal has steelmaking operations in 20 countries on four continents, including 65 integrated and minimill steelmaking facilities. Approximately 47% of its steel is produced in Europe, 35% in the Americas and 18% in other countries such as Kazakhstan, South Africa and the Ukraine.[527] ArcelorMittal, headquartered in Luxembourg and employing about 282,000 people, sells its products to the automotive, appliance, engineering, construction and machinery industries. The group recorded revenues of USD 65.1 billion during the financial year 2009, down from USD 124.9 billion in the previous year. The operating loss of the group was USD 1.7 billion during 2009, as compared to an operating profit of USD 12.3 billion in 2008.[528]

Being the world's largest steelmaker and having a truly global steel production footprint, ArcelorMittal is especially vulnerable to rising costs of its raw materials basket as well as to raw material price volatility. In response to this risk,

---

[525]Note that, due to the government control of the Chinese steel industry as explained in Section 3.2.2.3, Chinese steelmakers are consolidated into one single consumer in this paper.
[526]See ArcelorMittal (2010a), p. 2.
[527]See ArcelorMittal (2010b), p. 5.
[528]See Datamonitor (2010a), p. 4.

ArcelorMittal has traditionally pursued a raw material self-sufficiency strategy, acquiring mining assets complementary to its steel producing activities.[529]
Building on Mittal Steel's vertically integrated business model,[530] ArcelorMittal has continuously developed a strong global resource base in iron ore and
coking coal, designed to service its own steel mills. The company firmly be-
lieves there are numerous benefits to having own mining capabilities and that
self-sufficiency in key raw materials provides it with a competitive advantage.[531]
The company's long-life, low cost iron ore resources provide security of supply
and an important hedge against raw material price volatility as well as against
global supply constraints.[532] ArcelorMittal's steel units thus have access to iron
ore at its marginal production cost instead of at market price.[533]

ArcelorMittal's iron ore resource base is one of the largest privately-owned iron
ore resources in the world. Preliminary estimates put the company's iron ore
reserves at 19,000 Mt.[534] In 2009, ArcelorMittal produced 38.7 Mt of iron ore,
making it the sixth largest iron ore producer in the world (see Figure 3.3) and
thus supplying approximately 44% of its iron ore requirements from its own
mines.[535] Corresponding to it global steel production footprint, ArcelorMittal's
iron ore resource base is unique in its geographic diversity. The group currently
has iron ore mining activities in Algeria, Brazil, Bosnia, Canada, Kazakhstan,
Mexico, Ukraine and the USA.[536]

Aiming to build a truly integrated global steel production and to further increase
independence from mining companies, ArcelorMittal has announced ambitious
plans to further boost its global iron ore mining activities. The company's
near-term target is to invest USD 4 billion to expand annual iron ore production[537] to 100 Mt by 2015.[538] This target is to be achieved through operating
efficiency gains and brownfield expansions at existing mines as well as a significant greenfield projects.[539] For example, ArcelorMittal plans to triple its

---

[529]See ArcelorMittal (2011), p. 10.

[530]See De Smedt and Van Hoey (2008).

[531]See ArcelorMittal (2010a), p. 7.

[532]See ArcelorMittal (2011), p. 10.

[533]Note that ArcelorMittal prices externally marketable iron ore to the company's steel units at
"fair value", i.e. market price (see ArcelorMittal (2011), p. 22). From a group perspective
however, ArcelorMittal enjoys a cost advantage amounting to the difference between market
prices (charged to its steel units) and unit production cost (incurred by its mines).

[534]See ArcelorMittal (2011), p. 11.

[535]By inclusion of long-term supply contracts, captive supply in 2009 equaled 52.7 Mt, thus
raising self-sufficiency to approximately 59%.

[536]See ArcelorMittal (2010b), pp. 57–59.

[537]Including production sourced from long-term supply contracts.

[538]See ArcelorMittal (2011), p. 13; Woolley (2010).

[539]See ArcelorMittal (2011), p. 22.

iron ore output in Brazil to 15 Mt by 2014. It has reassumed control of the
Mina do Andrade mine[540] and will expand the mine's production capacity by
3.5 Mtpa.[541] 2011 also marked the beginning of iron ore production at Arcelor-
Mittal's greenfield project in Liberia, initially with 1.0 Mtpa.[542] On top of this,
ArcelorMittal recently acquired Baffinland Iron Mines Corporation in Canada,
which is expected to bring in a very high-grade and scalable resource.[543]

Including all information available to public knowledge as of March 1, 2011,
the 2020 base case assigns ArcelorMittal a total captive capacity of 105.1 Mt of
iron ore.[544] Half of this volume, 52.5 Mt, comes from mines in North America.
Captive mines in Africa & Middle East offer 20.1 Mt of capacity (19.1% of
Arcelormittal's captive capacity), while the remaining captive mines can be
found in CIS (17.4 Mt, 16.6%), South America (14.1 Mt, 13.4%) and Europe
(1.0 Mt, 1.0%).[545] With an expected iron ore demand of 159.1 Mt in 2020,
ArcelorMittal therefore reaches a maximum self-sufficiency of approximately
66.0% in the 2020 base case.[546]

Scenario H analyses the effects of the above described upstream integration of
the world's largest steel producer on the global iron ore market in general as well
as on the iron ore procurement cost of ArcelorMittal. Therefore, this scenario
simulates a fictive 2020 world market where ArcelorMittal does not own any
iron ore assets and is forced to purchase its required ore quantities entirely at
market prices. This situation is modeled based on the 2020 base case with the
difference that all mines actually owned by ArcelorMittal are allowed to sell to
the open market instead of being forced to send their output to ArcelorMittal's
plants.[547]

---

[540]Which the company had rented to Vale in 2004.

[541]See Euclid Infotech (2010); Luna and Ellsworth (2010).

[542]See ArcelorMittal (2011), p. 25.

[543]See ArcelorMittal (2011), p. 22.

[544]Not including long-term supply contracts.

[545]As it is not possible to anticipate greenfield project ArcelorMittal may choose to start or
what mines the company may purchase in the future, the 2020 base case assumes Arcelor-
Mittal's captive mines to consist of those mines captive as of March 1, 2011, plus announced
brownfield expansions at these sites and known greenfield projects.

[546]ArcelorMittal's 2020 iron ore demand is forecasted on individual steel plant level. Starting
from disclosed 2009 iron ore demand figures per plant, the 2020 demand is calculated by
assuming each plant to increase demand by the same ratio as the respective geographic
region.

[547]Recall that in the model, as described in Section 5.1.2.1, captive volume owned by steelmakers
is assigned to the regions in which the respective steelmaker has production facilities based
on geographic proximity.

6.1.2.1.2   China's captivity of iron ore mines (scenario I)

As described in Chapter 3, China has, since its opening up to the world market in 1978, transformed itself into the by far largest steel producing economy in the world. To satisfy its future needs, the country continues to build additional domestic steel production capacity. This immense hunger for steel consequently makes China the leading iron ore consumer in the world. Though historically self-sufficient and with a strong domestic mining sector, China's iron ores are of relatively low quality compared to those of other large producers, due to naturally low iron contents and high levels of impurities. Therefore, although one of the world's largest iron ore producers, China depends on significant levels of iron ore imports to fill the gap.

Having fully realized the magnitude of its future demand for steel and thus for iron ore, China has in the past years undertaken an urgent search for secure, low cost supplies. Aiming to sustain the development of its steel industry amidst high cost pressures, China has started to invest in iron ore mines overseas in a move to reduce its heavy reliance on imports from foreign miners.[548] This search has been even intensified after Rio Tinto, Vale and BHP Billiton denied China's demand for significant iron ore price discounts during the global financial crisis and finally abandoned the annual pricing system in favor of a more flexible, index-based system in 2009.[549] China has since had a fraught but symbiotic relationship with the Big Three, vowing to tackle the hegemony of the three major miners and cut its dependence on them.[550]

On the background of China's "Go Out Policy" (also referred to as the "Going Global Strategy") initiated in 1999,[551] the Chinese authorities have attributed great importance to developing global raw material sourcing activities in general.[552] Specifically, CISA has been very persistent in its calls for greater overseas investments of China's steel conglomerates, urging them to increase the share of directly controlled overseas iron ore resources in various forms of

---

[548]See Feng (1994); Lian et al. (2011).

[549]See Section 3.5.2.2 for a more detailed description of the change in the iron ore pricing mechanism.

[550]See Felix (2011a).

[551]As outlined in the Tenth and Eleventh Five Year Programs as well as the Iron and Steel Development Policy.

[552]Recall that, as described in detail in Section 3.2.2.3, China's steel enterprises are not operating in a competition-based domestic market environment, but are rather firmly embedded in a powerful state-business cartel referred to as "China Steel Inc.". All major industry developments, including import/export activities and outward bound FDI initiatives are co-determined and directed by government organizations, primarily the China Iron and Steel Association (CISA).

international ventures.[553] CISA targets to eventually reach an iron ore self-sufficiency of more than 50% of Chinese import demand.[554]

To encourage such moves, the Chinese central government provides support in the form of market information, preferential foreign currency denominated loan facilities and easing restrictions on international capital transfers.[555] A specific feature of government support are "FDI plus official development assistance" packages which provide for a complementary set of business investments and infrastructure development. Such activities, i.e. offering infrastructure build-up in exchange for access to resources, have in recent years been observed with increasing frequency in Africa and South America.[556] With respect to interests of the steel industry, Sierra Leone, Mauritania and Brazil have come into focus of this new approach. In Sierra Leone, for example, China Railways Materials Commercial Corporation invested USD 230 million in infrastructure as part of a deal between Chinese firms and miner African Minerals.[557] In Brazil, the Chinese government is complementing Baosteel's investments in local iron ore deposits with multi-billion USD investments in the Brazilian railway and port infrastructure.[558]

In consequence, Chinese steelmakers, especially large state-controlled enterprises, are making acquisitions abroad and forming alliances to win access to iron ore that could help sustain the country's phenomenal economic growth aspirations. Chinese companies have picked up a wide range of mining assets, though often at sizable premiums, and run them successfully.[559] Naturally, such investments have concentrated heavily on regions rich with iron ore resources, such as Australia as well as emerging markets in Africa and South America.[560] Chinese investments in Australian iron ore assets in 2008 accounted for USD 4.7 billion in exploration and mine development.[561] In 2009, Chinese companies completed 72 foreign investment deals involving natural resources assets with a combined value of USD 23.3 billion, one third of which in Australia.[562]

---

[553]See Taube and in der Heiden (2010), p. 202.
[554]See Felix (2011a).
[555]See Taube and in der Heiden (2010), p. 202; The Economist (2010a).
[556]Though Chinese officials have repeatedly claimed that China provides aid to Africa for friendship, not resources (see, e.g., Xinhua News Agency (2011)).
[557]See Felix (2011a).
[558]See Taube and in der Heiden (2010), pp. 202–203.
[559]See Hirt and Orr (2006); Kwong (2010); The Economist (2010a).
[560]See Bloomberg Businessweek (2010); Felix (2011a); Felix (2011b); Thomas and Regan (2009).
[561]See Australian Ministry of Treasury (2008); Australian Ministry of Treasury (2009).
[562]See Sprothen (2009).

Based on the original data set,[563] the 2020 base case assigns a total captive capacity of 539.0 Mt to Chinese owners, including steelmakers, government authorities and Chinese direct investment vehicles. Of this volume, 386.9 Mt stem from mines in mainland China while 152.2 Mt of captive capacity result from overseas direct investment stakes. The majority of these foreign stakes are located in Oceania (73.6 Mt, 48.4% of total Chinese captive capacity abroad), Africa & Middle East (34.3 Mt, 22.6%) and South America (26.7 Mt, 17.6%).

Scenario I aims to quantify the effects of the above described Chinese FDI initiative on the global iron ore market in general as well as specifically on the iron ore procurement cost of the Chinese steel industry.[564] Therefore, this scenario simulates a 2020 world market where China has refrained from foreign direct investment in iron ore mines. This situation is modeled based on the 2020 base case with the difference that all foreign mines owned by Chinese steelmakers or government authorities are allowed to sell to the open market instead of being forced to send their output to China. Domestic Chinese mines, however, continue to supply exclusively to the Chinese market.

6.1.2.2 Iron ore export taxes

Aiming to analyze the effectiveness of iron ore export taxes with respect to mitigating the risk arising from high iron prices and market volatility, two scenarios are defined in the following. These scenarios concern two of the main iron ore producers in the world, India and Brazil, one with export taxes already in place, the other currently debating their introduction.

Scenario J aims to analyze the effects of the iron ore export taxes currently in place in India, one of only two countries currently levying export taxes on iron ore in the world, on the global iron ore market in general as well as on Indian steelmakers' iron ore procurement cost.[565] Scenario K is defined in order to quantify the effects of a proposed introduction of iron ore export taxes in Brazil, one of the world's top iron ore exporters, on the global iron ore market as well as specifically on the iron ore procurement cost of the Brazilian steel industry.

---

[563]Including all information available to public knowledge as of March 1, 2011.

[564]Due to the collective-type structure of the Chinese iron and steel industries as described in Section 3.2.2.3, the captive capacity of individual Chinese owners is combined into a joint Chinese captive capacity in this scenario. Thus, the captive capacity is expected the affect the Chinese iron and steel industries as a whole, instead of just a few players.

[565]Note that China, the only other country currently charging export taxes on iron ore, would not be a suitable example as the country, due to its immense domestic demand, would not export iron ore even without the tax in place.

6.1.2.2.1   Iron ore export taxes in India (scenario J)

In the recent years, Indian miners have experienced a phase of repeated increases of export taxes on iron ore. At the beginning of 2009, Indian export taxes on iron ore were 5% ad valorem levied on lumps/pellets and 0% on fines.[566] Historically, this policy of allowing companies to export iron ore made sense. India required considerable foreign exchange and selling iron ore was one of the easy ways to achieve this. But, with India's steel consumption growing at an ever greater pace, a clear policy decision needed to be taken as to whether India should export its domestic iron ore for a profit or to encourage steel producers to use domestic ore for the manufacturing of steel within India.[567] In December 2009, the Indian government responded to the situation by raising the export tax on lumps/pellets to 10% and introducing a 5% export tax on iron ore fines.[568] Only five months later, export taxes on lumps/pellets were raised by another 5% to 15% ad valorem.[569] As of March 2011, India charges miners 20% ad valorem on all exports independent of the ore type.[570]

The underlying motives for these increases are twofold. By increasing the export tax on iron ore India aims to restrict exports of the ore and thus to

- Preserve the non-renewable natural resource for consumption by the domestic steel industry[571]

- Indirectly subsidize the local steel industry by giving them access to iron ore at low prices[572]

India's steel industry, and with it the Indian Steel Minister, has frequently lobbied for a complete ban on iron ore exports.[573] While the Indian state of Karnataka, the country's second-biggest iron ore producer, has a temporary iron ore export ban in place to smother illegal mining activities, other Indian states are considering following suit.[574] Calls for a nation-wide export ban, however, have not been heard so far.[575]

---

[566]See Moneycontrol (2010); Srivats (2009).
[567]See Bhaskar (2008).
[568]See Moneycontrol (2010); Srivats (2009).
[569]See Moneycontrol (2010).
[570]See Mayenkar (2011).
[571]See Bhaskar (2008); Moneycontrol (2010); Mayenkar (2011).
[572]See Moneycontrol (2010); Srivats (2009).
[573]See Moneycontrol (2010).
[574]See Gardiner (2011), p. 14; Steel Business Briefing (2011b).
[575]See Spiegel Online (2011).

As can be seen from the results of the 2020 base case (see Section 6.3.1.1), the latest increase in export taxes has had a significant impact on the competitiveness of India's iron ore exports. In fact, the export tax of 20% on all ores leaving the country have priced the ores out of the market, thus having an effect of a de-facto export ban. With India being a country rich in iron ore and geographically close to heavily demanding China, this tax increase cannot but have had an immense effect on the global iron ore trade flows and market prices.

This scenario aims to quantify the effects of the Indian export tax on the overall market, especially regarding global trade flows and market prices. In order to achieve this, the scenario is modeled as the 2020 base case except that the Indian export tax of 20% on all ore types is set to 0%.

6.1.2.2.2 Introduction of iron ore export taxes in Brazil (scenario K)

As described in Chapter 3, Brazil commands the largest high-quality iron ore deposits in the world. This wealth, combined with economic stability and a superior position in the global cost curve, has allowed Brazil to become the world's number three producer of iron ore as of 2009.

However, the domestic market for iron ore is small due to Brazil's underdeveloped steel industry.[576] Therefore, the vast majority of the country's iron ore production volume is exported, making Brazil the number two exporter of iron ore (see Table 3.4). This clear export-orientation is emphasized by the absence of an export tax on Brazilian iron ore.[577]

Recently, Brazilian policy makers have started to change their thinking. Brazil's president, Dilma Rousseff, has stated that she is seeking to expand domestic steelmaking in order to create jobs in the country and reduce reliance on natural resource exports. In this effort, Rousseff is calling on the country's leading iron ore producer Vale to concentrate less on exporting iron ore to China and more on investing in the domestic steel and shipbuilding industries.[578] Vale is in fact stepping up its involvement in steel projects in Brazil, e.g. a joint steel mill with South Korea's POSCO and Dongkuk Steel as well as the CSA steel complex with partner ThyssenKrupp.[579] This involvement is partly because of

---

[576]See Andrade et al. (2007).
[577]See Secretariat of the Federal Reserve of Brazil (2011).
[578]See The Financial Times (2011d).
[579]See Ellsworth (2011); Riveras (2011).

the government's pressure to add value to the iron ore before exporting and thus create jobs in South America's largest economy.[580]

It seems that Brazil's economic reorientation towards steel production may be successful as it meets excellent preconditions. Brazil is one of only two economies that can compete with new Chinese steelmaking capacity in a full range of cost of capital, fixed and variable operating cost and logistics. Steel mills in Brazil are 30–50% cheaper to build than comparable facilities in Japan, the United States and Western Europe and offer 15–30% lower variable operating costs.[581]

In order to further encourage the step change, Brazil's government is considering levying an iron ore export tax meant to spur investment in local steel production. Advisors to President Rousseff have asked the Ministry of Finance to study a measure consisting of a 5% export tax on iron ore in addition to an import tax on steel products as well as a removal of taxes on finished and value-added goods such as steel and steel plates.[582]

With Brazil being one of the world's major providers of iron ore, it is of great interest to quantify the effects of the introduction of such an export tax on the global market. This scenario analyzes these effects by adding a 5% export tax on iron ore from South America to the otherwise unchanged 2020 base case.[583] It must be noted that South America's 2020 base case iron ore demand already anticipates the increase in demand to arise from the newly formed Brazil steelmaking activity.

---

[580]It is interesting to note that Brazil is therefore following the typical path of economic development as outlined by Kumar (1997). In his analysis of the optimal capacity expansion for domestic processing of an exhaustible natural resource, Kumar states the clear economic advantage of such domestic processing vs. pure export of the resource. According to Kumar's analysis, a country will typically start as a pure extractive economy, engaging in no domestic processing whatsoever. Then it will steadily increases the proportion of its exports that undergo some domestic processing before finally reaching a phase where its exports comprise only the processed resource.

[581]See Bekaert et al. (2004).

[582]See Ellsworth and Colitt (2009); Ellsworth (2011); Rabello and Cortes (2010). Note that this escalation of tariffs along the value chain is referred to as "tariff escalation". For a detailed analysis of this type of trade policy, see Radetzki (2008), pp. 53–56.

[583]Note that Brazil is a member of the South American trade bloc MERCOSUR (along with Argentina, Paraguay and Uruguay), which promotes free trade between member countries. Thus, it makes sense to apply the tariff only to iron ore leaving the South American continent. Though this also means that the tax will be applied to iron ore exports from other South American countries, this error is negligible as Brazil accounts for roughly 90% of all South American iron ore production.

6.2 Description of methodology and scope of analyses

Now that all scenarios have been defined, this section describes the methodology and scope of the analyses performed on these scenarios to fulfill the primary aims stated in this paper, namely the characterization of the 2020 iron ore market and the evaluation of selected risk mitigation strategies.

In order to achieve the former goal, namely the characterization of the iron ore market in the year 2020, the results of the 2020 base case (scenario A) are described in detail and compared to the market setting as of 2009.[584] Afterwards, the detailed results of the six sensitivity scenarios (scenarios B–G) are individually described and compared to the results of the 2020 base case in order to illustrate the impact of the parameter changes on the output of the model. Subsequently, to even better quantify the impact of the various parameter changes on the economics of the iron ore market, the results of these scenarios are further consolidated and rediscussed in two sets. The outcomes of scenarios A through E, showing variations of the capacity and demand parameters, are jointly compared to analyze the market economics of supply and demand. Further, the results of scenarios A, F and G, defined by variations of the freight rate parameter, are compared to quantify the market economics of freight rates.

To evaluate the effectiveness of the selected risk mitigation strategies, captivity of mines and iron ore export taxes, the model results of the respective scenarios H through K are described individually in detail. As these scenarios represent slight alterations of the 2020 base case, their results are compared to said base case in order to show the impact of the scenario-specific settings and therefore the effect of the respective underlying risk mitigation strategy on the entire market economy as well as on the procurement cost of the affected demand-side player.

For the purpose of defining the exact scope of the analyses, it is necessary to precisely define what is to be understood by the vague term "model results" used in the methodology description above. As shown in Section 5.1.4, the iron ore model used in this paper generates a considerable amount of output per model run. Though all of these outputs are interesting from one point of view

---

[584]Recall that the 2009 market situation is defined as the status quo of the iron ore market in this paper due to the fact that this is the latest year for which complete market statistics are available. However, due to considerable inconsistencies between various data sources, the results of the 2020 base case are not compared to 2009 actuals, but rather to the results of the 2009 model run. As shown in Section 5.3, the results of this model run are sufficiently close to the 2009 actuals with respect to all key market figures.

or another, the scope of this paper only allows the discussion of a selection of these outputs. Thus it is necessary to define what model results required to arrive at a concise characterization of the global iron ore market and therefore to satisfy the main research objective of this paper. Taking this into account, the analyses in this chapter concentrate on the following outputs of the model:[585]

- Production, net trade and demand per region

    - Production of iron ore per region, in Mtpa

    - Net trade of iron ore per region, in Mtpa

    - Iron ore demand per region, in Mtpa

- Interregional iron ore trade flows

    - Top interregional iron ore trade flows, in Mtpa[586]

- Market prices, procurement cost of steelmakers and profit contribution of miners by region

    - Market price per region, in USD/t

    - Average iron ore procurement cost per region, in USD/t[587]

    - Total iron ore procurement cost of steelmakers per region, in USD billions[588]

    - Total profit contribution of iron ore miners per region of origin, in USD billions

- Structure of profit contributions of iron ore miners

    - Standardized FOB cost,[589] freight and export tax costs, profit contribution and revenues for all miners as well as for each of the three largest miners Vale, Rio Tinto and BHP Billiton

---

[585]Recall that all financial data is given in 2009 USD. It is especially to be taken into account that miners' profit contributions do not reflect currency exchange rates that may affect the magnitude of revenues and costs.

[586]In order to reduce complexity, only the top interregional trade flows are shown per scenario. While the number of flows displayed may vary from one scenario to another, the selected flows in each scenario sum up to more than 97% of the entire traded volume and thus provide a fairly unbiased overview.

[587]Taking into account captive supply priced at unit production cost.

[588]For scenarios concerning the analysis of risk mitigation strategies, iron ore procurement cost is displayed in greater detail for the consumer directly affected by the strategy.

[589]Note that, as described in detail in Section 5.1.2.1.2, the standardized FOB cost includes mining cost, mining royalties as well as grade and value-in-use corrections standardizing all ores to a 62% Fe fines equivalent.

6.3 Results of quantitative analyses

Following the methodology described in Section 6.2, this section provides the descriptive analysis of the results of the above described scenarios, structured as shown in Figure 6.2.

Sections

6.3.1 **Quantitative analysis of structure and dynamics of the 2020 iron ore market**	**6.3.1.1 Scenario A: 2020 base case**
	6.3.1.2 Market economics of supply and demand
	6.3.1.2.1 Scenario B: 2020 low capacity
	6.3.1.2.2 Scenario C: 2020 high capacity
	6.3.1.2.3 Scenario D: 2020 low demand
	6.3.1.2.4 Scenario E: 2020 high demand
	6.3.1.2.5 Summary of 2020 market economics of supply and demand
	6.3.1.3 Market economics of freight rates
	6.3.1.3.1 Scenario F: 2020 low freight rates
	6.3.1.3.2 Scenario G: 2020 high freight rates
	6.3.1.3.3 Summary of 2020 market economics of freight rates
6.3.2 **Evaluation of risk mitigation strategies for demand-side players in 2020**	**6.3.2.1 Captivity of iron ore mines**
	6.3.2.1.1 Scenario H: 2020 no captivity of iron ore mines by ArcelorMittal
	6.3.2.1.2 Scenario I: 2020 no Chinese captivity of iron ore mines abroad
	6.3.2.2 Iron ore export taxes
	6.3.2.2.1 Scenario J: 2020 no iron ore export taxes in India
	6.3.2.2.2 Scenario K: 2020 introduction of iron ore export taxes in Brazil

Figure 6.2: Structure of results of quantitative analyses [Own illustration]

The results of the descriptive analysis of key market characteristics in 2020 are shown in Section 6.3.1. First of all, in order to give an initial overview of the key characteristics of the iron ore market in the year 2020, Section 6.3.1.1 describes in detail the results of the 2020 base case (scenario A) and compares them to the results of the 2009 model run. Subsequently, the individual model results of the sensitivity scenarios B though E are described in Section 6.3.1.2, followed by a summary of the market economics of supply and demand (comparing scenarios A through E). Section 6.3.1.3 shows the individual results of freight rate scenarios F and G, which are further consolidated and compared to the base case to display the market economics of freight rates.

In Section 6.3.2, the model results of the scenarios analyzing the selected risk mitigation strategies are described in detail. The results of scenarios H and I, modeling the effect of captivity of iron ore mines, are described individually and compared to the base case results in Section 6.3.2.1. Finally, Section 6.3.2.2 shows the detailed model results for scenarios J and K, analyzing the effect of iron ore export taxes, which are described in detail together with a comparison to the results of the base case.

6.3.1 Quantitative analysis of structure and dynamics of the 2020 iron ore market

6.3.1.1 Scenario A: 2020 base case

As shown in Figure 6.3, the worldwide demand for iron ore modeled in the 2020 base case totals 2,360.5 Mt and is therefore 766.0 Mt higher than in 2009 (+48.0%). While demand for iron ore increases in all regions compared to 2009, the scale of increase differs from region to region. Due to its expected continued economic growth, China accounts for the largest absolute rise in annual demand (+226.0 Mt, +24.8% vs. 2009). China is followed in the demand ranking by South America (+152.5 Mt, +227.3%) and India (+101.1 Mt, +134.0%). Taking into account these increases, China is still by far the largest consumer of iron ore (1,136.8 Mt) in the 2020 base case, while CIS moves up to second place with 221.2 Mt (+99.6 Mt vs. 2009), closely followed by South America, now the third largest iron ore consumer with 219.6 Mt. Other Asia (186.5 Mt) and India (176.6 Mt) are placed fourth and fifth in terms of iron ore demand.

The above described global demand increase naturally leads to a rise in iron ore production of the same magnitude (+766.0 Mt, +48.0% vs. 2009). However, there are some considerable regional shifts in production, caused by the production capacity increase modeled in this scenario. In the 2020 base case, due to the completion of numerous green- and brownfield mining projects, overall iron ore mining capacity is modeled at 2,798.4 Mt, 68.8% higher than in 2009 (see Figure II.2). While all regions increase their production capacity, the largest absolute increases are modeled in South America (+348.9 Mt, +101.1% vs. 2009), Oceania (+346.0 Mt, +94.5%) and Africa & Middle East (+174.0 Mt, +180.6%). Taking this into account, Oceania continues to lead in terms of iron ore mining capacity with 712.1 Mt, now followed even more closely by South America with 693.9 Mt. China holds the world's third largest iron ore production capacity in the 2020 base case with 386.9 Mt.[590]

Consequently, due to their vast capacity increases and low-cost ore reserves, South America (+344.4 Mt, +99.8% vs. 2009), Oceania (+388.6 Mt, +92.5%) and Africa & Middle East (+174.0, +180.6%) are the regions with the largest absolute production volume increases in the 2020 base case. On the other hand, despite its slight capacity increase, China's iron ore production decreases significantly by 227.6 Mt to 78.8 Mt (−74.3% vs. 2009). Also India (−40.2 Mt,

---

[590]It is to be noted that China is modeled in the 2020 base case with a minor net capacity increase of 19.2 Mt compared to 2009 (+5.2%). This is due to the expected depletion of numerous Chinese mines, given that their annual production rates remain at or above the 2009 level.

−19.0%) and Other Asia (−0.9 Mt, −16.3%) reduce their production volumes compared to 2009. Thus, Oceania remains the largest iron ore producer with now 704.7 Mt, followed by South America (689.4 Mt), Africa & Middle East (270.3 Mt), CIS (228.1 Mt) and India (171.5 Mt).

Naturally, these changes in regional iron ore demand and production figures lead to altered net trade volumes. As in 2009, China is the world's leading net importer of iron ore, with a volume of 1,057.9 Mt in the 2020 base case. China thus compensates its demand increase and production decrease by additional net imports of 453.7 Mt compared to 2009. Besides China, only Other Asia (181.9 Mt, +12.3 Mt vs. 2009) and Europe (110.9 Mt, +10.3 Mt) are significant net importers in the base case. Fueled by the additional production capacity, the main net exporters in the 2020 base case are Oceania (692.4 Mt, +355.2 Mt compared to 2009), South America (469.8 Mt, +191.9 Mt) and Africa & Middle East (141.8 Mt, +100.0 Mt).

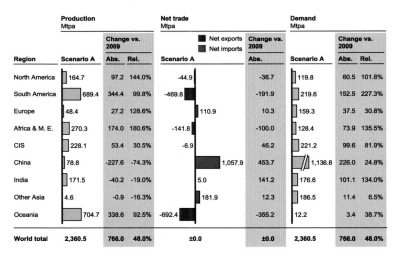

Figure 6.3: Scenario A: 2020 base case – Analysis of production, net trade and demand by region [Own illustration]

The above described changes in regional iron ore demand as well as additional production capacities in low-cost iron ore regions Oceania, South America and Africa & Middle East have substantial effects on the global iron ore trade flows in the 2020 base case (see Figure 6.4). As in 2009, the by-far largest flows run to China from Oceania (596.9 Mt) and South America (405.4 Mt). Due to higher production capacities and the favorable cost position of mines in these regions, the flows from these regions to China even show considerable increases of 340.5 Mt and 248.6 Mt respectively.[591] On account of this massive increased flow of low-cost ore into the market, China considerably reduces its more expensive domestic production vs. 2009 (-227.6 Mt) as well as its imports from India (-127.0 Mt). The latter is mainly due to India's increased export taxes of 20% ad valorem on all ore types in 2020 compared to a 5% tax on only lump and pellets in 2009.[592] This tax acts as a de facto export ban (by pricing the mines out of the market), thus allowing India to satisfy its increased domestic iron ore demand vs. 2009 entirely by means of domestic and captive South American production. Thanks to its increase in capacity and its favorable geographic and cost position, Africa & Middle East, apart from being able to satisfy its entire domestic iron ore demand, becomes a significant global supplier of ore in the 2020 base case. The region exports especially to Other Asia (87.1 Mt, +70.3 Mt vs. 2009), China (34.4 Mt, +4.9 Mt) and Europe (15.6 Mt, +2.7 Mt).

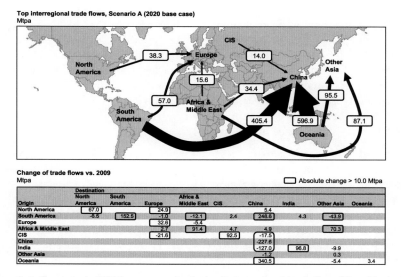

Top interregional trade flows, Scenario A (2020 base case)
Mtpa

Change of trade flows vs. 2009
Mtpa
☐ Absolute change > 10.0 Mtpa

Origin	Destination North America	South America	Europe	Africa & Middle East	CIS	China	India	Other Asia	Oceania
North America	67.0		24.9			5.4			
South America	-6.5	152.5	-1.0	-12.1	2.4	248.6	4.3	-43.9	
Europe			32.6	-5.4					
Africa & Middle East			2.7	91.4	4.7	4.9		70.3	
CIS			-21.6		92.5	-17.5			
China						-227.8			
India						-127.0	96.8	-9.9	
Other Asia						-1.2		0.3	
Oceania						340.5		-5.4	3.4

Figure 6.4: Scenario A: 2020 base case – Analysis of interregional trade flows [Own illustration]

Despite the overall increase in demand compared to 2009, the increased production capacity in regions with high-quality and thus low-cost ore resources such as Oceania, South America and Africa & Middle East and the resulting de-

---

[591] Despite having a similar capacity and production increase vs. 2009, the South American increase in exports to China is somewhat lower than Oceania's due to its stronger rise in domestic iron ore demand.

[592] See Section 5.1.2.2.1.

creased production in regions with higher costs, especially China, send regional market prices downwards (see Figure 6.5). Compared to 2009, the weighted world average market price for one ton of iron ore decreases by USD 9.92 to USD 77.05 (−11.4%). India shows the largest price decrease, down USD 19.93 to USD 53.41 (−27.2%). This above average price decrease stems from the increase of the country's iron ore export taxes, acting as a de facto export ban, and its resulting complete self-sufficiency through domestic production and captive supply abroad. Due to their significant iron ore demand and resulting dependency on imports, China and Other Asia also enjoy large price decreases, stemming from additional low-cost supply in the market. Nevertheless, China continues to hold the highest market price with USD 85.59 (USD −9.85, −10.3%), closely followed by Other Asia with USD 83.52 (USD −6.12, −6.8%).

The price changes in all other regions are caused not by supply or demand effects, but rather by the non-arbitrage condition of the model.[593] Thus, these changes are indirect effects of the combined market price decrease in the price-setting region China and the decreased freight rates in the 2020 base case compared to 2009. As freight rates sink, market prices in regions far from China, e.g. North and South America, are driven in an upward direction, closer to the Chinese market price. This is necessary in order to prevent arbitrage opportunities when regional markets move closer together in terms of freight costs.[594] For regions closer to China, e.g. Africa & Middle East and CIS, the effect of the reduced freight rates is overcompensated by the price decrease in China, thus leading to price decreases in the respective regions.

Compared to 2009, the increase in global iron ore demand increases steelmakers' total expenditure for iron ore by USD 41.2 billion to a total of USD 159.6 billion (+34.8%). Due to lower average market prices however, procurement costs on a per ton level are lower than in 2009. On average, iron ore consumers pay USD 67.61 per ton of ore, USD 6.62 less than in 2009 (−8.9%). It is to be mentioned that these average procurement costs per ton are lower than the respective regional market prices. This is due to the presence of captive iron ore mines which supply to steelmakers in these regions at unit production cost rather than at market price. Therefore, changes in the average iron ore

---

[593]See Section 5.1.3.2.4.

[594]For example, the unit production cost of South America's marginal supplier in the 2020 base case lies at USD 63.25. With freight rates to China at USD 18.42 per ton, however, the market price in South America must be at least USD 67.17 (China's market price of USD 85.59 minus USD 18.42) in order to prevent arbitrage between the two regions.

procurement cost per ton are influenced not only by changes in the market prices, but also by changes in the share of captive supply.[595]

Naturally, from a miner's point of view, the demand boom modeled in the 2020 base case is extremely advantageous. Despite lower average market prices, miners' joint profit contribution increases by USD 20.1 billion to USD 77.8 billion (+34.7% compared to 2009). Of course, regions with the largest production volume increase vs. 2009 are the ones profiting the most. Thus, iron ore miners in South America (USD +9.4 billion), Oceania (USD +8.6 billion) and Africa & Middle East (USD +4.5 billion) show the largest absolute increases in profit contribution. India's iron ore miners are the only ones suffering a profit contribution decrease, USD −4.7 billion to USD 3.2 billion (−59.1% compared to 2009). This is due to the increase of India's iron ore export tax, leading to the abolishment of iron ore exports on the one hand and the sharp decrease in the Indian market price on the other.

	Market price USD/t			Average iron ore procurement cost USD/t			Total iron ore procurement cost USD billions			Total profit contribution of miners (by origin) USD billions		
	Scenario A	Change vs. 2009		Scenario A	Change vs. 2009		Scenario A	Change vs. 2009		Scenario A	Change vs. 2009	
Region		Abs.	Rel.		Abs.	Rel.		Abs.	Rel.		Abs.	Rel.
North America	64.51	1.54	2.5%	42.13	3.26	8.4%	5.0	2.7	118.8%	2.3	0.4	19.5%
South America	67.17	0.10	0.1%	50.41	8.58	20.5%	11.1	8.3	294.4%	26.2	9.4	55.7%
Europe	67.65	-0.15	-0.2%	54.64	-6.05	-10.0%	8.7	1.3	17.8%	2.9	1.1	60.2%
Africa & M. E.	71.72	-2.35	-3.2%	68.01	-1.27	-1.8%	8.7	5.0	131.2%	9.6	4.5	86.7%
CIS	72.96	-3.02	-4.0%	47.40	18.59	64.5%	10.5	7.0	199.3%	4.7	0.8	19.2%
China	85.59	-9.85	-10.3%	79.73	-5.44	-6.4%	90.6	13.1	16.8%	0.0	±0.0	±0.0%
India	53.41	-19.93	-27.2%	50.23	-15.21	-23.2%	8.9	3.9	79.6%	3.2	-4.7	-59.1%
Other Asia	83.52	-6.12	-6.8%	82.73	-6.91	-7.7%	15.4	-0.3	-1.7%	0.1	0.1	125.7%
Oceania	78.07	-5.79	-6.9%	49.99	8.33	20.0%	0.6	0.2	66.4%	28.8	8.6	42.8%
World total	77.05	-9.92	-11.4%	67.61	-6.62	-8.9%	159.6	41.2	34.8%	77.8	20.1	34.7%

Figure 6.5: Scenario A: 2020 base case – Analysis of market prices, procurement cost and profit contribution of miners by region [Own illustration]

The detailed effects of the increases in regional iron ore demand as well as additional production capacities from 2009 to 2020 on iron ore miners' are shown in Figure 6.6. Fueled by the global demand and thus production increase, the overall standardized FOB cost rises by 47.5% to USD 65.4 billion. However, the standardized FOB cost declines slightly on a per ton basis (−0.4%). This

---

[595]For example, due to its overall increase in demand, CIS is forced to procure a larger share of its ore on the open market than in 2009. This leads to a considerable increase in the region's average iron ore procurement cost.

effect can be traced back to lower mining royalties (owing to lower market prices) slightly overcompensating lower grade and value-in-use premiums per ton. Regardless of the increase in production volume, the combined cost for freight and export taxes decreases in absolute terms, down 0.8% vs. 2009 to USD 16.4 billion. The larger decrease in combined freight and export tax costs on a per ton basis (−31.9%) is due to the significant decrease in average freight costs per ton modeled for 2020 as well as the absolute decrease in export taxes compared to 2009.[596] Despite the decrease in market prices, 2020 base case revenue increases by 34.8% to USD 159.6 billion due to the immense increase in iron ore demand. This leaves miners with a total profit contribution of USD 77.8 billion, 34.7% more than in 2009. On a per ton basis, however, revenues decrease by 8.9% due to lower market prices. Thus, miners' profit contribution per ton decreases by 9.0% to USD 32.98.

Due to above average capacity and production volume increases, the three largest miners profit from the market situation modeled in the 2020 base case. Vale increases its production by 85.9% to 436.4 Mt. The miner's total profit contribution rises to USD 21.3 billion (+57.0% vs. 2009). Rio Tinto's 2020 production volume rises to 247.5 Mt, up 52.6% compared to 2009. Consequently, its profit contribution increases by 29.8% to USD 13.1 billion. Also BHP Billiton increases its production by 77.2% to 188.5 Mt and enjoys an increased profit contribution of USD 9.3 billion (+45.7%). The reason for Vale's comparatively higher gain in total profit contribution can be found in its larger production volume increase compared to the other two major iron ore miners. Also, due to its significant share of domestic customers and the slight rise in the South American market price, Vale's revenues show a larger absolute increase than those of Rio Tinto and BHP Billiton. On a per ton level, however, all three major miners suffer profit contribution losses. Vale's profit contribution per ton sinks by 15.5% vs. 2009, Rio Tinto's is down 14.9% and BHP Billiton suffers the highest per ton profit contribution loss of 17.8%.

In terms of market share (based on profit contribution), the combined share of the Big Three increases by 4.2 percentage points compared to 2009 to 56.2%. Vale stays in first place, expanding its lead with a considerably increased share of 27.3% (+3.9 ppt vs. 2009). Rio Tinto's market share drops to 16.9% (−0.6 ppt) and BHP Billiton claims 12.0% of the overall profit contribution (+0.9 ppt). The main reason for the increased dominance of the Big Three in the 2020 base case compared to 2009 lies in the fact that all three players increase their production

---

[596]Note that in the 2020 base case neither of the two regions levying export taxes, China and India, actually export iron ore. Thus, overall global export tax costs are zero. By contrast, India exported considerable ore volumes to China and Other Asia in the 2009 model run, thus incurring export tax costs.

volume by more than the market average 48.0%. This is due to their immense increase in production capacity and the favorable position of their mines in the global industry cost curve.

	Production Mtpa	Analysis of profit contribution (USD billions)			
		Standardized FOB cost	Freight and export taxes	Profit contribution	Revenue
World total					159.6
		65.4	16.4	77.8	
Total	2,360.5				
Change vs. 2009	48.0%	47.5%	0.8%	34.7%	34.8%
Per ton (USD/t)		27.70	6.93	32.98	67.61
Change vs. 2009		-0.4%	-31.9%	-9.0%	-8.9%
Vale					
Total	436.4	7.6	5.2	21.3	34.0
Change vs. 2009	85.9%	834.6%	0.8%	57.0%	74.4%
Per ton (USD/t)		17.33	11.94	48.70	77.96
Change vs. 2009		402.7%	-45.8%	-15.5%	-6.2%
Rio Tinto					
Total	247.5	5.7	1.8	13.1	20.6
Change vs. 2009	52.6%	103.6%	-5.1%	29.8%	39.4%
Per ton (USD/t)		23.13	7.19	53.04	83.35
Change vs. 2009		33.5%	-37.8%	-14.9%	-8.6%
BHP Billiton					
Total	188.5	5.2	1.6	9.3	16.1
Change vs. 2009	77.2%	152.5%	9.9%	45.7%	62.4%
Per ton (USD/t)		27.43	8.63	49.53	85.59
Change vs. 2009		42.5%	-38.0%	-17.8%	-8.3%

Figure 6.6: Scenario A: 2020 base case – Analysis of individual profit contributions of miners [Own illustration]

6.3.1.2 Market economics of supply and demand

6.3.1.2.1 Scenario B: 2020 low capacity

As shown in Figure 6.7, the demand for iron ore in scenario B is identical to the demand in the base case. This is true for the total demand (2,360.5 Mt) as well as for the individual demand of the geographic regions. China thus continues to dominate demand with 1,136.8 Mt, followed by CIS (221.2 Mt) and South America (219.6 Mt).

Total world iron ore production in scenario B is equal to production in the base case (2,360.5 Mt). However, there are some considerable regional shifts in production, caused by the downsizing and/or delay of expansion projects modeled in this scenario. These project downsizings and delays lead to a decline in total production capacity vs. the base case by 7.2% or 200.1 Mt (see Figure II.2). Oceania (−74.7 Mt), South America (−51.1 Mt) and Africa & Middle East (−43.3 Mt), all home to numerous expansion projects, are especially affected. Despite this reduced capacity, Oceania and South America continue to lead global production as in the base case. South America is now the largest producer with 642.0 Mt (−6.9% vs. the base case), followed closely by Oceania with 636.3 Mt (−9.7%). India, with an increased production of 244.2 Mt (+42.4%) is now in third place, followed by Africa & Middle East (227.0 Mt, −16.0%). CIS (222.3 Mt, −2.5%) completes the top five. China's iron ore production more than doubles to 171.4 Mt compared to the base case (+117.4%).

Despite this significant increase in domestic production, China continues to lead net imports with 965.3 Mt (−92.6 Mt vs. the base case), followed by the only other two importing regions Other Asia (173.5 Mt, −8.5 Mt) and Europe (112.1 Mt, +1.2 Mt). As in the base case, the main net exporters in this scenario are Oceania (624.0 Mt, −68.4 Mt), South America (422.4 Mt, −47.4 Mt) and Africa & Middle East (98.5 Mt, −43.3 Mt). It is to be noted that India (despite its high export taxes) has become a significant net exporter in this scenario (67.7 Mt), compared to its net imports of 5.0 Mt in the base case.

The above described reduction of production capacities in low-cost iron ore regions Oceania, South America and Africa & Middle East has substantial effects on the global iron ore trade flows (see Figure 6.8). The by-far largest flows continue to run to China from Oceania (515.3 Mt) and South America (350.7 Mt). However, due to lower production capacities in these regions and thus lower production, these flows weaken significantly by 81.6 Mt and 54.7 Mt respectively. Africa & Middle East, China's number three supplier in the base case, is forced to reduce its supply to China by 14.3 Mt to 20.2 Mt due to its capacity constraints. With Chinese demand as strong as in the base case, this lacking

Region	Production Mtpa				Net trade Mtpa			Demand Mtpa		
	Scenario B	Change vs. base case			Scenario B	Change vs. base case		Scenario B	Change vs. base case	
		Abs.	Rel.			Abs.			Abs.	Rel.
North America	157.0	-7.8	-4.7%		-37.1	7.8		119.8	±0.0	±0.0%
South America	642.0	-47.4	-6.9%		-422.4	47.4		219.6	±0.0	±0.0%
Europe	47.2	-1.2	-2.4%		112.1	1.2		159.3	±0.0	±0.0%
Africa & M. E.	227.0	-43.3	-16.0%		-98.5	43.3		128.4	±0.0	±0.0%
CIS	222.3	-5.8	-2.5%		-1.1	5.8		221.2	±0.0	±0.0%
China	171.4	92.6	117.4%		965.3	-92.6		1,136.8	±0.0	±0.0%
India	244.2	72.7	42.4%		-67.7	-72.7		176.6	±0.0	±0.0%
Other Asia	13.0	8.5	183.8%		173.5	-8.5		186.5	±0.0	±0.0%
Oceania	636.3	-68.4	-9.7%		-624.0	68.4		12.2	±0.0	±0.0%
World total	2,360.5	±0.0	±0.0%		±0.0	±0.0		2,360.5	±0.0	±0.0%

(Net trade legend: ■ Net exports / Net imports)

Figure 6.7: Scenario B: 2020 low capacity – Analysis of production, net trade and demand by region [Own illustration]

supply from Oceania, South America and Africa & Middle East is compensated primarily by domestic Chinese iron ore production (171.4 Mt, +92.6 Mt vs. the base case), but also by imports from India (61.6 Mt, +61.6 Mt).

As can be expected, the reduced production capacity in regions with high-quality and thus low-cost ore resources such as Oceania, South America and Africa & Middle East and the resulting increased supply from regions with low-quality ore, especially China, force regional market prices upwards (see Figure 6.9). Compared to the base case, the weighted world average market price for one ton of iron ore increases by USD 15.86 to USD 92.91 (+20.6%). China continues to hold the highest market price with USD 101.68 (USD +16.09, +18.8%), closely followed by Other Asia with USD 97.92 (USD +14.40, +17.2%). All other regions show similar price gains, mainly due to the non-arbitrage condition of the model.[597]

Of course, this price increase is reflected in the total iron ore procurement cost. Compared to the base case, iron ore production capacity constraints increase steelmakers' expenditures for iron ore by USD 27.1 billion to a total of USD 186.7 billion (+17.0%). However, regions utilizing large amounts of captive iron ore supply manage to limit the effect of the increased market prices on their procurement costs. Therefore, the procurement costs increases

---

[597]See Section 5.1.3.2.4.

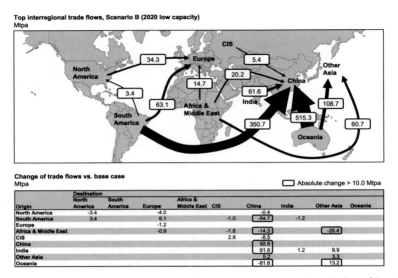

Figure 6.8: Scenario B: 2020 low capacity – Analysis of interregional trade flows [Own illustration]

of steelmakers in Oceania (+3.4%), North America (+13.1%), CIS (+13.9%) and China (+16.0%) are below the average 17.0% increase.

From a miner's point of view, the supply constraints modeled in this scenario are quite favorable. Increased market prices lead to an overall increase in profit contributions of iron ore miners of USD 22.7 billion to a total of USD 100.5 billion (+29.2% vs. the base case). Despite their loss in production volume vs. the base case, iron ore miners in South America (USD +8.4 billion), Oceania (USD +6.1 billion) and Africa & Middle East (USD +2.2 billion) show the largest absolute increases in profit contribution, mainly due to the sharp increase in the market price of their largest customers, China and Other Asia.

The detailed effects of the reduced production capacity on the iron ore miners' profit contributions are shown in Figure 6.10. Due to higher mining royalties (as they are based on market prices) as well as the above described substitution of low-cost capacity with increased production in regions with higher production costs per standardized ton, the overall standardized FOB cost increases by 5.5% to USD 69.0 billion. The combined cost for freight and export taxes also increases (+5.0%), although lower freight costs (owing to lower seaborne supply) are overcompensated by higher export taxes, as India now exports considerable volumes of ore to China and Other Asia compared to zero exports in the base case. Despite these higher cost positions, an increased total revenue of

Region	Market price USD/t			Average iron ore procurement cost USD/t			Total iron ore procurement cost USD billions			Total profit contribution of miners (by origin) USD billions		
	Scenario B	Change vs. base case		Scenario B	Change vs. base case		Scenario B	Change vs. base case		Scenario B	Change vs. base case	
		Abs.	Rel.		Abs.	Rel.		Abs.	Rel.		Abs.	Rel.
North America	80.60	16.09	24.9%	47.65	5.52	13.1%	5.7	0.7	13.1%	3.7	1.4	60.0%
South America	83.26	16.09	24.0%	61.17	10.75	21.3%	13.4	2.4	21.3%	34.6	8.4	32.1%
Europe	83.74	16.09	23.8%	65.66	11.03	20.2%	10.5	1.8	20.2%	4.0	1.1	37.0%
Africa & M. E.	87.81	16.09	22.4%	84.07	16.06	23.6%	10.8	2.1	23.6%	11.8	2.2	22.5%
CIS	92.49	19.53	26.8%	53.97	6.57	13.9%	11.9	1.5	13.9%	6.7	2.0	43.6%
China	101.68	16.09	18.8%	92.50	12.77	16.0%	105.2	14.5	16.0%	0.0	±0.0	±0.0%
India	63.95	10.54	19.7%	59.24	9.00	17.9%	10.5	1.6	17.9%	4.7	1.5	45.3%
Other Asia	97.92	14.40	17.2%	97.27	14.54	17.6%	18.1	2.7	17.6%	0.2	0.1	77.5%
Oceania	94.16	16.09	20.6%	51.67	1.68	3.4%	0.6	<0.1	3.4%	34.9	6.1	21.1%
World total	92.91	15.86	20.6%	79.10	11.50	17.0%	186.7	27.1	17.0%	100.5	22.7	29.2%

Figure 6.9: Scenario B: 2020 low capacity – Analysis of market prices, procurement cost and profit contribution of miners by region [Own illustration]

USD 186.7 billion (+17.0%), stemming from increased market prices, leads to a 29.2% rise in iron ore miners' combined profit contribution vs. the base case to USD 100.5 billion.

Analogical to the dynamics on the regional level, the largest three iron ore miners profit from higher market prices and overcompensate their loss in production volume with higher revenues per ton. Vale decreases its production by 4.8% to 415.6 Mt. The miner's total profit contribution, however, rises to USD 27.9 billion (+31.3% vs. the base case). Rio Tinto's production volume decreases to 226.6 Mt, down 8.5% compared to the base case. Nonetheless, its profit contribution increases by 20.2% to USD 15.8 billion. Also BHP Billiton shows a decrease in production by 5.1% to 178.8 Mt, but enjoys an increased profit contribution of USD 11.7 billion (+25.1%). Rio Tinto's comparatively larger decrease in profit contribution can be found in its higher share of mining projects, especially projects in an early development stage as of 2009. Thus, Rio Tinto is more exposed to the project risk modeled in this scenario than the other two major iron ore miners.

In terms of market share (based on profit contribution), the share of the Big Three decreases only slightly to 55.1% (−1.1 ppt vs. the base case). Vale stays in first place with 27.8% market share (+0.5 ppt), Rio Tinto's share drops to 15.7% (−1.2 ppt) and BHP Billiton claims 11.6% (−0.4 ppt).

Analysis of profit contribution (USD billions)

	Production Mtpa	Standardized FOB cost	Freight and export taxes	Profit contribution	Revenue
World total					186.7
		69.0	17.2	100.5	
Total	2,360.5				
Change vs. base case	±0.0%	5.5%	5.0%	29.2%	17.0%
Per ton (USD/t)		29.23	7.28	42.60	79.10
Change vs. base case		5.5%	5.0%	29.2%	17.0%
Vale					
Total	415.6	6.1	4.6	27.9	38.6
Change vs. base case	-4.8%	-19.4%	-11.5%	31.3%	13.5%
Per ton (USD/t)		14.67	11.09	67.16	92.92
Change vs. base case		-15.3%	-7.1%	37.9%	19.2%
Rio Tinto					
Total	226.6	5.0	1.7	15.8	22.4
Change vs. base case	-8.5%	-12.7%	-7.2%	20.2%	8.7%
Per ton (USD/t)		22.05	7.28	69.62	98.96
Change vs. base case		-4.7%	1.4%	31.3%	18.7%
BHP Billiton					
Total	178.8	4.9	1.6	11.7	18.1
Change vs. base case	-5.1%	-5.0%	-4.5%	25.1%	12.5%
Per ton (USD/t)		27.47	8.68	65.29	101.45
Change vs. base case		0.2%	0.6%	31.8%	18.5%

Figure 6.10: Scenario B: 2020 low capacity – Analysis of individual profit contributions of miners [Own illustration]

6.3.1.2.2   Scenario C: 2020 high capacity

As shown in Figure 6.11, the demand for iron ore in scenario C is identical to the demand in the base case. This is true for the total demand (2,360.5 Mt) as well as for the individual demand of the geographic regions. China thus continues to dominate demand with 1,136.8 Mt, followed by CIS (221.2 Mt) and South America (219.6 Mt).

Total world iron ore production in scenario C is equal to production in the base case (2,360.5 Mt). However, there are some regional shifts in production, caused by faster completion and/or higher capacity of expansion projects modeled in this scenario. This upscaling of projects and accelerated project completion leads to an increase in total production capacity vs. the base case by 5.0% or 138.9 Mt (see Figure II.2). Naturally, this additional capacity is mainly attributed to regions with many expansion projects, especially Oceania (+50.8 Mt), South America (+36.1 Mt) and Africa & Middle East (+30.5 Mt). Due to this increased capacity, Oceania and South America strengthen their lead in global production compared to the base case. Oceania remains the largest producer with now 731.7 Mt (+3.8% vs. the base case), followed by South America with 696.1 Mt (+1.0%). Africa & Middle East (281.4 Mt, +4.1%), CIS (212.1 Mt, −7.0%) and India (170.6 Mt, −0.5%) complete the top five. China's iron ore production decreases to 53.8 Mt (−31.7% compare to the base case).

This decrease in domestic production is compensated by an increase in Chinese net imports to 1,082.9 Mt (+25.0 Mt). China is followed in the net import ranking by Other Asia (183.3 Mt, +1.3 Mt) and Europe (109.8 Mt, −1.1 Mt). Fueled by additional production capacity, the main net exporters in this scenario are Oceania (719.4 Mt, +27.0 Mt), South America (476.5 Mt, +6.7 Mt) and Africa & Middle East (153.0 Mt, +11.2 Mt).

The above described additional production capacities in low-cost iron ore regions Oceania, South America and Africa & Middle East have substantial effects on the global iron ore trade flows (see Figure 6.12). The by-far largest flows continue to run to China from Oceania (618.3 Mt) and South America (413.9 Mt). Due to higher production capacities and the favorable cost position of mines in these regions, the flows from these regions even show increases of 21.4 Mt and 8.5 Mt respectively. Also due to higher capacity, the flow of iron ore from Africa & Middle East to China increases by 14.0 Mt to 48.4 Mt. On account of this increased flow of low-cost ore into the market, China no longer requires ore imports from CIS (−14.0 Mt) and reduces its higher cost domestic production by 25.0 Mt.

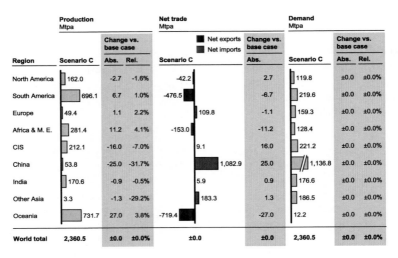

Region	Production Mtpa Scenario C	Change vs. base case Abs.	Change vs. base case Rel.	Net trade Mtpa Scenario C	Change vs. base case Abs.	Demand Mtpa Scenario C	Change vs. base case Abs.	Change vs. base case Rel.
North America	162.0	-2.7	-1.6%	-42.2	2.7	119.8	±0.0	±0.0%
South America	696.1	6.7	1.0%	-476.5	-6.7	219.6	±0.0	±0.0%
Europe	49.4	1.1	2.2%	109.8	-1.1	159.3	±0.0	±0.0%
Africa & M. E.	281.4	11.2	4.1%	-153.0	-11.2	128.4	±0.0	±0.0%
CIS	212.1	-16.0	-7.0%	9.1	16.0	221.2	±0.0	±0.0%
China	53.8	-25.0	-31.7%	1,082.9	25.0	1,136.8	±0.0	±0.0%
India	170.6	-0.9	-0.5%	5.9	0.9	176.6	±0.0	±0.0%
Other Asia	3.3	-1.3	-29.2%	183.3	1.3	186.5	±0.0	±0.0%
Oceania	731.7	27.0	3.8%	-719.4	-27.0	12.2	±0.0	±0.0%
World total	**2,360.5**	**±0.0**	**±0.0%**	**±0.0**	**±0.0**	**2,360.5**	**±0.0**	**±0.0%**

Figure 6.11: Scenario C: 2020 high capacity – Analysis of production, net trade and demand by region [Own illustration]

As can be expected, the increased production capacity in regions with high-quality and thus low-cost ore resources such as Oceania, South America and Africa & Middle East and the resulting decreased production in regions with higher costs, especially China and CIS, send regional market prices downwards (see Figure 6.13). Compared to the base case, the weighted world average market price for one ton of iron ore decreases by USD 15.16 to USD 61.89 (−19.7%). China continues to hold the highest market price with USD 68.42 (USD −17.17, −20.1%), closely followed by Other Asia with USD 64.66 (USD −18.86, −22.6%). All other regions, except for India, show price decreases of a similar magnitude.[598]

Naturally, this price decrease is reflected in the total iron ore procurement cost. Compared to the base case, additional iron ore production capacity reduces steelmakers' expenditures for iron ore by USD 26.5 billion to a total of USD 133.1 billion (−16.6%). Of course, relative cost reductions for regions using high shares of captive supply are lower than for regions that are more exposed to the open market. Therefore, the procurement cost decreases of

---

[598]The reason for India's below average price decrease can be found in its complete self-sufficiency (through domestic production and captive supply abroad) combined with high export taxes acting as an export ban (by pricing the mines out of the market). India therefore has a rather isolated position in the global iron ore market and does not profit from the additional global production capacity in this scenario.

Top interregional trade flows, Scenario C (2020 high capacity)
Mtpa

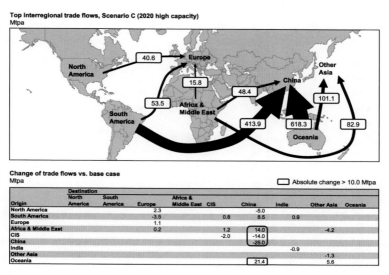

Change of trade flows vs. base case
Mtpa

Absolute change > 10.0 Mtpa

Origin	Destination North America	South America	Europe	Africa & Middle East	CIS	China	India	Other Asia	Oceania
North America			2.3			-5.0			
South America			-3.5		0.8	8.5	0.9		
Europe			1.1						
Africa & Middle East			0.2		1.2	14.0		-4.2	
CIS					-2.0	-14.0			
China						-25.0			
India							-0.9		
Other Asia								-1.3	
Oceania						21.4		5.6	

Figure 6.12: Scenario C: 2020 high capacity – Analysis of interregional trade flows [Own illustration]

steelmakers in Oceania (−3.6%), North America (−5.8%), CIS (−7.9%) and Europe (−12.1%) are below the average 16.6% decrease.[599]

From a miner's point of view, the additional supply modeled in this scenario is rather disadvantageous. Lower market prices lead to an overall decrease in profit contributions of iron ore miners of USD 27.9 billion to a total of USD 50.0 billion (−35.8%). Despite their increase in production volume vs. the base case, iron ore miners in South America (USD −10.2 billion), Oceania (USD −9.6 billion) and Africa & Middle East (USD −3.5 billion) show the largest absolute decreases in profit contribution, mainly due to the sharp decrease in the market price of their largest customers, China and Other Asia.

The detailed effects of the additional production capacity on the iron ore miners' profit contributions are shown in Figure 6.14. Despite the above described substitution of production in China and CIS with increased production in regions with lower production costs per standardized ton and lower mining royalties due to the lower market prices, the overall standardized FOB cost increases slightly by 1.8% to USD 66.5 billion. This effect can be traced back to lower grade

---

[599]Note that China, although it owns large volumes of captive capacity, does not fall into this category as it is not forced to utilize much of its captive capacity in this scenario (as in the base case).

Region	Market price USD/t			Average iron ore procurement cost USD/t			Total iron ore procurement cost USD billions			Total profit contribution of miners (by origin) USD billions		
	Scenario C	Change vs. base case		Scenario C	Change vs. base case		Scenario C	Change vs. base case		Scenario C	Change vs. base case	
		Abs.	Rel.		Abs.	Rel.		Abs.	Rel.		Abs.	Rel.
North America	52.77	-11.74	-18.2%	39.70	-2.43	-5.8%	4.8	-0.3	-5.8%	1.1	-1.2	-51.8%
South America	50.00	-17.17	-25.6%	40.48	-9.94	-19.7%	8.9	-2.2	-19.7%	16.0	-10.2	-38.9%
Europe	56.82	-10.83	-16.0%	48.03	-6.61	-12.1%	7.6	-1.1	-12.1%	2.0	-0.9	-30.6%
Africa & M. E.	54.75	-16.97	-23.7%	51.85	-16.16	-23.8%	6.7	-2.1	-23.8%	6.1	-3.5	-36.8%
CIS	58.71	-14.25	-19.5%	43.67	-3.73	-7.9%	9.7	-0.8	-7.9%	2.7	-1.9	-41.3%
China	68.42	-17.17	-20.1%	65.29	-14.44	-18.1%	74.2	-16.4	-18.1%	0.0	±0.0	±0.0%
India	51.69	-1.72	-3.2%	49.39	-0.85	-1.7%	8.7	-0.1	-1.7%	2.8	-0.5	-15.0%
Other Asia	64.66	-18.86	-22.6%	64.09	-18.64	-22.5%	12.0	-3.5	-22.5%	0.0	>-0.1	-50.5%
Oceania	60.90	-17.17	-22.0%	48.20	-1.79	-3.6%	0.6	>-0.1	-3.6%	19.2	-9.6	-33.4%
World total	61.89	-15.16	-19.7%	56.39	-11.22	-16.6%	133.1	-26.5	-16.6%	50.0	-27.9	-35.8%

Figure 6.13: Scenario C: 2020 high capacity – Analysis of market prices, procurement cost and profit contribution of miners by region [Own illustration]

and value-in-use premiums stemming from the decrease in market prices. The combined cost for freight and export taxes also increases, though insignificantly (+1.5%) due to higher freight costs owing to higher seaborne supply.[600] In addition to these higher cost positions, a decreased total revenue of USD 133.1 billion (−16.6%), stemming from lower market prices, leads to a 35.8% reduction of iron ore miners' combined profit contribution vs. the base case to USD 50.0 billion.

The three largest miners are equally hard hit. Vale's total profit contribution sinks to USD 13.6 billion (−36.2% vs. the base case), Rio Tinto retains a profit contribution of USD 9.1 billion (−30.4%) and BHP Billiton's profit contribution is reduced to USD 6.3 billion (−32.5%). The reason for Rio Tinto's comparatively low loss in total profit contribution can be found in its 5.6% increase in production volume vs. the base case. Therefore, Rio Tinto profits from having more capacity in expansion projects than the other two large players.

In terms of market share (based on profit contribution), the share of the Big Three increases to 58.1%. Vale stays in first place with 27.2% market share (−0.1 ppt vs. the base case), Rio Tinto's share rises to 18.3% (+1.4 ppt) and BHP Billiton claims 12.6% (+0.6 ppt).

---

[600] Note that, as in the base case, neither of the two regions levying export taxes, China and India, actually export iron ore in this scenario. Thus, the decrease in market prices has no effect on overall global export tax costs, which remain zero.

Analysis of profit contribution (USD billions)

	Production Mtpa	Standardized FOB cost	Freight and export taxes	Profit contribution	Revenue
World total					133.1
		66.5	16.6	50.0	
Total	2,360.5				
Change vs. base case	±0.0%	1.8%	1.5%	-35.8%	-16.6%
Per ton (USD/t)		28.19	7.04	21.16	56.39
Change vs. base case		1.8%	1.5%	-35.8%	-16.6%
Vale					
Total	430.4	7.8	5.1	13.6	26.5
Change vs. base case	-1.4%	3.5%	-2.6%	-36.2%	-22.2%
Per ton (USD/t)		18.19	11.79	31.52	61.50
Change vs. base case		5.0%	-1.3%	-35.3%	-21.1%
Rio Tinto					
Total	261.4	6.3	1.9	9.1	17.3
Change vs. base case	5.6%	9.5%	4.9%	-30.4%	-16.3%
Per ton (USD/t)		23.97	7.14	34.98	66.09
Change vs. base case		3.7%	-0.7%	-34.1%	-20.7%
BHP Billiton					
Total	194.1	5.3	1.7	6.3	13.3
Change vs. base case	3.0%	2.8%	2.8%	-32.5%	-17.7%
Per ton (USD/t)		27.37	8. 61	32.44	68.42
Change vs. base case		-0.2%	-0.2%	-34.5%	-20.1%

Figure 6.14: Scenario C: 2020 high capacity – Analysis of individual profit contributions of miners [Own illustration]

6.3.1.2.3   Scenario D: 2020 low demand

As shown in Figure 6.15, the worldwide demand for iron ore modeled in scenario D totals 2,050.8 Mt and is therefore 309.7 Mt lower than in the base case (−13.1%). While demand for iron ore decreases in all regions compared to the base case, the scale of decline differs from region to region. China accounts for the largest absolute drop in demand (−115.3 Mt, −10.1% vs. the base case), followed by South America (−50.7 Mt, −23.1%), Other Asia (−40.3 Mt, −21.6%), India (−34.1 Mt, −19.3%), Europe (−29.4 Mt, −18.4%) and North America (−23.4 Mt, −19.5%). Despite leading the demand decline ranking, China is still by far the largest consumer of iron ore (1,021.5 Mt).

Although production capacities in this scenario are identical to those in the base case, the above described global demand decline naturally leads to a drop in iron ore production of the same magnitude (−309.7 Mt, −13.1%). All regions reduce their supply of iron ore vs. the base case, though some are forced to stronger production cuts than others. As can be expected, export-oriented regions are among those with the largest absolute decline in production. The leading exporter in the base case, Oceania, is forced to reduce its output by 50.4 Mt to 654.2 Mt (−7.2% vs. the base case). South America's production even drops by 87.8 Mt (−12.7%) to 601.6 Mt. Nevertheless, these two regions remain the by far largest suppliers of iron ore. Africa & Middle East, also a major exporter in the base case, reduces its iron ore output to 245.2 Mt (−25.1 Mt, −9.3%). Although a strong importer of iron ore in the base case, China's immense decline in demand forces it to reduce its domestic output by 51.0 Mt (−64.6%) to a mere 27.9 Mt. Also India (−31.2 Mt, −18.2%), CIS (−30.7 Mt, −13.4%) and North America (−29.0 Mt, −17.6%) are among those regions with the largest absolute drop in production volume.

In terms of net trade, China, though with reduced imports of 64.3 Mt compared to the base case, remains the largest importer of iron ore (993.6 Mt). China is followed in the net import ranking by Other Asia (143.0 Mt, −38.9 Mt) and Europe (84.7 Mt, −26.2 Mt). Despite their reduction in iron ore output, the top three exporting regions in the base case maintain their relative positions. Oceania leads net exports with 643.2 Mt (−49.3 Mt), followed by South America (432.7 Mt, −37.1 Mt) and Africa & Middle East (128.3 Mt, −13.6 Mt).

The above described global demand erosion has substantial effects on the global iron ore trade flows (see Figure 6.16). In general, it can be observed that all regions reduce their intraregional supply (i.e. supply from local mines to local consumers). In addition, as described above, major importing regions China, Other Asia and Europe considerably reduce their imports as a result of their demand decline. However, China's imports still account for the by far largest

Region	Production Mtpa			Net trade Mtpa		Demand Mtpa		
	Scenario D	Change vs. base case Abs.	Rel.	Scenario D	Change vs. base case Abs.	Scenario D	Change vs. base case Abs.	Rel.
North America	135.7	-29.0	-17.6%	-39.3	5.6	96.4	-23.4	-19.5%
South America	601.6	-87.8	-12.7%	-432.7	37.1	169.0	-50.7	-23.1%
Europe	45.2	-3.2	-6.6%	84.7	-26.2	129.9	-29.4	-18.4%
Africa & M. E.	245.2	-25.1	-9.3%	-128.3	13.6	116.9	-11.6	-9.0%
CIS	197.4	-30.7	-13.4%	20.0	26.8	217.4	-3.9	-1.7%
China	27.9	-51.0	-64.6%	993.6	-64.3	1,021.5	-115.3	-10.1%
India	140.4	-31.2	-18.2%	2.1	-2.9	142.4	-34.1	-19.3%
Other Asia	3.3	-1.3	-29.2%	143.0	-38.9	146.2	-40.3	-21.6%
Oceania	654.2	-50.4	-7.2%	-643.2	49.3	11.1	-1.2	-9.6%
World total	2,050.8	-309.7	-13.1%	±0.0	±0.0	2,050.8	-309.7	-13.1%

(Net trade legend: ■ Net exports, ■ Net imports)

Figure 6.15: Scenario D: 2020 low demand – Analysis of production, net trade and demand by region [Own illustration]

trade flows, originating in Oceania (573.0 Mt) and South America (383.9 Mt). The flows from these regions show decreases of 23.9 Mt and 21.5 Mt vs. the base case respectively. Other Asia reduces its imports from Oceania by 25.4 Mt to 70.2 Mt and its imports from Africa & Middle East by 13.6 Mt to 73.5 Mt. European imports from South America are considerably reduced by 25.5 Mt to 31.4 Mt.

As can be expected, the significant demand reduction vs. the base case leads to lower market prices (see Figure 6.17). Compared to the base case, the weighted world average market price for one ton of iron ore decreases by USD 20.13 to USD 56.92 (−26.1%). China continues to show the highest market price with USD 63.23 (USD −22.36, −26.1%), followed by Other Asia with a market price of USD 59.47 (USD −24.05, −28.8%). All other regions show similar price decreases. However, it is noticeable that the largest exporting countries are among those with the highest relative market price decreases. The price in Africa & Middle East drops by 31.1% to USD 49.43, the South American price weakens by 33.3% to USD 44.81 and Oceanian consumers now pay USD 55.71 per ton of iron ore, 28.6% less than in the base case. The reason for this can be found in the fact that, as described above, the reduced demand from abroad drives down exports. In consequence, capacity utilization in exporting countries sinks and capacity is freed at low-cost mines for the satisfaction of domestic demand.

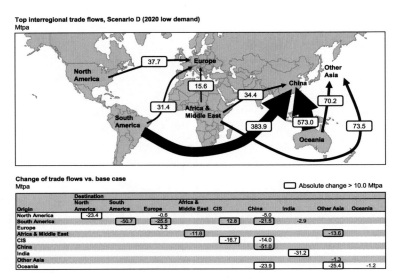

Figure 6.16: Scenario D: 2020 low demand – Analysis of interregional trade flows [Own illustration]

Consistently, this global market price decrease is reflected in the total iron ore procurement cost. Compared to the base case, the decline in demand reduces steelmakers' expenditures for iron ore by USD 52.1 billion to a total of USD 107.5 billion (−32.6%). Of course, due to lower market prices, procurement costs are also lower on a per ton level. On average, iron ore consumers pay USD 52.42 per ton of ore, USD 15.19 less than in the base case (−22.5%). It is to be mentioned that, as in scenario C, relative cost reductions for regions using high shares of captive supply are lower than for regions that are more exposed to the open market. Therefore, the procurement costs decreases of steelmakers in Oceania (−9.1%), CIS (−10.4%), North America (−11.7%) and Europe (−16.5%) are below the average 22.5% decrease.[601]

Naturally, from a miner's point of view, the demand decline modeled in this scenario is rather disadvantageous. Lower market prices lead to an overall decrease in profit contributions of iron ore miners of USD 39.6 billion to a total of USD 38.2 billion (−50.9%). Due to having the largest production volume decrease vs. the base case, iron ore miners in Oceania (USD −13.7 billion), South

---

[601]Note that China, although it owns large volumes of captive capacity, does not fall into this category as it is not forced to utilize much of its captive capacity in this scenario (as in the base case).

America (USD −13.5 billion) and Africa & Middle East (USD −4.9 billion) are hardest hit in absolute terms.

Region	Market price USD/t Scenario D	Change vs. base case Abs.	Rel.	Average iron ore procurement cost USD/t Scenario D	Change vs. base case Abs.	Rel.	Total iron ore procurement cost USD billions Scenario D	Change vs. base case Abs.	Rel.	Total profit contribution of miners (by origin) USD billions Scenario D	Change vs. base case Abs.	Rel.
North America	50.51	-14.00	-21.7%	37.20	-4.93	-11.7%	3.6	-1.5	-28.9%	0.9	-1.4	-62.8%
South America	44.81	-22.36	-33.3%	36.04	-14.37	-28.5%	6.1	-5.0	-45.0%	12.7	-13.5	-51.6%
Europe	54.14	-13.51	-20.0%	45.62	-9.01	-16.5%	5.9	-2.8	-31.9%	1.8	-1.1	-39.0%
Africa & M. E.	49.43	-22.29	-31.1%	47.44	-20.57	-30.2%	5.5	-3.2	-36.5%	4.7	-4.9	-51.1%
CIS	55.02	-17.94	-24.6%	42.44	-4.95	-10.4%	9.2	-1.3	-12.0%	2.1	-2.6	-55.5%
China	63.23	-22.36	-26.1%	61.17	-18.56	-23.3%	62.5	-28.2	-31.1%	0.0	±0.0	±0.0%
India	39.36	-14.05	-26.3%	38.73	-11.50	-22.9%	5.5	-3.4	-37.8%	0.9	-2.3	-71.6%
Other Asia	59.47	-24.05	-28.8%	59.01	-23.73	-28.7%	8.6	-6.8	-44.1%	<0.1	-0.1	-63.7%
Oceania	55.71	-22.36	-28.6%	45.42	-4.57	-9.1%	0.5	-0.1	-17.9%	15.2	-13.7	-47.4%
World total	**56.92**	**-20.13**	**-26.1%**	**52.42**	**-15.19**	**-22.5%**	**107.5**	**-52.1**	**-32.6%**	**38.2**	**-39.6**	**-50.9%**

Figure 6.17: Scenario D: 2020 low demand – Analysis of market prices, procurement cost and profit contribution of miners by region [Own illustration]

The detailed effects of the demand drop on the iron ore miners' profit contributions are shown in Figure 6.18. Fueled by the global production decrease, the overall standardized FOB cost shrinks by 16.9% to USD 54.3 billion. However, the standardized FOB cost also declines on a per ton basis (−4.3%), mainly due to lower mining royalties owing to lower market prices. Naturally, the combined cost for freight and export taxes also decreases in absolute terms, down 8.7% vs. the base case to USD 14.9 billion. However, per ton of ore sold, freight and export tax costs increase by 5.1%. This is because of higher average freight costs per ton stemming from the relative increase of seaborne vs. intraregional and domestic supply.[602] The decrease in total revenue vs. the base case, −32.6% to USD 107.5 billion, leaves miners with a total profit contribution of USD 38.2 billion (−50.9%). Similarly on a per ton basis, average revenue sinks to USD 52.42 per ton (−22.5%), putting the average profit contribution at USD 18.64 per ton (−43.5%).

The three largest miners are equally hard hit. Vale's total profit contribution sinks to USD 11.0 billion (−48.1% vs. the base case), Rio Tinto retains a profit contribution of USD 7.5 billion (−42.9%) and BHP Billiton's profit contribution

---

[602]Note that, as in the base case, neither of the two regions levying export taxes, China and India, actually export iron ore in this scenario. Thus, the decrease in market prices has no effect on overall global export tax costs, which remain zero.

is reduced to USD 5.1 billion (−45.0%). The reason for Vale's comparatively more severe loss in total profit contribution can be found in its 4.1% decrease in production volume vs. the base case. In comparison, Rio Tinto is forced to reduce production by only 0.6% vs. the base case and BHP Billiton even manages to keep production at the base case level. This difference in output reduction stems from the strong demand reduction in Vale's home region South America and the relative cost disadvantage of Vale's mines vs. those of the other two players with respect to supply to China.[603] Therefore, in times of lower demand, Rio Tinto and BHP Billiton profit from the geographic proximity of their mines to the number one consumer.

In terms of market share (based on profit contribution), the share of the Big Three increases by 5.7 percentage points compared to the base case to 61.8% in this scenario. Vale stays in first place with an increased share of 28.8% (+1.5 ppt vs. the base case), Rio Tinto's market share leaps to 19.6% (+2.7 ppt) and BHP Billiton claims 13.4% of the overall profit contribution (+1.5 ppt). This increased dominance of the three largest players is based on the overall advantageous cost position of their mines in the global cost curve compared to the mines of the other players. Thus, in times of low demand, the Big Three show below average production volume decreases.

---

[603]Recall that Vale's production capacity is located almost entirely in South America while Rio Tinto's and BHP Billiton's mines are situated in Oceania.

Analysis of profit contribution (USD billions)

	Production Mtpa	Standardized FOB cost	Freight and export taxes	Profit contribution	Revenue
World total					107.5
		54.3	14.9	38.2	
Total	2.050.8				
Change vs. base case	-13.1%	-16.9%	-8.7%	-50.9%	-32.6%
Per ton (USD/t)		26.50	7.28	18.64	52.42
Change vs. base case		-4.3%	5.1%	-43.5%	-22.5%
Vale					
Total	418.4	7.7	5.7	11.0	24.5
Change vs. base case	-4.1%	1.9%	10.1%	-48.1%	-28.1%
Per ton (USD/t)		18.41	13.71	26.35	58.47
Change vs. base case		6.3%	14.8%	-45.9%	-25.0%
Rio Tinto					
Total	246.1	5.8	1.7	7.5	15.1
Change vs. base case	-0.6%	2.1%	-3.3%	-42.9%	-27.0%
Per ton (USD/t)		23.76	6.99	30.44	61.19
Change vs. base case		2.7%	-2.8%	-42.6%	-26.6%
BHP Billiton					
Total	188.5	5.2	1.6	5.1	11.9
Change vs. base case	±0.0%	-0.3%	±0.0%	-45.0%	-26.1%
Per ton (USD/t)		27.34	8.63	27.26	63.23
Change vs. base case		-0.3%	±0.0%	-45.0%	-26.1%

Figure 6.18: Scenario D: 2020 low demand – Analysis of individual profit contributions of miners [Own illustration]

6.3.1.2.4   Scenario E: 2020 high demand

As shown in Figure 6.19, the worldwide demand for iron ore modeled in scenario E totals 2,704.0 Mt and is therefore 343.5 Mt higher than in the base case (+14.6%). While demand for iron ore increases in all regions compared to the base case, the scale of increase differs from region to region. China accounts for the largest absolute rise in demand (+106.3 Mt, +9.4% vs. the base case), followed by India (+100.6 Mt, +57.0%) and Other Asia (+40.0 Mt, +21.4%). Taking into account these increases, China is still by far the largest consumer of iron ore (1,243.1 Mt) while India moves up to second place with 277.1 Mt.

Although production capacities in this scenario are identical to those in the base case, the above described global demand increase naturally leads to a rise in iron ore production of the same magnitude (+343.5 Mt, +14.6%). In order to satisfy this vast demand, all regions except for China produce at their maximum annual capacity.[604] The regions with the largest absolute production volume increases are China (+214.6 Mt, +272.2%) and India (+105.6 Mt, +61.5%). Oceania and South America, though already almost at their maximum capacity in the base case and thus not able to significantly further increase supply, continue to lead global production with 712.1 Mt and 693.9 Mt respectively.

In terms of net trade, China, though with reduced imports of 108.3 Mt compared to the base case, remains the largest importer of iron ore (949.6 Mt). China is followed in the net import ranking by Other Asia (212.5 Mt, +30.5 Mt) and Europe (137.9 Mt, +27.0 Mt). The top three exporting regions in the base case maintain their relative positions. Oceania leads net exports with 697.9 Mt (+5.5 Mt), followed by South America (449.1 Mt, −20.7 Mt) and Africa & Middle East (128.5 Mt, −13.3 Mt).

The above described vast global demand increase has substantial effects on the global iron ore trade flows (see Figure 6.20). As mentioned above, all regions except China produce at their maximum capacity. In general, in accordance with the total cost minimization objective of the allocation mechanism as defined in Section 5.1.3.1, the following trade flow dynamic can be observed: First, all regions (except for China due to its unfavorably high-cost ore) use their domestic production to satisfy as much of their own demand as possible. Then, any excess volume is exported to the geographically closest regions with unsatisfied demand (in order to minimize freight costs). Thus, with production capacities at a threshold, geographic proximity becomes the key factor for deciding who

---

[604]China is the only region not producing at full capacity due to the unfavorable cost position of its mines in the global cost curve. It is to be noted that although Other Asia still has 1.0 Mt of idle capacity left, this capacity is captive to an Indian steelmaker and thus not freely accessible.

Region	Production Mtpa Scenario E	Change vs. base case Abs.	Change vs. base case Rel.	Net trade Mtpa Scenario E	Change vs. base case Abs.	Demand Mtpa Scenario E	Change vs. base case Abs.	Change vs. base case Rel.
North America	164.7	±0.0	±0.0%	-20.3	24.6	144.4	24.6	20.5%
South America	693.9	4.5	0.6%	-449.1	20.7	244.8	25.2	11.5%
Europe	49.3	1.0	2.0%	137.9	27.0	187.3	28.0	17.6%
Africa & M. E.	270.3	±0.0	±0.0%	-128.5	13.3	141.8	13.3	10.4%
CIS	229.1	1.0	0.4%	-4.3	2.6	224.8	3.6	1.6%
China	293.4	214.6	272.2%	949.6	-108.3	1,243.1	106.3	9.4%
India	277.1	105.6	61.5%	0.0	-5.0	277.1	100.6	57.0%
Other Asia	14.0	9.4	205.5%	212.5	30.5	226.5	40.0	21.4%
Oceania	712.1	7.5	1.1%	-697.9	-5.5	14.2	2.0	16.1%
World total	2,704.0	343.5	14.6%	±0.0	±0.0	2,704.0	343.5	14.6%

Figure 6.19: Scenario E: 2020 high demand – Analysis of production, net trade and demand by region [Own illustration]

supplies to whom. South America, in addition to its slight increase in production, reduces its exports to China (−73.8 Mt) in order to satisfy its own demand increase (+25.2 Mt) and to send additional supply to geographically closer regions North America (+23.9 Mt) and Europe (+27.7 Mt). Africa & Middle East reduces its exports to Other Asia (+13.3 Mt) in order to satisfy its increased domestic demand (+13.3 Mt). Following the same scheme, Oceania, in addition to its production increase, reduces its supply to China (−44.2 Mt) in oder to satisfy its own demand increase (+2.0 Mt) and to send additional supply to Other Asia (+49.7 Mt) for which it is the nearest possible supplier. Therefore, in addition to its increased demand, China is forced to compensate lacking supply from South America and Oceania (−73.8 Mt and −44.2 Mt respectively) by means of an increase in domestic production (+214.6 Mt).

As can be expected, the immense demand increase vs. the base case leads to significantly higher market prices (see Figure 6.21). Compared to the base case, the weighted world average market price for one ton of iron ore more than doubles to USD 155.69 (USD +78.64, +102.1%). The reason for this dramatic price increase lies in the fact that the global capacity constraints modeled in this scenario force China to utilize significant amounts of ore from its lower quality domestic mines, rather than being able to rely on additional imported low-cost ore. China, as the price-setting region, has the highest market price with USD 168.38 (USD +82.79, +96.7%), closely followed by Other Asia with

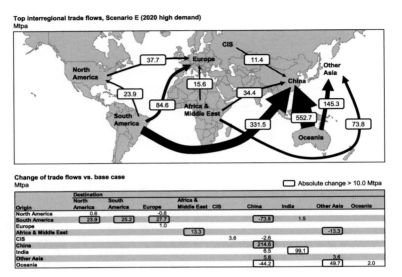

Figure 6.20: Scenario E: 2020 high demand – Analysis of interregional trade flows [Own illustration]

USD 164.62 (USD +81.10, +97.1%). Due to the non-arbitrage condition,[605] all other regions (except for India) show price increases of a similar magnitude. India's considerably lower absolute price increase (USD +51.30) has two reasons: Its complete self-sufficiency (through low-cost domestic production and captive supply abroad) and the its high export taxes shielding it from increased prices caused by the non-arbitrage condition (see Section 5.1.3.2.4).

Consistently, this global market price increase is reflected in the total iron ore procurement cost. Compared to the base case, the jump in demand increases steelmakers' expenditures for iron ore by USD 166.6 billion to a total of USD 326.1 billion (+104.4%). Of course, due to higher market prices, procurement costs are also higher on a per ton level. On average, iron ore consumers pay USD 120.62 per ton of ore, USD 53.01 more than in the base case (+78.4%). It is to be mentioned that, as in scenario B, relative cost increases for regions using high shares of captive supply are lower than for regions that are more exposed to the open market. Therefore, the rise in procurement costs for steelmakers in Oceania (+45.7%), CIS (+51.2%) and China (+70.1%) are below the average 78.4% increase.

---

[605]See Section 5.1.3.2.4.

Naturally, from a miner's point of view, the demand boom modeled in this scenario is extremely advantageous. Higher market prices more than triple iron ore miners' profit contributions to a total of USD 237.4 billion (USD +159.6 billion, +205.0%). Despite their only slight increase in production volume vs. the base case, iron ore miners in South America (USD +52.9 billion), Oceania (USD +50.7 billion) and Africa & Middle East (USD +18.6 billion) show the largest absolute increases in profit contribution, mainly due to their large export volume and the sharp rise in the market prices of their largest customers, China and Other Asia.

Region	Market price USD/t Scenario E	Change vs. base case Abs.	Rel.	Average iron ore procurement cost USD/t Scenario E	Change vs. base case Abs.	Rel.	Total iron ore procurement cost USD billions Scenario E	Change vs. base case Abs.	Rel.	Total profit contribution of miners (by origin) USD billions Scenario E	Change vs. base case Abs.	Rel.
North America	147.30	82.79	128.3%	81.58	39.45	93.6%	11.8	6.7	133.4%	9.9	7.6	330.8%
South America	149.96	82.79	123.3%	101.57	51.16	101.5%	24.9	13.8	124.6%	79.1	52.9	201.7%
Europe	150.44	82.79	122.4%	110.66	56.03	102.5%	20.7	12.0	138.1%	8.7	5.8	199.3%
Africa & M. E.	154.51	82.79	115.4%	144.75	76.74	112.8%	20.5	11.8	135.0%	28.2	18.6	193.0%
CIS	155.75	82.79	113.5%	71.64	24.25	51.2%	16.1	5.6	53.6%	16.1	11.4	244.7%
China	168.38	82.79	96.7%	135.65	55.92	70.1%	168.6	78.0	86.1%	0.0	±0.0	±0.0%
India	104.71	51.30	96.0%	92.42	42.19	84.0%	25.6	16.7	188.8%	15.5	12.2	375.9%
Other Asia	164.62	81.10	97.1%	162.80	80.07	96.8%	36.9	21.4	139.0%	0.6	0.5	576.9%
Oceania	160.86	82.79	106.0%	72.85	22.86	45.7%	1.0	0.4	69.3%	79.5	50.7	175.7%
World total	155.69	78.64	102.1%	120.62	53.01	78.4%	326.1	166.6	104.4%	237.4	159.6	205.0%

Figure 6.21: Scenario E: 2020 high demand – Analysis of market prices, procurement cost and profit contribution of miners by region [Own illustration]

The detailed effects of the demand increase on the iron ore miners' profit contributions are shown in Figure 6.22. Fueled by the global production increase, the overall standardized FOB cost rises by 11.5% to USD 72.9 billion. However, despite higher mining royalties owing to higher market prices, the standardized FOB cost declines on a per ton basis (−2.7%). This effect can be traced back to higher grade and value-in-use premiums stemming from the increase in market prices. Regardless of the increase in production volume, the combined cost for freight and export taxes decreases in absolute terms, down 3.2% vs. the base case to USD 15.8 billion. The larger relative decrease in freight and export tax costs on a per ton basis (−15.5%) is due to the fact that slightly higher export taxes (as India now exports ore to China compared to zero exports in the base case) are overcompensated by an immense decrease in average freight costs per ton, stemming from the relative decrease of seaborne vs. intraregional and domestic supply (especially in China). The rise in market prices and thus in total revenue vs. the base case, +104.4% to USD 326.1 billion, leaves miners with a total profit contribution of USD 237.4 billion (+205.0%). Similarly on a per ton basis, average revenue rises to USD 120.62 per ton (+78.4%), putting the average profit contribution at USD 87.81 per ton (+166.3%).

The three largest miners equally profit from this market situation. Vale's total profit contribution rises to USD 61.0 billion (+187.1% vs. the base case), Rio Tinto generates a profit contribution of USD 34.2 billion (+160.7%) and BHP Billiton's profit contribution reaches USD 24.7 billion (+165.1%). The reason for Vale's comparatively higher gain in total profit contribution can be found in its larger reduction in standardized FOB costs as well as in freight and export taxes vs. its main competitors. The former is due to the higher average Fe content of Vale's ores (65.5% vs. Rio Tinto's 62.5% and BHP Billiton's 60.9%) as well as its higher share of pellet production (10.3% of total production vs. 3.3% for Rio Tinto and 4.8% for BHP Billiton). Thanks to these differences in its resource base and production portfolio, Vale profits from higher price-based premiums than its main competitors. Vale's larger reduction in freight and export tax costs result from the geographic concentration of its production in South America (compared to Rio Tinto's and BHP Billiton's focus in Oceania). As described above, overall trade flows from South America to China are reduced in this scenario in favor of satisfaction of domestic demand and additional supply to geographically closer regions North America and Europe. The same dynamic is valid for Vale's trade flows, thus resulting in considerably lower freight costs per ton (−17.0%).

In terms of market share (based on profit contribution), the share of the Big Three decreases by 5.6 percentage points in this scenario compared to the base case. Vale stays in first place with a reduced share of 25.7% (−1.6 ppt vs. the base case), Rio Tinto's market share drops to 14.4% (−2.4 ppt) and BHP Billiton claims 10.4% of the overall profit contribution (−1.6 ppt). The reason for this decreased dominance of the Big Three in this scenario lies in the fact that all three players already produced at their maximum capacity in the base case (due to the favorable positions of their mines in the global industry cost curve). Thus, although they reach above average profit contribution gains on a per ton level, they are not able to profit as much from the increased market demand as the other iron ore miners are.

	Production Mtpa	Analysis of profit contribution (USD billions)			
		Standardized FOB cost	Freight and export taxes	Profit contribution	Revenue
World total					326.1
		72.9	15.8	237.4	
Total	2,704.0				
Change vs. base case	14.6%	11.5%	-3.2%	205.0%	104.4%
Per ton (USD/t)		26.95	5.86	87.81	120.62
Change vs. base case		-2.7%	-15.5%	166.3%	78.4%
Vale					
Total	436.4	3.3	4.3	61.0	68.7
Change vs. base case	±0.0%	-55.7%	-17.0%	187.1%	101.9%
Per ton (USD/t)		7.67	9.91	139.81	157.39
Change vs. base case		-55.7%	-17.0%	187.1%	101.9%
Rio Tinto					
Total	247.5	5.0	1.8	34.2	41.0
Change vs. base case	±0.0%	-13.0%	-0.8%	160.7%	98.6%
Per ton (USD/t)		20.12	7.13	138.28	165.54
Change vs. base case		-13.0%	-0.8%	160.7%	98.6%
BHP Billiton					
Total	188.5	5.2	1.6	24.7	31.6
Change vs. base case	±0.0%	1.2%	0.5%	165.1%	96.0%
Per ton (USD/t)		27.76	8.68	131.31	167.75
Change vs. base case		1.2%	0.5%	165.1%	96.0%

Figure 6.22: Scenario E: 2020 high demand – Analysis of individual profit contributions of miners [Own illustration]

6.3.1.2.5   Summary of 2020 market economics of supply and de-mand

In this section, in order to better quantify the impact of variations of the available production capacity and demand on the economics of the iron ore market, the outcomes of scenarios B through E are jointly compared to the results of the base case (scenario A).[606]

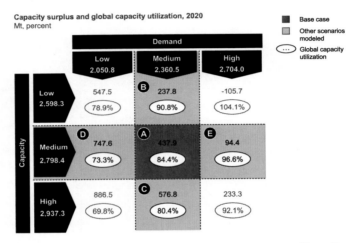

Figure 6.23: 2020 global capacity surplus and utilization per scenario [Own illustration]

As these five scenarios each differ in terms of the modeled production capacity and demand in the market, each scenario portrays a very specific market setting. In order to be able to compare these scenarios in a reasonable manner, it is important to realize that, as shown in Figure 6.23, the specific changes in the capacity and demand parameters of these scenarios inevitably lead to changes in global production capacity utilization.[607] This utilization can be seen as an indicator for the tightness of the global iron ore market. In other words, the higher the overall capacity utilization, the lower the amount of idle production capacity and, hence, the tighter the market. Thus, in the following, independent of whether the value of the capacity or demand parameter deviates from the respective base case value, the scenarios are arranged in ascending order according to their modeled global capacity utilization:

1. *Scenario D: 2020 low demand* – Global capacity utilization: 73.3%

---

[606]The respective 2009 model results are given for comparison only and are not described.

[607]Note that Figure 6.23, in addition to the five modeled scenarios A through E, also indicates four parameter value combinations that are not within the scope of this paper.

2. *Scenario C: 2020 high capacity* – Global capacity utilization: 80.4%

3. *Scenario A: 2020 base case* – Global capacity utilization: 84.4%

4. *Scenario B: 2020 low capacity* – Global capacity utilization: 90.8%

5. *Scenario E: 2020 high demand* – Global capacity utilization: 96.6%

First of all, the effect of the level of global capacity utilization on the iron ore trade flows is analyzed. However, as shown in the detailed results of the scenarios, these trade flows are too complex as to allow a detailed comparison of five scenario results. Therefore, the iron ore trade flows directed at China, the nucleus of world demand, are taken as a proxy for the key characteristics of the global trade flows. Figure 6.24 shows the split of supply to China by region of origin for each of the five scenarios.

Notably, China's share of domestic supply increases as the market becomes tighter. At the same time, imports from key suppliers Oceania and especially South America recede with increasing global capacity utilization. In scenario D (73.3% global capacity utilization), China satisfies only 2.7% of its iron ore demand through domestic supply, while importing 93.7% of its demand from Oceania and South America. In the scenario representing an extremely tight market (scenario E, 96.6% global capacity utilization), China's domestic production is increased to supply 23.6% of its required ore, while the share of the two largest external suppliers is reduced to 71.2%. The same effect can be seen in terms of China's utilization of its domestic production capacity. In scenario D, only 7.2% of China's available capacity is in operation, while scenario E shows a 75.9% utilization of China's capacity.

From this, it can be deduced that, the tighter the market is, the higher the domestic capacity utilization becomes in all regions. This is valid also and especially for those regions with low-quality and thus high-cost domestic ore resources. With increasing market tightness, the share of imports to these regions decreases and they are forced to increase utilization of their domestic capacity.

With respect to regional iron ore market prices, the effect of the level of global capacity utilization is displayed in Figure 6.25. For each scenario, sorted in ascending order according to the overall capacity utilization, the values for the maximum and minimum market prices are shown together with the weighted average price, while the other seven regional prices are depicted only as markers for reasons of clarity.

As can be expected, the tighter the market becomes, the higher the price level moves. The world average price per ton increases from USD 56.92 in scenario

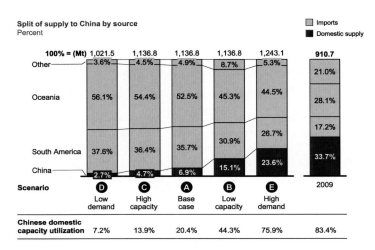

Figure 6.24: Scenarios A–E – Split of supply to China by source [Own illustration]

D to USD 154.51 in scenario E. Similarly, the values for the maximum and minimum market prices increase from USD 59.47 and USD 39.36 in scenario D to USD 168.38 and USD 104.71 in scenario E respectively. Interestingly, while prices show a more or less proportionate increase for global capacity utilizations between 73.3% (scenario D) and 90.8% (scenario B), prices rise disproportionately when the market becomes even tighter: The weighted average market price increases by 64.1% when global capacity utilization increases from 90.8% to 96.6%. This is due to the fact that the increased global capacity utilization forces China to put disproportionately expensive domestic mines into operation, thus considerably increasing the Chinese market price and with it, due to the non-arbitrage condition of the model,[608] the remaining market prices. For example, the European market price increases from USD 54.14 in scenario D to USD 150.44 in scenario E (+177.9%).

The absolute span between the maximum and the minimum market price changes considerably as the global capacity utilization increases. As indicated by the shades in Figure 6.25, this is due to the fact that the minimum market price (India) does not react as sensitively to changes in the level of global capacity utilization as the prices in the remaining markets do. This is because of India's complete self-sufficiency (through low-cost domestic production and captive supply abroad) and, more importantly, its high export taxes shielding it from a price increase caused by the non-arbitrage condition. The span be-

---

[608]See Section 5.1.3.2.4.

tween the maximum and the second lowest market price, however, is more or less constant at approximately USD 20.00 in all scenarios.

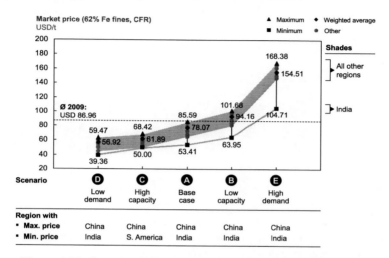

Figure 6.25: Scenarios A–E – Market prices by region [Own illustration]

Figure 6.26 aims to evaluate the effect of global capacity utilization on the overall iron ore procurement cost of the world's steelmakers. Apart from showing the absolute value of these costs per scenario, the figure splits the procurement costs into their three main constituents: standardized FOB costs, freight and export tax costs as well as miners' profit contributions.

Not surprisingly, overall iron ore procurement costs increase significantly as the market become tighter. While steelmakers pay a total of USD 107.5 billion in scenario D, their procurement costs increase to USD 326.1 billion in scenario E (+203.3%). On a regional level, for example, the joint iron ore procurement cost of European steelmakers increases from USD 5.9 billion in scenario D to USD 20.7 billion in scenario E (+250.8%). In line with the above described dynamics of the market prices, these costs show only a proportionate increase for global capacity utilizations between 73.3% (scenario D) and 90.8% (scenario B). When global capacity utilization increases from 90.8% to 96.6% however (scenario E), the steelmakers' iron ore procurement costs increase disproportionately by 74.7%. Interestingly, the overall increase in iron ore procurement cost as the market tightens is driven almost entirely by increases in the iron ore miners' profit contribution. Overall standardized FOB costs as well as freight and export tax costs, though fluctuating due to different demand levels per scenario, show only slight changes from one scenario to another.

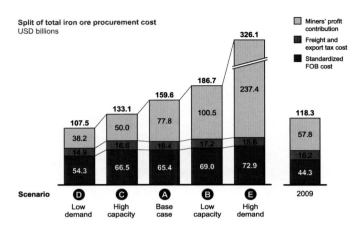

Figure 6.26: Scenarios A–E – Split of total iron ore procurement cost [Own illustration]

The impact of the global capacity utilization level on the iron ore miners' profit contribution is displayed in Figure 6.27. The overall industry profit contribution is split by player, showing the individual values for each of the Big Three and the remaining amount titled "Others". Also, the figure shows the corresponding market shares based on profit contribution for each of these players per scenario.

As mentioned above, the overall iron ore miners' profit contribution increases with rising global capacity utilization.[609] In scenario D, miners jointly pocket USD 38.2 billion in profit contribution, while this amount rises to USD 237.4 billion in scenario E. As with the above described market prices and iron ore procurement costs, miners' profit contributions show a disproportionately higher increase as the global capacity utilization rises from 90.8% (scenario B) to 96.6% (scenario E). This 5.8% increase in utilization boosts iron ore miners' joint profit contribution by 135.8%. This dynamic is mirrored on an individual player level. The individual profit contributions of the Big Three also show a positive correlation with global capacity utilization. Vale's profit increases from USD 11.0 billion in scenario D to USD 61.0 billion in scenario E. Similarly, Rio Tinto and BHP Billiton increase their profit contributions from USD 7.5 billion and USD 5.1 billion to USD 34.2 billion and USD 24.7 billion respectively.

---

[609]Note that, global capacity utilization increases with increasing demand and with decreasing supply. Therefore, a positive correlation between miners' profit contributions and global capacity utilization means that profit contributions are negatively correlated with supply and positively correlated with demand.

However, the profit contributions of the Big Three react less sensitive to changes in global capacity utilization than the profit contributions of the other miners do. This can be seen in terms of the changes of the individual market shares. The overall market dominance of the three largest iron ore producers decreases with rising global capacity utilization (and vice versa). The Big Three reach a joint market share of 61.9% in scenario D, but only 50.5% in scenario E. The reason for this lower sensitivity of the Big Three with respect to changes in the global capacity utilization is twofold: From a demand perspective, the Big Three profit from the favorable positions of their mines in the global industry cost curve. Due to this, all members of the Big Three already produce at or near maximum capacity in scenario D, where global capacity utilization is only 73.3%. Thus, although they profit from rising market prices when global demand increases, they are not able to increase their production volumes as many of the other iron ore miners are. Also, in terms of changes in global capacity utilization triggered by changes in supply (scenarios C, A and B), the Big Three show an decreased sensitivity. Although they profit from rising market prices when global supply decreases, the joint supply volume of the three largest iron ore miners decreases disproportionately due to their larger share of mining projects, including many projects in an early development stage as of 2009, and their resulting above average exposure to project risk in terms of changes in probability of realization and project delay.[610] Thus, as profit contributions are negatively correlated with supply levels, the major miners' joint increased exposure to project risk translates into a decreased sensitivity with respect to changes in global capacity utilization.

Therefore, in general terms, the key 2020 market economics of supply and demand can be summarized as follows:

- With increasing global capacity utilization, also regions with low-quality and thus high-cost domestic ore resources (especially China) are forced to increase the utilization of their domestic capacity and reduce their share of imports

- Market prices in all regions show a positive correlation with the level of global capacity utilization. India's market price reacts considerably less sensitive to capacity utilization changes than the prices in the remaining markets do.[611] However, market prices in all regions increase disproportionately when the global capacity utilization exceeds approximately 90%

---

[610]On an individual player level, this increased exposure is valid especially for Rio Tinto and somewhat less for BHP Billiton. Vale, on the other hand, shows a below average exposure due to its more mature projects and thus manages to increase its relative market share with decreasing supply.

[611]Due to a level of self-sufficiency and high Indian iron ore export taxes.

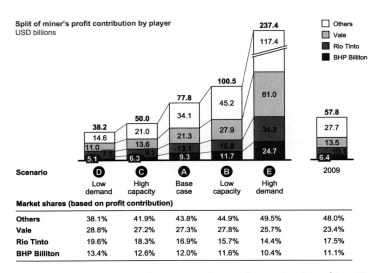

Figure 6.27: Scenarios A–E – Split of miner's profit contribution by player [Own illustration]

Market shares (based on profit contribution)

	D (Low demand)	C (High capacity)	A (Base case)	B (Low capacity)	E (High demand)	2009
Others	38.1%	41.9%	43.8%	44.9%	49.5%	48.0%
Vale	28.8%	27.2%	27.3%	27.8%	25.7%	23.4%
Rio Tinto	19.6%	18.3%	16.9%	15.7%	14.4%	17.5%
BHP Billiton	13.4%	12.6%	12.0%	11.6%	10.4%	11.1%

- Steelmakers' overall iron ore procurement costs increase as the market become tighter, rising disproportionately when the global capacity utilization exceeds approximately 90%. The cost increase is driven almost entirely by rising profit contribution of iron ore miners

- Iron ore miners' profit contributions show a negative correlation with supply levels and a positive correlation with demand levels. This results in an overall positive correlation of profit contribution with global capacity utilization, growing disproportionately when global capacity utilization exceeds approximately 90%. However, the individual profit contributions of the Big Three react less sensitive to changes in global capacity utilization than the profit contributions of the other miners do. Thus, the dominance of the Big Three in terms of joint market share (based on profit contribution) is negatively correlated with the level of global capacity utilization

6.3.1.3 Market economics of freight rates

6.3.1.3.1 Scenario F: 2020 low freight rates

As shown in Figure 6.28, the demand for iron ore in scenario F is identical to the demand in the base case. This is true for the total demand (2,360.5 Mt) as well as for the individual demand of the geographic regions. China thus continues to dominate demand with 1,136.8 Mt, followed by CIS (221.2 Mt) and South America (219.6 Mt).

Total world iron ore production in scenario F is equal to production in the base case (2,360.5 Mt). However, there are some minor regional changes in production, caused by the 47.0% freight rate decrease modeled in this scenario.[612] Oceania continues to lead production with 708.5 Mt (+3.8 Mt, +0.5% vs. the base case), followed by Oceania with 693.1 Mt (+3.7 Mt, +0.5%) and Africa & Middle East with 270.3 Mt (unchanged). The largest absolute production volume change vs. the base case can be found in China, now producing only 67.4 Mt (−11.4 Mt, −14.5%). Besides China, India is the only other region reducing its production in this scenario (−0.7 Mt, −0.4%).

China's decrease in domestic production is compensated by an equally sized increase in net imports to 1,069.3 Mt (+11.4 Mt). China is followed in the net import ranking by Other Asia (177.3 Mt, −4.7 Mt) and Europe (110.9 Mt, unchanged). The top three exporting regions in the base case maintain their relative positions. Oceania leads net exports with 696.2 Mt (+3.8 Mt), followed by South America (473.4 Mt, +3.7 Mt) and Africa & Middle East (141.8 Mt, unchanged).

The above described freight rate decrease vs. the base case has some effects on the global iron ore trade flows (see Figure 6.29). The by-far largest flows continue to be directed to China from Oceania (600.7 Mt) and South America (408.3 Mt). These flows increase slightly by 3.8 Mt and 3.0 Mt respectively. In general, in accordance with the total cost minimization objective of the allocation mechanism as defined in Section 5.1.3.1, it can be observed that, due to the reduced freight rates, some of the capacity in low-cost overseas regions that was idle in the base case now squeezes out some of the domestic production in regions with higher domestic production costs. Following this logic, China reduces its domestic supply by 11.4 Mt in exchange for addition less expensive import volumes from Other Asia (+4.7 Mt), Oceania (+3.8 Mt) and South America (+3.0 Mt). India's 0.7 Mt drop in domestic production is compensated by an equally sized additional import from South America (Indian

---

[612]Average of decrease on all routes. See Table II.5 for overview of freight rates per route.

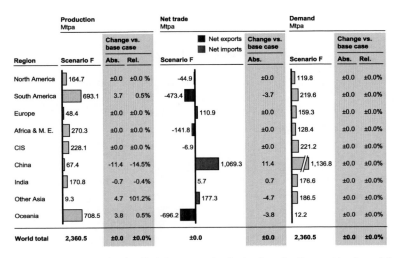

Figure 6.28: Scenario F: 2020 low freight rates – Analysis of production, net trade and demand by region [Own illustration]

captive supply). In other words, due to the reduced freight rates, some of the mines in Other Asia, Oceania and South America that are priced out of the market on a landed cost basis in the base case, now become capable of competing in regions with high demand.

Contrary to what may be expected, the reduced freight rates lead to a slight increase in the weighted world average market price for one ton of iron ore by +2.2% to USD 78.72 (see Figure 6.30). On a more detailed level, however, the change in freight rates shows a more sophisticated effect on market prices. Three regions, China, India and Other Asia, have slightly lower market prices than in the base case, while the remaining six regions show considerable price increases. The reasons for this heterogeneous market price development are two-fold: the change in global trade flows on the one hand and the increased logistic proximity between regions due to the lower freight rates on the other hand. As described above, China and India profit from lower-cost supply from abroad

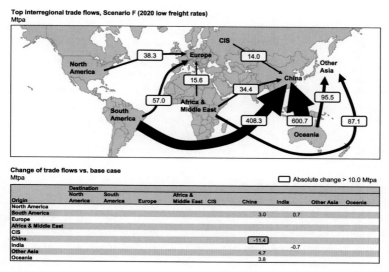

Top interregional trade flows, Scenario F (2020 low freight rates)
Mtpa

Change of trade flows vs. base case
Mtpa

☐ Absolute change > 10.0 Mtpa

Origin	North America	South America	Europe	Africa & Middle East	CIS	China	India	Other Asia	Oceania
North America									
South America						3.0	0.7		
Europe									
Africa & Middle East									
CIS									
China						-11.4			
India							-0.7		
Other Asia						4.7			
Oceania						3.8			

Figure 6.29: Scenario F: 2020 low freight rates – Analysis of interregional trade flows [Own illustration]

which squeezes out more expensive domestic ore.[613] In consequence, China's market price sinks slightly to USD 84.24 (USD −1.35, −1.6% vs. the base case), while the market price in India is reduced by USD 0.13 to USD 53.28 (−0.2%). Other Asia's market price reduction by USD 0.02 to USD 83.50, however, stems not from a change in supply, but rather from a slight decrease in domestic mining royalties.[614] Nevertheless, as in the base case, China continues to hold the highest market price with USD 84.24, closely followed by Other Asia with USD 83.50.

The price changes in all other regions, which maintain procurement mixes identical to those in the base case, are caused not by supply or demand effects,

---

[613]Note that the presence of domestic mines near the right end of the cost curve leads to a lower absolute market price decrease in these regions than would be expected based on the magnitude of the freight rate decrease. For example, as the landed cost of the Oceanian mine that is China's marginal supplier in the base case is decreased in this scenario, it moves to the left in the Chinese cost curve. Therefore, a domestic mine with unchanged landed cost is pushed to the right and becomes the new marginal mine. Thus, China's price decrease in this scenario is not equal to the freight cost decrease, but rather equal to the difference in landed cost between the marginal mine in the base case and the domestic mine now representing the marginal supplier.

[614]As these are based on the slightly decreased Chinese market price.

but rather by the non-arbitrage condition of the model.[615] Thus, these changes are an indirect effect of the decreased freight rates in this scenario. As freight rates sink, market prices especially in regions far from China are driven in an upward direction, closer to the Chinese market price. This is necessary in order to prevent arbitrage opportunities when regional markets move closer together in terms of freight costs.[616] Remarkably, despite this price increasing effect and its geographic proximity to China, India holds the by far lowest market price at USD 53.28. This is due to its complete self-sufficiency (through low-cost domestic production and captive supply abroad) and, more importantly, its high export taxes shielding it from a price increase caused by the non-arbitrage condition.

Compared to the base case, the slightly increased global average market price leads to a minor increase in steelmakers' overall expenditures for iron ore by USD 1.1 billion to a total of USD 160.7 billion (+0.7%). Naturally, the iron ore procurement costs per region reflect the individual regional price changes. With the largest regional price increase, North American steelmakers are confronted with a procurement cost increase of 12.3% to a total of USD 5.7 billion. Also South American iron ore consumers face a considerable 8.6% iron ore procurement cost increase to USD 12.0 billion. Chinese steelmakers profit from the price drop in their regional market, now paying a total of USD 88.6 billion for their ore, 2.2% less than in the base case. As in the scenarios described before, regions with high shares of captive supply manage to reduce the impact of increased market prices on their overall procurement costs compared to regions that are more exposed to the open market.

From a miner's point of view, the increase in the world average market price is rather advantageous. Overall profit contributions of iron ore miners increase by USD 8.4 billion to a total of USD 86.2 billion (+10.8%). The change of miners' profit contributions by region of origin depends greatly on the destination mix of their ore and the market price development in those regions. For example, North American miners boast the highest relative profit contribution increase (+24.2% vs. the base case) due to their large share of domestic sales and the considerable increase of the North American market price. Despite the slight market price decrease in their main target markets China and Other Asia, miners from South America (USD 30.6 billion, USD +4.3 billion) and Oceania (USD 30.5 billion, USD +1.6 billion) increase their profit due to lower freight

---

[615]See Section 5.1.3.2.4.

[616]For example, the unit production cost of South America's marginal supplier lies at USD 63.22. With freight rates to China down to USD 9.71 per ton, however, the market price in South America must be at least USD 74.53 (China's market price of USD 84.24 minus USD 9.71) in order to prevent arbitrage between the two regions.

costs and continue to lead the profit contribution ranking. South America's jump to first place in the ranking is due to two factors: a comparatively higher revenue increase per ton due to its miners' broader destination mix, including considerable supply to intraregional and European customers (where market prices increased) and comparatively higher freight cost savings per ton due to its geographic position vs. the regions of high import demand and thus larger exposure to freight rates.

Region	Market price USD/t			Average iron ore procurement cost USD/t			Total iron ore procurement cost USD billions			Total profit contribution of miners (by origin) USD billions		
	Scenario F	Change vs. base case		Scenario F	Change vs. base case		Scenario F	Change vs. base case		Scenario F	Change vs. base case	
		Abs.	Rel.		Abs.	Rel.		Abs.	Rel.		Abs.	Rel.
North America	73.15	8.64	13.4%	47.31	5.18	12.3%	5.7	0.6	12.3%	2.9	0.6	24.2%
South America	74.53	7.36	11.0%	54.76	4.35	8.6%	12.0	1.0	8.6%	30.6	4.3	16.6%
Europe	74.78	7.13	10.5%	57.88	3.25	5.9%	9.2	0.5	5.9%	3.2	0.3	10.6%
Africa & M. E.	77.10	5.38	7.5%	72.98	4.98	7.3%	9.4	0.6	7.3%	10.8	1.2	12.1%
CIS	77.54	4.58	6.3%	49.40	2.00	4.2%	10.9	0.4	4.2%	5.1	0.4	9.3%
China	84.24	-1.35	-1.6%	77.94	-1.79	-2.2%	88.6	-2.0	-2.2%	0.0	±0.0	±0.0%
India	53.28	-0.13	-0.2%	50.01	-0.23	-0.5%	8.8	>-0.1	-0.5%	3.2	>-0.1	-1.3%
Other Asia	83.50	-0.02	>-0.1%	82.63	-0.10	-0.1%	15.4	>-0.1	-0.1%	0.1	<0.1	0.3%
Oceania	80.21	2.14	2.7%	50.40	0.41	0.8%	0.6	<0.1	0.8%	30.5	1.6	5.7%
World total	78.72	1.68	2.2%	68.07	0.46	0.7%	160.7	1.1	0.7%	86.2	8.4	10.8%

Figure 6.30: Scenario F: 2020 low freight rates – Analysis of market prices, procurement cost and profit contribution of miners by region [Own illustration]

The detailed effects of the lower freight rates on the iron ore miners' profit contributions are shown in Figure 6.31. The overall standardized FOB cost increases slightly by 0.5% to USD 65.7 billion. This can be traced back to the net effect of the regional production shift as well as slightly lower royalties and lower premiums stemming from the slight decrease in the price-setting region's market price. Not surprisingly in the low freight rate scenario, the combined cost for freight and export taxes decreases significantly by 46.6% to USD 8.7 billion.[617] Based on the above described heterogeneous market price changes, the total revenue rises by only 0.7% to USD 160.7 billion. This slightly reduced total revenue combined with the considerably lower sum of the cost positions lead to a 10.8% increase in miners' profit contributions to USD 86.2 billion.

The effects on the three largest miners' profit contribution follow a similar pattern. Vale's total profit contribution rises to USD 24.6 billion (+15.9%

---

[617]Note that, as in the base case, neither of the two regions levying export taxes, China and India, actually export iron ore in this scenario. Thus, the decrease in the price-setting region's market price has no effect on overall global export tax costs, which remain zero.

vs. the base case), Rio Tinto shows a profit contribution of USD 13.9 billion (+5.6%) and BHP Billiton's profit contribution increases to USD 9.8 billion (+5.4%). The reason for Vale's comparatively higher profit contribution gain lies in its larger exposure to freight rates due to its geographic production focus in South America. Thus, Vale profits disproportionately high from the decrease in freight rates modeled in this scenario.

In terms of market share (based on profit contribution), the share of the Big Three decreases insignificantly to 56.0% (−0.2 ppt). Vale stays in first place with 28.5% market share (+1.2 ppt vs. the base case), Rio Tinto's share sinks to 16.1% (−0.8 ppt) and BHP Billiton claims 11.4% (−0.6 ppt).

	Production Mtpa	Analysis of profit contribution (USD billions)			
		Standardized FOB cost	Freight and export taxes	Profit contribution	Revenue
World total					160.7
		65.7	8.7	86.2	
Total	2,360.5				
Change vs. base case	±0.0%	0.5%	-46.6%	10.8%	0.7%
Per ton (USD/t)		27.83	3.70	36.54	68.07
Change vs. base case		0.5%	-46.6%	10.8%	0.7%
Vale					
Total	436.4	7.6	2.8	24.6	35.0
Change vs. base case	±0.0%	0.9%	-47.1%	15.9%	2.9%
Per ton (USD/t)		17.48	6.32	56.43	80.23
Change vs. base case		0.9%	-47.1%	15.9%	2.9%
Rio Tinto					
Total	247.5	5.7	1.0	13.9	20.6
Change vs. base case	±0.0%	0.2%	-46.4%	5.7%	-0.3%
Per ton (USD/t)		23.18	3.85	56.04	83.07
Change vs. base case		0.2%	-46.4%	5.7%	-0.3%
BHP Billiton					
Total	188.5	5.2	0.9	9.8	15.9
Change vs. base case	±0.0%	±0.0%	-46.5%	5.4%	-1.6%
Per ton (USD/t)		27.42	4.62	52.19	84.23
Change vs. base case		±0.0%	-46.5%	5.4%	-1.6%

Figure 6.31: Scenario F: 2020 low freight rates – Analysis of individual profit contributions of miners [Own illustration]

6.3.1.3.2   Scenario G: 2020 high freight rates

As shown in Figure 6.32, the demand for iron ore in scenario G is identical to the demand in the base case. This is true for the total demand (2,360.5 Mt) as well as for the individual demand of the geographic regions. China thus continues to dominate demand with 1,136.8 Mt, followed by CIS (221.2 Mt) and South America (219.6 Mt).

Total world iron ore production in scenario G is equal to production in the base case (2,360.5 Mt). However, there are some regional changes in production, caused by the 94.0% freight rate increase modeled in this scenario.[618] Oceania continues to lead production with 703.5 Mt (−1.2 Mt, −0.2% vs. the base case), followed by Oceania with 662.9 Mt (−26.5 Mt, −3.8%) and Africa & Middle East with 257.6 Mt (−12.7 Mt, −4.7%). The largest absolute production volume change vs. the base case can be found in China, now producing 129.9 Mt, 51.1 Mt more than in the base case (+64.8%). Besides China, India (+2.9 Mt, +1.7%) and Other Asia (+0.1 Mt, +2.1%) are the only other regions increasing their production in this scenario. All other regions, except for Europe (with unhcnaged production volume), reduce their production slightly compared to the base case.

China's increase in domestic production is compensated by an equally sized decrease in net imports to 1,006.8 Mt (−51.1 Mt). China is followed in the net import ranking by Other Asia (181.8 Mt, −0.1 Mt) and Europe (110.9 Mt, unchanged). The top three exporting regions in the base case maintain their relative positions. Oceania leads net exports with 691.2 Mt (−1.2 Mt), followed by South America (443.3 Mt, −26.5 Mt) and Africa & Middle East (129.2 Mt, −12.7 Mt).

The above described freight rate increase vs. the base case has some effects on the global iron ore trade flows (see Figure 6.33). The by-far largest flows continue to be directed to China from Oceania (587.8 Mt) and South America (381.8 Mt). These flows decrease by 9.1 Mt and 23.6 Mt respectively. In general, in accordance with the total cost minimization objective of the allocation mechanism as defined in Section 5.1.3.1, it can be observed that in some regions, due to the increased freight rates, domestic production capacity that was idle in the base case now squeezes out imported ore volumes from overseas. In other words, some of the mines in North America, South America, Africa & Middle East, CIS and Oceania that export ore in the base case are now priced out of the market on a landed cost basis in some regions. Following this logic, China increases its domestic supply by 51.1 Mt in exchange for a reduction of more

---

[618]Average of increase on all routes. See Table II.5 for overview of freight rates per route.

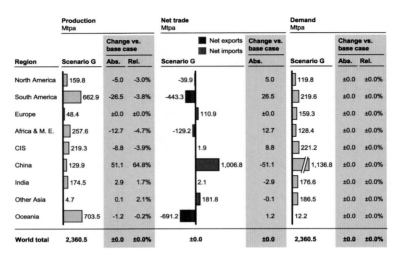

Figure 6.32: Scenario G: 2020 high freight rates – Analysis of production, net trade and demand by region [Own illustration]

expensive import volumes from South America (−23.6 Mt), CIS (−13.5 Mt), Oceania (−9.1 Mt), North America (−5.0 Mt). Likewise, imports to CIS from Africa & Middle East are reduced by 4.7 Mt in favor of domestic production. India's 2.9 Mt drop in imports from South America (Indian captive supply) is compensated by an equally sized increase in domestic production. Other Asia indirectly profits from China's reduction of imports by substituting imports from further-away Africa & Middle East for additional iron ore volume from Oceania.

Contrary to what may be expected, the increased freight rates lead to a slight decrease in the weighted world average market price for one ton of iron ore by 3.2% to USD 74.59 (see Figure 6.34). On a more detailed level, however, the change in freight rates shows a more sophisticated effect on market prices. Three regions, China, India and Other Asia, have slightly higher market prices than in the base case, while the remaining six regions show considerable price declines. The reasons for this heterogeneous market price development are two-fold: the change in global trade flows on the one hand and the lower logistic proximity between regions due to the higher freight rates on the other hand. As described above, due to the increased freight rates, China, Other Asia and India suffer from reduced low-cost supply from abroad which is squeezed out

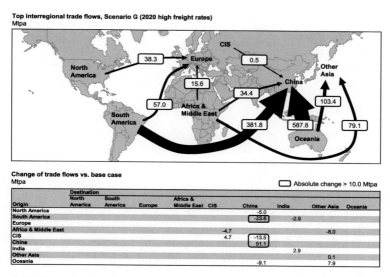

Top interregional trade flows, Scenario G (2020 high freight rates)
Mtpa

Change of trade flows vs. base case
Mtpa

☐ Absolute change > 10.0 Mtpa

Origin	Destination North America	South America	Europe	Africa & Middle East	CIS	China	India	Other Asia	Oceania
North America						-5.0			
South America						-23.8	-2.9		
Europe									
Africa & Middle East					-4.7			-8.0	
CIS					4.7	-13.5			
China						51.1			
India							2.9		
Other Asia								0.1	
Oceania						-9.1		7.9	

Figure 6.33: Scenario G: 2020 high freight rates – Analysis of interregional trade flows [Own illustration]

by supply from geographically nearer mines that are idle in the base case.[619] In consequence, China's market price rises slightly to USD 87.82 (USD +2.23, +2.6% vs. the base case), the Other Asian market price increases by USD 2.68 to USD 86.20 (+3.2%) and the market price in India increases by USD 0.64 to USD 54.05 (+1.2%). Thus, China continues to hold the highest market price with USD 87.82, closely followed by Other Asia with USD 86.20.

The market price decreases in all other regions, which mainly have procurement mixes identical to those in the base case, are caused not by supply or demand effects, but rather by the non-arbitrage condition of the model.[620] Thus, these price reductions are an indirect effect of the increased freight rates in this scenario. Recall that, in the base case, market prices in most regions[621] are not

---

[619]Note that the presence of domestic mines idle in the base case leads to a lower absolute market price increase in these regions than would be expected based on the magnitude of the freight rate increase. For example, as the landed cost of the Oceanian mine that is China's marginal supplier in the base case is increased in this scenario, it is replaced in the cost curve by a domestic mine that is idle in the base case. Thus, China's price increase in this scenario is not equal to the freight cost increase, but rather equal to the difference in landed cost between the marginal mine in the base case and the domestic mine now representing the marginal supplier.

[620]See Section 5.1.3.2.4.

[621]North America, South America, Europe, Africa & Middle East, CIS and Oceania.

determined by the unit production cost of the marginal supplier, but rather by the non-arbitrage condition of the model. This condition leads to a higher market price than required by the marginal supplier in order to prevent arbitrage opportunities between regions.[622] As freight rates increase significantly in scenario G, the geographic proximity of these regions to the price-setting region China decreases. Thus, market prices are given more slack and move to or at least closer to the prices required by the respective marginal suppliers.

Compared to the base case, the slightly decreased global average market price leads to a minor decrease in steelmakers' overall expenditures for iron ore by USD 0.8 billion to a total of USD 158.8 billion (−0.5%). Naturally, the iron ore procurement costs per region reflect the individual regional price changes. With the largest regional price decrease, North American steelmakers benefit from a procurement cost decrease of 18.0% to a total of USD 4.1 billion. Also iron ore consumers in South America (USD 9.1 billion, −17.8%) and Africa & Middle East (USD 7.4 billion, −15.3%) see their procurement costs reduced considerably. Chinese steelmakers on the other hand are confronted with a procurement cost increase of USD 3.5 billion to USD 94.2 billion (+3.9%). Regions with high shares of captive supply manage to reduce the impact of changes in market prices on their overall procurement costs compared to regions that are more exposed to the open market.

From a miner's point of view, the decrease in the world average market price is fairly disadvantageous. Overall profit contributions of iron ore miners decrease by USD 15.3 billion to a total of USD 62.5 billion (−19.7%). The change of miners' profit contributions by region of origin depends greatly on the destination mix of their ore and the market price development in those regions. For example, North American miners suffer the highest relative profit contribution decrease (−34.6% vs. the base case) due to their large share of domestic sales and the considerable decrease of the North American market price. Despite the slight market price increase in their main target markets China and Other Asia, miners from South America (USD 18.0 billion, USD −8.2 billion) and Oceania (USD 25.5 billion, USD −3.3 billion) face the largest absolute profit contribution decreases due to their significant export shares and thus high exposure to the freight rate increase.

The detailed effects of the higher freight rates on the iron ore miners' profit contributions are shown in Figure 6.35. The overall standardized FOB cost increases slightly by 1.4% to USD 66.3 billion. This can be traced back to the

---

[622]For example, the unit production cost of South America's marginal supplier in this scenario lies at USD 46.91. With freight rates to China at USD 35.84 per ton, however, the market price in South America must be at least USD 51.98 (China's market price of USD 87.82 minus USD 35.84) in order to prevent arbitrage between the two regions.

Region	Market price USD/t			Average iron ore procurement cost USD/t			Total iron ore procurement cost USD billions			Total profit contribution of miners (by origin) USD billions		
	Scenario G	Change vs. base case		Scenario G	Change vs. base case		Scenario G	Change vs. base case		Scenario G	Change vs. base case	
		Abs.	Rel.		Abs.	Rel.		Abs.	Rel.		Abs.	Rel.
North America	52.00	-12.51	-19.4%	34.56	-7.57	-18.0%	4.1	-0.9	-18.0%	1.5	-0.8	-34.6%
South America	51.98	-15.19	-22.6%	41.46	-8.95	-17.8%	9.1	-2.0	-17.8%	18.0	-8.2	-31.3%
Europe	64.68	-2.97	-4.4%	55.62	0.98	1.8%	8.9	0.2	1.8%	2.8	-0.1	-3.1%
Africa & M. E.	60.49	-11.23	-15.7%	57.63	-10.38	-15.3%	7.4	-1.3	-15.3%	7.5	-2.1	-22.3%
CIS	63.31	-9.65	-13.2%	43.14	-4.25	-9.0%	9.5	-0.9	-9.0%	3.7	-0.9	-20.4%
China	87.82	2.23	2.6%	82.83	3.10	3.9%	94.2	3.5	3.9%	0.0	±0.0	±0.0%
India	54.05	0.64	1.2%	50.95	0.71	1.4%	9.0	0.1	1.4%	3.4	0.1	4.2%
Other Asia	86.20	2.68	3.2%	85.52	2.79	3.4%	16.0	0.5	3.4%	0.1	<0.1	10.6%
Oceania	73.33	-4.74	-6.1%	49.13	-0.86	-1.7%	0.6	>-0.1	-1.7%	25.5	-3.3	-11.4%
World total	74.59	-2.46	-3.2%	67.25	-0.35	-0.5%	158.8	-0.8	-0.5%	62.5	-15.3	-19.7%

Figure 6.34: Scenario G: 2020 high freight rates – Analysis of market prices, procurement cost and profit contribution of miners by region [Own illustration]

net effect of the regional production shift as well as slightly higher royalties and higher premiums stemming from the slight increase in the price-setting region's market price. Not surprisingly in the high freight rate scenario, the combined cost for freight and export taxes increases significantly by 82.9% to USD 29.9 billion.[623] Based on the above described heterogeneous market price changes, the total revenue decreases by only 0.5% to USD 158.8 billion. This slightly decreased total revenue combined with the considerably higher cost positions lead to a 19.7% decrease in miners' profit contributions to USD 62.5 billion.

The effects on the three largest miners' profit contribution follow a similar pattern. Vale's total profit contribution sinks to USD 15.0 billion (−29.5% vs. the base case), Rio Tinto reaches a profit contribution of USD 11.7 billion (−10.7%) and BHP Billiton's profit contribution decreases to USD 8.2 billion (−12.0%). The reason for Vale's comparatively higher profit contribution loss lies in its larger exposure to freight rates due to its geographic production focus in South America. Thus, Vale suffers disproportionately high from the increase in freight rates modeled in this scenario.

In terms of market share (based on profit contribution), the share of the Big Three decreases insignificantly to 55.0% (−0.3 ppt vs. the base case). Despite a considerable market share decrease of 3.3 ppt, Vale stays in first place with

---

[623]Note that, as in the base case, neither of the two regions levying export taxes, China and India, actually export iron ore in this scenario. Thus, the increase in the price-setting region's market price has no effect on overall global export tax costs, which remain zero.

24.0% market share. Rio Tinto's share increases to 18.8% (+1.9 ppt) and BHP Billiton claims 13.1% (+1.1 ppt).

	Production Mtpa	Analysis of profit contribution (USD billions)			
		Standardized FOB cost	Freight and export taxes	Profit contribution	Revenue
World total			29.9	62.5	158.8
		66.3			
Total	2,360.5				
Change vs. base case	±0.0%	1.4%	82.9%	-19.7%	-0.5%
Per ton (USD/t)		28.10	12.67	26.49	67.25
Change vs. base case		1.4%	82.9%	-19.7%	-0.5%
Vale					
Total	420.5	6.6	9.3	15.0	30.8
Change vs. base case	-3.6%	-13.0%	78.2%	-29.5%	9.3%
Per ton (USD/t)		15.64	22.07	35.65	73.36
Change vs. base case		-9.8%	84.9%	-26.8%	-5.9%
Rio Tinto					
Total	247.5	5.7	3.4	11.7	20.9
Change vs. base case	±0.0%	-0.3%	93.4%	-10.7%	1.2%
Per ton (USD/t)		23.05	13.90	47.36	84.31
Change vs. base case		-0.3%	93.4%	-10.7%	1.2%
BHP Billiton					
Total	188.5	5.2	3.1	8.2	16.5
Change vs. base case	±0.0%	±0.0%	93.5%	-12.0%	2.5%
Per ton (USD/t)		27.44	16.70	43.58	87.71
Change vs. base case		±0.0%	93.5%	-12.0%	2.5%

Figure 6.35: Scenario G: 2020 high freight rates – Analysis of individual profit contributions of miners [Own illustration]

6.3.1.3.3 Summary of 2020 market economics of freight rates

In this section, in order to better quantify the impact of variations of the freight rates on the economics of the iron ore market, the outcomes of scenarios F (low freight rates) and G (high freight rates) are jointly compared to the results of the base case (scenario A, medium freight rates).[624] As these three scenarios each differ in terms of the modeled freight rate levels, each scenario portrays a very specific market setting.

First of all, the effect of the freight rate levels on the iron ore trade flows is analyzed. However, as shown in the detailed results of the scenarios, these trade flows are too complex as to allow a detailed comparison of three scenario results for reasons of limited space. Therefore, the iron ore trade flows directed at China, the nucleus of world demand, are taken as a proxy for the key characteristics of the global trade flows. Figure 6.36 shows the split of supply to China by region of origin for each of the three scenarios.

Notably, China's share of domestic supply increases as freight rates rise. At the same time, imports from key suppliers Oceania and South America recede with increasing freight rates. In scenario F (low freight rates), China satisfies only 5.9% of its iron ore demand through domestic supply, while importing 88.7% of its demand from Oceania and South America. In the scenario representing high freight rates (scenario G), China's domestic production is increased to supply 11.4% of its required ore, while the share of the two largest external suppliers is reduced to 85.3%. The same effect can be seen in terms of China's utilization of its domestic production capacity. In scenario F, only 17.4% of China's available capacity is in operation, while scenario G shows a 33.6% utilization of China's domestic capacity. From this, it can be deduced that, with increasing freight rate levels, domestic capacity in import-oriented regions partially squeezes out seaborne supply. This is valid also and especially for those regions with low-quality and thus high-cost domestic ore resources. With increasing freight rates, seaborne imports to these regions increase in cost and domestic mines that are priced out of the market when imports are less expensive come online.

With respect to regional iron ore market prices, the effect of changes in freight rates is displayed in Figure 6.37. For each scenario, sorted in ascending order according to the freight rate level, the values for the maximum and minimum market prices are shown together with the weighted average price, while the other seven regional prices are depicted only as markers for reasons of clarity.

As can be expected, the higher freight rates rise, the higher the maximum market price moves. This price, belonging to the Chinese market in all sce-

---

[624]The respective 2009 model results are given for comparison only and are not described.

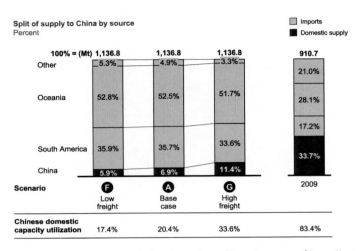

Figure 6.36: Scenarios F, A, G – Split of supply to China by source [Own illustration]

narios, increases from USD 84.24 for low freight rates, to USD 87.82 for high freight rates. The world average price per ton, however, decreases slightly from USD 78.72 in scenario F to USD 74.59 in scenario G. The minimum market price remains more or less constant, varying from USD 53.28 in scenario F to USD 52.00 in scenario G.

In order to understand these heterogeneous price effects, one must first of all distinguish three separate groups of regions as indicated by the shades in Figure 6.37. China and Other Asia make up the first group. These regions, due to their large iron ore consumption and their comparatively low domestic production, have the highest import demand of all regions. Thus, their market prices are not only the highest in all scenarios per se, but are also especially exposed to changes in freight rate levels. Therefore, Chinese and Other Asian market prices rise when freight rate levels increase (and vice versa).[625] The second group consists of North America, South America, Europe, Africa & Middle East, CIS and Oceania. Due to their comparatively low-cost marginal suppliers, these regions' prices are not directly influenced by supply and demand, but rather by the non-arbitrage condition of the model.[626] Thus, in order to prevent arbitrage opportunities between these markets and the higher-priced markets China and

---

[625]Note that these market prices do not vary in the same magnitude as the freight rates, since resulting changes in the order of mines in the regions' cost curves, especially substitutions between domestic and seaborne suppliers, significantly weaken the effect of changing freight rates on the market prices.

[626]See Section 5.1.3.2.4.

Other Asia, their market prices are determined by the Chinese market price minus the respective costs of transporting ore to China.[627] In consequence, as overall freight rate levels rise, the geographic proximity of these regions to the price-setting region China decreases. Thus, market prices are given more slack and move to or at least closer to the prices required by the respective marginal suppliers. On the other hand, when freight rates decrease, the higher geographic proximity to price-setting China forces market prices upward, closer to the Chinese market price.[628] The overall resulting effect is shown in the large shade in Figure 6.37.[629] For example, the European market price drops from USD 74.78 in scenario F to USD 64.68 in scenario G (-13.4%). India's market price, despite the geographic proximity to China, holds the by far lowest market price in two of the three scenarios. Also, its market price stays more or less constant and does not react as sensitively to changes in freight rate levels as the prices in the remaining markets do. This is due to its complete self-sufficiency (through low-cost domestic production and captive supply abroad) and, more importantly, its high export taxes shielding it from a price increase caused by the above described non-arbitrage condition.

Figure 6.38 aims to evaluate the effect of freight rate levels on the iron ore procurement cost of the world's steelmakers. Apart from showing the absolute value of these costs per scenario, the figure splits the procurement costs into their three main constituents: standardized FOB costs, freight and export tax costs as well as miners' profit contributions.

As is shown, the overall iron ore procurement costs mirror the weighted average market prices, thus only barely decreasing as freight rates increase. Steelmakers pay a total of USD 160.7 billion with low freight rates (scenario F) and a slightly lower amount of USD 158.8 billion with high freight rates (scenario G). On a regional level, for example, European steelmakers' joint iron ore procurement costs equal USD 9.2 billion in scenario F and USD 8.9 billion in scenario G. Interestingly, with overall standardized FOB costs almost identical in all of the three scenarios, the increase in freight cost from USD 8.7 billion in scenario F to USD 29.9 billion in scenario G is entirely at the expense of miners' profit

---

[627]As China is the price-setting region in all three scenarios.

[628]It must be noted that if freight rates between regions were zero, all regional market prices would converge to the cost of the global marginal mine. On the other hand, if freight rates were infinite, each market's price would be set at the cost of the regions marginal supplier, independent of the supply and demand situations in the other regional markets.

[629]Note that, as freight rates change, not only the price levels, but also the spread of the respective market prices is affected. This is due to the fact that changes in freight rate levels are modeled on a percentage basis. Thus, those regions further away from China (e.g., North and South America) observe a more extreme relative price change effect than regions closer to China (e.g., CIS and Oceania).

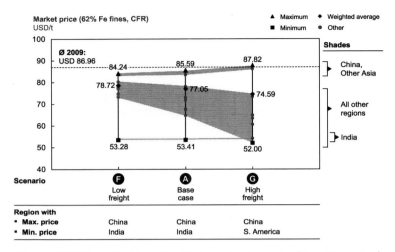

Figure 6.37: Scenarios F, A, G – Market prices by region [Own illustration]

contribution. Although the individual regions' iron ore procurement costs are not displayed here, it can be summarized that these move in line with the above described respective regional market prices.

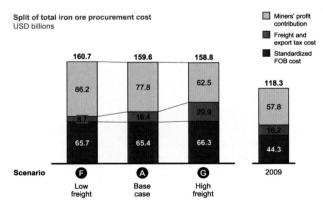

Figure 6.38: Scenarios F, A, G – Split of total iron ore procurement cost [Own illustration]

The impact of the freight rate level on the iron ore miners' profit contribution is displayed in Figure 6.39. The overall industry profit contribution is split by player, showing the individual values for each of the Big Three and the remaining amount titled "Others". Also, the figure shows the corresponding market shares based on profit contribution for each of these players per scenario.

As mentioned above, due to a more or less unaffected world average market price, the overall iron ore miners' profit contribution are negatively correlated with the level of freight rates. In scenario F (low freight rates), miners jointly pocket USD 86.2 billion in profit contribution, while this amount sinks to USD 62.5 billion in scenario G (high freight rates). This dynamic is mirrored on an individual player level. The individual profit contributions of all three major iron ore miners are reduced with increasing freight rates (and vice versa). However the Big Three show different sensitivities with respect to freight rate variations. This is best displayed in terms of their individual market shares. While the order of the Big Three remains unchanged throughout all scenarios, Vale loses market shares as freight rates increase while Rio Tinto and BHP Billiton gain market shares. This effect can be traced back to Vale's greater exposure to freight rates due to the focus of its mining operations in South America compared to Rio Tinto's and BHP's focus in Oceania. Thus, Vale shows a higher sensitivity to changes in freight rate levels than the other two large iron ore miners do. However, the joint market dominance of the three largest iron ore producers is more or less unaffected by changes in freight rates.

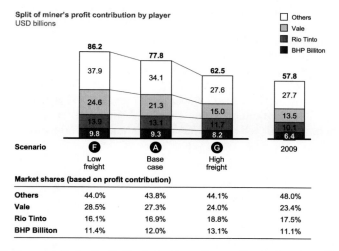

Figure 6.39: Scenarios F, A, G – Split of miner's profit contribution by player [Own illustration]

Therefore, in general terms, the key 2020 market economics of freight rates can be summarized as follows:

- With increasing freight rate levels, idle domestic capacity in import-oriented regions squeezes out seaborne supply, especially in regions with low-quality and thus high-cost domestic ore resources (especially China, but also Other Asia)

- Changes in freight rate levels have heterogeneous effects on regional market prices. The regions with highest import demand (China and Other Asia) show a positive correlation of their market prices with freight rates.[630] India's market price is more or less constant at an extremely low level, independent of freight rate changes.[631] All other regions' market prices are negatively correlated with the freight rate level, although regions further from China (e.g., North and South America) show a higher price elasticity than regions with higher geographic proximity to China (e.g., CIS and Oceania)

- Steelmakers' overall iron ore procurement costs stay more or less constant as freight rates change. Changes in overall absolute freight costs are counterbalanced by commensurate changes in global miners' profit contributions. On a regional level, however, iron ore procurement costs mirror the respective market price changes

- The overall iron ore miners' profit contribution decreases with rising freight rates (and vice versa). Due to its geographic production focus in South America, Vale's profit contribution shows a considerably higher sensitivity to freight rate changes than the other two major iron ore miners' profit contributions do. Thus, Vale's market share (based on profit contribution) shows a negative correlation with freight rates, while Rio Tinto's and BHP Billiton's shares are positively correlated with freight rates. The dominance of the Big Three in terms of joint market shares remains more or less constant, independent of freight rate levels

---

[630] However, these market prices do not vary in the same magnitude as the freight rates, since resulting changes in the order of mines in the regions' cost curves, especially substitutions between domestic and seaborne suppliers, significantly weaken the effect of changing freight rates on the market prices.

[631] Due to a level of self-sufficiency and high Indian iron ore export taxes.

6.3.2 Evaluation of risk mitigation strategies for demand-side players in 2020

6.3.2.1 Captivity of iron ore mines

6.3.2.1.1 Scenario H: 2020 no captivity of iron ore mines by Arcelor-Mittal

As shown in Figure 6.40, the demand for iron ore in scenario H is identical to the demand in the base case. This is true for the total demand (2,360.5 Mt) as well as for the individual demand of the geographic regions. China thus continues to dominate demand with 1,136.8 Mt, followed by CIS (221.2 Mt) and South America (219.6 Mt).

Also, production capacities in this scenario are identical to those in the base case, as are the production volumes per region. Therefore, total world iron ore production equals 2,360.5 Mt, with Oceania leading production with 704.7 Mt, closely followed by South America with 689.4 Mt.

With demand, capacities and production identical to the base case, net trade also remains unchanged. China therefore continues to lead net imports with 1,057.9 Mt, followed by the only other net importers Other Asia (181.9 Mt) and Europe (110.9 Mt). Main net exporters are Oceania (692.4 Mt), South America (469.8 Mt) and Africa & Middle East (141.8 Mt).

Despite the unchanged demand, capacity and production figures, the abolition of ArcelorMittal's captive capacity modeled in this scenario has effects on the global iron ore trade flows (see Figure 6.41). The by-far largest flows continue to be directed to China from Oceania (611.1 Mt) and South America (391.1 Mt).

To understand the change in trade flows in this scenario it is important to note that in the base case the allocation is slightly distorted due to the forced destinations attributed to ArcelorMittal's captive mines. Once these forced destinations are removed (by allowing these mines to sell to the open market), the cost minimization objective of the model's allocation mechanism finds a slightly improved allocation in terms of total freight costs.[632] Starting from the trade flows in the base case, this new allocation can be retraced by means of a circular swap of 14.3 Mt of ore supply. Europe imports 14.3 Mt from South America instead of from Africa & Middle East. Instead, Africa & Middle East supplies these 14.3 Mt to Other Asia, which in turn reduces its supply from

---

[632]Total freight costs are reduced by approximately USD 0.1 billion (−0.7%) compared to the base case.

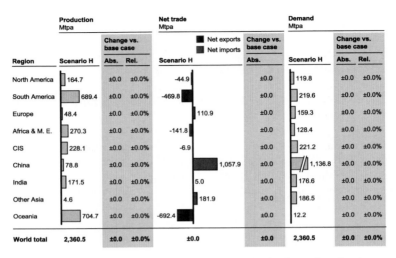

Figure 6.40: Scenario H: 2020 no captivity ArcelorMittal – Analysis of production, net trade and demand by region [Own illustration]

Oceania by 14.3 Mt. China imports these vacant 14.3 Mt of ore from Oceania and reduces its imports from South America by the same amount.

The above described circular swap of 14.3 Mt of supply does not affect the marginal supplier in any region, but rather affects mines within the respective industry cost curves. In consequence, the change in trade flows vs. the base case has no effect on market prices (see Figure 6.42). China, the price-setting region, has the highest market price with USD 85.59, followed by Other Asia (USD 83.52) and Oceania (USD 78.07). India holds the lowest market price at USD 53.41 per ton.

Though market prices are identical to those in the base case, total iron ore procurement costs increase by USD 4.8 billion to USD 164.4 billion (+3.0%). This increase is due to the fact that the mines captive to ArcelorMittal in the base case and thus supplying to ArcelorMittal at unit production cost, now sell to consumers at the respective market price. In consequence, the five regions where ArcelorMittal's steelmaking facilities are located (North America, South America, Europe, Africa & Middle East and CIS) now show an increase in iron ore procurement costs. The magnitude of these increases depends on the amount of captive capacity allocated to the respective regions in the base case.[633] Thus, Europe suffers the largest increase in total iron ore procurement

---

[633]This allocation within ArcelorMittal's complex network of mining and steelmaking facilities is performed using a freight cost minimization approach.

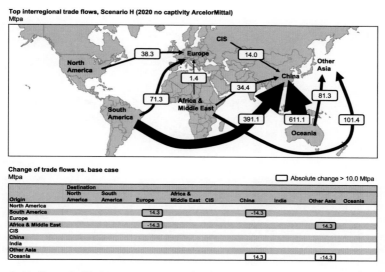

Figure 6.41: Scenario H: 2020 no captivity ArcelorMittal – Analysis of interregional trade flows [Own illustration]

cost by USD 2.0 billion (+23.2%), followed by North America (USD +1.1 billion, +19.9%), CIS (USD +0.9 billion, +8.6%), South America (USD +0.5 billion, +4.9%) and Africa & Middle East (USD +0.3 billion, +3.3%). Though not increased compared to the base case, China's iron ore procurement costs remain highest with USD 90.6 billion.

The overall profit contribution of the iron ore industry increases by USD 4.9 billion to USD 82.7 billion (+6.2%). This increase stems mainly from the additional revenue generated by mines formerly captive to ArcelorMittal now selling at market prices instead of at unit production cost.[634] Due to this, the rise in profit contribution is not distributed evenly among supplying regions, but rather mainly according to the location of mines formerly captive to ArcelorMittal. The most considerable increases are thus to be found in North America (USD +2.7 billion, +119.3%), CIS (USD +0.9 billion, +19.3%), Africa & Middle East (USD +0.7 billion, +7.8%) and South America (USD +0.4 billion, +1.5%).

---

[634]Note that, as described above, the improved allocation of supply in this scenario reduces total freight costs by approximately USD 0.1 billion compared to the base case. Therefore, the increase of miners' total profit contribution compared to the base case is roughly USD 0.1 billion higher than the steelmakers' total iron ore procurement cost increase.

	Market price USD/t			Average iron ore procurement cost USD/t			Total iron ore procurement cost USD billions			Total profit contribution of miners (by origin) USD billions		
		Change vs. base case			Change vs. base case			Change vs. base case			Change vs. base case	
Region	Scenario H	Abs.	Rel.	Scenario H	Abs.	Rel.	Scenario H	Abs.	Rel.	Scenario H	Abs.	Rel.
North America	64.51	±0.00	±0.0%	50.50	8.37	19.9%	6.1	1.1	19.9%	5.0	2.7	119.3%
South America	67.17	±0.00	±0.0%	52.86	2.45	4.9%	11.6	0.5	4.9%	26.6	0.4	1.5%
Europe	67.65	±0.00	±0.0%	67.29	12.65	23.2%	10.7	2.0	23.2%	2.9	<0.1	1.0%
Africa & M. E.	71.72	±0.00	±0.0%	70.26	2.26	3.3%	9.0	0.3	3.3%	10.4	0.7	7.8%
CIS	72.96	±0.00	±0.0%	51.46	4.07	8.6%	11.4	0.9	8.6%	5.6	0.9	19.3%
China	85.59	±0.00	±0.0%	79.73	±0.00	±0.0%	90.6	±0.0	±0.0%	0.0	±0.0	±0.0%
India	53.41	±0.00	±0.0%	50.23	±0.00	±0.0%	8.9	±0.0	±0.0%	3.2	±0.0	±0.0%
Other Asia	83.52	±0.00	±0.0%	82.73	±0.00	±0.0%	15.4	±0.0	±0.0%	0.1	±0.0	±0.0%
Oceania	78.07	±0.00	±0.0%	49.99	±0.00	±0.0%	0.6	±0.0	±0.0%	28.9	<0.1	0.1%
World total	77.05	±0.00	±0.0%	69.62	2.01	3.0%	164.4	4.8	3.0%	82.7	4.9	6.2%

Figure 6.42: Scenario H: 2020 no captivity ArcelorMittal – Analysis of market prices, procurement cost and profit contribution of miners by region [Own illustration]

The detailed effects of the annulment of ArcelorMittal's captivity on the iron ore miners' profit contributions are shown in Figure 6.43. Due to stable production and demand levels per region, total standardized FOB costs are identical to those in the base case (USD 65.4 billion). Owing to the improved supply allocation and the resulting slight reduction in total freight costs, the combined cost for freight and export taxes is reduced by 0.7% to USD 16.3 billion.[635] As described above, total industry revenue increases by 3.0% to USD 164.4 billion, due to mines formerly captive to ArcelorMittal now selling at market prices instead of at unit production cost. The combination of decreased cost positions and increased revenue leaves miners with an increased total profit contribution of USD 82.7 billion (+6.2%).

In contrast to the development observed for the iron ore mining industry as a whole, the abolition of ArcelorMittal's upstream integration has no effect on the profit contribution of the three largest iron ore mining companies. Vale's total profit contribution remains at USD 21.3 billion, Rio Tinto continues to generate a profit contribution of USD 13.1 billion and BHP Billiton's profit contribution equals USD 9.3 billion. The reason for the lacking change is that the Big Three participate neither in the freight cost reduction (due to their unchanged trade flows), nor in the revenue increase (due to the constant market prices) compared to the base case.

---

[635]Note that neither of the two regions levying export taxes, China and India, actually export iron ore in this scenario. Thus, as in the base case, overall global export tax costs are zero.

In terms of market share (based on profit contribution), the share of the Big Three consequently decreases by 3.3 percentage points in this scenario compared to the base case. Vale stays in first place with a reduced share of 25.7% (−1.6 ppt vs. the base case), Rio Tinto's market share drops to 15.9% (−1.0 ppt) and BHP Billiton claims 11.3% of the overall profit contribution (−0.7 ppt). The reason for this decreased dominance of the Big Three in this scenario lies in the fact that all three players are unable to profit from the increased revenues, as these are directed exclusively towards mines formerly captive to ArcelorMittal.

	Production Mtpa	Analysis of profit contribution (USD billions)			
		Standardized FOB cost	Freight and export taxes	Profit contribution	Revenue
World total					164.4
		65.4	16.3	82.7	
Total	2,360.5				
Change vs. base case	±0.0%	±0.0%	-0.7%	6.2%	3.0%
Per ton (USD/t)		27.70	6.88	35.03	69.62
Change vs. base case		±0.0%	-0.7%	6.2%	3.0%
Vale					
Total	436.4	7.6	5.2	21.3	34.0
Change vs. base case	±0.0%	±0.0%	±0.0%	±0.0%	±0.0%
Per ton (USD/t)		17.33	11.94	48.70	77.96
Change vs. base case		±0.0%	±0.0%	±0.0%	±0.0%
Rio Tinto					
Total	247.5	5.7	1.8	13.1	20.6
Change vs. base case	±0.0%	±0.0%	±0.0%	±0.0%	±0.0%
Per ton (USD/t)		23.13	7.19	53.04	83.35
Change vs. base case		±0.0%	±0.0%	±0.0%	±0.0%
BHP Billiton					
Total	188.5	5.2	1.6	9.3	16.1
Change vs. base case	±0.0%	±0.0%	±0.0%	±0.0%	±0.0%
Per ton (USD/t)		27.43	8.63	49.53	85.59
Change vs. base case		±0.0%	-0.0%	-0.0%	±0.0%

Figure 6.43: Scenario H: 2020 no captivity ArcelorMittal – Analysis of individual profit contributions of miners [Own illustration]

Having now fully analyzed the effect of the annulment of ArcelorMittal's captivity on the iron ore and steel industries as a whole, it becomes necessary to determine the effects on ArcelorMittal itself (see Figure 6.44).

In the base case, ArcelorMittal utilizes its entire available captive capacity of 105.1 Mt to supply its steelmaking facilities with iron ore. According to the model assumptions, this volume is transferred from ArcelorMittal's mines to its blast furnaces at unit production cost (plus freight and export tax costs where applicable). Thus, the average cost of a ton of captive supply equals USD 23.04. Based on the company's assumed total iron ore demand of 159.1 Mt,[636] this

---

[636]Note that ArcelorMittal's 2020 iron ore demand is calculated by applying the region-specific demand growth rates assumed in the medium demand scenario to the company's 2009 actual iron ore demand per region.

corresponds to a self-sufficiency of 66.0%. The remainder of the required ore (54.0 Mt) is purchased on the open market at an average cost of USD 68.17 per ton (based on the regional split of residual demand and the respective market prices). In total, the average cost per ton therefore equals USD 38.36 with ArcelorMittal's total procurement cost summing up to USD 6.1 billion.

Assuming the complete absence of captive supply for ArcelorMittal as modeled in scenario H, the steel company is forced to procure its entire required ore volume (159.1 Mt) on the open market. Based on the regional distribution of ArcelorMittal's steelmaking facilities and the respective market prices in these regions, the average cost per ton equals USD 68.19.[637] Thus, ArcelorMittal's iron ore procurement costs without captive supply totals USD 10.9 billion.

Summarizing, due to its extensive upstream integration, steelmaker Arcelor-Mittal enjoys a considerable annual iron ore procurement cost reduction of USD 4.8 billion (−43.7%) in 2020.[638]

---

[637] Note that the difference between average free market cost in the base case and in scenario H derives from the slight difference in regional distribution of residual demand in the base case and ArcelorMittal's overall demand in scenario H.

[638] Note that this cost advantage does not take into account the original cost of acquiring the respective mines, nor the fix costs incurred in running these mines. It must be noted that the procurement cost reduction effect through captivity of mines is derived from the difference between the marginal production cost of the ore and the prevailing market price. Naturally, the same amount would be achieved by a financial investor owning equity shares in iron ore mines and selling ore on the open market. ArcelorMittal therefore could choose to regard its iron ore mining assets purely as investment vehicles. Selling the captive ore on the open market instead of charging it into the own blast furnaces would lead to the same profit as the above described iron ore procurement cost reduction.

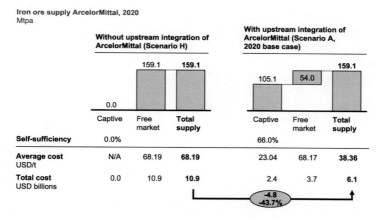

Figure 6.44: Scenario H: 2020 no captivity ArcelorMittal – Analysis of procurement cost of ArcelorMittal [Own illustration]

6.3.2.1.2 Scenario I: 2020 no Chinese captivity of iron ore mines abroad

As shown in Figure 6.45, the demand for iron ore in scenario I is identical to the demand in the base case. This is true for the total demand (2,360.5 Mt) as well as for the individual demand of the geographic regions. China thus continues to dominate demand with 1,136.8 Mt, followed by CIS (221.2 Mt) and South America (219.6 Mt).

Also, production capacities in this scenario are identical to those in the base case, as are the production volumes per region. Therefore, total world iron ore production equals 2,360.5 Mt, with Oceania leading production with 704.7 Mt, closely followed by South America with 689.4 Mt.

With demand, capacities and production identical to the base case, net trade also remains unchanged. China therefore continues to lead net imports with 1,057.9 Mt, followed by the only other net importers Other Asia (181.9 Mt) and Europe (110.9 Mt). Main net exporters are Oceania (692.4 Mt), South America (469.8 Mt) and Africa & Middle East (141.8 Mt).

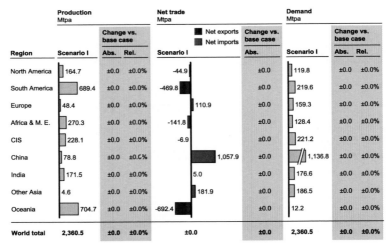

Figure 6.45: Scenario I: 2020 no Chinese captivity abroad – Analysis of production, net trade and demand by region [Own illustration]

Despite the unchanged demand, capacity and production figures, the abolition of China's foreign captive capacity modeled in this scenario has effects on the global iron ore trade flows (see Figure 6.46).[639] The by-far largest flows continue to be directed to China from Oceania (637.1 Mt) and South America (406.9 Mt).

To understand the change in trade flows in this scenario it is important to note that in the base case the allocation is slightly distorted due to the forced destination attributed to China's captive mines abroad. Once this forced supply to China is removed (by allowing these mines to sell to the open market), the cost minimization objective of the model's allocation mechanism finds a slightly improved allocation in terms of total freight costs.[640] In consequence, China no longer imports ore from Africa & Middle East (−34.4 Mt), North America (−6.6 Mt) and Other Asia (−0.7 Mt). These former captive volumes are offset by additional imports from main suppliers Oceania (+40.2 Mt) and South America (+1.5 Mt). The respective volume freed in Africa & Middle East is sent to Other Asia (+34.4 Mt), which in turn decreases its imports from Oceania (−40.2 Mt). The formerly Chinese captive production in North America (6.6 Mt) is sent to Other Asia and Europe, leading to the latter reducing its import volume from South America accordingly.

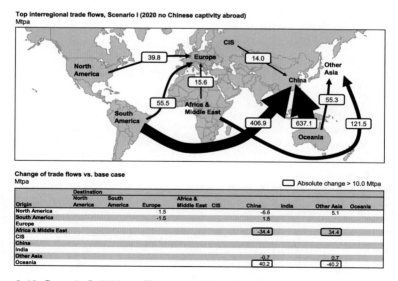

Figure 6.46: Scenario I: 2020 no Chinese captivity abroad – Analysis of interregional trade flows [Own illustration]

---

[639]Note that China's complete domestic iron ore production remains captive in this scenario.

[640]Total freight costs are reduced by approximately USD 0.1 billion (−0.3%) compared to the base case.

The above described change in trade flows does not affect the marginal supplier in any region, but rather affects mines within the respective industry cost curves. In consequence, the change in trade flows vs. the base case has no effect on market prices (see Figure 6.47). China, the price-setting region, has the highest market price with USD 85.59, followed by Other Asia (USD 83.52). India holds the lowest market price at USD 53.41 per ton.

Despite identical market prices in all regions, China's iron ore procurement costs increase by USD 4.9 billion to USD 95.5 billion (+5.4%) due to the annulment of Chinese captivity of iron ore mines outside of China modeled in this scenario. This increase is due to the fact that Chinese steelmakers must now purchase additional ore on the open market at market price instead of receiving iron ore volumes from their mines abroad at unit production cost. Procurement costs in all other regions, however, are identical to those shown in the base case. The global total of iron ore procurement costs thus increases to 164.5 Mt (+3.1%).

The overall profit contribution of the iron ore industry increases by USD 5.0 billion to USD 82.8 billion (+6.4%). This increase stems mainly from the additional revenue generated by mines formerly captive to China now selling at market prices instead of at unit production cost.[641] Due to this, the rise in profit contribution is not distributed evenly among supplying regions, but rather mainly according to the location of mines formerly captive to China. The most considerable absolute increases are thus to be found in Oceania (USD +2.2 billion, +7.6%), Africa & Middle East (USD +1.5 billion, +15.5%) and South America (USD +1.1 billion, +4.2%).

The detailed effects of the annulment of China's captivity abroad on the iron ore miners' profit contributions are shown in Figure 6.48. Due to stable production and demand levels per region, total standardized FOB costs are identical to those in the base case (USD 65.4 billion). Owing to the improved supply allocation and the resulting slight reduction in total freight costs, the combined cost for freight and export taxes is reduced by 0.3% to USD 16.3 billion.[642] As described above, total industry revenue increases by 3.1% to USD 164.5 billion, due to mines formerly captive to China now selling at market prices instead of at unit production cost. The combination of decreased cost positions and increased revenue leaves miners with an increased total profit contribution of USD 82.8 billion (+6.4%).

---

[641] Note that, as described above, the improved allocation of supply in this scenario reduces total freight costs by approximately USD 0.1 billion compared to the base case. Therefore, the increase of miners' total profit contribution compared to the base case is roughly USD 0.1 billion higher than the steelmakers' total iron ore procurement cost increase.

[642] Note that neither of the two regions levying export taxes, China and India, actually export iron ore in this scenario. Thus, as in the base case, overall global export tax costs are zero.

Region	Market price USD/t			Average iron ore procurement cost USD/t			Total iron ore procurement cost USD billions			Total profit contribution of miners (by origin) USD billions		
	Scenario I	Change vs. base case		Scenario I	Change vs. base case		Scenario I	Change vs. base case		Scenario I	Change vs. base case	
		Abs.	Rel.		Abs.	Rel.		Abs.	Rel.		Abs.	Rel.
North America	64.51	±0.00	±0.0%	42.13	±0.00	±0.0%	5.0	±0.0	±0.0%	2.4	0.1	5.7%
South America	67.17	±0.00	±0.0%	50.41	±0.00	±0.0%	11.1	±0.0	±0.0%	27.3	1.1	4.2%
Europe	67.65	±0.00	±0.0%	54.64	±0.00	±0.0%	8.7	±0.0	±0.0%	2.9	±0.0	±0.0%
Africa & M. E.	71.72	±0.00	±0.0%	68.01	±0.00	±0.0%	8.7	±0.0	±0.0%	11.1	1.5	15.5%
CIS	72.96	±0.00	±0.0%	47.40	±0.00	±0.0%	10.5	±0.0	±0.0%	4.7	<0.1	0.3%
China	85.59	±0.00	±0.0%	84.05	4.32	5.4%	95.5	4.9	5.4%	0.0	±0.0	±0.0%
India	53.41	±0.00	±0.0%	50.23	±0.00	±0.0%	8.9	±0.0	±0.0%	3.2	±0.0	±0.0%
Other Asia	83.52	±0.00	±0.0%	82.73	±0.00	±0.0%	15.4	±0.0	±0.0%	0.1	<0.1	47.9%
Oceania	78.07	±0.00	±0.0%	49.99	±0.00	±0.0%	0.6	±0.0	±0.0%	31.0	2.2	7.6%
World total	**77.05**	**±0.00**	**±0.0%**	**69.69**	**2.08**	**3.1%**	**164.5**	**4.9**	**3.1%**	**82.8**	**5.0**	**6.4%**

Figure 6.47: Scenario I: 2020 no Chinese captivity abroad – Analysis of market prices, procurement cost and profit contribution of miners by region [Own illustration]

In contrast to the development observed for the iron ore mining industry as a whole, the abolition of China's iron ore mining activities outside of China has no effect on the profit contribution of the three largest iron ore mining companies. Vale's total profit contribution remains at USD 21.3 billion, Rio Tinto continues to generate a profit contribution of USD 13.1 billion and BHP Billiton's profit contribution equals USD 9.3 billion. The reason for the lacking change is that the Big Three participate neither in the freight cost reduction (due to their unchanged trade flows), nor in the revenue increase (due to the constant market prices) vs. the base case.

In terms of market share (based on profit contribution), the share of the Big Three consequently decreases by 3.3 percentage points in this scenario compared to the base case. Vale stays in first place with a reduced share of 25.7% (−1.6 ppt vs. the base case), Rio Tinto's market share drops to 15.9% (−1.0 ppt) and BHP Billiton claims 11.3% of the overall profit contribution (−0.7 ppt). The reason for this decreased dominance of the Big Three in this scenario lies in the fact that all three players are unable to profit from the increased revenues, as these are directed exclusively towards mines formerly captive to China.

Having now fully analyzed the effect of the annulment of China's foreign iron ore mine captivity on the iron ore and steel industries as a whole, it becomes necessary to determine the effects on the Chinese steel industry itself (see Figure 6.49).

	Production Mtpa	Analysis of profit contribution (USD billions)			
		Standardized FOB cost	Freight and export taxes	Profit contribution	Revenue
World total					164.5
		65.4	16.3	82.8	
Total	2,360.5				
Change vs. base case	±0.0%	±0.0%	-0.3%	6.4%	3.1%
Per ton (USD/t)		27.70	6.91	35.08	69.69
Change vs. base case		±0.0%	-0.3%	6.4%	3.1%
Vale					
Total	436.4	7.6	5.2	21.3	34.0
Change vs. base case	±0.0%	±0.0%	±0.0%	±0.0%	±0.0%
Per ton (USD/t)		17.33	11.94	48.70	77.96
Change vs. base case		±0.0%	±0.0%	±0.0%	±0.0%
Rio Tinto					
Total	247.5	5.7	1.8	13.1	20.6
Change vs. base case	±0.0%	±0.0%	±0.0%	±0.0%	±0.0%
Per ton (USD/t)		23.13	7.19	53.04	83.35
Change vs. base case		±0.0%	±0.0%	±0.0%	±0.0%
BHP Billiton					
Total	188.5	5.2	1.6	9.3	16.1
Change vs. base case	±0.0%	±0.0%	±0.0%	±0.0%	±0.0%
Per ton (USD/t)		27.43	8.63	49.53	85.59
Change vs. base case		±0.0%	-±0.0%	-±0.0%	±0.0%

Figure 6.48: Scenario I: 2020 no Chinese captivity abroad – Analysis of individual profit contributions of miners [Own illustration]

In the base case, China utilizes 142.0 Mt of overseas captive capacity (mainly in Oceania, Africa & Middle East and South America) and 78.8 Mt of domestic production capacity to supply its steelmaking facilities with iron ore.[643] According to the model assumptions, volume from these mines are transferred to blast furnaces in mainland China at unit production cost (plus freight and export tax costs where applicable). Thus, the average total cost of a ton of captive supply equals USD 51.00 from abroad and USD 63.37 per domestic ton. Based on the country's assumed 2020 iron ore demand of 1,136.8 Mt, this corresponds to a self-sufficiency of 19.4%.[644] The remainder of the required ore (916.0 Mt) is purchased on the open market at a price of USD 85.59 per ton (Chinese market price). In total, the average cost per ton of iron ore for a Chinese steelmaker therefore equals USD 79.73 with China's total procurement cost summing up to USD 90.6 billion.

Assuming the complete absence of foreign captive supply for China as modeled in scenario I, the country's steelmakers are left with 78.8 Mt of utilized domestic supply and are forced to procure the remainder of the required ore volume

---

[643] Note that China only utilizes 93.3% of its entire captive capacity abroad and only 20.4% of its domestic capacity due to unfavorable cost positions of the remaining mines.

[644] Utilization of the entire Chinese-owned foreign and domestic production capacity would lead to a self-sufficiency of 47.4%.

(1,058.0 Mt) on the open market.[645] Thus, Chinese self-sufficiency drops from 19.4% to 6.9%. With an average unit cost of domestic supply of USD 63.37 and the Chinese market price at USD 85.59, the average procurement cost per ton equals USD 84.05. Therefore, without captive iron ore mines abroad, China's steel industry faces total iron ore procurement costs of USD 95.5 billion.

Summarizing, due to its strategy of iron ore mine captivity abroad, China enjoys an annual iron ore procurement cost reduction of USD 4.9 billion (−5.1%) in 2020.[646]

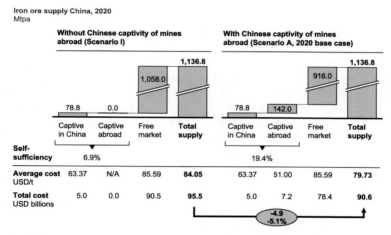

Figure 6.49: Scenario I: 2020 no Chinese captivity abroad – Analysis of procurement cost of China [Own illustration]

---

[645] As in the base case, China utilizes only 20.4% of its domestic production capacity due to unfavorable cost positions of the remaining mines.

[646] Note that this cost advantage does not take into account the original cost of acquiring the respective mines, nor the fix costs incurred in running these mines. It must be noted that the procurement cost reduction effect through captivity of mines is derived from the difference between the marginal production cost of the ore and the prevailing market price. Naturally, the same amount would be achieved by a financial investor owning equity shares in iron ore mines and selling ore on the open market. China therefore could choose to regard its iron ore mining assets purely as investment vehicles. Selling the captive ore on the open market instead of charging it into the own blast furnaces would lead to the same profit as the above described iron ore procurement cost reduction.

6.3.2.2 Export taxes on iron ore

6.3.2.2.1   Scenario J: 2020 no iron ore export taxes in India

As shown in Figure 6.50, the demand for iron ore in scenario J is identical to the demand in the base case. This is true for the total demand (2,360.5 Mt) as well as for the individual demand of the geographic regions. China thus continues to dominate demand with 1,136.8 Mt, followed by CIS (221.2 Mt) and South America (219.6 Mt).

Total world iron ore production in scenario J is equal to production in the base case (2,360.5 Mt). However, there are some regional shifts in production, caused by the annulment of Indian export taxes modeled in this scenario. This improvement of the cost position of Indian mines leads to a strong increase in the Indian iron ore production of 87.1 Mt to 258.6 Mt (+50.8%) compared to the base case. Other regions, especially China (−25.0 Mt, −31.7%), South America (−20.6 Mt, −3.0%), CIS (−14.0 Mt, −6.1%) and Oceania (−13.2 Mt, −1.9%) reduce their production volumes. Oceania remains the largest producer with now 691.5 Mt, followed by South America with 668.8 Mt and Africa & Middle East with 262.3 Mt (−8.0 Mt, −3.0%).

With demand per region constant, this shift in regional production leads to equivalent changes in net trade. Despite this, China continues to lead net imports with 1,082.9 Mt (−25.0 Mt), followed by the only other significant net importers Other Asia (183.3 Mt, +1.3 Mt) and Europe (110.9 Mt, unchanged). The top three net exporters are Oceania (679.2 Mt, −13.2 Mt), South America (449.2 Mt, −20.6 Mt) and Africa & Middle East (133.9 Mt, −8.0 Mt). It is to be noted that India, due to the annulment of its iron ore export taxes, has become a significant net exporter in this scenario (82.1 Mt), compared to its net imports of 5.0 Mt in the base case.

The abolition of export taxes on ores from India and the resulting increased Indian ore exports have substantial effects on the global iron ore trade flows (see Figure 6.51). The by-far largest flows continue to run to China from Oceania (574.4 Mt) and South America (384.0 Mt). In general, in accordance with the total cost minimization objective of the allocation mechanism as defined in Section 5.1.3.1, it can be observed that, due to the reduced Indian export taxes, some of the Indian production capacity that is idle in the base case now squeezes out production in other regions. Following this logic, China reduces its domestic supply by 25.0 Mt as well as imports from Oceania (−22.5 Mt), South America (−21.3 Mt), CIS (−14.0 Mt) and North America (−5.0 Mt) in exchange for 87.8 Mt of imports from neighboring India. In other words, due to the reduced export taxes, some of the mines in India that are priced out of the

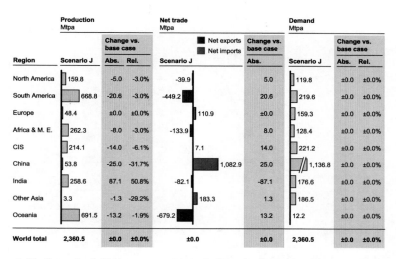

Figure 6.50: Scenario J: 2020 no export taxes India – Analysis of production, net trade and demand by region [Own illustration]

market on a landed cost basis in the base case, now become capable of selling ore on the Chinese market. Other Asia indirectly profits from India's exports to China, as it substitutes domestic production (−1.3 Mt) and imports from Africa & Middle East (−8.0 Mt) for vacant lower-cost production volumes from Oceania (+9.3 Mt).

As can be expected, the increased production volume in India, a region with high-quality and thus low-cost ore resources, and the resulting decreased production in regions with higher costs, especially China and CIS, sends market prices downwards (see Figure 6.52). Compared to the base case, the weighted world average market price for one ton of iron ore decreases by USD 13.32 to USD 63.73 (−17.3%). As described above, Other Asia and China especially profit from India's increase in exports to China and thus reduce their market prices considerably. The Other Asian market price drops by USD 17.63 to USD 65.89 (−21.1%) while China, still the price-setting region, continues to hold the highest market price with USD 69.65 (USD −15.94, −18.6%). Due to the non-arbitrage condition,[647] all other regions (except for India) show similar market price decreases. The Indian market price, however, increases by USD 7.87 to USD 61.28 (+14.7%). The reason for this price increase is twofold: The annulment of the export tax and the resulting outflow of significant low-cost volumes to neighboring consumer China forces India to utilize some of

---

[647]See Section 5.1.3.2.4.

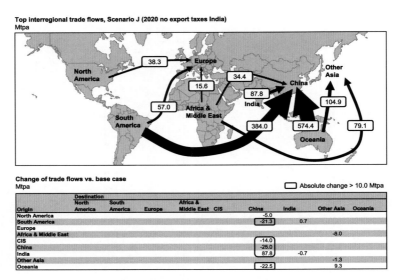

Figure 6.51: Scenario J: 2020 no export taxes India – Analysis of interregional trade flows [Own illustration]

its higher-cost mines to satisfy domestic demand. Also, with the export tax no longer in place, the Indian market price is no longer shielded from the influence of the Chinese market price based on the non-arbitrage condition (see, e.g., Section 6.3.1.2.4). Thus, without the export tax, India is now fully exposed to the dynamics of the iron ore market.

Naturally, these price changes are reflected in the total iron ore procurement cost. Compared to the base case, the additional iron ore production in India reduces global steelmakers' expenditures for iron ore by USD 22.3 billion to a total of USD 137.3 billion (−14.0%). In accordance with the respective regional market price changes, steelmakers in Other Aisa and China are among those profiting the most. Procurement costs in Other Asia drop by USD 3.2 billion (−20.9%) and Chinese steelmakers pay USD 14.8 billion less for their ore than in the base case (−16.3%). Relative cost reductions for regions using high shares of captive supply are lower than for regions that are more exposed to the open market. Therefore, the procurement costs decreases of steelmakers in Oceania (−3.3%), North America (−6.3%), CIS (−6.8%) and Europe (−11.4%) are below the average 14.0% decrease.[648] Following the rise in market price,

---

[648]Note that China, although it owns large volumes of captive capacity, does not fall into this category as it is not forced to utilize much of its captive capacity in this scenario (as in the base case).

India's steelmakers face increased iron ore procurement costs of USD 10.2 billion (USD +1.3 billion, +14.5%).

From the iron ore miner's point of view, the additional low-cost supply from India entering the market is rather disadvantageous. Lower market prices lead to an overall decrease in profit contributions of iron ore miners of USD 26.2 billion to a total of USD 51.7 billion (−33.6%). The change of miners' profit contributions by region of origin depends greatly on the destination mix of their ore and the market price development in those regions. Iron ore miners in Oceania (USD −9.9 billion), South America (USD −9.8 billion) and Africa & Middle East (USD −3.5 billion) show the largest absolute decreases in profit contribution, mainly due to the sharp decrease in the market price of their largest customers, China and Other Asia. Indian iron ore miners are the only once profiting from the annulment of the Indian export tax. Their joint profit contribution increases by USD 1.0 billion to USD 4.2 billion (+30.9%) as they benefit from higher production volumes, the increase in the domestic market price and new export opportunities to even higher-priced China.

One can attempt to evaluate the annulment of the Indian export tax from the Indian government's point of view by comparing its effect on the iron ore procurement cost of the country's steelmakers and the effect on the Indian iron ore miners' profit contribution. As described above, procurement costs incurred by Indian steelmakers increase by USD 1.3 billion while the total profit contribution generated by the country's iron ore miners rises by USD 1.0 billion. On an extremely simplified basis, it can be said that, due to the annulment of the export tax on iron ore, India's joint iron ore and steel industries incur a net loss of USD 0.3 billion in profit contribution.[649] The reason for this lies in the relative weight of the two industries. Although the size of India's iron ore mining industry is considerable, India's steelmaking industry is even larger and thus of greater importance from a national economic perspective.

The detailed effects of the annulment of the Indian iron ore export tax on the global iron ore miners' profit contributions are shown in Figure 6.53. Despite the above described substitution of production in China and CIS with increased low-cost production in India and lower mining royalties due to the lower market prices, the overall standardized FOB cost increases by 6.0% to USD 69.3 billion. This effect can be traced back to lower grade and value-in-use premiums stemming from the decrease in market prices. The combined cost for freight and export taxes decreases, though insignificantly (−0.3%) due to lower total freight

---

[649]This calculation is to be interpreted with extreme caution, as it does not take into account potential revenue changes for the Indian government in terms of taxes and royalties, nor any other macroeconomic effects or effects in other industries that may be associated with the annulment of the export tax.

Region	Market price USD/t			Average iron ore procurement cost USD/t			Total iron ore procurement cost USD billions			Total profit contribution of miners (by origin) USD billions		
	Scenario J	Change vs. base case		Scenario J	Change vs. base case		Scenario J	Change vs. base case		Scenario J	Change vs. base case	
		Abs.	Rel.		Abs.	Rel.		Abs.	Rel.		Abs.	Rel.
North America	52.72	-11.79	-18.3%	39.45	-2.68	-6.3%	4.7	-0.3	-6.3%	1.1	-1.2	-51.4%
South America	52.13	-15.04	-22.4%	42.16	-8.26	-16.4%	9.3	-1.8	-16.4%	16.4	-9.8	-37.3%
Europe	56.58	-11.07	-16.4%	48.38	-6.26	-11.4%	7.7	-1.0	-11.4%	2.0	-0.9	-30.4%
Africa & M. E.	57.22	-14.50	-20.2%	54.76	-13.25	-19.5%	7.0	-1.7	-19.5%	6.1	-3.5	-36.2%
CIS	59.96	-13.00	-17.8%	44.16	-3.23	-6.8%	9.8	-0.7	-6.8%	2.8	-1.9	-40.4%
China	69.65	-15.94	-18.6%	66.73	-13.00	-16.3%	75.9	-14.8	-16.3%	0.0	±0.0	±0.0%
India	61.28	7.87	14.7%	57.50	7.27	14.5%	10.2	1.3	14.5%	4.2	1.0	30.9%
Other Asia	65.89	-17.63	-21.1%	65.41	-17.32	-20.9%	12.2	-3.2	-20.9%	0.1	>-0.1	-47.4%
Oceania	62.13	-15.94	-20.4%	48.33	-1.66	-3.3%	0.6	>-0.1	-3.3%	18.9	-9.9	-34.4%
World total	63.73	-13.32	-17.3%	58.16	-9.45	-14.0%	137.3	-22.3	-14.0%	51.7	-26.2	-33.6%

Figure 6.52: Scenario J: 2020 no export taxes India – Analysis of market prices, procurement cost and profit contribution of miners by region [Own illustration]

costs owing to volumes from near-by India replacing volumes from regions further away as a supplier to China.[650] In addition to these higher cost positions, a decreased total revenue of USD 137.3 billion (−14.0%), stemming from lower market prices, leads to a 33.6% reduction of iron ore miners' combined profit contribution vs. the base case to USD 51.7 billion.

The three largest miners are equally hard hit. Vale's total profit contribution sinks to USD 14.0 billion (−34.3% vs. the base case), Rio Tinto retains a profit contribution of USD 9.0 billion (−31.5%) and BHP Billiton's profit contribution is reduced to USD 6.3 billion (−32.1%). In terms of market share (based on profit contribution), the share of the Big Three even increases slightly to 56.7% (+0.5 ppt vs. the base case). Vale stays in first place with a slightly reduced market share of 27.0% (−0.3 ppt), Rio Tinto's share rises to 17.4% (+0.5 ppt) and BHP Billiton claims 12.3% (+0.3 ppt).

---

[650]Note that in the base case, neither of the two regions levying export taxes, China and India, actually export iron ore. Thus, despite the resulting Indian export increase, the annulment of India's export tax has no effect on overall global export tax costs, which remain zero as in the base case.

Analysis of profit contribution (USD billions)

	Production Mtpa	Standardized FOB cost	Freight and export taxes	Profit contribution	Revenue
World total					137.3
		69.3	16.3	51.7	
Total	2,360.5				
Change vs. base case	±0.0%	6.0%	-0.3%	-33.6%	-14.0%
Per ton (USD/t)		29.36	6.91	21.90	58.16
Change vs. base case		6.0%	-0.3%	-33.6%	-14.0%
Vale					
Total	420.5	7.5	4.8	14.0	26.3
Change vs. base case	-3.6%	-1.0%	-7.3%	-34.3%	-22.8%
Per ton (USD/t)		17.80	11.49	33.19	62.48
Change vs. base case		2.8%	-3.8%	-31.8%	-19.9%
Rio Tinto					
Total	247.5	5.9	1.8	9.0	16.6
Change vs. base case	±0.0%	2.5%	0.4%	-31.5%	-19.3%
Per ton (USD/t)		23.71	7.22	36.32	67.24
Change vs. base case		2.5%	0.4%	-31.5%	-19.3%
BHP Billiton					
Total	188.5	5.2	1.6	6.3	13.1
Change vs. base case	±0.0%	-0.2%	±0.0%	-32.1%	-18.6%
Per ton (USD/t)		27.36	8.63	33.64	69.64
Change vs. base case		-0.2%	±0.0%	-32.1%	-18.6%

Figure 6.53: Scenario J: 2020 no export taxes India – Analysis of individual profit contributions of miners [Own illustration]

6.3.2.2.2   Scenario K: 2020 introduction of iron ore export taxes in Brazil

As shown in Figure 6.54, the demand for iron ore in scenario K is identical to the demand in the base case. This is true for the total demand (2,360.5 Mt) as well as for the individual demand of the geographic regions. China thus continues to dominate demand with 1,136.8 Mt, followed by CIS (221.2 Mt) and South America (219.6 Mt).

Total world iron ore production in scenario K is equal to production in the base case (2,360.5 Mt). However, there are some regional shifts in production, caused by the introduction of Brazilian export taxes modeled in this scenario.[651] This increase of the cost position of Brazilian mines leads to a decrease in the South American iron ore production of 4.6 Mt to 684.8 Mt (-0.7%) compared to the base case. Consequently, other regions, especially Oceania ($+3.8$ Mt, $+0.5\%$), Inida ($+0.4$ Mt, $+0.3\%$) and Other Asia ($+0.4$ Mt, $+8.1\%$), increase their production volumes. Oceania remains the largest producer with now 708.5 Mt, followed by South America with 684.8 Mt and Africa & Middle East with 270.3 Mt (unchanged).

With demand per region constant, this shift in regional production leads to equivalent changes in net trade. Despite this, China continues to lead net imports with 1,057.9 Mt (unchanged), followed by the only other significant net importers Other Asia (181.5 Mt, -0.4 Mt) and Europe (110.9 Mt, unchanged). The top three net exporters are Oceania (696.2 Mt, $+3.8$ Mt), South America (465.2 Mt, -4.6 Mt) and Africa & Middle East (141.8 Mt, unchanged).

The introduction of export taxes on iron ore from Brazil and the resulting decreased South American ore exports have some minor effects on the global iron ore trade flows (see Figure 6.55). The by-far largest flows continue to run to China from Oceania (600.7 Mt) and South America (401.2 Mt). In general, in accordance with the total cost minimization objective of the allocation mechanism as defined in Section 5.1.3.1, it can be observed that, due to the export taxes levied in this scenario, part of the South American production capacity that supplies China and India in the base case is now squeezed out by capacity in other regions that was idle in the base case. In other words, some of the mines in South America that export ore in the base case are now priced out of the market on a landed cost basis in China and India. Following this logic,

---

[651] As described in Section 6.1.2.2.2, due to the regional structure of the model, this scenario adds a 5% export tax on iron ore from all South American countries (not just Brazil). However, this error is negligible as Brazil accounts for roughly 90% of all South American iron ore production. For reasons of simplicity, this export tax will therefore be referred to as being Brazilian in the following.

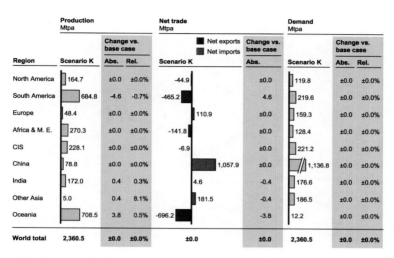

Figure 6.54: Scenario K: 2020 introduction export taxes Brazil – Analysis of production, net trade and demand by region [Own illustration]

China reduces its imports from South America (−4.2 Mt) in exchange for increased imports from Oceania (+3.8 Mt) and Other Asia (+0.4 Mt). Similarly, India reduces its imports from South America by 0.4 Mt and increases domestic production by the same amount.

As can be expected, the increased landed cost positions of ore volumes from South America and the resulting change in trade flows described above has some influence on the iron ore market prices (see Figure 6.56). In total, compared to the base case, the weighted world average market price for one ton of iron ore decreases slightly by USD 0.15 to USD 76.90 (−0.2%). A more significant impact, however, can be found in the South American and European market prices. The South American market price decreases significantly by USD 6.74 to USD 60.43 (−10.0%). The reason for this price decrease is the reduced outflow of low-cost volumes to China and India due to the introduction of the export tax. This allows South America to utilize some of its lower-cost mines to satisfy domestic demand. Europe suffers considerably from the introduction of Brazilian export taxes. Its market price increases by USD 5.09 to USD 72.74 (+7.5%). This increase is due to South America being Europe's marginal supplier combined with the fact that there existis no idle mine in the global cost curve able to supply to Europe at a lower price than the increased cost of this marginal mine. For China and India, being forced to slightly change their supply sources from South America, a region with high-quality and thus low-cost ore resources, to

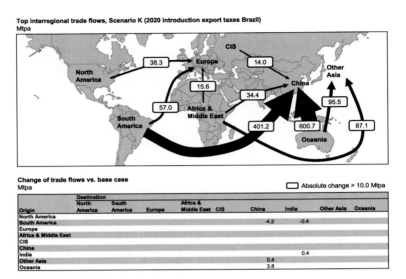

Figure 6.55: Scenario K: 2020 introduction export taxes Brazil – Analysis of interregional trade flows [Own illustration]

mines idle in the base case for cost reasons leads to an increase in market price of USD 0.18 and USD 0.10 respectively. Consequently, China, as the price-setting region, continues to hold the highest market price with USD 85.77 (+0.2%). Due to the non-arbitrage condition,[652] all other regions (except for Other Asia and South America) show similar market price increases.[653]

Despite the slight reduction in the world average market price, the introduced Brazilian export tax increases global steelmakers' expenditures for iron ore by USD 0.1 billion to a total of USD 159.7 billion (−0.1% compared to the base case). This is due to the presence of Chinese and Indian captive mines in South America, which increase in terms of their unit production cost. In accordance with the respective regional market price changes, steelmakers in South America profit from the iron ore export tax. Their iron ore procurement costs decrease by USD 0.9 billion to USD 10.2 billion (−7.8%). Europe shows the largest increase with USD 0.5 billion, now paying USD 9.2 billion for its iron ore (+6.1%). China's iron ore procurement costs also increase, up USD 0.3 billion to USD 91.0 billion (+0.4%), due to its slight increase in market price and

---

[652]See Section 5.1.3.2.4.

[653]Note that Other Asia's price increase of USD 0.01 stems from an increase in royalties due to the higher market price in the price-setting region.

the cost increase in its South American captive mines. All other regions show rather insignificant cost increases of less than USD 0.1 billion per region.

From the iron ore miner's point of view, the introduction of export taxes on iron ore leaving Brazil is rather disadvantageous. Although most regions show an increase in market price, the decreased world average market price leads to an overall decrease in profit contributions of iron ore miners of USD 3.1 billion to a total of USD 74.8 billion (−4.0%). However, on a regional level, South American iron ore miners are the only ones suffering a profit contribution decrease, USD −3.5 billion to USD 22.7 billion (−13.4%). This is due to their significant share of domestic customers and the sharp decrease in the South American market price. European miners profit from the domestic market price increase. Their profit contribution increases by USD 0.2 billion to USD 3.1 billion (+8.5%). Miners from all other regions show profit contribution increases of around USD 0.1 billion per region.

One can attempt to evaluate the introduction of Brazilian export taxes on iron ore from the Brazilian government's point of view by comparing its effect on the iron ore procurement cost of South American steelmakers and the effect on the region's iron ore miners' profit contribution. As described above, procurement costs incurred by South American steelmakers decrease by USD 0.9 billion while the total profit contribution generated by the region's iron ore miners is reduced by USD 3.5 billion. On an extremely simplified basis, it can be said that, due to the introduction of the export tax on iron ore, South America's joint iron ore and steel industries incur a net loss of USD 2.6 billion in profit contribution.[654] The reason for this lies in the relative weight of the two industries. Although, as described in the Section 6.1.2.2.2, there is an attempt to encourage the growth of the Brazilian steelmaking industry, Brazil's iron ore mining industry is considerably larger and thus of greater importance from a national economic perspective.

The detailed effects of the introduction of Brazilian iron ore export taxes on the global iron ore miners' profit contributions are shown in Figure 6.57. Despite the above described substitution of low-cost imports from South America with higher-cost production in India, Other Asia and Oceania, the overall standardized FOB cost remains constant at USD 65.4 billion. This is due to the minor scale of the volume substitution. The combined cost for freight and export taxes increases significantly to USD 19.5 billion (+19.4%), due to the introduction of the Brazilian export tax. The considerably higher total cost of supply combined

---

[654]This calculation is to be interpreted with extreme caution, as it does not take into account potential revenue changes for the Brazilian government in terms of taxes and royalties, nor any other macroeconomic effects or effects in other industries that may be associated with the introduction of the export tax.

Region	Market price USD/t			Average iron ore procurement cost USD/t			Total iron ore procurement cost USD billions			Total profit contribution of miners (by origin) USD billions		
	Scenario K	Change vs. base case		Scenario K	Change vs. base case		Scenario K	Change vs. base case		Scenario K	Change vs. base case	
		Abs.	Rel.		Abs.	Rel.		Abs.	Rel.		Abs.	Rel.
North America	64.69	0.18	0.3%	42.19	0.06	0.1%	5.1	<0.1	0.1%	2.3	<0.1	0.9%
South America	60.43	-6.74	-10.0%	46.47	-3.94	-7.8%	10.2	-0.9	-7.8%	22.7	-3.5	-13.4%
Europe	72.74	5.09	7.5%	57.98	3.34	6.1%	9.2	0.5	6.1%	3.1	0.2	8.5%
Africa & M. E.	71.90	0.18	0.3%	68.17	0.16	0.2%	8.8	<0.1	0.2%	9.6	<0.1	0.3%
CIS	73.14	0.18	0.2%	47.52	0.13	0.3%	10.5	<0.1	0.3%	4.7	<0.1	0.5%
China	85.77	0.18	0.2%	80.01	0.29	0.4%	91.0	0.3	0.4%	0.0	±0.0	±0.0%
India	53.51	0.10	0.2%	50.51	0.27	0.5%	8.9	<0.1	0.5%	3.3	<0.1	0.6%
Other Asia	83.53	0.01	<0.1%	82.74	0.01	<0.1%	15.4	<0.1	<0.1%	0.1	<0.1	<0.1%
Oceania	78.25	0.18	0.2%	50.01	0.02	<0.1%	0.6	<0.1	<0.1%	28.9	0.1	0.3%
World total	76.90	-0.15	-0.2%	67.65	0.04	0.1%	159.7	0.1	0.1%	74.8	-3.1	-4.0%

Figure 6.56: Scenario K: 2020 introduction export taxes Brazil – Analysis of market prices, procurement cost and profit contribution of miners by region [Own illustration]

with a slight increased total revenue of USD 159.7 billion (+0.1%), stemming from increased iron ore procurement costs, leads to a 4.0% reduction of iron ore miners' combined profit contribution vs. the base case to USD 74.8 billion.

The effect on the profit contribution of the three largest miners is heterogeneous. Vale's total profit contribution sinks to USD 18.7 billion (−11.8% vs. the base case), Rio Tinto slightly increases its profit contribution to USD 13.2 billion (+0.3%) and BHP Billiton's profit contribution is reduced to USD 9.3 billion (−0.3%). The reason for Vale's immense profit contribution loss is two-fold: due to the miner's geographic focus of production in Brazil and its large share of exports, Vale's freight and export tax costs are increased by 38.5% because of the introduction of the export tax. Additionally, the decreased South American market price affects Vale negatively in terms of supply to domestic customers, shrinking the miner's total revenues by 1.5%.

In terms of market share (based on profit contribution), the total share of the Big Three decreases slightly to 55.1% (−1.0 ppt vs. the base case) due to Vale's considerable decrease in profit contribution. Despite its loss, Vale stays in first place with 25.1% market share (−2.2 ppt), Rio Tinto's share increases to 17.6% (+0.7 ppt) and BHP Billiton claims 12.4% (+0.5 ppt).

Analysis of profit contribution (USD billions)

	Production Mtpa	Standardized FOB cost	Freight and export taxes	Profit contribution	Revenue
World total					159.7
		65.4	19.5	74.8	
Total	2,360.5				
Change vs. base case	±0.0%	<0.1%	19.4%	-4.0%	0.1%
Per ton (USD/t)		27.71	8.27	31.67	67.65
Change vs. base case		<0.1%	19.4%	-4.0%	0.1%
Vale					
Total	436.4	7.6	7.2	18.7	33.5
Change vs. base case	±0.0%	-0.1%	38.5%	-11.8%	-1.5%
Per ton (USD/t)		17.30	16.54	42.93	76.77
Change vs. base case		-0.1%	38.5%	-11.8%	-1.5%
Rio Tinto					
Total	247.5	5.7	1.8	13.2	20.7
Change vs. base case	±0.0%	±0.0%	±0.0%	0.3%	0.2%
Per ton (USD/t)		23.12	7.19	53.18	83.49
Change vs. base case		±0.0%	±0.0%	0.3%	0.2%
BHP Billiton					
Total	188.5	5.2	1.7	9.3	16.2
Change vs. base case	±0.0%	±0.0%	3.9%	-0.3%	0.2%
Per ton (USD/t)		27.43	8.96	49.38	85.77
Change vs. base case		±0.0%	3.9%	-0.3%	0.2%

Figure 6.57: Scenario K: 2020 introduction export taxes Brazil – Analysis of individual profit contributions of miners [Own illustration]

6.4 Discussion of results

Following the descriptive analysis of the scenario results in the previous section, this section aims to summarize the characteristics and dynamics of the 2020 iron ore market as well as to provide an evaluation of the selected risk mitigation strategies for demand-side players.

6.4.1 Discussion of results of quantitative analysis of structure and dynamics of the 2020 iron ore market

The scenarios presented above cover a broad spectrum of possible market constellations for the 2020 iron ore market. The results of these scenarios vary strongly in terms of regional market prices, iron ore procurement costs and profit contributions of iron ore miners. Some general market characteristics, however, are common to all. Thus, with all the necessary qualifications to the accuracy and reliability of the model, the following general characteristics of the 2020 iron ore market can be assumed:[655]

- *Increased global demand* – It is probable that the 2020 iron ore market will be characterized by considerably higher global iron ore demand than in 2009. This demand increase will stem particularly from regions with booming economies, especially China, South America, India and CIS.[656] Therefore, as in 2009, the nucleus of global iron ore demand will presumably be in Asia

- *Increased global production capacity* – It can be assumed that this demand surge will be compensated by considerably higher global iron ore production capacities compared to 2009. These additional capacities will stem from numerous green- and brownfield expansion projects already under development, especially in South America, Oceania and Africa & Middle East. All having particularly high-quality and thus low-cost ore resources, South America and Oceania will strengthen their positions as the world's largest suppliers of iron ore, while Africa & Middle East is expected to establish itself as the indisputable number three supplier by 2020

---

[655]Note that the levels of 2020 supply and demand in the model are based on data from McKinsey & Company (2011b); McKinsey & Company (2010a). Though therefore exogenous to the model, the relative levels compared to 2009 are summarized here in order to provide a complete overview of the key characteristics of the 2020 iron ore market.

[656]See Section 4.1.1 for details on demand-side developments.

- *Increased seaborne trade flows* – In terms of iron ore trade, it can be expected that the main flows will be directed from the three largest supplying regions to China and the remaining Asian economies. This effect will be reinforced by a considerable decrease in China's domestic production due to depletion of mines and the presence of lower-cost production capacity abroad. Therefore, the global share of seaborne supply is set to increase compared to 2009

Depending on the exact level of global demand, production capacity and freight rates, however, the resulting 2020 regional market prices as well as the steelmakers' overall iron ore procurement costs and the iron ore miners' profit contributions vary from levels considerably below the 2009 actuals to a multiple of their 2009 values.

6.4.1.1 Discussion of 2020 market economics of supply and demand

As shown in Section 6.3.1.2.5, regional market prices, steelmakers' overall iron ore procurement costs and iron ore miners' profit contributions all show a positive correlation with global capacity utilization,[657] increasing disproportionately when global capacity utilization exceeds approximately 90%. Thus, the exact levels of these key market figures depend on respective levels of global demand and global production capacity.

In terms of 2020 global iron ore demand, the BRIC countries will clearly be the main drivers, showing by far the largest potential demand increases. Therefore, as outlined in Section 4.1.1, global capacity utilization from a demand perspective depends considerably on the rate of the BRICs' economic growth and their resulting demand for steel and thus for iron ore. While some sources, based on economic arguments, indicate that the BRIC countries' growth may slow quite abruptly, one can equally find renowned economists claiming that the speed of the BRICs' economic development is generally being underestimated.[658] This paper, relying on GDP scenarios defined by McKinsey & Company (2010a),[659] can and will not join in the discussion as to what the exact magnitude of the BRIC countries' economic growth will be through 2020. Fact is, however, that

---

[657]Defined as the ratio of global demand to global production capacity.

[658]For a general discussion of the BRICs' growth perspectives, see Wilson and Purushothaman (2003). For a discussion of China's economic growth, see, e.g., BBC News (2011); Davies and Emmett (2010); Johnson and Wassener (2011); Wolf (2011). A detailed scenario-based analysis of the potential economic developments in Russia, India and China through 2025 can be found in World Economic Forum (2010a); World Economic Forum (2010b); World Economic Forum (2010c).

[659]See Section 5.1.2.3.

the function of GDP per capita and iron ore demand per capita cannot be actively manipulated by any player in the market.[660] Therefore, the BRICs, though with a particular incentive to keep global capacity utilization low, will, like all other countries, have to accept the iron ore demand set by its respective economic growth.

From the supply side, however, global capacity utilization is more easily influenced. Iron ore miners, especially the Big Three, have a significant incentive to keep the market tight, preferably above a global capacity utilization of 90%. This would, as shown in Section 6.3.1.2.5, lead to considerably higher market prices and thus higher profit contributions.[661] While it is not probable that iron ore miners will cut capacity at mines in operation,[662] they may decide to delay announced expansion projects in order to avoid lower global capacity utilization. Small iron ore miners, apart from lacking sufficient leverage to influence global capacity utilization in this manner, will not voluntarily delay their expansion projects as they are forced to achieve returns on their invested capital in order to stay in business. Major iron ore miners, such as the Big Three, however, have sufficiently large projects to create enough leverage and command enough disposable capital to delay projects and thus keep global supply low while ensuring at least supply-demand equilibrium. As shown in Section 6.3.1.2.5, delaying expansion projects would mean a reduction in market dominance of the Big Three.[663] However, their significantly increased profit contributions resulting from higher market prices would justify this move.[664]

Interestingly, recent events suggest that, despite having repeatedly announced massive expansion projects,[665] the major iron ore miners may already be pursuing this strategy. The consensus view about a rapid drop in market prices has

---

[660]Due to the significance of steel for industry growth and necessary infrastructure projects as well as the lack of substitute materials, see Section 5.1.2.3.

[661]However, it is to be noted that maximizing the market price is not always to the miners' advantage. As described in detail in Section 2.2.2, the capital required for the setup of new mining operations represents an effective barrier to entry. When market prices are extremely high, new junior miners may decide to enter the market and engage in iron ore mining activities, thus threatening the market shares of the incumbents (see Eckel (1914), pp. 175–176; Koscianski and Mathis (1995); Mathis and Koscianski (1997); O'Keefe and Burke (2007)). Recall also that, as mentioned in Section 4.1.2, the available level of iron ore production capacity reacts to demand increases with a time lag of three to seven years, leading to a cyclicality in the market.

[662]Due to the significant economies of scale involved in iron ore mining activities, see Section 5.1.2.1.1.2.

[663]In terms of reduced joint market share due to new production capacity of other miners coming online through 2020.

[664]However, due to their market-dominating position, the Big Three are well advised to consider whether or not this would attract the attention of the competition watchdogs.

[665]See Section 4.1.2.

started to fracture as the list of delayed new mining projects grows. The latest additions to this list include Vale, which recently cut its iron ore production capacity target for 2015 by about 10%. Also, according to BHP Billiton, additional global iron ore production capacity for 2010 was announced at 500 Mt, but actual new capacity was less than half of that.[666]

On the other hand, China and other large iron ore consuming entities may also try to influence global capacity utilization to their favor by encouraging the build-up of additional production capacity. As described in Section 6.1.2.1.2, especially China has been extremely active in funding junior miners' capacity expansion projects and developing own projects abroad. However, these projects jointly have little chance of outbalancing capacity expansion decisions of the major miners, who have a higher leverage in terms of total capacity of current green- and brownfield expansion projects.

Summarizing, in terms of market economics of supply and demand, this paper arguments that, due to the significant amount of expansion projects commanded by the Big Three and their incentive to delay capacity coming online, it is probable that the 2020 market constellation will be somewhere near scenario B (low supply).[667] This would lead to considerably higher market prices than in 2009 and with it higher overall iron ore procurement costs for steelmakers and increased profit contributions for iron ore miners. Apart from a probable higher base-level in 2020, market prices are expected be more volatile than in 2009 and with them, steelmakers' iron ore procurement costs and miners' profit contributions. As described in detail in Section 4.1.3, this is due to the new spot market-liked iron ore pricing mechanism and the shift to shorter pricing periods as well as speculation effects arising from the newly established iron ore derivatives market.[668]

6.4.1.2 Discussion of 2020 market economics of freight rates

With respect to market economics of freight rates, as shown in Section 6.3.1.3.3, the results of the corresponding scenarios show that changes in freight rate levels have heterogeneous effects on regional market prices and therefore on the iron

---

[666]See The Financial Times (2011b).

[667]Recall that, as described in Section 6.1.1, the base case, though representing what is considered a "typical" 2020 market constellation in this paper, is not necessarily the most probable scenario.

[668]Although the iron ore model used in this paper is static and therefore does not directly reflect price volatility, it suggests a magnitude to the effects of volatility in terms of the here discussed demand and production capacity levels by allowing the comparison of the results of the respective sensitivity scenarios.

ore procurement costs of individual regions. The regions with highest import demand (China and Other Asia) show a positive correlation of their market prices and procurement costs with freight rates.[669] All other regions (with the exception of India)[670] show a negative correlation.[671] On a global scale, however, the weighted average market price and steelmakers' overall iron ore procurement costs remain largely unaffected by freight rate variations. Miners' profit contributions, however, are negatively correlated with freight cost levels. South American miner Vale, due to its disadvantageous geographic position with respect to delivery to Asia and its resulting larger exposure to freight rates, shows a particularly high sensitivity to freight rate changes. Thus, freight rate volatility represents a considerable risk for iron ore miners, especially for those with mining operations far from Asia, the nucleus of global demand.

This paper, building on freight rate predictions by Gardiner (2011),[672] does not aim to predict the correct freight rate level in 2020. However, as described in detail in Section 4.1.3, it can be assumed that freight rates will show considerable volatility as they depend on the interaction of vessel supply and demand on the world market and therefore reflect the general volatility in the market for raw materials in general and for iron ore in particular.[673]

While most iron ore miners use derivatives and freight forward agreements to hedge against this volatility, recent developments show that Vale is addressing its increased risk by establishing its own fleet.[674] The world's number one iron ore producer is investing almost USD 4.4 billion to build 35 "Valemax" iron ore carriers. These giants, the first of which was commissioned in Mai 2011, will be the world's largest bulk carriers, boasting an overall length of 360 meters and a tonnage of 400,000 dwt.[675] According to company sources, Vale's mega-ships will be used predominantly to ship iron ore from Brazil to China, while chartered ships will be used on other routes.[676]

---

[669]However, as described above, these market prices and costs haven an extremely low elasticity with respect to freight rates changes.

[670]India shows a more or less constant low market price due to its self-sufficiency and iron ore export taxes.

[671]Although regions further from China show a higher price elasticity than regions with higher geographic proximity to China.

[672]See Section 5.1.2.2.2.

[673]Although the iron ore model used in this paper is static and therefore does not directly reflect volatility, it suggests a magnitude to the effects of freight rate volatility by allowing the comparison of the results of the respective sensitivity scenarios.

[674]See Steel Business Briefing (2011d). Note that, due to the recency of this development, Vale's fleet is not reflected in the here discussed model.

[675]On its maiden voyage the "Vale Brasil" carried more than 391,000 tons of ore.

[676]See, e.g., Antonioli (2011b); Ellsworth et al. (2011); Fernandez and Fabi (2010); Steel Business Briefing (2011d).

Using its own fleet creates two fundamental advantages for Vale. First of all, Vale will be able to reduce its freight rates to the actual cost of shipping by cutting out the margin of the shipping company.[677] Therefore, Vale will be able to reduce the freight rate advantage traditionally held by Australian iron ore miners with respect to supply to Asia. Secondly, in addition to the lower base-level freight costs, Vale will no longer face freight rate volatility caused by supply and demand changes in the market for bulk freight capacity.[678] It will rather be able to calculate with more stable freight costs, having to take into account only the inflation of factor costs.[679]

6.4.2 Discussion of evaluation of selected risk mitigation strategies

In combination with the market trends described in Section 4.1, the above discussed market economics of supply, demand and freight rates lead to the expectation of a high-priced and volatile 2020 iron ore market. Therefore, steelmakers will no longer be able to rely on business-as-usual scenarios when it comes to the procurement of iron ore. They must factor in higher base-level prices and increased market volatility and devise strategies to cope with the new market situation. The scenarios presented in Section 6.3.2 of this paper aimed to analyze the effectiveness of two such risk mitigation strategies: captivity of mines and introduction of iron ore export taxes. In the following, the results of these scenarios will be summarized and the effectiveness of the underlying strategies discussed.

6.4.2.1 Discussion of captivity of mines

The scenarios discussed in Section 6.3.2.1 analyzed the effect of ArcelorMittal's as well as China's captivity of iron ore mines. As shown, the captivity of mines leads to considerable iron ore procurement cost reductions for the respective players. ArcelorMittal, due to its extensive upstream integration resulting in a

---

[677]Note that, on the other hand, Vale faces a significant amount of cost of capital due to the tied capital invested in the ships. Also, the managerial challenges involved in managing a fleet is not to be underestimated. In order to reduce this burden, Vale has recently offered to sell its new ships to shipping companies in exchange for a long-term contract with the new shipowners that will ensure the ships will only be used to transport Vale's iron ore. The freight price Vale will pay to the owners will be based on a cost plus return of investment basis (see Antonioli and Saul (2011)).

[678]Of course, this is valid only for the routes on which the own ships are employed. Freight rate volatility will still remain an issue for the remaining routes.

[679]Note that this cost inflation may be considerable, especially in terms of carbon and energy prices. Nevertheless, these factor cost increases also apply to chartered freight rates.

self-sufficiency of 66.0%, enjoys an annual iron ore procurement cost reduction of USD 4.8 billion (-43.7%) compared to no captivity (see results of scenario H in Section 6.3.2.1.1). Similarly, China's steel industry, due to its strategy of iron ore mine captivity abroad leading to a self-suffiency of 19.4%, realizes an annual iron ore procurement cost reduction of USD 4.9 billion (-5.1%) compared to only domestic captive supply (see results of scenario I in Section 6.3.2.1.2).[680]

It must be noted that this procurement cost reduction effect through captivity of mines is derived from the difference between the marginal production cost of the ore and the prevailing market price. Naturally, the same amount would be achieved by a financial investor owning equity shares in iron ore mines and selling ore on the open market. In the scenarios examined above, ArcelorMittal and China therefore could choose to regard their iron ore mining assets purely as investment vehicles. Selling the captive ore on the open market instead of charging it into the own blast furnaces would lead to the same profit as the above described iron ore procurement cost reduction. ArcelorMittal's and China's specific advantage in using the captive ore to satisfy own demand, however, lies in the security of supply, especially with respect to the specific quality of the required ore. This security may be of increased value in the future, if the global iron ore demand surge continues.

In addition to the considerable absolute procurement cost reductions, the scenarios analyzed in the sensitivity analysis in Section 6.3.1 of this paper show that captivity of mines also leads to a reduced exposure to market price volatility.[681] Throughout these scenarios, regions with high shares of captive supply show a lower elasticity of their iron ore procurement costs with respect to market price changes than regions with low shares of captive supply.[682] Therefore, by locking in low cost supply by means of captivity and thus increasing self-sufficiency, steelmakers become less exposed to the price volatility of the open market.

---

[680]Note that these absolute cost decreases result from steelmakers tapping into the upstream shift of the industry profit pools (as shown in Section 4.2). Thus, by means of captivity of iron ore mines, steelmakers mitigate the current structural disadvantages of being pure midstream players.

[681]Recall that, although the iron ore model used in this paper is static and therefore does not directly reflect price volatility, it suggests a magnitude to the effects of volatility in terms of demand, production capacity and freight levels by allowing the comparison of the results of the respective sensitivity scenarios.

[682]Though observed here on a regional level, it can be assumed that this finding is also valid for individual demand-side players. Note that this lower elasticity of procurement costs can be observed for price changes in both directions. Price increases lead to below average relative procurement cost increases and price decreases lead to below average relative procurement cost decreases.

As captivity therefore surely has an iron ore procurement cost reducing and cost-stabilizing effect for the individual steelmaker, it is necessary to briefly analyze the effect of captive mines from a global industry perspective. As shown in both the case of ArcelorMittal and China, captivity of mines has no effect on the market price in any region, nor on the iron ore procurement costs or profit contributions of the remaining steel and iron ore players.[683] However, it is possible that significant increases in the amount of overall captive supply will lead to increasing market prices in the future. If, for example, China acquired significant existing production capacity in Africa, this would force European and Other Asian customers to change their suppliers to ones further away. This would lead to higher inefficiencies in the market in terms of allocation costs and thus possibly to higher market prices. Also, any player locking up more existing annual iron ore production capacity than required in terms of its annual demand would lead to a tightening of the market and thus to increased market prices.

In the current high-price environment, and with long-term supply contracts being linked to the volatile spot market, it could pay off for steelmakers to integrate upstream and thereby secure iron ore at unit production cost, thus reducing the risk of procurement cost volatility and giving themselves more flexibility in terms of supply sources. Such integrations can take on many forms, ranging from joint ventures with major mining companies[684] to stakes in smaller mining companies[685] or even own greenfield mining projects.[686]

While large mining companies, especially in the current iron ore boom, commonly have a dismissive attitude towards joint ventures and takeover bids, some smaller mines are available for sale in locations that were previously too expensive to explore and exploit. However, the initial cost of acquiring or setting up an own a mine (i.e., the cost of capital), may represent a severe roadblock to this strategy. Buying into the supply chain to secure iron ore supply at low

---

[683]This is in line with findings in the livestock/meat packing markets, where captivity in the form of exclusive supply contracts is shown to have no effect on the open market price (see U.S. Department of Agriculture, Agricultural Marketing Service (1996), p. 30). The report argquments that, as is the case in the 2020 iron ore market, if 20% of the market supply is removed by means of captivity, so is 20% of demand, leading to a net effect on market prices of zero.

[684]Note that joint ventures with mining companies that do not provide the respective steelmaker with a guaranteed stake in production and thus access to iron ore at unit production cost are not considered captive supply in this model.

[685]Often in exchange for financial support or infrastructure (see Section 6.1.2.1.2).

[686]For a classification of different types of vertical integration, see Jaspers and van den Ende (2006). The decision as to which type of integration is best depends on many factors, including the involved transaction costs. For an analyses of vertical integration using the transaction cost approach, see Fauser (2004), pp. 49–53; Joskow (1985); Perry (1989), pp. 212–221.

cost means placing a considerable bet. It means tying up significant amounts of capital in order to get more control over supply security as well as reduced procurement costs and protection against price volatility. The ownership of ore reserves and mining operations and implies a steady burden on the company owning them in terms of fixed costs, necessary infrastructure investments and reserves for contingencies.[687] Additionally, owning mines exposes a steelmaker to additional risks, such as risks arising from infrastructure and logistics, mining laws and environmental policies. Therefore, if a steelmaker were assured of being able to cover its ore requirements on the open market at acceptable prices in the future it would not be financially justified to own iron ore reserves, unless when obtainable at a bargain price. However, with the current market setting, such assurance cannot be given. Depending only on ore from the open market means being entirely at the mercy of general market conditions and thus being open to price volatility.

A steelmaker's decision as to whether or not to acquire stakes in iron ore mines depends also on the relative size of its iron ore demand. If the capacity acquired is small relative to the size of the steelmaker's iron ore demand, upstream vertical integration can be seen as a no-regret move. It increases the steelmaker's insight into the iron ore market and thus improves its position in the new market environment. At the same time, captive supply gives the steelmaker continuous access to low-cost ore, thus also providing more flexibility in terms of procurement sources. This allows the steelmaker to better cope with market volatility and potentially increase its margin. If, on the other hand, a steelmaker acquires access to iron ore capacity that is large compared to its overall demand, then upstream integration would be equivalent to taking a long position in iron ore and would need to be in line with the company's long-term view on the developments of the iron ore market.

While the scenarios calculated in this paper for ArcelorMittal and China deal with the captive supply of large demand-side players, smaller steelmakers may shy away from owning mining operations due to the above mentioned capital requirements and other operational risks involved. However, recent developments in Germany, a country that depends greatly on raw materials from abroad to power its export-driven economy, show that a viable option for smaller companies may be to join forces and jointly acquiring stakes in mines. Following the announced of a German raw materials strategy in October 2010,[688] Rainer

---

[687]It must be noted that the 2020 procurement cost savings calculated for ArcelorMittal and China in this paper do not take into account the cost of acquiring and managing the respective mines, nor the fix costs incurred in running them.

[688]See Bundesministerium für Wirtschaft und Technologie (2010), especially pp. 10–12 regarding the diversification of raw materials procurement sources.

Brüderle, German Federal Minister of Economics and Technology at that time, urged German industrial firms to jointly set up a "Deutsche Rohstoff AG", or "German Raw Materials, Inc.", to find and secure raw materials needed by the German industrial sector and thus shield it from price volatility. The aim of the proposed company is to secure low cost access to crucial raw materials, for example iron ore, copper, nickel and coal, by means of acquiring stakes in foreign mining operations as well as own exploration projects. Ideas on how exactly it would operate are currently being discussed between the German Federal Ministry of Economics and Technology and the Federation of German Industries (BDI).[689] Though Brüderle ruled out the state's taking a stake in it, government sources say Berlin could support the company by giving state guarantees to its investments.[690] There is great interest among German industrial players for such a company, especially among those in the steel industry. ThyssenKrupp, Germany's biggest steelmaker, has announced its eagerness to participate in such a joint raw materials sourcing initiative, offering to bring in its own raw materials purchasing business.[691] However, the potential hurdles of such a venture are manifold: It may prove difficult to achieve mutual consent between companies with various different interests and specific raw materials requirements. Also, it is unclear whether the joint scale of raw materials demand of the participating companies will be sufficient to justify the required investments. Finally, and most profoundly, antitrust authorities may not permit the joint procurement of raw materials by competing firms.

6.4.2.2 Discussion of introduction of export taxes on iron ore

The scenarios discussed in Section 6.3.2.2 analyzed the effect of existing Indian export taxes on iron ore as well as the potential introduction of such taxes in Brazil.[692] As shown in both cases, the presence of iron ore export taxes leads to a considerable domestic market price reduction and thus to reduced iron ore procurement costs for steelmakers of the respective region.[693] India, due to its 20.0% export tax on iron ore, enjoys a domestic market price reduction

---

[689]See, e.g., Buchenau and Palm (2011); Die Welt (2010); Spiegel Online (2010).

[690]See Dunkel (2011).

[691]See Die Welt (2010); Schlandt (2010).

[692]In contrast to the strategy of captivity, export taxes cannot be levied by individual steelmakers. However, a strong national steel lobby may be able to influence a government's trade policy accordingly.

[693]As described above, this is due to the fact that export taxes reduce the export competitiveness of domestic mines by pricing them out of the market in other regions. The resulting reduced export of low-cost production volumes allows the respective regions to utilize more of its lower-cost mines to satisfy domestic demand. This is in line with findings from analyses of export taxes in the Indonesian palm oil industry, see Hasan et al. (2001); Marks et al. (1998).

of USD 7.87 (-12.8%)[694] and reduced annual iron ore procurement costs of USD 1.3 billion (-12.7%)[695] compared to no export tax (see results of scenario J in Section 6.3.2.2.1).[696] Similarly, Brazil, if it were to introduce a 5.0% export tax on iron ore, would see its domestic market price reduced by USD 6.74 (-10.0%) and would therefore realize an iron ore procurement cost reduction for its steelmakers of USD 0.9 billion (-7.8%) compared to no export tax (see results of scenario K in Section 6.3.2.2.2).[697]

In addition to these considerable absolute market price and procurement cost reductions, the scenarios analyzed in the sensitivity analysis in Section 6.3.1 of this paper show that export taxes on iron ore lead to a reduced exposure to market price volatility.[698] Throughout these scenarios, India, due its 20.0% export tax on iron ore, shows a considerably lower elasticity of its domestic iron ore market price and procurement cost with respect to changes in global demand, production capacity and freight rate levels than regions without an export tax. This reduced exposure to market volatility is due to India's complete self-sufficiency on an extremely low cost level, achieved by preventing the outflow of low-cost production volumes by means of the export tax.[699] Therefore, India is effectively detached from the remaining world market and thus hardly

---

[694] Note that this section discusses the effect of the introduction of export taxes. As India already levies export taxes in the 2020 base case, the effect described here is the reverse of the one described in Section 6.3.2.2.1. Therefore, relative changes of Indian market figures differ from those displayed above.

[695] Recall that relative changes of iron ore procurement costs can differ from relative changes in market price due to the presence of captive mines supplying at unit production cost.

[696] Note that, due to its proximity to price-setting region China, India's export taxes also help to shield its market price from the non-arbitrage effect. As explained in Section 5.1.3.2.4, the absolute difference between market prices of two regions in a global state of equilibrium may not exceed the sum of costs incurred in transporting ore from one region to the other (i.e., freight and export tax costs). Thus, as export taxes increase the cost of transporting ore from the respective region to the price-setting region, they allow a lower market price than without the tax.

[697] Recall that, as described in Section 6.1.2.2.2, due to the regional structure of the model, this scenario adds a 5% export tax on iron ore from all South American countries (not just Brazil). However, this error is negligible as Brazil accounts for roughly 90% of all South American iron ore production. For reasons of simplicity, this export tax and the resulting outcomes are therefore referred to as affecting only Brazil in this section.

[698] Recall that, although the iron ore model used in this paper is static and therefore does not directly reflect price volatility, it suggests a magnitude to the effects of volatility in terms of demand, production capacity and freight levels by allowing the comparison of the results of the respective sensitivity scenarios. Furthermore, this effect can only be shown for India, as it is the only country effectively levying export taxes in the base case and the scenarios of the sensitivity analysis. China, although levying an export tax of 10.0% on iron ore, cannot be considered, as its immense domestic demand would not allow exports even without an export tax in place.

[699] As shown above, the 20.0% export tax levied on Indian iron ore acts as a de facto export ban.

exposed to any global market volatility, be it in the form of global demand, capacity or freight rate changes.[700]

Therefore, by levying export taxes on iron ore and therefore encouraging domestic miners to satisfy domestic demand, a region's steelmakers enjoy a reduction in market price and iron ore procurement costs and are also less exposed to the price volatility of the open market. However, apart from these positive effects for the region's steelmakers, it is necessary to take into account the effect of export taxes on the region's iron ore miners. In the case of Indian export taxes, domestic miners' profit contributions are decreased by USD 1.0 billion (−23.8%). The introduction of export taxes in Brazil would lead to a reduction of the Brazilian miners' profit contributions of USD 3.5 billion (−13.4%). In both cases, the reasons for the reduced profit contributions are twofold: First of all, miners suffer from their reduced ability to compete on a landed cost basis in foreign markets. This prevents miners from exporting ore and thus from profiting from higher market prices abroad. Secondly, miners now confined to the domestic market are confronted with a reduced domestic market price.

Due to these converse effects, a region's decision as to whether or not to introduce export taxes on iron ore must be proceeded by a detailed analysis of the effects on both the steel and the iron ore industries. In the cases presented here, the effect of protectionism of the steel industry by means of iron ore export taxes on the joint profit contributions of both industries results in a net gain of USD 0.3 billion for India and a net loss of USD 2.6 billion for Brazil.[701] The reason for this difference lies in the relative weight of the iron ore and steel industries in the respective regions. India's steel industry is considerably larger and thus of greater importance from a national economic perspective than its iron ore mining industry. The situation is quite the opposite in Brazil.[702]

To complete the discussion of the effect of iron ore export taxes, it is necessary to briefly analyze their effect from a global industry perspective. Both the case of India and Brazil analyzed in this paper show that export taxes on iron ore

---

[700]It must be mentioned, however, that India is of course still prone to volatility of demand and production capacity within its own country. However, this is presumably much easier to anticipate and control than on a global scale.

[701]These calculations are to be interpreted with extreme caution, as they do not take into account potential revenue changes for the respective governments in terms of taxes and royalties, nor any other macroeconomic effects or effects in other industries that may be associated with the introduction of the export taxes.

[702]Note that, as described in Section 6.1.2.2.2, the Brazilian government is currently debating a reduced reliance on natural resource exports in exchange for increased domestic steelmaking activities. Thus, from a government point of view, the profit contribution loss of the iron ore industry resulting from such protectionism might be acceptable in order to foster the growth of the domestic steel industry.

have an increasing effect on the prices in the other regions in the market.[703] This, naturally, results in higher iron ore procurement costs for steelmakers and, on the other hand, increased profit contributions for iron ore miners in these regions.[704]

Without going into detail on the overall welfare effects of export taxes,[705] it is important to mention the recent debate about the welfare and environmental effects of trade liberalization vs. protectionism. Some fear that free trade may harm both welfare and natural resource stocks in exporting countries, while others are convinced that most, if not all, countries will benefit from increased trade.[706] However, policy advisers and international economic policy organizations have traditionally defended the free trade paradigm of the neoclassical economic theory[707] and have thus repeatedly stood up for the reduction of export taxes and other trade barriers.[708] Especially the World Trade Organization has underlined the necessity of free global trade in raw materials.[709] In this respect, the current challenges in raw materials markets, as highlighted in this paper for iron ore, are leading to a new global "raw materials diplomacy". For example, within its newly defined trade strategy for raw materials, the European Union aims to secure global free trade of raw materials by proposing trade disciplines on export restrictions (including bans, quotas, taxes and non-automatic export licenses).[710]

6.4.3 Discussion of results from a European perspective

The final section of this chapter discusses the model results from a European perspective. In the 2020 base case, as described in detail in Section 6.3.1.1,

---

[703]This is due to the fact that export taxes in both cases lock up low-cost iron ore supplies that otherwise would be used to partially satisfy demand in other regions. This creates imbalances in the global market and forces the remaining regions to pay high prices.

[704]Recall that the price increasing effect is particularly high for Europe in the case of the introduction Brazilian export taxes, due to its strong dependency on iron ore imports from Brazil.

[705]For a complete overview of the general welfare effects of trade policy instruments as well as an analysis of optimum export tax levels, refer to Corden (1974), pp. 158–200; Dixit and Norman (1980), pp. 149–195; Helpman and Krugman (1989), pp. 15–16; Krugman and Obstfeld (1988), pp. 185–217.

[706]For discussions see, e.g., Bulte and Barbier (2005); Emran (2005); Flaaten and Schulz (2010); Nielsen (2006).

[707]See, e.g., the fundamental pleas for global free trade in Smith (1776) and later in Ricardo (1951).

[708]See Flaaten and Schulz (2010).

[709]See World Trade Organization (2010).

[710]See European Commission (2011), p. 12.

Europe more than doubles its iron ore production from 21.2 Mt in 2009 to 48.4 Mt (+27.2 Mt, +128.6%). At the same time, the European iron ore demand increases by 37.5 Mt to 159.3 Mt (+30.8%). In consequence, Europe imports a total of 110.9 Mt of iron ore (+10.3 Mt vs. 2009), the primary sources being South America (57.0 Mt), North America (38.3 Mt) and Africa & Middle East (15.6 Mt). The 2020 base case puts the European iron ore market price at USD 67.65, only slightly lower than in 2009 (USD −0.15, −0.2%). The total iron ore procurement cost of European steelmakers totals USD 8.7 billion, USD 1.3 billion higher than the corresponding 2009 figure (+17.8%).

The sensitivity analyses show that the level of global demand, production capacity and freight rates have a strong influence on the 2020 regional market prices and steelmakers' iron ore procurement costs. Thus, depending on these key market parameters, also the European market price as well as the European steelmakers' iron ore procurement costs vary from levels considerably below the 2009 actuals to a multiple of their 2009 values.

With respect to the market economics of supply and demand, Section 6.3.1.2.5 shows that market prices in all regions are positively correlated with the level of global capacity utilization.[711] Also, as can be seen in Figure 6.25, market prices in all regions increase disproportionately when the global capacity utilization exceeds approximately 90%. Europe is no exception, with its market price ranging from USD 54.14 in scenario D (73.3% capacity utilization) to USD 150.44 in scenario E (96.6% capacity utilization). This dynamic is mirrored by the total iron ore procurement cost of European steelmakers, which increases from USD 5.9 billion in scenario D to USD 20.7 billion in scenario E.

While scenarios D and E analyze the effect of changes in the global iron ore demand level (see Sections 6.3.1.2.3 and 6.3.1.2.4), the influence of changes in demand figures of individual key iron ore consuming regions should not be neglected. Figure 6.58 shows the effect of changes in the Chinese and South American demand levels on the European market price.[712] These regions are of specific interest from a European perspective as China is the by-far largest overall consumer of iron ore and South America is the largest provider of iron ore to Europe.[713] As stated above, the European market price in the 2020 base case, where China has a demand of 1,136.8 Mt, is USD 67.65. The sensitivity

---

[711]Defined as the ratio of global demand to global production capacity.

[712]The respective analyses are based on the 2020 base case, with the individual regions' demand figures altered ceteris paribus. These results are therefore not directly comparable with the demand scenarios D and E described above, which alter the demand levels of multiple regions vs. the base case.

[713]Recall also that, as described in Section 6.1.2.2.2, Brazilian officials are seeking to expand domestic steelmaking in the future in order to reduce reliance on natural resource exports.

of Europe's iron ore price to changes in Chinese demand is significant. If the Chinese demand in 2020 were 950.0 Mt (16.4% less than in the base case), the European market price would drop to USD 56.08 (-17.1% vs. the base case). Should, on the other hand, Chinese demand be 1,300.0 Mt ($+14.4\%$), the European iron ore price would rise to USD 85.15 ($+25.9\%$). The influence of the South American iron ore demand level on the European price is considerably lower. If South American demand, defined as 219.6 Mt in the 2020 base case, were to reach only 100.0 Mt (-54.5% compared to the base case), the European market price would decrease to USD 57.12 (-15.6%). If, however, the demand were 300.0 Mt ($+36.6\%$), the European market price would increase slightly to USD 69.87 ($+3.3\%$).

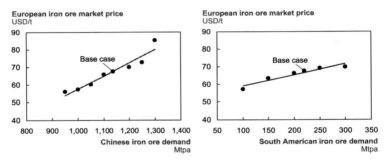

Figure 6.58: Influence of 2020 Chinese and South American iron ore demand on European market price [Own illustration]

As described in detail in Section 6.3.1.3.3, the effects of freight rate levels on regional market prices are rather inhomogeneous. Europe's market price, as the price of most other regions, is negatively correlated with freight rates.[714] Therefore, the European market price drops from USD 74.78 in scenario F (low freight rates) to USD 64.68 in scenario G (high freight rates). Due to its considerable distance from China, Europe shows a higher price elasticity with respect to freight rate changes than regions with higher geographic proximity to China (e.g., CIS and Oceania).

With respect to the evaluated risk mitigation strategies, only iron ore export taxes prove to have an effect on market prices. Figure 6.59 shows the effect of Brazilian and Indian iron ore export taxes ranging from 0% to 20% on the

---

[714]Recall that this is due to the fact that, because of its comparatively low-cost marginal supplier, Europe's market price is not directly influenced by supply and demand, but rather by the non-arbitrage condition of the model (see Section 5.1.3.2.4).

European iron ore market price.[715] While Brazil has 0% iron ore export tax in the 2020 base case, scenario K (see Section 6.1.2.2.2) analyzes the effect of a 5% export tax on Brazilian iron ore, leading to a European market price increase of 7.5% to USD 72.72. An additional increase in export tax would be even more disadvantageous for European steelmakers. For example, a 20% tax on Brazilian iron ore exports would result in a European market price of USD 93.43, 38.1% higher than in the base case. The sensitivity of the European iron ore price with respect to the Indian iron ore export tax is considerably lower. The 2020 base case models a 20% tax on iron ore exports from India, thus acting as a de facto export ban (see Section 6.3.1.1). At the other extreme, scenario J (see Section 6.3.2.2.1) shows that the European market price is reduced to USD 56.58 (−16.4% vs. the base case). In consequence, Europe should keep a close eye on the developments regarding iron ore export taxes. If possible, Europe should push for an annulment or at least a reduction of the Indian export tax and prevent the introduction of such a tax in Brazil and other iron ore exporting countries.

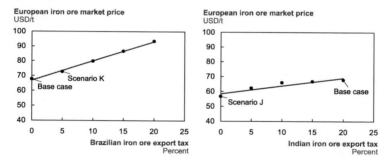

Figure 6.59: Influence of 2020 Brazilian and Indian iron ore export tax on European market price [Own illustration]

---

[715]The respective analyses are based on the 2020 base case, with the individual regions' iron ore export taxes altered ceteris paribus. Note that, due to the regional structure of the model, the Brazilian export tax applies to iron ore from all South American countries. However, this error is negligible as Brazil accounts for roughly 90% of all South American iron ore production. For reasons of simplicity, this export tax is referred to as being Brazilian in the following.

7 Wrap-up and outlook

The final chapter of this paper aims to provide a concluding summary as well as to give an outlook regarding possibilities for future related research. Section 7.1 reviews the attainment of the goals set out in Chapter 1 and briefly summarizes the guiding ideas of this paper. Subsequently, Section 7.2 gives a critical appraisal of the methodology used and finally suggests areas for future research regarding the iron ore market.

7.1 Review of goal attainment and conclusion

As defined in Section 1.2, the starting point of this paper was to seek the answer to the following two fundamental questions against the background of recent radical changes in the iron ore market:

- What general structure and dynamics will characterize the global iron ore market in the year 2020?

- How can demand-side players mitigate the risks arising from higher and more volatile iron ore prices?

The first question, representing the main focus of this paper, was a response to the general uncertainty in the market, with market participants seeking indications as to what direction the development of the iron ore industry will take. The second research question aimed to specifically address demand-side players' rising concern regarding increased iron ore market prices and short-term price fluctuations, by proposing risk mitigation strategies and evaluating their effectiveness together with their influence on the iron ore market in general. In order to further substantiate these research questions, the following five practical objectives were defined:

1. Describe in detail the iron ore value chain, the relevant technical characteristics of iron ore as a product and its role in the steelmaking process

2. Gain an in-depth understanding of the current structure and fundamental mechanics of the iron ore market, taking into account the status quo supply and demand situation, as well as identifying key market participants

3. Describe in detail the recent developments and trends in the market and determine the effects especially on demand-side players. Derive potential risk mitigation strategies for these players and select those to be analyzed in greater detail

4. Propose a 2020 iron ore market model reflecting the market's fundamental structure and mechanics, including the changes caused by the recent developments

5. Employ the proposed model to derive and discuss quantitative results with respect to the structure and dynamics of the 2020 iron ore market as well as the effectiveness and influences of the selected risk mitigation strategies for demand-side players

The first objective was attained in Chapter 2, where a technical introduction to iron ore was given. Section 2.1 provided a precise definition of iron ore and examined the nature and occurrence of the material in the form of resources and reserves. Also, various differentiating factors of natural iron ores were outlined. Subsequently, Section 2.2 described in detail the mine-to-market supply route of iron ore. Finally, Section 2.3 highlighted iron ore's economic importance by describing its significance for iron- and steelmaking. The section consequently included an overview of the most common steelmaking process routes and discussed the quality of iron ores with respect to their use in these process routes.

Objective two was addressed in Chapter 3 by means of an extensive overview of the current structure and mechanics of the global iron ore market along the 2009 market situation. Section 3.1 provided some introductory comments regarding the accepted routines and practices for presenting iron ore data and statistics. Sections 3.2 and 3.3 described the global demand and supply situations for iron ore in 2009, by discussing the respective geographic distribution and portraying key market participants on both sides. The, Section 3.4 briefly introduced the market for dry bulk freight and highlighted the influence of freight rates on the iron ore market. Section 3.5 dealt with the actual iron ore market mechanism and included descriptions of the modes of iron ore transactions, the pricing of iron ore and the 2009 iron ore trade flows. Finally, Section 3.6 outlined the effects of public policy on the iron ore market, with a strong focus on the taxation of the industry.

The third objective was achieved in Chapter 4, which gave a comprehensive overview of the recent developments and trends in the global iron ore market. These respective market developments and trends were presented in Section 4.1. Subsequently, Section 4.2 highlighted the impact of those market changes on the world's steelmakers. Based on this impact, Section 4.3 provided an overview of potential risk mitigating strategies for demand-side players. Due to their expected significant impact on the iron ore market, captivity of mines and introduction of iron ore export taxes were selected as those strategies to be analyzed in greater detail.

Based on the fundamental characteristics and mechanics of the market derived in previous chapters, Chapter 5 addressed the fourth objective by proposing a model for the 2020 iron ore market. Assuming perfect competition on the supply side, this model takes the form of a deterministic nine-region spatial equilibrium model cleared by merit order. The development of this model represents the heart of the present paper. Key features of the model are its bottom-up structure, modeling supply volumes and costs on an individual mine level, and its novel standardization method, allowing the integration of all ore types and grades into the same cost curve. Also, the model's simulation of global trade flows using a linear optimization approach is mentionable. Section 5.1 gave an overview of the general structure of the model and described in detail the key input components, the market mechanism and outputs of the model. Section 5.2 outlined the technical implementation of the model with a special focus on the implementation of the allocation mechanism. Finally, Section 5.3 presented a validation of the proposed model by comparing selected results to respective 2009 actuals.

The fifth and final objective was attained in Chapter 6, where the results of the quantitative analyses derived using the market model were described and discussed. First, Section 6.1 set the scope of the market evaluation, by defining capacity, demand and freight rates as the key market parameters and defining the exact values leading to a realistic market constellation for the 2020 base case. Additional settings for these market parameters were further defined for a sensitivity analysis, allowing the evaluation of the impact of changes of these parameters on the market. Also, the scenarios were defined with which the selected risk mitigation strategies were evaluated. In Section 6.2, the methodology and depth of the analyses were defined in terms of which output factors were to be analyzed. Finally, Section 6.3 described the quantitative model results for the 2020 base case and each of the prior defined scenarios along the criteria presented in Section 6.2. In the discussion in Section 6.4, an effort was made to summarize in general terms the key characteristics and dynamics of the global iron ore market in 2020 and to give an evaluation of the effectiveness of the selected risk mitigation strategies for demand-side players as well as their influence on the iron ore market.

In order to avoid redundancy, this section will refrain from repeating in detail the results of the key analyses discussed in Section 6.4. However, the following concluding remarks are offered:

As in recent years, the surge in global steel demand stemming from the economic growth of the BRIC countries will continue to have a significant impact on the iron ore market going forward. The ratio of iron ore demand and available iron ore production capacity, as shown by the analyses of this paper, represents one of the fundamental parameters defining the iron ore market. Naturally, iron ore miners have an incentive to keep the market tight, and the Big Three have sufficient leverage in the form of expansion projects and disposable cash to maintain high global capacity utilization by delaying announced expansions. It therefore can be expected that the 2020 iron ore market setting will be characterized by higher market prices than observed in 2009, thus leading to increased iron ore procurement costs for steelmakers and increased profit contributions for miners.

Also, the impact of dry bulk freight rates on the iron ore market should not be underestimated. Contrary to what may be expected, the weighted average global market price in 2020 remains largely unaffected by freight rate variations. However, iron ore miners' profit contributions show an extreme negative correlation with freight rate levels. Especially Vale, due to its larger exposure to freight rates, shows a particularly high sensitivity. Thus, freight rate volatility represents a considerable risk for iron ore miners, though not so much for consumers of iron ore.

In addition to the impact of production capacity, demand and freight rate levels, the recent radical change in the pricing mechanism for iron ore marks the beginning of an irreversible trend. Supported by increasing liquidity in the newly emerged derivatives market, the contract price for iron ore will continue to move closer to the daily spot market price in the coming years, thus following the examples of the transformation in the pricing systems of crude oil, aluminum and thermal coal. This will result in increased market price volatility, affecting the payoffs of all market participants going forward.

The clear implication for steelmakers is that they can no longer rely on business-as-usual scenarios when it comes to the procurement of iron ore. They must factor in higher base-level prices as well as increased volatility and consider the longer-range implications for profitable growth under multiple scenarios. Such fundamental developments can be addressed only by making substantial operational and strategic moves. According to the motto "You can't stop the tide, but you can ride the waves",[716] this paper has proposed several risk mitigation strategies and analyzed captivity of mines as well as the introduction of iron ore export taxes in greater detail. In summary, the perspective for steelmakers is an encouraging one. The evolution of the iron ore market offers steelmakers a new source of competitive differentiation. While the new market characteristics will make business more risky, each risk also holds an upside. It is this upside that steelmakers should be searching for.

7.2 Critical assessment and areas for future research

In giving a critical appraisal of this paper, this section will focus primarily on the mechanics of the iron ore market model proposed in Chapter 5. It must be kept in mind that this iron ore market model is one that, due to the immense complexity of the underlying iron ore market, does not claim to constitute an identical representation of reality. Instead, the model aims to capture the key characteristics and dynamics of the market while yielding to certain necessary simplifications of the real market. The most crucial of these simplifications are discussed in the following and possible remedies, to be interpreted as potentials for improvement of the model, are suggested:

- *Regional structuring of the global iron ore market* – As described in Section 5.1.1, the iron ore market model proposed in this paper splits the world into nine geographic regions, each with a port defined as the iron ore trading hub of the respective region. The global iron ore market is therefore modeled as a network of nine punctiform markets. While this surely represents a considerable simplification of the real world, this paper maintains that the error is negligible given the research objectives of the model. The allocation of countries and territories to a region was dictated mainly by membership in federations or trade blocs, as these entities play an important role in terms of trade policies. Also, special care was taken in the selection of the regions' hubs, aiming to reflect geographically the focal points of the regions' iron ore supply and demand.[717] It would be possible, however, to change the model structure to a more granular, e.g., country level, assuming that it is possible to obtain iron ore demand on this level. This would require the calculation of freight costs for a considerably higher number of point-to-point connections, while complicating the allocation of supply. Apart from adding complexity to the calculations

---

[716]Verhoeven et al. (2010).
[717]This legitimates that intraregional freight costs are zero in the model.

and the model results, however, it is not clear how a more granular market structure would help gain additional insight with respect to market characteristics and dynamics

- *Standardization of iron ore supply and demand* – Despite the fact that, as described in Section 2.1.3, iron ore is not a homogeneous product, the model presented in this paper standardizes the global iron ore supply and demand to 62% Fe fines with 0% moisture content (see Sections 5.1.2.1.1.4 and 5.1.2.3.2). This "commoditization" of iron ore is justifiable by the increased complexity that would be caused by reflecting the real-world heterogeneity of iron ore in terms of ore type, grade and moisture content in the model. While the model goes to great lengths to make amends for this commoditization in terms of recalculation of supply/demand volumes, production costs and market prices,[718] this simplification may be considered rather harsh, especially from a demand perspective. It must be kept in mind that, due to the general complexity of steelmaking processes (see Section 2.3.1), many steelmakers actually seek to buy ore with particular physical and chemical attributes for optimum efficiency in their plants.[719] In reality, demand for iron ore is therefore split into an almost infinite number of different segments. While the present model assumes that demand differences are smoothed out on a regional level, an improved iron ore market model might aim to at least differentiate supply and demand for iron ore by type,[720] while retaining the standardization of the remaining ore characteristics. Although this would require a more detailed derivation of demand and a more complex allocation mechanism, it would allow the analysis of the effect of the region-specific steel process route mix[721] and its change over time

- *Allocation mechanism based on total cost minimization* – As described in detail in Section 5.1.3.1, the iron ore model proposed in this paper uses a linear optimization approach similar to the classical transportation problem to allocate iron ore supplies to consuming regions by minimizing total cost in the objective function. Though this mechanism is adapted to reflects the presence of captive mines, it does not take into account the effect of long-term supply contracts between iron ore miners and steelmakers on global trade flows. The reason for this neglect is the fact that

---

[718]Recall that, as described in 5.1.2.1.2.2, premiums and penalties are applied to the mining cost of certain ores in order to reflect differences in market prices based on efficiency in the blast furnace.

[719]See Banks (1979); Frost (1986); Manners (1971), p. 145.

[720]Iron ore fines, lump, pellets and concentrates.

[721]For example, share of primary vs. secondary steelmaking or abundance of pelletizing plants at the steel mills allowing the use of fines instead of pellets.

information on such supply contracts is not publicly available. Nevertheless, the model proposed in this paper assumes that, in the long-run, rising cost pressures will force steelmakers to terminate potentially existing adverse contracts in favor of contracts with miners offering more cost-efficient ore, thus leading again to an overall cost-efficient allocation. However, taking into account the above described preference of steelmakers for particular physical and chemical attributes of iron ores, it may be assumed that there may exist significant long-term contracts contradicting a purely cost-efficient ore allocation. Therefore, further research may be necessary as to the effect of long-term supply contracts on iron ore supply allocation

- *Neglect of exchange rate effects* – All financial input data, calculations and results of the present iron ore market model, as stated in Section 3.1.2, are entirely in U.S. dollars and therefore do not take into account potential exchange rate effects. This was deemed necessary as exchange rate effects may have distorted fundamental market characteristics or interfered with market dynamics, thus making it difficult to achieve the main objectives of this paper. Also, applying different local currencies in the model would have required the estimation of their respective exchange rates vs. the U.S. dollar in the year 2020, which appears a difficult, if not impossible, task. In the real iron ore market, however, exchange rates have a significant effect on the competitiveness of individual mines and the financial result of mining companies. This is due to the fact that miners' costs are commonly incurred in the local currency of the mine, while all iron ore sales are commonly in U.S. dollars.[722] Thus, if the local currency of a miner appreciates against the U.S. dollar, its costs increase compared to the market price of the ore.[723] Thus, an improved iron ore market model might take into account and analyze the effects of such exchange rate changes by modeling miners' costs in their local currency.

Although the iron ore market model presented in this paper therefore does not fully capture the iron ore market in all its details, it is a reasonable starting point and adequately reflects the key characteristics and dynamics of the market. Future generations of researchers could improve the mechanics of the model

---

[722]See Kinch (2011); Peaple (2011).

[723]For example, the Australian dollar was 12% higher in the first half of 2011 against 2010's average rate vs. the U.S. dollar, thus decreasing Australian miners' profit which is reported in U.S. dollars (see Peaple (2011)). Also the profit of Brazil's Vale is being increasingly eroded by a currency squeeze: the U.S. dollar lost 4.2% against the Brazilian real in the second quarter of 2011 alone (see Kinch (2011)).

based on the above discussion. In addition, the findings presented in this paper mandate further research, in particular in the following areas:

- *Expansion of descriptive market analysis further into the future* – With one of its primary goals being to analyze the fundamental effects of the recent disruptive changes in the market, this paper limits itself to a fairly reasonable forecast period. Future researchers, however, may attempt to take a more macroscopic view by expanding this descriptive iron ore market analysis further into the future, e.g. to the year 2050. This would allow the analysis of various major demand- and supply-side trends which are forecasted to take shape beyond the time scope of the present paper. These trends include a continued global demand increase, especially from emerging markets as well as constrained supply, as easy-to-tap and high-quality reserves are slowly depleted. While new iron ore mining projects may still boast good resources, they may have issues with infrastructure and local cultural and political concerns. Thus, future iron ore supply is expected to stem mainly from harder-to-access, more costly and more politically unstable environments.[724] Also, as described in Section 5.1.2.3.2, China is expected to enter into a period of high steel scrap availability as considerable amounts of steel products from the millennium production boom enter into the scrap cycle sometime after 2020. This will jump-start the Chinese scrap market and presumably lead to a shift in the steelmaking process route mix towards secondary steelmaking using EAFs. Naturally, such an increase in Chinese secondary steel production would lead to a relative decrease in iron ore demand.[725] In terms of the iron ore market model, this type of analysis would require a considerable effort. Apart from a general update of the input data to adequately reflect supply and demand conditions in the future, the mechanics of the model would have to be remodeled in order to take into account the steel process route mix per region as well as the supply and demand conditions in the global scrap market

- *Analysis of the effect of resource nationalism and public policy measures* – High raw materials prices have seen a resurgence in resource nationalism. Governments of countries rich in iron ore are seeking a larger share of the profits of the price boom. Also, governments are rediscovering the security of raw materials supply as a key part of their strategic agenda. Although, as discussed in Section 2.1.2, the depletion of global iron ore supplies is not a probable scenario, many traditional industrialized countries that see locally produced steel as being of strategic importance, are seeking ways

---

[724]See, e.g., Bisson et al. (2010).
[725]See, e.g., Reck et al. (2010); Steel Business Briefing (2009).

to ensure affordable and secure iron ore supply well into the future. This resource nationalism is taking a variety of forms, such as the proposal of a Resource Super Profit Tax (RSPT) in Australia, the Indigenization Act in Zimbabwe, increases in mining taxes and royalties in various African countries and restrictions on foreign mine ownership in India and China.[726] These public policy measures are bound to have an immense effect on the profits and the competitiveness of iron ore players as well as on the structure of the iron ore industry. Therefore, building on the exemplary analysis of the effect of iron ore export taxes in this paper, further research is required as to the magnitude of the effects of different policy measures on individual industry players and the market in general. Also, from a policymaker's perspective, one may aim to analyze the effects of various policy measures on the welfare of the economy and attempt to define key characteristics of an optimal public policy with respect to iron ore

- *Analysis of miners' capacity expansion strategies* – As discussed in detail in Section 6.4.1, iron ore miners, especially the Big Three, have a significant collective incentive to delay expansion projects in order to keep the market tight as this results in higher market prices and thus in overall higher profit contributions. On an individual player level, however, delaying expansion projects leads to reduced available capacity and therefore may result in lower revenues for the respective miner despite higher market prices. If one rules out collusion, this has miners facing an interesting dilemma. On the one hand, they can increase market prices by jointly slowing capacity expansions, but on the other hand, those miners actually delaying their projects will suffer from lower production volumes while the other miners skim the additional profits. This dilemma mandates a detailed analysis of iron ore miners' capacity expansion decision using a multi-period game-theoretical approach.[727]. Within such an analysis, the competition between miners could be simulated in two stages, where miners first simultaneously decide how much capacity they want to expand and then compete with this new capacity using a realistic market mechanism as described in Section 5.1.3 of this paper. By comparing the payoffs of various capacity expansion strategy combinations, this will allow the evaluation of these strategies and possibly even the derivation of dominant strategies for specific miners or certain market situations. In order to be able to analyze these strategies correctly, it would be necessary to take

---

[726]See, e.g., Blas (2011); Bloomberg Businessweek (2010); Ernst & Young (2011a); Fischermann (2011); Sprothen (2009); The Financial Times (2010d); The Financial Times (2011d).
[727]See, e.g., the Strategic Business Wargaming approach as adopted in Nordhoff (2009).

into account the capital expenditures involved in setting up new mining projects, as well as an NPV-based evaluation of such investment decisions

The above described suggestions for improvements and extensions of the model and the additional research areas outlined represent only a small fraction of the possibilities. It is hoped that the market model proposed in this paper as well as the resulting insights will serve as a sound basis for further analyses of the iron ore market.

Appendix

I Alphabetical list of countries/territories and geographic regions

Country/territory	Geographic region
Afghanistan	Africa & Middle East
Albania	Europe
Algeria	Africa & Middle East
American Samoa	Oceania
Andorra	Europe
Angola	Africa & Middle East
Antigua and Barbuda	South America
Argentina	South America
Armenia	CIS
Aruba	South America
Australia	Oceania
Austria	Europe
Azerbaijan	CIS
Bahamas	South America
Bahrain	Africa & Middle East
Bangladesh	Other Asia
Barbados	South America
Belarus	CIS
Belgium	Europe
Belize	South America
Benin	Africa & Middle East
Bermuda	South America
Bhutan	Other Asia
Bolivia	South America
Bosnia and Herzegovina	Europe
Botswana	Africa & Middle East
Brazil	South America
Brunei Darussalam	Other Asia
Bulgaria	Europe
Burkina Faso	Africa & Middle East
Burundi	Africa & Middle East
Cambodia	Other Asia
Cameroon	Africa & Middle East
Canada	North America
Cape Verde	Africa & Middle East
Cayman Islands	South America
Central African Republic	Africa & Middle East
Chad	Africa & Middle East
Channel Islands	Europe
Chile	South America
China	China
Colombia	South America
Comoros	Africa & Middle East
Congo, Democratic Republic	Africa & Middle East
Congo, Republic	Africa & Middle East

Continued on next page

Country/territory	Geographic region
Costa Rica	South America
Côte d'Ivoire	Africa & Middle East
Croatia	Europe
Cuba	South America
Cyprus	Africa & Middle East
Czech Republic	Europe
Denmark	Europe
Djibouti	Africa & Middle East
Dominica	South America
Dominican Republic	South America
Ecuador	South America
Egypt	Africa & Middle East
El Salvador	South America
Equatorial Guinea	Africa & Middle East
Eritrea	Africa & Middle East
Estonia	Europe
Ethiopia	Africa & Middle East
Faeroe Islands	Europe
Fiji	Oceania
Finland	Europe
France	Europe
French Polynesia	Oceania
Gabon	Africa & Middle East
Gambia	Africa & Middle East
Georgia	CIS
Germany	Europe
Ghana	Africa & Middle East
Gibraltar	Europe
Greece	Europe
Greenland	North America
Grenada	South America
Guam	Other Asia
Guatemala	South America
Guinea	Africa & Middle East
Guinea-Bissau	Africa & Middle East
Guyana	South America
Haiti	South America
Honduras	South America
Hong Kong SAR, China	China
Hungary	Europe
Iceland	Europe
India	India
Indonesia	Other Asia
Iran	Africa & Middle East
Iraq	Africa & Middle East
Ireland	Europe
Isle of Man	Europe
Israel	Africa & Middle East
Italy	Europe
Jamaica	South America
Japan	Other Asia
Jordan	Africa & Middle East
Kazakhstan	CIS
Kenya	Africa & Middle East
Kiribati	Oceania
Korea, DPR	Other Asia
Korea, Republic	Other Asia
Kosovo	Europe
Kuwait	Africa & Middle East
Kyrgyz Republic	CIS
Laos	Other Asia
Latvia	Europe
Lebanon	Africa & Middle East
Lesotho	Africa & Middle East
Liberia	Africa & Middle East
Libya	Africa & Middle East
Liechtenstein	Europe
Lithuania	Europe
Luxembourg	Europe

Continued on next page

Country/territory	Geographic region
Macao SAR, China	China
Macedonia	Europe
Madagascar	Africa & Middle East
Malawi	Africa & Middle East
Malaysia	Other Asia
Maldives	Africa & Middle East
Mali	Africa & Middle East
Malta	Europe
Marshall Islands	Oceania
Mauritania	Africa & Middle East
Mauritius	Africa & Middle East
Mayotte	Africa & Middle East
Mexico	North America
Micronesia, Federated States	Oceania
Moldova	CIS
Monaco	Europe
Mongolia	CIS
Montenegro	Europe
Morocco	Africa & Middle East
Mozambique	Africa & Middle East
Myanmar	Other Asia
Namibia	Africa & Middle East
Nepal	Other Asia
Netherlands	Europe
Netherlands Antilles	South America
New Caledonia	Oceania
New Zealand	Oceania
Nicaragua	South America
Niger	Africa & Middle East
Nigeria	Africa & Middle East
Northern Mariana Islands	Other Asia
Norway	Europe
Oman	Africa & Middle East
Pakistan	Other Asia
Palau	Other Asia
Panama	South America
Papua New Guinea	Oceania
Paraguay	South America
Peru	South America
Philippines	Other Asia
Poland	Europe
Portugal	Europe
Puerto Rico	South America
Qatar	Africa & Middle East
Romania	Europe
Russian Federation	CIS
Rwanda	Africa & Middle East
Samoa	Oceania
San Marino	Europe
São Tomé and Principe	Africa & Middle East
Saudi Arabia	Africa & Middle East
Senegal	Africa & Middle East
Serbia	Europe
Seychelles	Africa & Middle East
Sierra Leone	Africa & Middle East
Singapore	Other Asia
Slovak Republic	Europe
Slovenia	Europe
Solomon Islands	Oceania
Somalia	Africa & Middle East
South Africa	Africa & Middle East
Spain	Europe
Sri Lanka	Other Asia
St. Kitts and Nevis	South America
St. Lucia	South America
St. Vincent and the Grenadines	South America
Sudan	Africa & Middle East
Suriname	South America
Swaziland	Africa & Middle East

Continued on next page

Country/territory	Geographic region
Sweden	Europe
Switzerland	Europe
Syrian Arab Republic	Africa & Middle East
Taiwan	Other Asia
Tajikistan	CIS
Tanzania	Africa & Middle East
Thailand	Other Asia
Timor-Leste	Other Asia
Togo	Africa & Middle East
Tonga	Oceania
Trinidad and Tobago	South America
Tunisia	Africa & Middle East
Turkey	Africa & Middle East
Turkmenistan	CIS
Turks and Caicos Islands	South America
Tuvalu	Oceania
Uganda	Africa & Middle East
Ukraine	CIS
United Arab Emirates	Africa & Middle East
United Kingdom	Europe
United States	North America
Uruguay	South America
Uzbekistan	CIS
Vanuatu	Oceania
Vatican City	Europe
Venezuela	South America
Vietnam	Other Asia
West Bank and Gaza	Africa & Middle East
Yemen	Africa & Middle East
Zambia	Africa & Middle East
Zimbabwe	Africa & Middle East

Table I.1: Alphabetical list of countries/territories and geographic regions [Own illustration]

II Model input data by scenario

| | 2009 | |
Region	Capacity Mtpa	Demand Mtpa
North America	67.5	59.4
South America	345.0	67.1
Europe	21.8	121.7
Africa & Middle East	96.3	54.5
CIS	175.2	121.6
China	367.6	910.7
India	211.7	75.5
Other Asia	6.2	175.1
Oceania	366.1	8.8
World total	**1,657.4**	**1,594.4**

Table II.1: Input data 2009 capacity and demand [Own illustration]

| | 2020 low capacity | | | 2020 medium capacity | | | 2020 high capacity | | |
| | Capacity | Change vs. 2020 medium | | Capacity | Change vs. 2009 | | Capacity | Change vs. 2020 medium | |
Region	Mtpa	Abs.	Rel.	Mtpa	Abs.	Rel.	Mtpa	Abs.	Rel.
North America	157.0	-7.8	-4.7%	164.7	97.2	144.0%	170.1	5.4	3.3%
South America	642.8	-51.1	-7.4%	693.9	348.9	101.1%	730.0	36.1	5.2%
Europe	48.1	-1.2	-2.4%	49.3	27.5	125.9%	50.4	1.1	2.2%
Africa & M. E.	227.0	-43.3	-16.0%	270.3	174.0	180.6%	300.8	30.5	11.3%
CIS	222.3	-6.8	-3.0%	229.1	53.9	30.8%	232.9	3.8	1.7%
China	386.9	±0.0	±0.0%	386.9	19.2	5.2%	386.9	±0.0	±0.0%
India	262.9	-14.2	-5.1%	277.1	65.4	30.9%	287.1	10.0	3.6%
Other Asia	13.9	-1.1	-7.6%	15.0	8.8	142.3%	16.2	1.1	7.6%
Oceania	637.4	-74.7	-10.5%	712.1	346.0	94.5%	763.0	50.8	7.1%
World total	**2,598.3**	**-200.1**	**-7.2%**	**2,798.4**	**1,141.0**	**68.8%**	**2,937.3**	**138.9**	**5.0%**

Table II.2: Input data 2020 capacity [Own illustration]

| | 2020 low demand | | | 2020 medium demand | | | 2020 high demand | | |
| | Demand | Change vs. 2020 medium | | Demand | Change vs. 2009 | | Demand | Change vs. 2020 medium | |
Region	Mtpa	Abs.	Rel.	Mtpa	Abs.	Rel.	Mtpa	Abs.	Rel.
North America	96.4	-23.4	-19.5%	119.8	60.5	101.8%	144.4	24.6	20.5%
South America	169.0	-50.7	-23.1%	219.6	152.5	227.3%	244.8	25.2	11.5%
Europe	129.9	-29.4	-18.4%	159.3	37.5	30.8%	187.3	28.0	17.6%
Africa & M. E.	116.9	-11.6	-9.0%	128.4	73.9	135.5%	141.8	13.3	10.4%
CIS	217.4	-3.9	-1.7%	221.2	99.6	81.9%	224.8	3.6	1.6%
China	1,021.5	-115.3	-10.1%	1,136.8	226.0	24.8%	1,243.1	106.3	9.4%
India	142.4	-34.1	-19.3%	176.6	101.1	134.0%	277.1	100.6	57.0%
Other Asia	146.2	-40.3	-21.6%	186.5	11.4	6.5%	226.5	40.0	21.4%
Oceania	11.1	-1.2	-9.6%	12.2	3.4	38.7%	14.2	2.0	16.1%
World total	**2,050.8**	**-309.7**	**-13.1%**	**2,360.5**	**766.0**	**48.0%**	**2,704.0**	**343.5**	**14.6%**

Table II.3: Input data 2020 demand [Own illustration]

2009 freight rates

USD/t

Origin \ Destination		North America Port Duluth, USA	South America Tubarão, Brazil	Europe Rotterdam, Netherlands	Africa & Middle East Saldanha Bay, South Africa	CIS Novorossiysk, Russia	China Qingdao, China	India Mormugao, India	Other Asia Fukuyama, Japan	Oceania Port Hedland, Australia
North America	Port Duluth, USA	0.00	17.79	13.90	22.13	18.58	32.47	24.54	31.28	31.32
South America	Tubarão, Brazil	17.79	0.00	16.06	11.14	17.67	28.37	20.88	29.42	22.58
Europe	Rotterdam, Netherlands	13.90	16.06	0.00	17.53	12.09	27.64	18.05	28.09	24.83
Africa & Middle East	Saldanha Bay, South Africa	22.13	11.14	17.53	0.00	18.67	21.37	14.10	20.92	15.80
CIS	Novorossiysk, Russia	18.58	17.67	12.09	18.67	0.00	19.46	13.61	23.65	20.40
China	Qingdao, China	32.47	28.37	27.64	21.37	19.46	0.00	14.40	5.80	11.58
India	Mormugao, India	24.54	20.88	18.05	14.10	13.61	14.40	0.00	14.84	11.80
Other Asia	Fukuyama, Japan	31.28	29.42	28.09	20.92	23.65	5.80	14.84	0.00	12.00
Oceania	Port Hedland, Australia	31.32	22.58	24.83	15.80	20.40	11.58	11.80	12.00	0.00

Table II.4: Input data 2009 freight rates [Own illustration]

2020 low freight rates

USD/t

		Destination								
		North America	South America	Europe	Africa & Middle East	CIS	China	India	Other Asia	Oceania
		Port Duluth, USA	Tubarão, Brazil	Rotterdam, Netherlands	Saldanha Bay, South Africa	Novorossiysk, Russia	Qingdao, China	Mormugao, India	Fukuyama, Japan	Port Hedland, Australia
Origin	North America — Port Duluth, USA	0.00	6.13	4.82	7.60	6.40	11.09	8.41	10.69	10.71
	South America — Tubarão, Brazil	6.13	0.00	5.78	3.89	6.09	9.71	7.18	10.22	7.75
	Europe — Rotterdam, Netherlands	4.82	5.78	0.00	6.04	4.21	9.46	6.22	9.61	8.51
	Africa & Middle East — Saldanha Bay, South Africa	7.60	3.89	6.04	0.00	6.43	7.14	4.88	7.04	5.46
	CIS — Novorossiysk, Russia	6.40	6.09	4.21	6.43	0.00	6.70	4.72	8.11	7.01
	China — Qingdao, China	11.09	9.71	9.46	7.14	6.70	0.00	4.99	2.08	4.03
	India — Mormugao, India	8.41	7.18	6.22	4.88	4.72	4.99	0.00	5.14	4.11
	Other Asia — Fukuyama, Japan	10.69	10.22	9.61	7.04	8.11	2.08	5.14	0.00	4.13
	Oceania — Port Hedland, Australia	10.71	7.75	8.51	5.46	7.01	4.03	4.11	4.13	0.00

2020 medium freight rates

USD/t

		Destination								
		North America	South America	Europe	Africa & Middle East	CIS	China	India	Other Asia	Oceania
		Port Duluth, USA	Tubarão, Brazil	Rotterdam, Netherlands	Saldanha Bay, South Africa	Novorossiysk, Russia	Qingdao, China	Mormugao, India	Fukuyama, Japan	Port Hedland, Australia
Origin	North America — Port Duluth, USA	0.00	11.55	9.02	14.37	12.06	21.08	15.93	20.31	20.33
	South America — Tubarão, Brazil	11.55	0.00	10.42	7.23	11.47	18.42	13.55	19.10	14.66
	Europe — Rotterdam, Netherlands	9.02	10.42	0.00	11.38	7.85	17.94	11.71	18.23	16.12
	Africa & Middle East — Saldanha Bay, South Africa	14.37	7.23	11.38	0.00	12.12	13.87	9.15	13.58	10.25
	CIS — Novorossiysk, Russia	12.06	11.47	7.85	12.12	0.00	12.63	8.84	15.36	13.24
	China — Qingdao, China	21.08	18.42	17.94	13.87	12.63	0.00	9.35	3.76	7.52
	India — Mormugao, India	15.93	13.55	11.71	9.15	8.84	9.35	0.00	9.63	7.66
	Other Asia — Fukuyama, Japan	20.31	19.10	18.23	13.58	15.36	3.76	9.63	0.00	7.79
	Oceania — Port Hedland, Australia	20.33	14.66	16.12	10.25	13.24	7.52	7.66	7.79	0.00

2020 high freight rates

USD/t

		Destination								
		North America	South America	Europe	Africa & Middle East	CIS	China	India	Other Asia	Oceania
		Port Duluth, USA	Tubarão, Brazil	Rotterdam, Netherlands	Saldanha Bay, South Africa	Novorossiysk, Russia	Qingdao, China	Mormugao, India	Fukuyama, Japan	Port Hedland, Australia
Origin	North America — Port Duluth, USA	0.00	22.38	17.43	27.90	23.39	41.05	30.96	39.54	39.59
	South America — Tubarão, Brazil	22.38	0.00	19.71	13.93	22.23	35.84	26.31	36.85	28.47
	Europe — Rotterdam, Netherlands	17.43	19.71	0.00	22.05	15.13	34.91	22.71	35.47	31.33
	Africa & Middle East — Saldanha Bay, South Africa	27.90	13.93	22.05	0.00	23.50	27.33	17.68	26.65	19.84
	CIS — Novorossiysk, Russia	23.39	22.23	15.13	23.50	0.00	24.51	17.07	29.84	25.70
	China — Qingdao, China	41.05	35.84	34.91	27.33	24.51	0.00	18.07	7.13	14.49
	India — Mormugao, India	30.96	26.31	22.71	17.68	17.07	18.07	0.00	18.63	14.78
	Other Asia — Fukuyama, Japan	39.54	36.85	35.47	26.65	29.84	7.13	18.63	0.00	15.10
	Oceania — Port Hedland, Australia	39.59	28.47	31.33	19.84	25.70	14.49	14.78	15.10	0.00

Table II.5: Input data 2020 freight rates [Own illustration]

III Overview of formulae and mechanisms of the market model

This section gives an overview of the key formulae and mechanisms of the iron ore market model proposed in this paper. For an explanation of the symbols used, see page xix.

Standardization of supply volumes:

$$x_m = x_m^{ROM} \cdot (1 - mc_m) \cdot \frac{fc_m}{62.0\%}$$

CFR cost calculation:

$$c_{mij}^{CFR} = c_m^{FOB} + c_m^{ex} + c_{mij}^{freight}$$

FOB cost calculation:

$$c_m^{FOB} = c_m^{mining} + corr_m^{grade} + corr_m^{VIU} + c_m^{royalty}$$

Standardization of mining cost:

$$c_m^{mining} = c_m^{mining,ROM} \cdot \frac{62.0\%}{fc_m \cdot (1 - mc_m)}$$

Inflation of mining cost:

$$c_m^{mining,2020} = c_m^{mining,2009} \cdot [0.20 \cdot 1.02^{(2020-2009)} + 0.30 \cdot 1.03^{(2020-2009)} + 0.50]$$

Standardization of freight cost:

$$c_{mij}^{freight} = \frac{c_{ij}^{freight} \cdot x_m^{ROM}}{x_m}$$

Demand calculation:

$$d_j = d_j^{steel} \cdot 1.6 \cdot (s_j^{BOF} \cdot 0.9 + s_j^{OHF} \cdot 0.5 + s_j^{DR} \cdot 0.9)$$

Allocation of supply volumes:

$$\min \quad \sum_{m=1}^{M} \sum_{j=1}^{R} c_{mij}^{CFR} \cdot x_{mj}$$

$$\text{subject to} \quad \sum_{j=1}^{R} x_{mj} \leq \bar{x}_m \quad \text{for } m = 1, \ldots, M$$

$$\sum_{m=1}^{M} x_{mj} = d_j \quad \text{for } j = 1, \ldots, R$$

$$x_{mj} \geq 0 \quad \text{for } m = 1, \ldots, M; j = 1, \ldots, R$$

Market clearing per regional market:

$$\min \quad \sum_{m=1}^{M} p_m \cdot x_m$$

$$\text{subject to} \quad \sum_{m=1}^{M} x_m = d_j \quad (\lambda)$$

$$0 \leq x_m \leq \bar{x}_m \quad \text{for } m = 1, \ldots, M$$

The market-clearing production levels can be expressed in terms of λ_j, the market price or Lagrange multiplier associated with the fulfillment of demand:

$$x_m(\lambda) = \left\{ \begin{array}{ll} \bar{x}_m & \text{if } \lambda_j > p_m \\ 0 \leq \Delta d_j \leq \bar{x}_m & \text{if } \lambda_j = p_m \\ 0 & \text{if } \lambda_j < p_m \end{array} \right\} \text{ for } m = 1, \ldots, M$$

The market price λ_j is found by solving

$$\sum_{m=1}^{M} x_m(\lambda_j) = d_j$$

The profit contribution of each mine segment is defined as

$$\pi_m = (\lambda_j - c_{mij}^{CFR}) \cdot x_m$$

Price adjustment to prevent arbitrage:

$$\bar{\lambda}_j = \left\{ \begin{array}{ll} \lambda_p - c_{pj}^{freight} - c_p^{ex} & \text{if } \lambda_p - c_{pj}^{freight} - c_p^{ex} \geq \lambda_j \\ \lambda_j & \text{if } \lambda_p - c_{pj}^{freight} - c_p^{ex} < \lambda_j \end{array} \right.$$

Bibliography

Adelman, M. A. (1990). Mineral depletion with special reference to petroleum. *Review of Economics and Statistics 72*(1), 1–10.

Andrade, E., R. M. Fantoni, and W. B. Jones, Jr. (2007, May). What's ahead for business in Brazil. *The McKinsey Quarterly*, 1–10.

Anglo American (2010, November). Kumba Iron Ore Limited. Deutsche Bank BRICS Global Metals and Mining Conference 2010.

Antonioli, S. (2011a). Vale keeps steelmakers sweet on pricing. *Reuters News*. March 18, 2011.

Antonioli, S. (2011b). Vale mega ships to cut freight costs by 20–25 pct. *Reuters News*. June 17, 2011.

Antonioli, S. and J. Saul (2011). Vale in talks to sell giant ships to China. *Reuters News*. September 5, 2011.

ArcelorMittal (2010a). ArcelorMittal annual report 2009. http://www.arcelormittal.com/rls/data/upl/638-17-0-AnnualReport2009-ManagementReport.pdf. Accessed January 9, 2011.

ArcelorMittal (2010b). ArcelorMittal fact book 2009. http://www.arcelormittal.com/index.php?lang=en&page=658. Accessed January 9, 2011.

ArcelorMittal (2011). ArcelorMittal annual report 2010. http://www.arcelormittal.com/rls/data/upl/638-22-0-AM_AR10.pdf. Accessed August 9, 2011.

Astier, J. E. (2001). Evolution of the world iron ore market. *Minerals & Energy 16*(4), 23–30.

Australian Bureau of Agricultural and Resource Economics (2009a). Australian commodities: December quarter 2009.

Australian Bureau of Agricultural and Resource Economics (2009b). Australian mineral statistics 2009: December quarter 2009.

Australian Ministry of Treasury (2008). Foreign investment approval no. 100. Media release. September 21, 2008.

Australian Ministry of Treasury (2009). Foreign investment decision no. 032: Sinosteel's interests in Murchison Metals Ltd. Media release. March 31, 2009.

Bain & Company (2010). Stahl: Höhere Preise, mehr Risiko, aber weniger Rendite. Media release. April 19,2010.

Baldursson, F. M. (1999). Modelling the price of industrial commodities. *Economic Modelling 16*(3), 331–353.

Banks, F. E. (1979, June). The 'new' economics of iron and steel. *Resources Policy 5*(2), 95–103.

Barnes, R. S. (1974). The material resources for the iron and steel industries. *Resources Policy 1*(2), 66–74.

Barnett, D. F. and R. W. Crandall (1986). *Up from the ashes: the rise of the steel minimill in the United States*. The Brookings Institution, Washington, D.C.

Barnett, D. F. and R. W. Crandall (2002). *Industry Studies*, Chapter 5 – Steel: Decline and Renewal, pp. 118–139. M.E. Sharpe, Armonk.

Barnett, H. J. and C. Morse (1963). *Scarcity and Growth*. The Johns Hopkins Press, Baltimore.

BBC News (2011). China's economic growth slows amid monetary tightening. *BBC News*. July 13, 2011.

Beja, A. and N. H. Hakansson (1977, May). Dynamic market processes and the rewards to up-to-date information. *The Journal of Finance 32*(2), 291–304.

Beja, A. and N. H. Hakansson (1979). *Impending changes for securities markets: What role for the exchanges?*, Chapter – From Orders to Trades: Some Alternative Market Mechanisms. JAI Press, Greenwich.

Bekaert, F., C. Françoise, and R. Verhoeven (2004). The China factor in global steel. *The McKinsey Quarterly 2*, 20–22.

Bhaskar, R. (2008). Iron ore: it's a steal. *Daily News and Analysis*. April 4, 2008.

BHP Billiton (2010). BHP Billiton annual report 2009. http://www. arcelormittal.com/rls/data/upl/638-22-0-AM_AR10.pdf. Accessed January 9, 2011.

Bisson, P., E. Stephanson, and S. P. Viguerie (2010, June). Pricing the planet. *The McKinsey Quarterly*, 1–7.

Blas, J. (2009). Iron ore pricing emerges from stone age. *The Financial Times*. October 26, 2009.

Blas, J. (2011). Resource nationalism returns to commodities. *The Financial Times*. June 14, 2011.

Blas, J., C. O'Murchu, and S. Bernard (2009). Iron ore pricing war. *The Financial Times*. October 14, 2009.

Bloomberg Businessweek (2010). The deal is simple. Australia gets money, China gets Australia. *Bloomberg Businessweek*. September 2, 2010.

Bor, A. (1999). Power games. http://mba.tuck.dartmouth.edu/paradigm/back_ issues/fall1999/letters/bor.html. Accessed December 12, 2010.

Bottke, H. (1981). *Lagerstättenkunde des Eisens*. Glückauf Verlag, Essen.

Bowie, C. (2009). A review of mining royalties in Australia. http://www.minterellison.com/public/connect/Internet/Home/Legal% 2BInsights/Newsletters/Previous%2BNewsletters/A-ERU3%2Bmining% 2Broyalties%2Boverview/. Accessed June 30, 2010.

Braid, D. (2011). Coking coal sees changing dynamics and prices. *Steel Business Briefing Insight*. June 14, 2011.

Branch, A. E. (2007). *Elements of Shipping*. Routledge, New York.

Brazil Steel Institute (2010). Steel – Building a sustainable future. http://www.acobrasil.org.br/site%5Cportugues%5Cbiblioteca%5CFolder_ Institucional_ingles.pdf. Accessed March 21, 2011.

Buchenau, M.-W. and R. Palm (2011). Deutschlands geheimer Rohstofffriese. *Handelsblatt*. August 2, 2011.

Bulte, E. H. and E. B. Barbier (2005). Trade and renewable resources in a second best world: An overview. *Environmental & Resource Economics 30*, 423–463.

Bundesministerium für Wirtschaft und Technologie (2010, October). Rohstoff-strategie der Bundesregierung. http://www.bmwi.de/Dateien/BMWi/ PDF/rohstoffstrategie-der-bundesregierung,property=pdf,bereich=bmwi, sprache=de,rwb=true.pdf. Accessed March 18, 2011.

Burgo, J. A. (1999). *The Making, Shaping and Treating of Steel*, Volume 2 – Ironmaking, Chapter 10 – The Manufacture of Pig Iron in the Blast Furnace, pp. 721–761. Association for Iron and Steel Technology, Warrendale.

Cabral, L. M. B. (2000). *Introduction to Industrial Organization*. The MIT Press, Cambridge.

Cairns, R. D. (1998). Are mineral deposits valuable? A reconciliation of theory and practice. *Resources Policy 24*(1), 19–24.

Caney, R. W. and J. E. Reynolds (2010). *Reeds Marine Distance Tables*. A&C Black, London.

Carlton, D. W. (1989). *Handbook of Industrial Organization*, Volume 1, Chapter 15 – The Theory and the Facts of How Markets Clear: Is Industrial Organization Valuable for Understanding Macroeconomics?, pp. 909–947. North-Holland, Amsterdam.

Cattaneo, B. (2006). Managing political risk in mining operations. http://www.lbma.org.uk/assets/3e_cattaneo_lbma2006.pdf. Accessed March 21, 2011.

Cavallaro, N. (2010). The iron ore pricing rainbow. *Metal Bulletin*. June 16, 2010.

Chang, H.-S. (1994). Estimating Japanese import shares of iron ore. *Resources Policy 20*(2), 87–93.

China Customs (2011). E-mail received from China Customs on January 6, 2011 regarding iron ore export tax 2009 and 2020. No. 6 Jianguomennei Avenue, Dongcheng District, Beijing, China.

China Daily (2010). Iron ore trio may face China's anti-monopoly investigation. *China Daily*. April 16, 2010.

Clarkson Research Services Ltd. (2010). Shipping intelligence network, tripcharter rates time series. http://www.clarksons.net/sin2010/ts/Default.aspx. Accessed March 31, 2010.

Coeyman, M. (1994). Polymer price gains could foster thoughts of substitution. *Chemical Week 155*(7), 11.

Considine, T. J. (1991). Economic and technological determinants of the material intensity of use. *Land Economics 67*(1), 99–115.

Consiglieri, J. F. (2004). *Mining royalties*, Chapter 2 – Mining Royalty as Compensation Not Tax, pp. 4–6. Mining Policy Research Initiative, International Development Research Centre, Montevideo.

Corden, W. M. (1974). *Trade Policy and Economic Welfare*. Clarendon Press, Oxford.

Creamer, M. (2008). World has arrived at new iron ore futures market, says BHP Billiton's Randolph. *Mining Weekly*. July 4, 2008.

Crompton, P. (2000). Future trends in Japanese steel consumption. *Resources Policy 26*(2), 103–114.

Crowson, P. C. F. (1992). *Competitiveness in Metals*, Chapter 3 – Copper, pp. 68–126. Mining Journal Books, London.

Crowson, P. C. F. (1997, November). Mining during the next 25 years: Issues and challenges. *Natural Resources Forum 21*(4), 231–238.

Crowson, P. C. F. (2006). *Australian Mineral Economics: A Survey of Important Issues*, Chapter 7 – Mineral Markets, Prices and the Recent Performance of the Minerals and Energy Sector, pp. 59–78. Australasian Institute of Mining and Metallurgy, Carlton.

Crowson, P. C. F., G. Jackson, and D. Corlett (1978). Minerals availability – Trends and problems. *Engineering and Process Economics 3*, 3–9.

Crust, J. (2010). Raw Materials Group sees LME iron ore contract. *Reuters News*. February 19, 2011.

Czerwensky Intern (2009). Rohstoffe: Banken und Börsen gewinnen bei Eisenerz an Gewicht. *Czerwensky Intern 64*. June 15, 2009.

Dantzig, G. B., A. Orden, and P. Wolfe (1954). The generalized Simplex method for minimizing a linear form under linear inequality restraints. Rand Research Memorandum RM-1264. April 5, 1954.

Datamonitor (2006). International steel SWOT analysis. http://www.datamonitor.com. Accessed January 9, 2011.

Datamonitor (2010a). ArcelorMittal company profile. http://www.datamonitor.com. Accessed January 9, 2011.

Datamonitor (2010b). BHP Billiton Group company profile. http://www.datamonitor.com. Accessed January 9, 2011.

Datamonitor (2010c). Rio Tinto company profile. http://www.datamonitor.com. Accessed January 9, 2011.

Datamonitor (2010d). Vale S.A. company profile. http://www.datamonitor.com. Accessed January 9, 2011.

Davies, K. and F. Emmett (2010). Economists have consistently underestimated Chinese growth. *Royal Bank of Scotland Economics Weekly*. December 6, 2010.

de Long, J. B., A. Schleifer, L. H. Summers, and R. J. Waldmann (1990). Positive feedback investment strategies and destabilizing rational speculation. *Journal of Finance 45*(2), 379–395.

De Smedt, S. and M. Van Hoey (2008, February). Integrating steel giants: An interview with the ArcelorMittal postmerger managers. *The McKinsey Quarterly*, 1–11.

Degner, M., R. Fandrich, G. Endemann, J. T. Ghenda, K. Letz, B. Lüngen, I. Steller, H.-J. Wieland, A. Winkhold, R. Bartos, and R. Winkelgrund (2007). *Stahlfibel*. Verlag Stahleisen, Düsseldorf.

Der Spiegel (2011). Ungewöhnlich, richtig, notwendig. *Der Spiegel*. August 1, 2011.

Deutsches Institut für Normung e. V. (2000). DIN EN 10020:2000 – Begriffsbestimmungen für die Einteilung der Stähle. Beuth Verlag, Berlin.

Die Welt (2010). ThyssenKrupp plädiert für Deutsche Rohstoff AG. *Die Welt*. November 16, 2010.

Dillinger Hütte GTS (2011). Vom Eisenerz zum Roheisen: Eisen – Produkt des Hochofens. http://www.dillinger.de/cdstahlherstellung/cd/screens/htmlscopt/b10.html. Accessed May 12, 2011.

Dixit, A. and V. Norman (1980). *Theory of International Trade*. Cambridge University Press, Cambridge.

Du, X., C. L. Yu, and D. J. Hayes (2011). Speculation and volatility spillover in the crude oil and agricultural commodity markets: A Bayesian analysis. *Energy Economics 33*, 497–503.

Dunkel, M. (2011). Rohstoffversorgung bleibt Aufgabe der Wirtschaft. *Financial Times Deutschland*. January 20, 2011.

Dvořáček, J. (2005). *New Technologies in Underground Mining, Safety and Sustainable Development – Proceedings of the Sixth International Mining Forum 2005*, Chapter 1 – The Royalties as the Tool of Raw Material Policy of the European Union Countries, pp. 1–4. Taylor & Francis, Florence.

Ebeling, Paul A., J. (2011). Brazil to increase global steel demand. *Live Trading News*. June 3, 2011.

Eckel, E. C. (1914). *Iron Ores; Their Occurence, Valuation and Control.* McGraw-Hill, New York.

Eggert, R. G. (1992). *Competitiveness in Metals*, Chapter 2 – Exploration, pp. 21–67. Mining Journal Books, London.

Ellsworth, B. (2011). Brazil gov't studying iron ore export tax. *Reuters News.* April 1, 2011.

Ellsworth, B., J. Blount, S. Antonioli, and J. Saul (2011). Vale reroutes China-bound iron cargo to Italy. *Reuters News.* June 21, 2011.

Ellsworth, B. and R. Colitt (2009). Brazil considering iron ore export tax. *Reuters News.* October 19, 2009.

Emran, M. S. (2005). Revenue-increasing and welfare-enhancing reform of taxes on exports. *Journal of Development Economics 77*, 277–292.

Ericsson, M. (2009). Iron ore, the China factor. *Reuters News.* October 9, 2009.

Ernst & Young (2011a). Business risks facing mining and metals 2011–2012.

Ernst & Young (2011b). Global steel – 2010 trends, 2011 outlook. http://www.ey.com/Publication/vwLUAssets/Global_Steel_Report_2010-2011/$FILE/Global%20Steel%20Report%202010-2011%20FULL%20REPORT.pdf. Accessed June 14, 2011.

Erreygers, G. (2009). Hotelling, Rawls, Solow: How exhaustible resources came to be integrated into the neoclassical growth model. *History of Political Economy 41*, 263–281.

Euclid Infotech (2010). ArcelorMittal will triple iron-ore output in Brazil. *Euclid Infotech.* April 16, 2010.

European Commission (2011). Tackling the challenges in commodity markets and on raw materials. http://ec.europa.eu/enterprise/policies/raw-materials/files/docs/communication_en.pdf. Accessed May 28, 2011.

Farthing, K. (2009). Iron-ore price war. *Mining Weekly.* July 24, 2009.

Fauser, B. (2004). *Horizontale und vertikale Integration im Bereich der Leistungsverwertung.* Rainer Hampp Verlag, München.

Fehling, L. (1977). *Die Eisenerzwirtschaft Australiens.* Selbstverlag im wirtschafts- und sozialgeographischen Institut der Universität zu Köln, Köln.

Felix, B. (2011a). China steps up iron ore drive in Africa. *Reuters News.* August 18, 2011.

Felix, B. (2011b). China's iron ore ventures in west Africa. *Reuters News*. August 18, 2011.

Felix, B. (2011c). Key political risks to watch in Guinea. *Reuters News*. September 5, 2011.

Feng, L. (1994). China's steel industry: It's rapid expansion and influence on the international steel industry. *Resources Policy 20*(4), 219–234.

Fernandez, C. and R. Fabi (2010). World's largest ships. *Reuters News*. December 10, 2010.

Fey, L. (2010). Turbulence in the steel market. *Deutsche Bank Research Briefing*. July 29, 2010.

Fischer, K. (1988). *Oligopolistische Marktprozesse: Einsatz verschiedener Preis-Mengen-Strategien unter Berücksichtigung von Nachfrageträgheit*. Physica-Verlag, Heidelberg.

Fischermann, T. (2011). Teurer Stoff. *Die ZEIT*. January 13, 2011.

Flaaten, O. and C. E. Schulz (2010). Triple win for trade in renewable resource goods by use of export taxes. *Ecological Economics 69*, 1076–1082.

Frankfurter Allgemeine Sonntagszeitung (2010). Eisenerz ist heiß. *Frankfurter Allgemeine Sonntagszeitung*. April 11, 2010.

Frankfurter Allgemeine Zeitung (2010). Salzgitter fürchtet den Anstieg der Rohstoffpreise. *Frankfurter Allgemeine Zeitung*. March 27, 2010.

Frondel, M., P. Grösche, D. Huchtemann, A. Oberheitmann, J. Peters, C. Vance, G. Angerer, C. Sartorius, P. Buchholz, S. Röhling, and M. Wagner (2007). Trends der Angebots- und Nachfragesituation bei mineralischen Rohstoffen. Rheinisch-Westfälisches Institut für Wirtschaftsforschung, Fraunhofer-Institut für System- und Innovationsforschung, Bundesanstalt für Geowissenschaften und Rohstoffe.

Frontline Systems, Inc. (2010a). Risk Solver Platform reference guide. http://www.solver.com/suppxlsguide.htm. Accessed September 28, 2010.

Frontline Systems, Inc. (2010b). Risk Solver Platform user guide. http://www.solver.com/suppxlsguide.htm. Accessed September 28, 2010.

Frost, A. J. and J. Prechter, Robert R. (1998). *Elliott Wave Principle*. New Classics Library, Gainesville.

Frost, F. (1986). Strategic alternatives for Australian iron-ore producers. *Long Range Planning 19*(1), 89–98.

Fuentes, J. E., T. George, and J. Whittikar (2008). Measuring and mitigating risk in mining operations. http://crugroup.com/consultancy/CRUStrategies/performanceimprovement/Documents/Measuring_and_mitigating_risk_Copper%20Studies.pdf. Accessed April 12, 2011.

Fylstra, D., L. Lasdon, J. Watson, and A. Waren (1998). Design and use of the Microsoft Excel Solver. *INFORMS Interfaces 28*(5), 29–55.

Galdón-Sánchez, J. E. and J. A. Schmitz, Jr. (2002). Competitive pressure and labor productivity: World iron-ore markets in the 1980s. *The American Economic Review 92*(4), 1222–1235.

Gardiner, N. (2011). Dry Bulk Forecaster, 4Q10 – Quarterly forecasts of the dry bulk market. Drewry Maritime Research.

Geoscience Australia (2011). Iron fact sheet. http://www.australianminesatlas.gov.au/education/fact_sheets/iron.jsp#ozresdep. Accessed April 9, 2011.

GHD Pty Ltd. (2011). Infrastructure for the mining industry. http://www.ghd.com/PDF/InfrastructurefortheMiningIndustry.pdf. Accessed February 2, 2011.

Ghosh, S. (2006). Steel consumption and economic growth: Evidence from India. *Resources Policy 31*, 7–11.

Global Ports Ltd. (2010). Global ports dry cargo port database. http://www.g-ports.com/. Accessed March 12, 2010.

Goldman Sachs Global Economics Group (2007). BRICS and beyond. http://www2.goldmansachs.com/ideas/brics/book/BRIC-Full.pdf. Accessed August 10, 2011.

González, P. (2004). *Mining royalties*, Chapter 1 – Distributing Mining Wealth through Royalties, pp. 3–4. Mining Policy Research Initiative, International Development Research Centre, Montevideo.

Gravelle, J., L. Paton, L. Fitzgerald, R. Albert, and G. Eng (2009). Canadian mining taxation 2009. Pricewaterhouse Coopers LLP.

Grootjans, W. and A. Verweij (2009). The influence of financial derivatives in global commodity markets. http://www.accenture.com/SiteCollectionDocuments/PDF/Accenture_The_Influence_of_Financial_Derivatives_in_Global_Commodity_Markets.pdf. Accessed May 27, 2011.

Hajek, S. and M. Kamp (2010). Rohstoffmarkt mit neuen Erzfeinden. *WirtschaftsWoche*. May 27, 2010.

Hakala, D. R. (1970). Basic determinants and consequences of shifts in the supply of iron ore. *Land Economics 46*(2), 195–199.

Hanssmann, F. (1987). *Einführung in die Systemforschung: Methodik der modellgestützten Entscheidungsvorbereitung.* Oldenbourg Verlag, München.

Hart, O. D. and D. M. Kreps (1986). Price destabilizing speculation. *Journal of Political Economy 94*(5), 927–952.

Hasan, E. and F. D. Galiana (2008a, May). Electricity markets cleared by merit order – Part I: Finding the market outcomes supported by pure strategy Nash equilibria. *IEEE Transactions of Power Systems 23*(2), 361–371.

Hasan, E. and F. D. Galiana (2008b, May). Electricity markets cleared by merit order – Part II: Strategic offers and market power. *IEEE Transactions of Power Systems 23*(2), 372–379.

Hasan, E. and F. D. Galiana (2010, May). Fast computation of pure strategy Nash equilibria in electricity markets cleared by merit order. *IEEE Transactions of Power Systems 25*(2), 722–728.

Hasan, M. F., M. R. Reed, and M. A. Marchant (2001). Effects of an export tax on competitiveness: The case of the Indonesian palm oil industry. *Journal of Economic Development 26*(2), 77–90.

Hashimoto, H. and T. Sihsobhon (1981, June). *World Bank Commodity Models*, Chapter 4 – A World Iron and Steel Economy Model: the WISE Model. World Bank Staff Commodity Working Paper No. 6. The World Bank, Washington, D.C.

Hatayama, H., I. Daigo, Y. Matsuno, and Y. Adachi (2010). Outlook of the world steel cycle based on the stock and flow dynamics. *Environmental Science & Technology 44*(16), 6457–6463.

Hellmer, S. (1997a). *Competitive Strength in Iron Ore Production*, Chapter 1 – Testing Cournot behavior with conjectural variation in the European market for iron ore. PhD thesis, Luleå University of Technology.

Hellmer, S. (1997b). *Competitive Strength in Iron Ore Production*, Chapter 2 – Competitive strength in iron ore production: Why LKAB is still in business. PhD thesis, Luleå University of Technology.

Helpman, E. and P. R. Krugman (1989). *Trade Policy and Market Structure.* The MIT Press, Cambridge.

Henderson, J. M. (1958). *The Efficiency of the Coal Industry: An Application of Linear Programming.* Harvard University Press, Cambridge.

Herfindahl, O. C. (1950). Concentration in the U.S. steel industry. PhD thesis, Columbia University.

Hillier, F. S. and G. J. Lieberman (1995). *Introduction to Operations Research*. McGraw-Hill, New York.

Hirt, M. and G. Orr (2006, August). Helping China's companies master global M&A. *McKinsey on Strategy*. Published by The McKinsey Quarterly.

Hook, L. (2011). Rare earth prices soar as China stocks up. *The Financial Times*. June 19, 2011.

Hoovers (2011a). BHP Billiton Limited company profile. http://www.hoovers.com. Accessed February 12, 2011.

Hoovers (2011b). Rio Tinto Limited company profile. http://www.hoovers.com. Accessed February 12, 2011.

Hoovers (2011c). Vale S.A. company profile. http://www.hoovers.com. Accessed February 12, 2011.

Hotelling, H. (1931). The economics of exhaustible resources. *Journal of Political Economy 392*, 137–175.

Hull, J. C. (2006). *Options, Futures, and Other Derivatives*. Pearson Prentice Hall, Upper Saddle River.

ICAP (2010). Iron ore derivatives. http://steelguru.com/article/details/NDI%3D/Iron_Ore_Derivatives.html. Accessed February 9, 2010.

Indiastat (2010). India iron ore production statistics. http://www.indiastat.com/industries/18/stats.aspx. Accessed October 28, 2010.

Intercontinental Exchange (2010). ICE iron ore product guide. https://www.theice.com/publicdocs/ICE_Iron_Ore_Product_Guide_ENG.pdf. Accessed March 28, 2011.

International Chamber of Commerce (2010). Incoterms 2010.

Iron and Steel Statistics Bureau (2010). Iron ore trade flows 2000–2009.

Isern, J. and C. Pung (2007). Driving radical change. *The McKinsey Quarterly 4*, 1–12.

Jaspers, F. and J. van den Ende (2006). The organizational form of vertical relationships: Dimensions of integration. *Industrial Marketing Management 35*, 819–828.

Jefferson, G. H. (1990). China's iron and steel industry: Sources of enterprise efficiency and the impact of reform. *Journal of Development Economics 33*, 329–355.

Jeffrey, K. (2006). *Industrial Minerals & Rocks – Commodities, Markets and Uses*, Chapter 1 – Characteristics of the Industrial Minerals Sector, pp. 3–19. Society for Mining, Metallurgy and Exploration, Littleton.

Johnson, I. and B. Wassener (2011). China's economy grew 10.3 percent in 2010. *The New York Times*. January 19, 2011.

Johnston, R. and D. Reddy (2011). Political risk in mining. http://origin-pwc. pwc.com/ca/en/mining/publications/2011-04-political-risk-in-mining.pdf. Accessed March 21, 2011.

Jones, A. (1986). Prospects for an iron ore cartel. *Resources Policy 12*(2), 103–115.

Jorgenson, J. D. (2011). Mineral commodity summary iron ore. U.S. Geological Survey.

Joskow, P. L. (1985, Spring). Vertical integration and long-term contracts: The case of coal-burning electric generating plats. *Journal of Law, Economics & Organization 1*(1), 33–80.

Kaiser, A. (2010). Die neue Opec. *Manager Magazin*. April 6, 2010.

Kästner, H., C. Kippenberger, M. Kruszona, H. Schmidt, L. Steiner, J. Priem, and E. Wettig (1979). Untersuchungen über Angebot und Nachfrage mineralischer Rohstoffe: XII Eisenerz. Bundesanstalt für Geowissenschaften und Rohstoffe, Deutsches Institut für Wirtschaftsforschung.

Kay, J. and J. Mirrlees (1975). *The Economics of Natural Resource Depletion*, Chapter 9 – The desirability of natural resource depletion, pp. 140–176. Macmillan, London.

Kinch, D. (2009). Iron-ore futures may start by April. *Bloomberg*. November 26, 2009.

Kinch, D. (2010). Global iron ore industry likely to adopt monthly pricing. *Dow Jones International News*. July 20, 2010.

Kinch, D. (2011). Brazil vale disappoints some analysts as it grapples with cost inflation. *Dow Jones International News*. August 1, 2011.

Kirk, W. S. (1999). Metals prices in the United States through 1998 – iron ore. U.S. Geological Survey Special Report.

Köhn, R. (2011). Auf dem falschen Fuß. *Frankfurter Allgemeine Zeitung*. September 6, 2011.

Koscianski, J. and S. Mathis (1995). Excess capacity and the probability of entry: An application to the US titanium industry. *Resources Policy 21*(1), 43 – 51.

Krugman, P. R. and M. Obstfeld (1988). *International Economics: Theory and Policy*. Scott Foresman, Chicago.

Kuck, P. (2010). Iron ore statistical compendium. U.S. Geological Survey Special Report.

Kumar, R. C. (1997). On optimal capacity expansion for domestic processing of an exhaustible, natural resource. *Journal of Environmental Economics and Management 32*(2), 154–169.

Kuyek, J. (2004). *Mining royalties*, Chapter 3 – Myth and Reality: Understanding Mining Taxation in Canada, pp. 5–6. Mining Policy Research Initiative, International Development Research Centre, Montevideo.

Kwong, R. (2010). Baosteel and China Steel in iron ore move. *The Financial Times*. November 17, 2010.

Labson, B. S. (1997). Changing patterns of trade in the world iron ore and steel market: An econometric analysis. *Journal of Policy Modeling 19*(3), 237.

Lam, E. (2011). Fortify your portfolio with some iron ore. *Financial Post*. March 10, 2011.

Latoff, R. (2009, April). Enduring ideas: The industry cost curve. *The McKinsey Quarterly*.

Law, A. M. and W. D. Kelton (2006). *Simulation Modeling and Analysis*. McGraw-Hill, Boston.

Leach, J. (1991, February). Rational speculation. *Journal of Political Economy 99*(1), 131–144.

Lewis, H. G. (1941, March). The nature of the demand for steel. *Journal of the American Statistical Association 36*(216), 110–115.

Lian, R., J. Hua, and T. Miles (2011). China to study iron ore, coal reserve plan. *Reuters News*. February 24, 2011.

Liebl, F. (1995). *Simulation: Problemorientierte Einführung*. Oldenbourg Verlag, München.

Lindstädt, H. (1997). *Optimierung der Qualität von Gruppenentscheidungen – Ein simulationsbasierter Beitrag zur Principal-Agent-Theorie.* Physica-Verlag, Heidelberg.

Lindstädt, H. and R. Hauser (2004). *Strategische Wirkungsbereiche des Unternehmens – Spielräume und Integrationsgrenzen erkennen und gestalten.* Gabler Verlag, Wiesbaden.

Luna, D. and B. Ellsworth (2010). Brazil's Vale returning iron ore mine to ArcelorMittal. *Reuters News.* March 2, 2010.

Lundgren, N.-G. (1996). Bulk trade and maritime transport costs: The evolution of global markets. *Resources Policy 22*(1/2), 5–32.

Malenbaum, W. (1975). Laws of demand for minerals. Proceedings of the Council of Economics, 104th Annual Meeting of the AIME. February 16-20, 1975.

Manners, G. (1971). *The Changing World Market for Iron Ore 1950–1980.* The Johns Hopkins Press, Baltimore.

Marks, S. V., D. F. Larson, and J. Pomeroy (1998). Economic effects of taxes on exports of palm oil products. *Bulletin of Indonesian Economic Studies 34*(3), 37–58.

Mas-Colell, A., M. D. Whinston, and J. R. Green (1995). *Microeconomic Theory.* Oxford University Press, New York.

Mathis, S. and J. Koscianski (1997). Excess capacity as a barrier to entry in the US titanium industry. *International Journal of Industrial Organization 15*(2), 263 – 281.

Mayenkar, S. (2011). India hikes iron ore export duty to 20 pct. *Reuters News.* February 28, 2011.

McKinsey & Company (2010a). GDP scenarios. McKinsey Global Institute. Internal document.

McKinsey & Company (2010b). Global steel demand outlook. McKinsey Basic Materials Institute. Internal document.

McKinsey & Company (2011a). Iron ore demand model. McKinsey Basic Materials Institute. Internal model.

McKinsey & Company (2011b). Iron ore supply database. McKinsey Basic Materials Institute. Internal database.

Meadows, D. H., D. L. Meadows, J. Randers, and W. W. Behrens III (1972). *The Limits to Growth*. The New American Library, New York.

Mendelson, H. (1982). Market behavior in a clearing house. *Econometrica 50*(6), 1505–1524.

Merriam-Webster, Inc. (2011). Merriam-Webster online dictionary. http://www.merriam-webster.com. Accessed June 12, 2011.

Microsoft (2006). Solver limits for constraints and adjustable cells. http://support.microsoft.com/kb/75714. Accessed March 29, 2010.

Millbank, P. (2011). Tight supply to keep iron ore prices high. *Steel Business Briefing Insight*. February 3, 2011.

Miller, G. L. and S. F. Harris (1972). Price formation, price projections and commodity marketing research. Occasional Paper No. 13. Bureau of Agricultural and Resource Economics.

Moneycontrol, C. (2010). Iron ore export duty should be around 20%. *CNBC Moneycontrol*. July 16, 2010.

Movshuk, O. (2004). Restructuring, productivity and technical efficiency in China's iron and steel industry, 1988-2000. *Journal of Asian Economics 15*, 135–151.

Neely, J. (2011). Vale open to shorter iron ore pricing formulas. *Reuters News*. June 17, 2011.

Nenov, I. P. and D. H. Fylstra (2003). Interval methods for accelerated global search in the Microsoft Excel Solver. *Reliable Computing 9*, 143–159.

Neumann, K. and M. Morlock (1993). *Operations Research*. Carl Hanser Verlag, München.

Niedhart, N. (2009). *Simulation von Wettbewerbsstrategien in liberalisierten Eisenbahnmärkten – Mehrperiodige spieltheoretische Analyse von Wettbewerb im Hochgeschwindigkeitsverkehr*. Rainer Hampp Verlag, München.

Nielsen, M. (2006). Trade liberalisation, resource sustainability and welfare: The case of East Baltic cod. *Ecological Economics 58*, 650–664.

Nordhoff, O. (2009). *Quasihomogenität in Multi-Markt-Oligopolen*. Rainer Hampp Verlag, München.

Oakley, D. and J. Blas (2010). Iron ore swaps could grow to $200bn. *The Financial Times*. March 30, 2010.

Obert, M. (2009). *Energy Trading and its Relevance for European Energy Companies*. Rainer Hampp Verlag, München.

O'Driscoll, M. (2006). *Industrial Minerals & Rocks – Commodities, Markets and Uses*, Chapter 4 – International Trade in Industrial Minerals, pp. 49–59. Society for Mining, Metallurgy and Exploration, Littleton.

O'Keefe, B. and D. Burke (2007). The new iron age. *Fortune 156*(11), 112–124. November 26, 2007.

O'Neill, J. (2001). Building better global economic BRICs. Goldman Sachs Global Economics Paper.

O'Sullivan, A. and S. M. Sheffrin (2002). *Economics: Principles in action*. Pearson Prentice Hall, Upper Saddle River.

Otto, J. M. (2000, November). Mining taxation in developing countries. Study of the United Nations Conference on Trade and Development.

Otto, J. M., C. Andrews, F. Cawood, M. Doggett, P. Guj, S. Frank, J. Stermole, and J. Tilton (2006). *Mining Royalties: A Global Study of Their Impact on Investors, Government, and Civil Society*. The International Bank for Reconstruction and Development / The World Bank, Washington, D.C.

Pamuk, H. (2010). Iron ore swap contracts: Who's doing what? *Reuters News*. July 28, 2010.

Panama Canal Authority (2010). Panama Canal expansion program description. http://www.pancanal.com/eng/expansion/index.html. Accessed December 18, 2010.

Parker, B. (2006). *Industrial Minerals & Rocks – Commodities, Markets and Uses*, Chapter 9 – Ship and Barge Transportation of Industrial Minerals, pp. 99–108. Society for Mining, Metallurgy and Exploration, Littleton.

Peaple, A. (2011). Miners face a hole that's getting deeper. *Dow Jones News Service*. July 28, 2011.

Peck, M. J., H. H. Landsberg, and J. E. Tilton (1992). *Competitiveness in Metals*. Mining Journal Books, London.

Peel, G. (2009). The magnetite revolution. *FN Arena Weekly*. August 10, 2009.

Perry, M. K. (1989). *Handbook of Industrial Organization*, Volume 1, Chapter 4 – Vertical Integration: Determinants and Effects, pp. 183–255. North-Holland, Amsterdam.

Pilling, D. (2011). Tax threat to Australian mining all hot air. *The Financial Times*. July 26, 2011.

Pizarro, R. (2004). *Mining royalties*, Chapter 4 – The Establishment of Royalty in Chile, pp. 7–8. Mining Policy Research Initiative, International Development Research Centre, Montevideo.

Porter, M. E. (2008). The five competitive forces that shape strategy. *Harvard Business Review*, 78–93.

Poveromo, J. J. (1999). *The Making, Shaping and Treating of Steel*, Volume 2 – Ironmaking, Chapter 8 – Iron ores, pp. 569–720. Association for Iron and Steel Technology, Warrendale.

Poveromo, J. J. (2006). *Industrial Minerals & Rocks – Commodities, Markets and Uses*, Chapter 108 – Agglomeration Processes: Pelletizing and Sintering, pp. 1391–1404. Society for Mining, Metallurgy and Exploration, Littleton.

PriceWaterhouseCoopers (2010). Total tax contribution: A study of the economic contribution mining companies make to public finances. http://www.pwc.co.uk/eng/issues/total_tax_contribution.html. Accessed June 13, 2011.

Priovolos, T. (1987). An econometric model of the iron ore industry. World Bank staff commodity working papers. The World Bank, Washington D.C.

Rabello, M. L. and K. Cortes (2010). Brazil may tax ore exports, seek more steel plants. *Bloomberg*. February 9, 2010.

Radetzki, M. (2008). *A Handbook of Primary Commodities in the Global Economy*. Cambridge University Press, Cambridge.

Rankin, B. (2006). Value of land. http://www.radicalcartography.net/?manhattan-value. Accessed August 2, 2011.

Reck, B. K., M. Chambon, S. Hashimoto, and T. E. Graedel (2010). Global stainless steel cycle exemplifies China's rise to metal dominance. *Environmental Science & Technology 44*(10), 3940–3946.

Regan, J. (2009). Rio-BHP iron ore venture could free small miners. *Reuters News*. October 28, 2009.

Regan, J. (2011). Rio Tinto to speed up iron ore expansion on strong demand. *Reuters News*. June 14, 2011.

Regan, J. and M. Smith (2011). BHP Billiton sees weak European, U.S. growth for years. *Reuters News*. August 10, 2011.

Reuters News (2010). Taxes and tariffs in the mining sector. *Reuters News*. October 6, 2010.

Ricardo, D. (1821). On the principles of political economy and taxation. Library of Economics and Liberty, http://www.econlib.org/library/Ricardo/ricP1.html. Accessed June 7, 2011.

Ricardo, D. (1951). *Principles of Political Economy and Taxation*. Cambridge University Press, Cambridge.

Rio Tinto (2010). Rio Tinto annual report 2009. http://www.riotinto.com/annualreport2009/pdf/rio_tinto_full_annualreport2009.pdf. Accessed January 9, 2011.

Rio Tinto (2011). Rio Tinto Iron Ore's global operations. http://www.riotintoironore.com/ENG/operations/index_operations.asp. Accessed May 27, 2011.

Riveras, I. (2011). Vale to keep stake in steel mill venture till 2014. *Reuters News*. April 28, 2011.

Roberts, M. C. (1996). Metal use and the world economy. *Resources Policy 22*(3), 183–196.

Rogers, C. D., K. Robertson, and K. Robertson (1987, March). Long term contracts and market stability: The case of iron ore. *Resources Policy 13*(1), 3–18.

Rogers, J. (2004). *Hot Commodities*. Random House, New York.

Roman, P. A. and L. Daneshmend (2000). Economies of scale in mining – Assessing upper bounds with simulation. *The Engineering Economist 45*(4), 326–338.

Röttges, S. and W. Sturbeck (2010). Stahlkocher unter Zugzwang. *Frankfurter Allgemeine Zeitung* (52). March 3, 2010.

Samuelson, P. A. (1952). Spatial price equilibrium and linear programming. *American Economic Review 42*, 283–303.

Sato, R. (2010). The TEX Iron Ore Manual 2009. The TEX Report, Ltd.

Schlandt, J. (2010). Thyssen-Krupp forciert Deutsche Rohstoff AG. *Frankfurter Rundschau*. November 16, 2010.

Secretariat of the Federal Reserve of Brazil (2011). Common external tariff. http://www.receita.fazenda.gov.br/Principal/Ingles/Versao2/default.asp. Accessed March 21, 2011.

Sensfuß, F., M. Ragwitz, and M. Genoese (2008). The merit-order effect: A detailed analysis of the price effect of renewable electricity generation on spot market prices in Germany. *Energy Policy 36*, 3086–3094.

Serapio, Manolo, J. (2011). Iron ore contracts may be priced daily in 3–5 years. *Reuters News*. June 28, 2011.

Sergeant, B. (2008). Iron ore, king of resources. *Mineweb*. April 4, 2008.

Sergeant, B. (2009). Seaborne iron ore – the world's quietest, greatest franchise. *Mineweb*. June 5, 2009.

Simon, J. L. (1981). *The Ultimate Resource*. Princeton University Press, Princeton.

Simon, J. L. (1996). *The Ultimate Resource 2*. Princeton University Press, Princeton.

Smith, A. (1776). *An Inquiry into the Nature and Causes of the Wealth of Nations*. W. Strahan and T. Cadell, London.

Smith, M. (2011). Rio Tinto moves towards monthly pricing contracts. *Reuters News*. June 21, 2011.

Smith, N. R. (1988). *China's Energy and Mineral Industries: Current Perspectives*, Chapter 6 – Present trends and outlook for minerals markets and trade in the Asia-Pacific region, pp. 67–98. Westview Press, Boulder.

Söderholm, P. and T. Ejdemo (2008). Steel scrap markets in Europe and the USA. *Minerals & Energy 23*(2), 57–73.

Solow, R. M. (1974). The economics of resources or the resources of economics. *American Economic Review 64*(2), 1–14.

Speltz, C. N. (2006). *Industrial Minerals & Rocks – Commodities, Markets and Uses*, Chapter 7 – Rail Transportation of Industrial Minerals, pp. 79–94. Society for Mining, Metallurgy and Exploration, Littleton.

Spiegel Online (2010). Brüderle fordert Rohstoff-Kartell gegen China. *Spiegel Online*. November 2, 2010.

Spiegel Online (2011). Indien erwägt Exportstopp für Eisenerz. *Spiegel Online*. January 12, 2011.

Sprothen, V. (2009). Chinesen am Schacht. *Die ZEIT*. May 20, 2009.

Srivats, K. R. (2009). Govt hikes iron ore export duty. *The Hindu Business Line*. Dezember 27, 2009.

Steel Business Briefing (2009). Scrap should give China an edge in iron ore talks. October 19, 2009.

Steel Business Briefing (2010a, December). BHPB makes great leap forward on pricing in 2010. *Raw Materials Xtra 11*.

Steel Business Briefing (2010b). Brazil's Vale links iron ore prices to a price index. *Steel Business Briefing*. April 6, 2010.

Steel Business Briefing (2010c, November). Iron ore juniors at mercy of giants on rail haulage. *Raw Materials Xtra 10*.

Steel Business Briefing (2010d, December). Little significant new tonnage from Australia before 2013. *Raw Materials Xtra 11*.

Steel Business Briefing (2011a, April). Japanese mills struggle to pass on higher raw materials costs. *Raw Materials Xtra 15*.

Steel Business Briefing (2011b, May). New Indian iron ore probe to curb exports. *Raw Materials Xtra 16*.

Steel Business Briefing (2011c). SBB Analytics China. http://www.steelbb.com/analyticschina/. Accessed January 31, 2011.

Steel Business Briefing (2011d, June). Vale launches first giant iron ore vessel. *Raw Materials Xtra 17*.

Steel Business Briefing (2011e, May). WA government to lift royalties for iron ore fines. *Raw Materials Xtra 16*.

Stein, J. C. (1987). Informational externalities and welfare-reducing speculation. *Journal of Political Economy 95*(6), 1123–1145.

Steinfeld, E. S. (1998). *Forging Reform in China*. Cambridge Books. Cambridge University Press, Cambridge.

Stiglitz, J. E. (1989). *Handbook of Industrial Organization*, Volume 1, Chapter 13 – Imperfect Information in the Product Market, pp. 769–847. North-Holland, Amsterdam.

Suez Canal Authority (2010). Stages of developing the Suez Canal. http://www.suezcanal.gov.eg/sc.aspx?show=12. Accessed December 18, 2010.

Sukagawa, P. (2010). Is iron ore priced as a commodity? Past and current practice. *Resources Policy 35*, 54–63.

Supatgiat, C., R. Zhang, and J. R. Birge (2001). Equilibrium values in a competitive power exchange market. *Computer Economics 17*, 93–121.

Tasker, S.-J. (2010). Iron ore price could double in BHP push. *The Australian*. February 15, 2010.

Taube, M. and P. in der Heiden (2010). *China Steel Inc. – State-owned and state-run?* Metropolis Verlag, Marburg.

The Economist (2010a). Chinese takeovers: Being eaten by the dragon. *The Economist*. November 17, 2010.

The Economist (2010b). Fixed ore floating. *The Economist*. July 3, 2010.

The Economist (2010c). Making the earth move. *The Economist*. August 21, 2010.

The Economist (2011a). Everyday higher prices. *The Economist*. February 24, 2011.

The Economist (2011b). Geology or geography? *The Economist*. August 27, 2011.

The Economist (2011c). A rocky patch. *The Economist*. May 14, 2011.

The Financial Times (2010a). Annual iron ore contract system collapses. *The Financial Times*. March 30, 2010.

The Financial Times (2010b). Big three rule. *The Financial Times*. October 19, 2010.

The Financial Times (2010c). Ore struck. *The Financial Times*. April 6, 2010.

The Financial Times (2010d). Race for resources tests trade openness. *The Financial Times*. November 5, 2010.

The Financial Times (2010e). Super profit tax needs superpolitics. *The Financial Times*. June 17, 2010.

The Financial Times (2011a). BHP points to strong growth. *The Financial Times*. July 21, 2011.

The Financial Times (2011b). Iron ore set to remain 'stronger for longer'. *The Financial Times*. July 20, 2011.

The Financial Times (2011c). Vale sees Africa as new raw-materials frontier. *The Financial Times*. April 26, 2011.

The Financial Times (2011d). Vale: signs of growing resource nationalism. *The Financial Times*. April 3, 2011.

The Joint Ore Reserves Committee (2004). The JORC Code – Australasian code for reporting of exploration results, mineral resources and ore reserves. http://www.jorc.org, The Australasian Institute of Mining and Metallurgy, Australian Institute of Geoscientists and Minerals Council of Australia. Accessed June 25, 2010.

The New York Times (2009). Where boom times slow, but never end. *The New York Times*. August 14, 2009.

The New York Times (2010). Rio Tinto goes to quarterly pricing on iron ore. *The New York Times*. April 10, 2010.

The Steel Index (2011). The Steel Index iron ore price series, historical spot price database. http://www.thesteelindex.com/. Accessed June 7, 2011.

The Wall Street Journal (2010). Vale buys iron-ore stake in Guinea. *The Wall Street Journal*. May 1, 2010.

The Wall Street Journal (2011). BHP Billiton is wary of rising costs as profit soars. *The Wall Street Journal*. August 25, 2011.

The World Bank (2011). World development indicators database: Gross domestic product. http://data.worldbank.org/indicator/NY.GDP.MKTP.CD. Accessed July 7, 2011.

Thomas, D. and J. Regan (2009). China eyes stakes in Australian iron ore explorers. *Reuters News*. September 8, 2009.

Tilton, J. E. (1978). Impact of market instability for mineral materials. *World Economy 1*, 369–384.

Tilton, J. E. (2003). *On borrowed time? Assessing the threat of mineral depletion*. Resources for the Future, Washington, D.C.

Tirole, J. (1990). *The theory of industrial organization*. The MIT Press, Cambridge.

Toweh, S. H. and R. T. Newcomb (1991). A spatial equilibrium analysis of world iron ore trade. *Resources Policy 17*(3), 236–248.

Treadgold, T. (2009). Ore war. *Forbes Asia*. October 5, 2009.

United Nations Conference on Trade and Development (1974). The maritime transportation of iron ore.

United Nations Conference on Trade and Development (1994). Enhanced recuperation and recycling: Implications for primary commodity producers in developing countries – the case of ferrous scrap versus iron ore.

United Nations Conference on Trade and Development (2010). Iron ore market 2009–2011.

U.S. Department of Agriculture, Agricultural Marketing Service (1996). Concentration in agriculture: A report of the advisory committee on agricultural concentration.

U.S. Geological Survey (2010a). USGS 2008 minerals yearbook Australia.

U.S. Geological Survey (2010b). USGS 2008 minerals yearbook Brazil.

U.S. Geological Survey (2010c). USGS 2009 minerals yearbook China.

Vale (2010). Vale annual report 2009. http://2009.vale20f.com/. Accessed January 9, 2011.

van Vuuren, D. P., B. J. Strengers, and H. J. M. De Vries (1999). Long-term perspectives on world metal use – A system-dynamics model. *Resources Policy 25*(4), 239–255.

Varian, H. R. (2010). *Intermediate Microeconomics – A Modern Approach.* W. W. Norton & Company, New York.

Verhoeven, R., S. Mareels, C. Sürig, and B. Zeumer (2010). Short-selling the earth? McKinsey & Company, Metals & Mining Practice. Special Edition of McKinsey on Metals & Mining.

Wakelin, D. H. and J. Ricketts (1999). *The Making, Shaping and Treating of Steel,* Volume 2 – Ironmaking, Chapter 1 – The Nature of Ironmaking, pp. 1–35. Association for Iron and Steel Technology, Warrendale.

Waldmeir, P. and J. Farchy (2010). Vale denies iron ore price fixing accusations. *The Financial Times.* June 2, 2010.

Walras, L. (1874). *Eléments d'Économie Politique Pure.* L. Cobaz, Lausanne. Translated by William Jaffé, 1954: Elements of pure economics. Allen and Urwin, London.

Wärtsilä (2010). Shipping scenarios 2030. http://www.shippingscenarios.wartsila.com/Wartsila_Shipping_Scenarios_2030.pdf. Accessed January 12, 2011.

Watters, D. C. (2000). The industry cost curve as a strategic tool. *The McKinsey Quarterly.*

Wilson, D., A. L. Kelston, and S. Ahmed (2010, May). Is this the 'BRICs Decade'? *Goldman Sachs Global Economics BRICs Monthly.*

Wilson, D. and R. Purushothaman (2003). Dreaming with BRICs: The path to 2050. *Goldman Sachs Global Economics Paper*.

Wilson, R. (2004, April). Steel wants its bumpers back. *Automotive Industries*, 25–26.

Woetzel, J. R. (2001). Remaking China's giant steel industry. *The McKinsey Quarterly 4*, 93–102.

Wolf, M. (2011). How China could yet fail like Japan. *The Financial Times*. June 17, 2011.

Woolley, S. (2010). How companies are coping with unstable commodities. *Bloomberg Businessweek*. September 30, 2010.

Woolrich, N. (2010). Iron ore demand on the rise. *Australian Broadcasting Corporation*. May 2, 2010.

World Economic Forum (2010a). China and the world: Scenarios to 2025. http://www3.weforum.org/docs/WEF_Scenario_ChinaWorld2025_Report_2010.pdf. Accessed February 24, 2011.

World Economic Forum (2010b). India and the world: Scenarios to 2025. http://www3.weforum.org/docs/WEF_Scenario_IndiaWorld2025_Report_2010.pdf. Accessed February 24, 2011.

World Economic Forum (2010c). Russia and the world: Scenarios to 2025. http://www3.weforum.org/docs/WEF_Scenario_RussiaWorld2025_Report_2010.pdf. Accessed February 24, 2011.

World Economic Forum (2011). Global risks 2011. http://riskreport.weforum.org/global-risks-2011.pdf. Accessed February 24, 2011.

World Shipping Register (2010). Sea distances and voyage calculator. http://www.e-ships.net/dist.htm. Accessed October 11, 2010.

World Steel Association (1990). Steel statistical yearbook 1990. http://www.worldsteel.org/pictures/programfiles/SSY1990.pdf. Accessed January 24, 2010.

World Steel Association (2000). Steel statistical yearbook 2000. http://www.worldsteel.org/pictures/programfiles/SSY2000.pdf. Accessed January 24, 2010.

World Steel Association (2008). Fact sheet steel and energy. http://www.worldsteel.org/pictures/programfiles/Fact%20sheet_Energy.pdf. Accessed March 10, 2010.

World Steel Association (2010). Steel statistical yearbook 2010. http://www.
worldsteel.org/pictures/publicationfiles/SSY%202010.pdf. Accessed July 3,
2010.

World Steel Association (2011). World steel in figures 2011. http://www.
worldsteel.org/pictures/publicationfiles/WSIF_2011.pdf. Accessed August
12, 2011.

World Trade Organization (2010). Annual report 2010. http://www.wto.org/
english/res_e/booksp_e/anrep_e/anrep10_e.pdf. Accessed July 10, 2011.

Wu, Y. (2000). The Chinese steel industry: Recent developments and prospects.
Resources Policy 26, 171–178.

Xinhua News Agency (2010). Russian iron ore exports to China via inland port
almost double in Jan-May period. *Xinhua News Agency*. June 21, 2010.

Xinhua News Agency (2011). China's aid to Africa for friendship, not resources.
Xinhua News Agency. April 26, 2011.

Yamawaki, H. (1984). Market structure, capacity expansion, and pricing: A
model applied to the Japanese iron and steel industry. *International Journal
of Industrial Organization 2*(1), 29–62.

Yellishetty, M., G. M. Mudd, and P. G. Ranjith (2011). The steel industry,
abiotic resource depletion and life cycle assessment: A real or perceived issue?
Journal of Cleaner Production 19, 78–90.

Zhou, Z. (1998). An equilibrium analysis of hedging with liquidity constraints,
speculation, and government price subsidy in a commodity market. *Journal
of Finance 53*(5), 1705–1736.

Schriften zu
MANAGEMENT, ORGANISATION UND INFORMATION
Herausgegeben von Hagen Lindstädt (Auswahl)

Bernd Fauser: **Horizontale und vertikale Integration im Bereich der Leistungsverwertung. Entwurf eines heuristischen Erklärungsmodells und seiner Überprüfung anhand der Luftverkehrs- und Medienbranche**
Band 4, ISBN 3-87988-852-3, Rainer Hampp Verlag, München und Mering 2004, 338 S., € 32.80

Carsten Cramme: **Informationsverhalten als Determinante organisationaler Entscheidungseffizienz**
Band 6, ISBN 3-87988-937-6, Rainer Hampp Verlag, München und Mering 2005, 299 S., € 29.80

Hagen Lindstädt: **Beschränkte Rationalität. Entscheidungsverhalten und Organisationsgestaltung bei beschränkter Informationsverarbeitungskapazität**
Band 7, ISBN 3-87988-997-X, Rainer Hampp Verlag, München und Mering 2005, 412 S., € 32.80

Peter Nischalke: **Die Organisation wachsender Unternehmen. Eine Entwicklung idealtypischer Gestaltungsalternativen auf system- und kontingenztheoretischer Basis**
Band 8, ISBN 3-86618-019-5, Rainer Hampp Verlag, München und Mering 2006, 252 S., € 27.80

Tim Habermann: **Integrationstreiber in der Leistungserstellung. Entwurf eines Analyseschemas zur Betrachtung von Integration in Industriesegmenten mit Beispielen aus der Telekommunikations- und der Pharmaindustrie**
Band 9, ISBN 3-86618-027-6, Rainer Hampp Verlag, München und Mering 2006, 383 S., € 34.80

Marcus Schuster: **Absorptive Capacity und Anreizperspektive. Wissensabsorption und Innovativität aus organisationstheoretischer Sicht**
Band 10, ISBN 978-3-86618-061-1, Rainer Hampp Verlag, München und Mering 2006, 329 S., € 32.80

Juliane Schneider: **Optimale Delegation bei mehreren Agenten. Untersuchung eines zweistufigen Entscheidungsprozesses**
Band 11, ISBN 978-3-86618-068-0, Rainer Hampp Verlag, München und Mering 2006, 316 S., € 29.80

Kilian Sauerwald: **Effektivität und Effizienz: Zielbeziehungen organisationaler Entscheidungen**
Band 12, ISBN 978-3-86618-110-6, Rainer Hampp Verlag, München und Mering 2007, 338 S., € 32.80

Arne Kreitz: **Optimale Organisation der Wertschöpfung internationaler Unternehmen. Modellhafte Abbildung und Vergleich organisatorischer Idealtypen**
Band 14, ISBN 978-3-86618-293-6, Rainer Hampp Verlag, München und Mering 2008, 310 S., € 29.80

Rolf Heintzeler: **Strategische Frühaufklärung im Kontext effizienter Entscheidungsprozesse**
Band 15, ISBN 978-3-86618-301-8, Rainer Hampp Verlag, München und Mering 2008, 303 S., € 29.80

Amadeus Petzke: **Nähe zum Kerngeschäft als Kriterium für Portfolioentscheidungen**
Band 16, ISBN 978-3-86618-315-5, Rainer Hampp Verlag, München und Mering 2009, 317 S., € 29.80

Nicolas Niedhart: **Simulation von Wettbewerbsstrategien in liberalisierten Eisenbahnmärkten. Mehrperiodige spieltheoretische Analyse von Wettbewerb im Hochgeschwindigkeitsverkehr**
Band 17, ISBN 978-3-86618-317-9, Rainer Hampp Verlag, München und Mering 2009, 206 S., € 24.80

Christian Thiel: **Leitungsspanne und Hierarchietiefe von Organisationen. Modellierung und Simulation bei einfacher und stochastischer Informationsentstehung**
Band 18, ISBN 978-3-86618-336-0, Rainer Hampp Verlag, München und Mering 2009, 323 S., € 29.80

Michael Wagner: **Konfiguration und Koordination der internationalen Wertschöpfungskette**
Band 19, ISBN 978-3-86618-380-3, Rainer Hampp Verlag, München und Mering 2009, 293 S., € 29.80

Ole Nordhoff: **Quasihomogenität in Multi-Markt-Oligopolen. Eine analytische und simulationsgestützte Untersuchung von Preis-Mengen-Strategien**
Band 20, ISBN 978-3-86618-406-0, Rainer Hampp Verlag, München und Mering 2009, 272 S., € 27.80

Arne Schneemann: **Eintrittsabwehr und strategisches Commitment in Netzwerkindustrien**
Band 22, ISBN 978-3-86618-444-2, Rainer Hampp Verlag, München und Mering 2010, 256 S., € 27.80

Christian Frank: **Strategien in Post-Merger-Integrationen. Eine experimentelle Turniersimulation**
Band 23, ISBN 978-3-86618-446-6, Rainer Hampp Verlag, München und Mering 2010, 283 S., € 27.80

Mathias Gerlach: **Markteintrittswettbewerb in homogenen Oligopolen. Ein experimentelles Strategieturnier**
Band 24, ISBN 978-3-86618-453-4, Rainer Hampp Verlag, München und Mering 2010, 222 S., € 24.80

Tobias Bayer: **Integriertes Variantenmanagement. Variantenkostenbewertung mit faktorenanalytischen Komplexitätstreibern**
Band 25, ISBN 978-3-86618-454-1, Rainer Hampp Verlag, München und Mering 2010, 222 S., € 24.80

Daniel Kronenwett: **Strategische Konsistenz von M&A-Serien in Europa**
Band 26, ISBN 978-3-86618-496-1, Rainer Hampp Verlag, München und Mering 2010, 254 S., € 27.80

Jana Oehmichen: **Mehrfachmandate von Aufsichtsratsmitgliedern. Eine Panel-Analyse ihrer Wirkung in deutschen Unternehmen**
Band 27, ISBN 978-3-86618-605-7, Rainer Hampp Verlag, München und Mering 2011, 179 S., € 22.80

Jörn M. Andreas: **Determinanten der Aufsichtsratsvergütung in deutschen Aktiengesellschaften. Eine panelökonometrische Untersuchung zur Effektuierung der Anreizorientierung**
Band 28, ISBN 978-3-86618-606-4, Rainer Hampp Verlag, München und Mering 2011, 284 S., € 29.80

Yuldon Gyana Tshang: **Corporate Governance bei Organisationskomplexität. Eine empirische Untersuchung moderierender Effekte in deutschen Aktiengesellschaften**
Band 29, ISBN 978-3-86618-617-0, Rainer Hampp Verlag, München und Mering 2011, 252 S., € 24.80

Emily Bünn: **Partnerstrukturen und ihre Erfolgswirkung in Unternehmens-kooperationen. Eine empirische Analyse des europäischen Private Equity Marktes**
Band 30, ISBN 978-3-86618-623-1, Rainer Hampp Verlag, München und Mering 2011, 168 S., € 19.80

Andreas Habeck: **Das wiederholte Ultimatumspiel mit fixem Gegner. Multivariate Untersuchung und Verhaltensmodellierung**
Band 31, ISBN 978-3-86618-642-2, Rainer Hampp Verlag, München und Mering 2011, 173 S., € 19.80

Martin Strumpler: **Informationsbewertung unter Ambiguität. Eine experimentelle Untersuchung**
Band 32, ISBN 978-3-86618-651-4, Rainer Hampp Verlag, München und Mering 2011, 276 S., € 27.80

Ralf Berger: **Strategie und Eigentümerstruktur als Determinanten des Finanzmanagements. Eine empirische Untersuchung deutscher Blue Chips**
Band 33, ISBN 978-3-86618-655-2, Rainer Hampp Verlag, München und Mering 2011, 243 S., € 27.80

Philipp Rappold: **Macht von Vorstandsvorsitzenden. Eine Survival-Analyse der Determinanten erzwungener Entlassungen in deutschen Aktiengesellschaften**
Band 34, ISBN 978-3-86618-659-0, Rainer Hampp Verlag, München u. Mering 2011, 184 S., € 24.80

Heiko Peters: **Organisationsgestaltung durch explizite Verhaltensnormen. Eine agenten-basierte Simulation zur Organisation dezentraler Informationsverarbeitung**
Band 35, ISBN 978-3-86618-670-5, Rainer Hampp Verlag, München u. Mering 2012, 249 S., € 27.80